Time Lords & Tribbles, Winchesters & Muggles: The DePaul Pop Culture Conference A Five-year Retrospective

Edited By
Paul Booth and Isabella Menichiello

Paul Booth is Associate Professor at DePaul University. He is the author of *Crossing Fandoms* (Palgrave 2016), *Digital Fandom 2.0* (Peter Lang 2016), *Playing Fans* (University of Iowa 2015), *Game Play* (Bloomsbury 2015), *Time on TV* (Peter Lang 2012), and *Digital Fandom* (Peter Lang 2010). He has edited *Seeing Fans* (Bloomsbury 2016, with Lucy Bennett), *Controversies in Digital Ethics* (Bloomsbury 2016, with Amber Davisson), and *Fan Phenomena: Doctor Who* (Intellect 2013). He has published numerous articles on fans, social media, and technology. His research interests include fandom, new technologies and media, popular culture, and cult media. He is currently enjoying a cup of coffee.

Isabella Menichiello is an undergraduate student at DePaul University pursuing a degree in Film and Television.

Cover design by Julia Dourgarian

Time Lords & Tribbles, Winchesters & Muggles: The DePaul Pop Culture Conference A Five-year Retrospective
Edited by Paul Booth and Isabella Menichiello

Part II: Joss Whedon: A Celebration

Part III: A Celebration of Supernatural

Part IV: A Celebration of Star Trek

Part V: Harry Potter and the Pop Culture Conference

Paul dedicates this book to everyone who has made the Pop Culture Conference such a joy to put together.

Isabella dedicates this book to her family for their continual love and support.

Acknowledgments

Paul: Putting together a conference is never a one-person job, and I have been thankful for the support of my college at DePaul. But it truly wouldn't be possible to do the Pop Culture Conference without the unending support and help of my wife, Katie Booth. From brainstorming ideas to implementing new and exciting developments, Katie has been an amazing (and often unsung) partner in this event. It truly wouldn't be an event without her, and for that (and so many other things) I thank her with all my heart.

Bella: Thank you to Paul for the opportunity to do further work with subjects and content that I love. Thank you to my family for always indulging my intense interest in all forms of media.

Acknowledgements

A Celebration of Doctor Who: Grateful acknowledgement to Katie Booth, Kathleen Browne, Jef Burnham, Carolyn Bronstein, Elizabeth Gaytan, Matt Irvine, Fatenah Issa, Aisha Pulido, John Shananan, Lynne M. Thomas, and Latrina West-Shields.

Joss Whedon, A Celebration: Grateful acknowledgement to Katie Booth, Kathleen Browne, Jef Burnham, Cheryl Cain, Gina Christodoulou, Michael Deangelis, Mat Irvine, Fatenah Issa, Allison McCracken, Wilma Rodriguez, and Latrina West-Shields. Many thanks to Alien Entertainment and Deborah Liebow from DePaul University's Loop Barnes and Noble. Cover and layout design by Jeremy Kanne. See his other work and contract his services at: www.jeremykanne.com.

A Celebration of Supernatural: This Celebration wouldn't have been possible without help from the following: All of the speakers; All the volunteers (Laura Buczynski, Katie Capparelli, Michael Constantino, Sophia Dixon, Mary Doerries, Gordon Dymowski, Jess Glass, Sarah Kates, David LeGare, Michael Mulligan, Jenny Riley, Aubrie Rizzo, Mayra Sanchez, Kathleen Wright, and Stephanie Zahaitis); Jeremy Kanne, who created the fantastic cover; My incredible research assistant Jess Glass; Jennifer Willis-Rivera, Melanie Schmitz, and Annie Houston from Random Acts; The Winchester Family Business! (thewinchesterfamilybusiness.com); Katie Booth, Kathleen Browne, Gina Christodoulou, Michael Deangelis, Salma Ghanem, Kathy Larsen, Mark Oshiro, Wilma Rodriguez, Maureen Ryan, Alex Schneider, Robbie Thompson, and Lynn Zubernis!

A Celebration of Star Trek: This Celebration wouldn't have been possible without help from the following: All of the speakers; All the volunteers (Emily Baeza, Katie Caparelli, Thom Coates, Kaleb Davie, Jess Glass, Julianna Hartke, Rebecca Manion, Erica Marquis, Isabella Menichiello, Michael Mulligan, Jack Prey, Andrew Sharp, Laura Springman, TJ Watson, Kathleen Wright); Laura Bluett; Mariah Cowan; Ruth Frasier from Chimp Haven; Marc Malnakoff; Brannon Braga; Lisa Klink; Lincoln Geraghty; Heather Ash, Katie Booth,

Kathleen Browne, Gina Christodoulou, Marielle Galizio, Michael Deangelis, Salma Ghanem, & Wilma Rodriguez.

Harry Potter and the Pop Culture Conference: Many thanks to the following, without whom this conference would not have been possible! All the volunteers (Kaitlynn Aiken, Emily Baeza, Annalisa Baranowski, Noah Barth, Laura Buczynski, Gabe Bustoz, Katie Campos, Katie Capparelli, Thom Cote, Sophie Dixon, Mary Doerries, Carrie Emge, Jess Glass, PJ Krumpelman, Rutherford Manion, Cate Morrow, Michael Mulligan, Caitlin Nero, Katie Paul, Avery Riley, Jenny Riley, Chell Rodriguez, Kinga Rzezinowska, Gabi Sellers, William Staton, Maricar Tamayo, Brock Williams, Kathleen Wright), The Best Communication Research Assistants (Isabella Menichiello, Monika Sziron, and Zenaya Williams); Laura Bluett, Eti Berland and Anny Rusk of the *The Patronuses* and the Harry Potter Alliance; Alanna Bennett and Dr. Christopher Bell; Jennifer Jones; Kathleen Browne, Gina Christodoulou, Marielle Galizio, Michael DeAngelis, Salma Ghanem, and Wilma Rodriguez; the ever-amazing Katie Booth

Introduction
The DePaul Pop Culture Conference

Paul Booth

The DePaul Pop Culture Conference began with a question from a student. In late 2012, after a particularly good discussion about narrative complexity and the Timey-Wimey paradox of "Blink" in my class "Time Travel on Television," Spencer Flynn asked what I was planning to do for the 50th anniversary of *Doctor Who*. It was not an unwelcome question: Perhaps because we were talking about "Blink," or perhaps because of my *Doctor Who*-themed accessories (pins, ties, and teeshirts) and office door (festooned with *Doctor Who* images like an Ood mask), Spencer (as well as the other students) somehow seemed to pick up on my particular preference for this classic British television series. "Well, I'm seeing the fiftieth anniversary movie in the theater," I said. "And I'm definitely going to rewatch some old episodes! But other than that, I don't have any specific plans…"

"No, that's not what I mean," he responded. "Are you doing anything at DePaul? Can we have a screening? Or can you give a talk or something?"

What a great idea—a short talk about the importance and relevance of *Doctor Who* for the DePaul community! There are plenty of ties between the Doctor and Vincentian values, such as the care of disadvantaged people, the commitment to social reform, and always asking the question "What can be done?" I bet I could invite some of my colleagues and friends as well. We could have a screening and I could talk about it. But what episode? Classic or new? Which Doctor? A great episode, or a mediocre one?

And then I got to thinking for real. Who am I to give the talk? Isn't there so much more to talk about? And what about things I don't really know about? Maybe I could ask two other people to sit in on a panel with me? But then whom to ask? My mind was spinning and the ideas were flowing. (Spencer, I imagine, did not expect this flood of possibility.) My fannish sensibilities were on overdrive (would it be possible to get David Tennant as a guest?) and I thought the event, which I'd now in my head called *A Celebration of Doctor Who,* might be a cool fan convention.

At the same time, a different *Doctor Who* related event helped shape the start of the Pop Culture Conference. *Walking in Eternity*, a 2013 *Doctor Who* themed scholarly conference, was fresh in my mind when Spencer asked me about my academic plans for *Doctor Who's* 50th. I'd just written a paper for the conference which was to be delivered later that year (actually much closer to the 50th anniversary, in September). Like most scholarly conferences, each participant was expected to write and deliver a 20-minute presentation of research. There were academic books for us to browse through and purchase, and teaching materials on display. It was held at a college in the UK, the University of Hertfordshire. We also had well-attended sessions from four keynote speakers throughout the weekend, who focused their hour-long talks on different cultural and industrial aspects of the series. Unlike most scholarly conferences, however, we also were graced by a visit from *Doctor Who* icon K-9 (the robotic dog) and its owner/operator Mat Irvine; we had an AUTHENTIC DALEK (!!) on display, and we had specially made tee-shirts for the conference. It was, in many respects, a typical scholarly conference but with tinges of fandom garnishing the event. And it was magnificent.

Indeed, I thought, why not plan an event that was like *Walking in Eternity*, but reversed? A fan event but with tinges of academic conferencing?

In truth, fan conventions and academic conferences are not as different as many people might think. Fans and scholars participate in many of the same tasks, often debating, discussing, or analyzing texts using multiple methodologies. These differing methodologies become valued differently, depending on the context. For example, Matt Hills (2010, p. 4) has discussed the way fan research tends to be seen as affectively "intra-textual," as fans dig deeper into a text (something Jason Mittell (2013) has referred to as "drillable media"). Conversely, academic scholarship tends to be read in a scholarly "inter-textual" fashion, moving across, between, betwixt, and within multiple texts and discourses simultaneously (moving in a "spreadable" pattern, to co-opt a term from Jenkins, Ford, and Green (2013)). Each context (convention, conference) brings with it expectations from the participants. We assume that fans are emotionally invested and that academics are objective and scholarly. But these are not necessarily true: plenty of fan conventions feature analytic or "objective" discussions of media and cultural production and academics are nothing if not passionate about their research materials (sometimes they may be one of only a few people in the world who are passionate about them; other times they may study something as popular as, say, *Doctor Who*).

In addition, both conventions and conferences feature panels and roundtable discussions. Both offer workshop spaces, where fans can learn handicrafts from each other and scholars can work on CVs and cover letters. Fans often cosplay ('dress up') at cons; academics will wear the clothes of their profession. There are always things to purchase, whether that's collectibles and swag (the dealer's hall at fan conventions) or scholarly books (at conferences). Scholarly research into fan conventions has speculated on the communal and participatory nature of the space (Bacon-Smith 1992; Jenkins 1992; Zubernis and Larson 2012), and scholarly conferences are similarly spaces where academics can come together to share research and scholarship on a variety of topics and in fields, often in areas of interest.

In academic literature, the connection between fans and academics has been much discussed. In an article about fan studies for the *Journal of Fandom Studies* I wrote in 2013, I noted that:

> For many fan scholars, fan studies has already become meta: the discipline has been under scrutiny from the disciples. The ongoing discussion of aca-fandom, for example, stems from a need to reflect on where we have been and what we are doing. Although Jenkins's (2011) blog conversation demonstrates the multifaceted meanings of the term 'aca-fan', for the purposes of this article I will be defining aca-fandom as the hybridized identity between scholarship and fandom within one conception of being, much as in M. Hills' discussion of the scholar-fan and fan-scholar (2002: 11–20). That is, Hills' fan-scholar who analyses the object of her fandom could be using an aca-fan methodology, while an academic Hills' scholar-fan who researches something she is enamored of is also participating in aca-fandom. Far from separate, dichotomous identities, the fan and the researcher, as Hills (2007: 46) states 'can no longer be "set apart" from the culture and ideology it studies, but is rather "set in relation" with these contexts.' (123)

This brings up a number of salient points: the fan and the scholar are not so much binary opposites as set up on different sides of the same continuum. Academics who are also fans have been called the "aca-fan" (academic-fan, from aca-fan himself Henry Jenkins) and the "scholar-fan" (from Matt Hills). Conversely, fans who participate in more scholarly analyses of their object of fandom have been called "fan-scholars" in academic literature or "meta-fans" in fan parlance. We might call the *Walking in Eternity* conference a "scholar-fan" space, where scholars of *Doctor Who* would also be able to stretch their fannish identities. I wanted the Pop Culture Conference to be a place where scholar-fans and fan-scholars could congregate, where fans could stretch their scholarly muscles as well as scholars could become a bit more fannish. The Pop Culture Conference is a space to enable a fan-scholar/scholar-fan dialogue, one that relies on fannish enthusiasm for the show and couples it with scholarly analysis (Hills 2002).

Suddenly, I had a plan for *A Celebration of Doctor Who*—a full day of fannish scholarship (or scholarly fandom?) focused on *Doctor Who*. Why not invite all the local *Doctor Who* scholars I knew to come out and do some fun panels? So, I put the word out and people started to submit their ideas. In order to facilitate a more engaging style of discourse, however, the Pop Culture Conference would have to be a space where there were presentations by researchers as well as fans and members of the local community, but these presentations should not be strictly academic paper presentations. So, I asked participants to phrase their responses and topics as discussion points to be addressed in a roundtable format.

Putting together a conference is never a one-person job, and my wife Katie was immediately on board with the idea—the event could not have happened without (and continues to this day because of) her help. From day one she has been a partner in this event, helping to work with guests, brainstorming ideas for the conference, and working to make it better each year.

It was also fortuitous that I was able to invite *Doctor Who* alum Rob Shearman as a keynote speaker for this first conference; never underestimate the power of social media to put people in contact with each other! Rob's amazing interview and talk helped frame the event and helped make *A Celebration of Doctor Who* a success for those who attended.

The first Pop Culture Conference happened in May 2013 and I figured that was that. Maybe in 25 years, for *Doctor Who*'s 75th anniversary, I'd revisit. But it was a fun event (even Captain Jack himself—John Barrowman—recorded a video message for us!) and the people that attended seemed to have a good time, and I made some friends and had some interesting discussions. A great time, but just a one-time thing.

Until August 2013 and an email in my inbox—"What's next year's event going to be about?"

It's a question we ask every year now—what is the big anniversary for next year? We try to balance types of fandoms, levels of interest from the DePaul community, availability of academic expertise, and that all-important fun quotient. There may be an incredibly passionate fannish subculture for an obscure TV show from the 1970s, but finding a good mix of academic and fan can be tough.

Each year we try to improve from years before, through taking suggestions from attendees and trying new experiments for events and speakers. The second year we instituted an anti-harassment policy, following the best practices of fan conventions around the country. Interestingly, I was contacted a year later by a reporter from the *Chicago Tribune* hoping to do a story about harassment at local conventions—she was very surprised to hear that there had been none at the DePaul Pop Culture Conference. "Then why have a policy?" she asked. I explained that it wasn't so much focused on what *has* happened as it is a plan for what to do if something *does* happen, and it's in place to help people feel safe at the event. It has a list of what is not acceptable at the conference and a number of remedies if harassment is witnessed or experienced, and contact information for help. "So nothing has actually happened?" she repeated, and I replied again, "No." The story was never printed. A similar conversation happened with an academic, who emailed me to ask why such a policy was in place. It is not usual for academic conferences to include such policies at scholarly events, so for the academics coming to the Pop Culture Conference, it's often a new experience to read. This is a real learning experience, though, and one of the many reasons the intermingling of fans and academics at the Pop Culture Conference is useful: we all learn from each other.

The second Pop Culture Conference was also the first year we raised money for charity—the results of a small silent auction were donated to Equality Now, an organization supported by Joss Whedon (the subject of our second conference). Each year we've tried to increase our charitable giving (this book is another aspect of this, as all proceeds from sales will be donated to Global Girl Media), and we've donated to Random Acts, Chimp Haven, and the Harry Potter Alliance. Keynote speaker Cheryl Cain, a writer who worked on *Firefly*, gave a talk about working on the series and then held a workshop on writing for television. The next year, keynote Robbie Thompson, producer of TV's *Supernatural*, held the audience captivated with stories and advice for writing. The following year, writer/producer/director Brannon Braga discussed his history with the *Star Trek* series. And other speakers, like Lisa Klink (*Star Trek Voyager*), Dr. Lincoln Geraghty (*Living with Star Trek*), Mat Irvine (*Doctor Who*), Mark Oshiro (Mark Watches...), and Dr. Christopher Bell have explored many aspects of their particular fannish expertise. As I write this, Alanna Bennett (Buzzfeed writer about *Harry Potter*) will be speaking at the 2017 conference, and of course, there have been over 100 speakers and panel participants over the past five years that have all helped to make this event special for the over 1000 people who have attended.

2014's *Celebration of Joss Whedon* made way for 2015's *A Celebration of Supernatural* and 2016's *Celebration of Star Trek*. We've grown with each of these events—the *Supernatural* one had teeshirts for sale, the *Star Trek* one saw a new location with lots more vendors and keynote speakers. As I write this, planning is already underway for 2017's *A Celebration of Harry Potter*, which has seen more preregisters than any other Pop Culture Conference we've run. More people have submitted abstracts for consideration and there are more panels than ever before. We continue to grow, and improve, each year. I hope you'll join us for future events— and I hope you'll be there when we answer "What's next year's event going to be about?"

References
Bacon-Smith, Camile. 1992. *Enterprising Women*. Philadelphia, PA: University of Pennsylvania Press.
Booth, Paul. 2013. "Augmenting Fan/Academic Dialogue: New Directions in Fan Research." *Journal of Fandom Studies* 1, no. 2: 119-137.
Hills, Matt. 2002. *Fan Cultures*. London: Routledge.
Hills, Matt. 2007. "Media Academics as Media Audiences. In *Fandom: Identities and Communities in a Mediated World*, edited by Jonathan Gray, Cornel Sandvoss, and C. Lee Harrington, 33–47. New York: New York University Press.
Hills, Matt. 2010. *Triumph of a Time Lord: Regenerative Doctor Who in the Twenty-first Century*. London: IB Tauris.
Jenkins, Henry, Sam Ford, and Joshua Green. 2013. *Spreadable Media*. New York: New York University Press.
Jenkins, Henry. 1992. *Textual Poachers*. New York: Routledge.
Jenkins, Henry. 2011. "Aca-Fandom and Beyond." Blog series. *Confessions of an Aca-Fan*. Henryjenkins.org.

Mittell, Jason. 2013. "Forensic Fandom and the Drillable Text." *Spreadable Media Web Exclusive Essay*. http://spreadablemedia.org/essays/mittell/#.WOKH6BIrLUI

Zubernis, Lynn, and Katherine Larsen. *Fandom at the Crossroads*. Newcastle, UK: Cambridge Scholars Press.

A Celebration of *Doctor Who*

A Colloquium,
Discussion, and
Commemoration on
the Fiftieth
Anniversary of
BBC's *Doctor Who*

Saturday May 04, 2013   *DePaul University*

Introduction

Paul Booth

The first Pop Culture Conference focused on the 50th anniversary of *Doctor Who*, in the appropriately titled *A Celebration of Doctor Who*. Held 04 May 2013, this interdisciplinary conference celebrated *Doctor Who* by bringing together academics, fans, community members, and students—a wide swath of people with an interest in this cult BBC show.

Sparking debate and discussion about the changing values, meanings, and contexts of *Doctor Who* across its first half-century, the conference focused on speaking to multiple groups—the colloquium featured both fan and scholarly speakers, and both academics and fan groups were in attendance. Speakers and audience members explored the nuances of the program, discussed the mysteries of the protagonist, and debated the greatest enigmas throughout time and space.

The keynote speaker was *Doctor Who* luminary Robert Shearman, who wrote the first Series episode "Dalek" as well as a number of Big Finish audios, including "Chimes of Midnight," consistently voted the best audio adventure of all time. Shearman spoke about his writing process, offered anecdotes about his experiences working with Russell T Davies and Steven Moffat, and articulated his personal history with *Doctor Who*. During his hour-long interview/talk, Shearman revealed aspects of the production process, including how particular scenes are constructed in the editing room. He also performed a live commentary on his episode "Dalek" (14 April 2006) and read one of his short stories.

In addition, over 150 participants attended six roundtable discussions during the daylong celebration. The first Pop Culture Conference held just one panel at a time, so that each roundtable featured featured six speakers presenting multiple viewpoints and illuminating both scholarly and fan discourse. Topics included "The Long Appeal of *Doctor Who*," which focused on the changing fan base of the show; "*Doctor Who* and Philosophy," which examined the series' moral and ethical dimensions; and "*Doctor Who* Aesthetics," which looked at design challenges throughout the show's history. In the afternoon, thematic panels included "*Doctor Who* and Gender,"

"*Doctor Who* and Fandom," and "*Doctor Who* and Narrative," each of which offered analyses of the show's impact on fifty years of cultural studies.

Speakers at the colloquium ranged from academics who integrate *Doctor Who* into their research to fans who have published about the show. As befits the academic/fan amalgam of the conference, speakers were encouraged to discuss and debate, rather than present scholarly papers. In many ways, speakers at the colloquium embodied what Matt Hills has termed the "scholar-fan" model of academia and the "fan-scholar" model within fandom.

The fan-scholars in attendance included Erika Ensign and Lynne M. Thomas, contributors to the *Verity! Doctor Who* podcast. Thomas also co-edited, with fellow roundtable participant Tara O'Shea, the collection *Chicks Dig Time Lords* (2010). Other contributors to that collection who participated include novelists Mary Robinette Kowal, Kathryn Sullivan, and Jody Lynn Nye, and author Tammy Garrison. Additional fan-scholars in attendance include Philip Sandifer, author of the *TARDIS Eruditorum* blog and book series, Doctor Who columnist Rob Levy, and Jennifer Adams Kelley, coordinator of the Chicago TARDIS fan convention.

Scholar-fans who spoke came from varied inter-disciplinary backgrounds, including professor of design, and author of *TARDISBound* (2011), Piers Britton; philosophy professor Ann Hetzel Gunkel; religious studies professor Scott Paeth; historian, and author of *Doctor Who in Time and Space* (2013), Gillian Leitch; television scholar Derek Kompare; rhetorician Ashley Hinck; media professor Cary Elza; humanities professor, and author of *The Doctor Who Franchise* (2012), Lynnette Porter; cinema professor Michele Leigh; psychologist Sherry Ginn; professor of English Gerry Canavan; and writing professor Carole Barrowman, author of a novel set in the *Torchwood* universe. Her presence at the conference was exceptional, as her personal connection to the program (her brother is John Barrowman, who played Jack Harkness) facilitated a special video message from Captain Jack himself.

The *Celebration* also hosted screenings of key episodes from the series' fifty-year history, selected by a Facebook poll of attendees before the event, a book signing, and *Doctor Who* music played live by a fan Who-themed band, The Well-Tempered Schism.

The Celebration of Doctor Who was never intended to be the first Pop Culture Conference; it was simply The Pop Culture Conference and I thought it would end there. We learned a lot from this early event—from the big (it's useful to have more than one panel at a time) to the small (provide tablecloths). But my original intention worked: to bring together academics and fans in conversation.

Interestingly, there are two direct antecedents I can point to as helping me develop this idea, and both are directly related to *Doctor Who*. In 2013, I presented a paper at *Walking in Eternity*, a *Doctor Who* themed academic conference held in the UK in Sept. Although the conference took place after the *Celebration of Doctor Who*, I'd submitted the paper and was gearing up for my trip as I was planning the *Celebration*. The second event was doing interview research for the 2012 *Chicago TARDIS* fan convention. At this con I interviewed about one hundred fans about their experiences being fans of *Doctor Who*.

Researching fans at a convention; writing academic work for a convention. The two activities suddenly seemed to me to be linked. I knew I wasn't the first to see the comparison between fans and academics (Matt Hills has certainly written on the subject), but here was tangible evidence in front of my own eyes, done by me.

I'm a fan of *Doctor Who*.

I'm also an academic who studies *Doctor Who*.

There must be more of us.

So I made an event to find out.

Looking back at the first Pop Culture Conference is a bit like looking at your writing from years ago: you can see what you were trying to do and you now know how to make it better. There were a number of things that we changed over the years from this first event, but I'll always remember it incredibly fondly—it started this whole mess and, for that, I can only say thank you to all that were there at the start, thank you to the speakers and fans, and thank you to *Doctor Who*. I hope you enjoy reading some of the essays that emerged from the conference.

Portions of this summary were original published in 2013 in Science Fiction Studies, vol. 40.

Keynote

Robert Shearman

The truth is, I had never really watched *Doctor Who* when I was a little kid. I was far too frightened of it. Not, I think, by anything I had ever actually *seen* on the screen—my fear was such that I could never get beyond the opening title sequence, that psychedelic time tunnel, Tom Baker's terrifying face. But its *reputation* in the home counties of Great Britain in the seventies was immense—it was this unpleasant fixture in my childhood that I knew must always exist, but that I should steer well clear of, like crossing roads without pedestrian lights, like electrified railway lines, like strange men in cars offering sweets. I didn't have to have watched *Doctor Who* to know what it was. It was this temptation that sat squat in the BBC schedules on a Saturday evening— and a temptation that was offered in plain sight, and only the most daring of children, and the most wicked probably, would give into.

I was eleven years old when I changed my mind, and went over to the dark side. And it wasn't catching a glimpse of some metal monster that suddenly filled my imagination, it wasn't a cute metal dog or a leggy assistant.

In the lunch break at our school the Junior History Society sat in Room 10, next door to the library, and just across from the Prefect's Room. I liked history a lot. I liked the way there were lots of lists that came attached to history, and how I could memorize dates of battles, and the correct order for all the kings and queens since William the Conqueror. And sometimes the society would be made up of talks given to us by the schoolteachers—not just history teachers, but even biology teachers with a penchant for naval warfare. And sometimes, though more rarely, talks given by some of the older boys. These were usually the better talks, because even though they weren't delivered as well, they were delivered with *passion*—it takes an unfeigned passion to make a teenager stand up in front of kids younger than himself for half an hour. So, yes, we had William the Conqueror, and we had naval warfare —but the talk that really changed my life was the one called "The History of *Doctor Who*."

So this older boy—not quite a prefect yet, but nearly there, on his way—talked to us all about his favorite show on television. It sounded like a cop-out even then—until we realized that the show genuinely *did* have a history; it had been going on for *ages*, even before I was born! He explained how the series had evolved over the years, from being an educational vehicle to get children excited about history and science, into a military based adventure series, into something horrific, into something comic; he explained how the producers changed, how the lead actors changed, that it was a constantly changing thing. And he had a scroll—I remember the scroll very well—and on it he had written the names of every single *Doctor Who* adventure *ever*— and how exotic they all sounded, all the way from "An Unearthly Child" to "Logopolis." This huge list, of new things I could learn to recite, in order! I remember that scroll. I remember how he let it unroll, and that it ran right down the length of his body and spooled around his feet.

That boy's name was Owen Bywater. We are still good friends to this day—even though I rather plagued him for years for information about my new chosen obsession. Years later, when I wrote my own episode of *Doctor Who*, I wrote in a character called Bywater, as a thank you. He's the first person in the twenty-first century to get exterminated by a Dalek. I knew it was what he would have wanted.

The first *Doctor Who* books I read were not the Target novelizations—they were *The Making of Doctor Who* and *The Doctor Who Programme Guide*. I gobbled them up. I reread them so often that in my mind's eye I can still see the pages in my head, all the information clearly laid out, with production codes, cast list, and story synopsis. *Doctor Who* was off the air for its seasonal break at the time; when it came back, in the new year of 1982, I was already a *Doctor Who* fan, I simply hadn't got round to watching any of the episodes yet. When in episode one of "Castrovalva," Peter Davison's new Doctor makes allusions to the Brigadier and to the Ice Warriors, I could confidently turn to my family and tell them that their origin stories were "The Web of Fear" and "The Ice Warriors" respectively. I felt very proud. My parents, I think, less so.

What I hadn't realized, of course, was that I had fallen in love with the series at an unusual angle. I never went through the process of pretending it was in any way real. I was more fascinated by the changing styles of different script editors than I was in whether the Master's plans actually made any sense or not. And it was the first time too that I consciously realized that something I enjoyed was a work of art, a fiction created by multiple and contradictory artists. The thrill was always that it was a series that could be analyzed, poked apart, prodded at. I bought an expensive academic tome with my birthday money called *Doctor Who—The Unfolding Text*, and barely understood a word of it, but was nonetheless hugely excited that it was possible to look at fiction in this way. Owen Bywater and I started our own fanzine—in truth, it was already Owen's, but I forced my way on to it through sheer obsessive enthusiasm—and wrote barely coherent essays about the weaknesses of "The King's Demons" and the "Graham Williams era." It didn't matter that I hadn't seen any stories that Graham Williams had produced, and his "era" lasted two and a half years. I was, without knowing it, applying myself to academic study.

It was no surprise to anyone that I studied English literature at university, and cut a swathe through Wordsworth and Webster with the same sort of hungry passion I had found pointing out the flaws in *The Trial of a Time Lord*. It was suggested that I stay on and complete a doctorate on Renaissance drama, doing a bit of teaching on the side. But I had been dabbling in writing drama of my own, and had got lucky with some early scripts—I accepted instead an Arts Council residency to be attached to a local theatre and to develop my work as a playwright. In the end I chose writing fiction over academia, and at times it felt a little like a betrayal.

Of course, I knew I would never write for *Doctor Who*. The show had been cancelled in 1989 whilst I was an undergraduate. I was always terribly grateful to it, because I knew it had awakened the impulse in me to write at all. And that contradictory sense that is there, I think, in all good writing—of losing yourself in the imaginative thrust of the fantasy that you're creating, whilst also standing back from it coolly and remembering that it is something that is going to be criticized, analyzed and assessed. That any good piece of fiction has to be two things at once—it has to be a story worth the examining, and yet first and foremost, it has to be a *story* too.

That push-pull nature of writing is always there, I think. But it was never more true than when I was invited to write for the first season of the revived *Doctor Who* in 2004. (Yes, it came back. You could have knocked me down with a feather.) There's a tricky high wire balancing act when you write fiction, of calculating the effect you have upon the audience, whilst pretending the audience isn't there to begin with. With *Doctor Who* it was almost impossible to forget that the audience were waiting in the wings. Not just to see whether or not they enjoyed my Dalek story. But to *assess* the revival, to judge its place within that unfolding text of the show's history. I knew that whether the revival succeeded or not, my story would never now be forgotten, it would be forever upon all the lists. I had a dream one night about Owen Bowater's scroll, and my story at the very bottom of it, that it had been the last killing blow.

The great joy for me, of course, is that *Doctor Who* didn't end the year that we revived it. That it wasn't some final dying gasp for breath, but a new beginning. My story is number 161 (oh, trust me, I still know my lists), and at the time of writing, I'm waiting for next week's broadcast of number 265. In the mental scroll of my mind, that places me just under the halfway point, somewhere around Owen Bywater's ankle. That's not a bad place to be. It's strangely cozy, actually.

It was an honor to be invited to speak at DePaul university in 2013 about my time on *Doctor Who.* It was so tempting to go there and try to speak as the academic I might once have been. As the eleven-year-old fan who would have found my story fascinating (and been *very* harsh about it, I expect, because he was a humorless and unforgiving sort of sod). In the end I realized that the best I could do was speak about the process honestly, as well as I could recall it—but that the actual *analysis* of it would best be done by others. There is a bluntness to pure academic study, I think, that is almost gleeful—quite rightly, it can't afford to take into account good intentions, it can't worry about hurt feelings. As a writer I am proud of my contribution to *Doctor Who* (and relieved I didn't do anything to damage it). As an academic, I would have to be much more clinical.

They say of *Doctor Who* that it's like playing in a sandpit. This gorgeous, clever idea for a series, that over the decades has allowed so many different approaches and styles, some of them in direct opposition to the other. As writers we get into the sandpit for a little while, and get to build our own sandcastles with the finest (but very oddest) sand imaginable, and then we have to get out again, and let other people knock them down and build castles of their own. But I've always sort of understood—right beside that sandpit there's this *other* sandpit, where all the academics go to play. And they look at the sandcastles that we've had knocked down, and they *remember* them. They assess them, they compare them to the castles that came before or have come since. They don't apologize for them, but they do make sense of them—maybe they weren't even castles, as it turns out, maybe they were forts. And the passion is just as great as in the writer's sandpit, and the playing more thoughtful and more generous. Long may both play on, side by side— all of us, basically, just kids out in the sunshine having fun.

The Cultural Lives of *Doctor Who*: Celebrations, Conferences, Conventions

Paul Booth

Like many television programs with a strong fan base, *Doctor Who* has thrived not just on the television screen, but also through celebratory fan conventions. For fans in 2013, *Doctor Who*'s fiftieth anniversary celebrations arrived with pomp and circumstance, fanfare and flourish: This year, celebrations have been *de rigueur*.

[Image 1: Who Celebration]
(http://www.bbcamerica.com/anglophenia/2013/07/tickets-for-the-doctor-who-50th-anniversary-celebration-coming-soo/)

For *Doctor Who* the fiftieth anniversary, as Matt Hills has described, is not just a way of marking a milestone for the television series, but also an "epic collision between fandom and brand management." This collision can be seen not just in the way the BBC releases minisodes to appeal to fans, in a fashion that Hills has called "trans-transmedia," but also in the many in-person celebrations being held at the anniversary. These celebrations have taken many guises: from professionally-run, BBC-organized affairs, to academic conferences, to fan/scholar celebrations of *Doctor Who*, to fan-run conventions, to record-breaking cinema extravaganzas, to fan-oriented screening parties, the sheer number of fan celebrations demonstrate the continued affective and communal power of a cult television franchise like *Doctor Who.*

[Image 2: Chicago Tardis]

This past weekend (Nov 28–Dec 01) I attended (and presented at) Chicago TARDIS, a local fan-run convention with over 2500 attendees, 30 guests, and 160 panels and events. Chicago TARDIS manifests the collision between fandom and branding. The panels at Chicago TARDIS included both professional actor/crew presentations (three original Doctors were present, as were a number of companions and ancillary content creators), while also featuring more fan-oriented panels like "Fangirls are Real Fans, Too," "The Danger of Fandom Entitlement," and "Heroes (or Chumps?) of Cosplay."

TARDIS has been running under that name for thirteen years, and emerged after the demise of HME/Visions, a Chicago area *Doctor Who* convention that ran from 1990–1998. In her book *The Doctor Who Franchise*, Lynette Porter describes how "some guests prefer" attending smaller events like TARDIS or other fan-run US conventions like Gallifrey One and Hurricane Who, "because they provide that personal touch and are smaller, less stressful events" (151). Although fans of *Doctor Who* have met informally since the beginning of the show, organized fan conventions for *Doctor Who* started in earnest in the UK on Saturday 6th August 1977, with the *Doctor Who Appreciation Society*'s convention, later named Panopticon. The first US convention was held in December 1979, with Fourth Doctor Tom Baker and producer Graham Williams in attendance (there because of the last minute cancellation of the production of *Shada*).

Doctor Who fan conventions are different than *Doctor Who* exhibitions, as Philip Sandifer describes. In her chapter on the *Doctor Who* Experience in Cardiff Bay, Melissa Beattie points out the exhibition has served not only to revitalize Cardiff, but also to reinforce the dominant, commercial meanings of *Who*. Indeed, unlike fan-run conventions like Chicago TARDIS, more official, BBC-sanctioned events tend to seem "much more like a traditional museum with … displays and structures," according to Beattie (178). The famous *Doctor Who Exhibition* in Longleat or the *Doctor Who Exhibition* in Blackpool were both long-running museums of *Doctor Who* props, monsters, and memorabilia.

[Image 4: Blackpool] (http:// doctorwhotimevor tex.blogspot.com/ 2009/10/ blackpool-doctor- who-exhibition- to.html)

In general, professionally-run conventions like the *Doctor Who* Experience or the BBC's own 50th anniversary celebration tend to reinforce the dominant readings of the show with panels articulating authorized behind-the-scenes information or discussion with actors and crew. In contrast, smaller, more fan-run conventions tend to allow a plurality of voices, with panels discussing fannish activities like "Fandom Culture Clash" and "You Know You're a *Doctor Who* Fan When…" That being said, many fan-run conventions also have crew and special guests, and many professional feature fan-friendly fare. There may also be a UK/US difference in convention styles, and the line between guest and participant is often more blurred at fan-run conventions. According to Zubernis and Larsen's *Fandom at the Crossroads*, more corporate organizations like Creation Entertainment tend to reinforce the barrier between fan and celebrity, even while simultaneously seeming to erase it. At Chicago TARDIS, interaction with guests is less regulated and often happens seemingly on accident – in the hotel bar, in the lobby while waiting for a cab, even walking across the street to Target (last year I literally ran into *Sarah Jane Adventures* actress Anjli Mohindra while making my way through the hotel doors).

As we commemorate the fiftieth anniversary of *Doctor Who*, it's important to recognize that meeting in-person to celebrate the show is nothing new. Many *Doctor Who* conventions are now decades old. 2013 may mark a higher level of visibility for the program than ever before, but its fans have met for decades before now. What is different today is what Hills notes of TV anniversary celebrations: they "take on different meanings within reconfigured industry/audience contexts" (p. 217). Fan conventions are similar, and the annual *consistency* of conventions allows them to take on new dimensions. Unprecedented levels of access to behind-the-scenes news, celebrity personal lives, and production details make professional conventions often a reiteration rather than a revelation of information.

Meanwhile, the growing popularity of fan-run celebrations seems to be developing just as social media and the web provide copious avenues for fans to meet and congregate online. In my own research on *Doctor Who* fan conventions, I found that, for many fans, coming to Chicago TARDIS was less about meeting guests and more like "a family reunion," where they could see the friends that "got" each other's quirks. That TARDIS is always the weekend of Thanksgiving increases its familial quality: Thanksgiving is to celebrate with our family, to relax by the hearth, and to enjoy the company of those – and the shows – we love. The fiftieth anniversary of *Doctor Who* may be behind us, but like the Doctor himself, they will continue to develop and regenerate for many years to come – and, judging by these cosplayers, below, the future is assured.

[Figure 5: Cosplay] Photo Credit: Jef Burnham

My thanks to Ian Peters and Jennifer Adams Kelly for providing information about TARDIS as well as background on Doctor Who conventions in general help in the early stages of this post. Originally published in 2013 on Antenna blog, blog.commarts.wisc.edu/2013/12/03/the-cultural-lives-of-doctor-who-celebrations-conferences-conventions/

References
Beattie, Melissa. 2013. "The 'Doctor Who Experience' (2012–) and the Commodification of Cardiff Bay." In *New Dimensions of Doctor Who Exploring Space Time and Television*, edited by Matt Hills, 177–191. London: IB Tauris.
Booth, Paul. 2013. "Augmenting Fan/Academic Dialogue: New Directions in Fan Research." *Journal of Fandom Studies* 1, no. 2: 119-137.
Hills, Matt. 2013, "The Cultural Lives of Doctor Who: What's Special About Multiple Multi-Doctor Specials?" *Antenna.* http://blog.commarts.wisc.edu/2013/10/15/the-cultural-lives-of-doctor-who-whats-special-about-multiple-multi-doctor-specials/
Porter, Lynnette. 2012. *The Doctor Who Franchise.* Jefferson, NC: McFarland.
Sandifer, Philip. 2012. "You Were Expecting Someone Else 9 (Longleat, Doctor Who Monthly, the Peter Davison Comics)." *Tardis Eruditorum.* http://www.eruditorumpress.com/blog/you-were-expecting-someone-else-9-longleat-doctor-who-monthly-the-peter-davison-comics/
Zubernis, Lynn, and Katherine Larsen. *Fandom at the Crossroads.* Newcastle, UK: Cambridge Scholars Press.

The Cultural Lives of *Doctor Who*: Of Anniversaries and Authenticity, Costumes and Canon

Piers Britton

In many ways, *Doctor Who*'s Series 7 finale, "The Name of the Doctor," marked the beginning of the golden jubilee celebrations (albeit six months early): the episode echoed a cherished tradition for major Who anniversaries by including new footage of past Doctors, as well as archival material. However, for the first time the new footage relied entirely on non-speaking stand-ins, their faces out of focus or in shadow, with the result that the principal signifier for each Doctor was his distinctive sartorial look.

Compared to the decidedly impressionistic recreation of past Doctors' outfits by James Acheson and Colin Lavers in "The Three Doctors" (1972) and "The Five Doctors" (1983) respectively, Howard Burden's costumes for the "Name" cameos show considerable attention to detail. This is particularly striking in the case of the First Doctor, who appears in the pre-credits sequence on Gallifrey and again at the climax. The body double here is seen only in long shots, which alternate with close-ups and medium close-ups digitally incorporating footage of William Hartnell. Each shot of Hartnell is tight and short enough that in fact only the most general costume correspondence was needed to make the body double a credible match. Yet Burden was evidently taking no chances; his homage to Maureen Heneghan's original costume design was remarkably precise, at a stroke establishing "authentic" costume as a key value for the anniversary season. This use of costume as a marker of authenticity was to play out in unexpected ways, with various ramifications for *Who* tradition and canon, in both "The Day of the Doctor" and "The Night of the Doctor."

The culminating moments of "Name" introduced a past Doctor who was, from the audience's point of view, not a past Doctor at all – the "forgotten" incarnation of the Time Lord played by John Hurt. While this brief, tenebrous sequence allowed little opportunity to see the details of Hurt's richly textured costume, unofficial photographs from location filming had already revealed that in the fiftieth anniversary special Hurt would be wearing a leather "U-Boat" jacket similar to that chosen for Christopher Eccleston's Ninth Doctor. The likeness was enough to provoke speculation well before "The Name of the Doctor" aired, and even before Hurt himself had disclosed that he was playing "part of the Doctor." Fan interest was further piqued by the fact that Hurt's double-breasted waistcoat bore more than a passing resemblance to the one worn by Paul McGann as the Eighth Doctor in the 1996 TV movie. All this led to the quite reasonable supposition that Hurt might be "another version of the Eighth or Ninth Doctors."

As it turned out, the melding of sartorial images is a function of Hurt's, playing a missing incarnation between McGann and Eccleston. The logic of Howard Burden's costume choice in terms of branding and affect is easy to discern. The leather jacket, which is the dominant element of the outfit, reinforces the New Who aesthetic and allows the war-ravaged Hurt incarnation to stand in for the absent Eccleston. For the observant fan, the secondary detail of the waistcoat helps subtly to bridge New Who with the TV movie and thus Classic Who. (Hurt's "sawn-off" version of the Classic-era sonic screwdriver represents another such visual bridge.) What's particularly noteworthy about the War Doctor's costume is that rebranding is achieved through a strategic break with Who precedent. Hurt's outfit situates his Doctor "authentically" within the canon precisely by subverting the tradition that each Doctor's costume should be unlike his immediate predecessor's. Nor, as it turned out, was this to be the only such breach of this tradition in anniversary productions.

Among the biggest surprises of the jubilee season was the Eighth Doctor's scintillating return and regeneration into Hurt's incarnation in "The Night of the Doctor." For this "minisode" Howard Burden designed an entirely new outfit for McGann. At one level this was no doubt a response to the actor's well-known dissatisfaction with his original costume and wig. However, as with Hurt's costume, the main function of the new ensemble was surely to form a bridge, this time between the War Doctor and the Eighth Doctor's own prior image in the TV movie. For "Night," McGann once again wears a frock coat and patterned silk waistcoat, but this time more muted, the coat being earthier in tone than the TV Movie original and made of a soft, matt, woolen fabric rather than flashy panne velvet and satin. In other respects the costume tends "prophetically" toward the militarism of Hurt's outfit. Thus the canvas soldier's leggings worn by the War

Doctor are prefigured by the Eighth Doctor's leather gaiters, the War Doctor's khaki field trousers by his predecessor's tobacco brown twill work-pants, and even Hurt's tattered scarf by McGann's casually knotted silk neckerchief.

The Eighth Doctor's costume for "Night" was also interesting for what it was not. In 2012, Paul McGann secured approval to introduce a new outfit, satchel, and sonic screwdriver into publicity and packaging for the Eighth Doctor audio dramas he records for Big Finish Productions. The new costume was very close to Eccleston's: leather pea coat, tee shirt, and jeans. Clearly it was too close for the purposes of the anniversary specials, with their sleight-of-hand sartorial "retcon" of the War Doctor incarnation. There is slight irony in the rejection of the 2012 costume, given that one of the most discussed aspects of "The Night of the Doctor" has been the name checking of the Eighth Doctor's Big Finish companions, which effectively established his audio adventures as canon. Yet brand logic evidently required that this new inclusiveness apply only to the aural component of Big Finish's work, not to all its "televisual" trappings.[1]

[1] Matt Hills, "Televisuality without television? The Big Finish audios and discourses of 'tele-centric' Doctor Who," in *Time and Relative Dissertations in Space: Critical Perspectives on Doctor Who*, ed. David Butler (Manchester: Manchester University Press, 2008), 280–295.

Originally published on Antenna December 5, 2013 for *The Cultural Lives of Doctor Who: Of Anniversaries and Authenticity, Costumes and Canon*. http://blog.commarts.wisc.edu/2013/12/05/the-cultural-lives-of-doctor-who-of-anniversaries-and-authenticity-costumes-and-canon/

The End...or is it?: Poetic Endings, Time Travel, and the Satisfaction of Conditional Closure

Cary Elza

I

As the producers of science fiction—and especially British science fiction—have known for years, one of the pleasures of apocalypse narratives is the spectacle of the ultimate narrative closure...without the commitment. This image of temporary finality is at the heart of films about the end of the world, of course, but also features prominently in texts about time travel, from H.G. Wells' *The Time Machine* to *Doctor Who,* which (like Douglas Adams' *Hitchhikers' Guide to the Galaxy*) also has the added bonus of offering access to the end of the universe, not just planet Earth.

What does it mean to enjoy the moment when all stories end, and then pop back to London for a pint? *Doctor Who,* as a serial narrative about time travel, reveals something about our need, as audiences, to feel that we're a part of the last story—to fantasize about inclusion—while also flirting safely with the eventual reality of conclusion.

II

First, a bit about apocalyptic texts:

The word apocalypse comes from the Greek "apokalypsis," which means to reveal something, like the lifting of a veil. And in the tradition of Jewish apocalyptic literature, of which the book of Revelation is only the most well-known example, a divine messenger comes down and conveys privileged information to an agent of earth.

In Revelation, which was written around 96 C.E., scholars largely agree that a mystic called John of Patmos is the one in this privileged position.[1] Like Ezekiel before him, he's made a prophet by the heavenly transfer of information; he *knows* what's coming down the line, and can use this information to spread the word of God.

No one else knows. Humans are walking around with their little problems, living their little lives, and they *just have no idea.*

As Jon R. Stone writes in his analysis of apocalyptic fiction, all apocalypses share five general characteristics: 1) "a supernatural source from which a secret knowledge comes"; 2) "interest in otherworldly forces, usually angelic and demonic"; 3) "the firm belief in divine intervention in human history, usually culminating in the end of an evil person or power, or sometimes the end of time itself"; 4) "the restoration of paradise on Earth"; and 5) "the dispensing of rewards and punishments to men and women in the afterlife."2

These features of apocalyptic literature require the presence of an outsider with power, an agent of change, who intervenes in the lives of Earthlings, thwarts disaster, and shares the secret knowledge of the "true" nature of things with a chosen human. If this is sounding familiar so far, it's not a coincidence.

So what's so great about this? Why is it so appealing to *know*, to experience this image of the coming end of the world? Why is knowledge of the *end* so important?

Well, we know from popular culture, and from anecdotal evidence, and maybe from experiences we've had in our own lives, that when you know you're about to die, something in you changes. Food tastes different. Everyday actions take on greater significance. You appreciate the experience of living life. And importantly, that crystallization of experience, that sense of new meaning, *reveals* something about ourselves and about what's most important to us.

It's this element of revelation that's at the heart of the apocalypse…it's the knowledge of our own end writ large.

Here's the thing, though—if we're *not* about to die, it's really hard to *think* our own deaths. We don't like to do it, to imagine the world when we're gone. But even if we did, it's just…difficult.

III

Theorist and philosopher Walter Benjamin explains this to a certain extent in his essay "The Storyteller"—he says, basically, that a person's life, a person's story, can only really be told at the moment of his or her death—we need an *end* to make sense of the middle. He writes:

> …not only a man's knowledge or wisdom, but above all his real life—and this is the stuff that stories are made of—first assumes transmissible form at the moment of his death. Just as a sequence of images is set in motion inside a man as his life comes to an end —unfolding the views of himself under which he has

encountered himself without being aware of it—suddenly in his expressions and looks the unforgettable emerges and imparts to everything that concerned him that authority which even the poorest wretch in dying possesses for the living around him. This authority is at the very source of the story.3

But when it happens, we won't be part of it. We can't witness our own deaths from the outside, nor eulogize ourselves. *Others* will tell our story—*others* will make sense of our lives, once the end is known.

In other words, you need the end to make sense of the rest of it. This suggests that there is ultimate *value* in the end—there's authority, there's *significance*. The moment of death has the ability to change our very perception of time.

Frank Kermode, in his influential work on ideas of narrative closure in literature, *The Sense of an Ending*, suggests precisely this when he contrasts *kairos* with *chronos*. While *chronos* is "passing time" or "waiting time," "mere successiveness," "*kairos* is the season, a point in time filled with significance, charged with a meaning derived from its relation to the end."4

The presence of an *ending*, in other words, gives meaning to what comes before.

Kermode writes: "…it makes little difference—though it makes some—whether you believe the age of the world to be six thousand years or five thousand million years, whether you think time will have a stop or that the world is eternal; there is still a need to speak humanly of a life's importance in relation to it—a need in the moment of existence to belong, to be related to a beginning and to an end."5

Everyone needs to feel like their time is significant. And there's something to be said for the fear of missing out. We are aware, on an intellectual level, of the insignificance of our own existence. But we need to feel like it means something, like we're a part of something.

Again, Kermode says: "For to make sense of our lives from where we are, as it were, stranded in the middle, we need fictions of beginnings and fictions of ends, fictions which unite beginning and end and endow the interval between them with meaning."6

To do this, we tell stories to each other. **We can, through fiction, convert *chronos* into *kairos*.**

Benjamin, too, says: "The novel is significant…not because it presents someone else's fate to us, perhaps didactically, but because this

39

stranger's fate *by virtue of the flame which consumes it* yields us the warmth which we never draw from our own fate. What draws the reader to the novel is the *hope of warming his shivering life with a death he reads about.*"7

In other words, if you believe that existence just stops when you die and that there's no afterlife of any kind, we are not a part of our own death. By definition, we can't be. It's a melancholic thought—we embody our own eventual loss, the loss of ourselves.

But—and here's the key—we *can* imagine death in more diffuse forms. We can use fiction, and use film, to imagine the end of ourselves, and the end of all things.

And the best part is that, having confronted the truth of our eventual end—I know that postmodernism suggests that there's no essential truth—but guess what: there IS one essential truth. We're all going to die one day—we can take a step back, go get a cup of coffee or a beer, and come down from our melancholic musings.

So this is the beauty of apocalyptic narratives—they let us imagine the end, and then recover.

IV

That brings me, finally, to *Doctor Who*, which revels in its ability to visualize extravagant conclusions—to a single life, to a species, to a planet, to the universe—and then rewinds the clock and allows us, alongside the companion, to consider the magnitude of what we've just seen. In fact, in time travel narratives in general, we can experience a vision of the end of the world—not just the prevention of it—over and over again.

In other words, we can witness the moment when all stories end, and then pop back to the pub for a pint and chips.

In the second episode of the first season of the new series, Nine takes Rose to see the end of the world—the moment when the earth is burned up by the sun (it's held there by gravity until everyone's ready to watch, not unlike Douglas Adams' *Restaurant at the End of the Universe*, another melancholic musing on ends staged for our convenience and viewing pleasure). A romantic date, to be sure, and one that sets the tone of their relationship.

Rose is disturbed by this, by the prospect of witnessing the end of the world, especially for "fun." But shenanigans and intrigue distract her from the original purpose of their trip, as they're wont to do. By the end of the episode, the earth has been destroyed, but no one saw it because they were busy doing other stuff.

And no one was there to eulogize it. Rose, visibly wilted, finds this a really melancholy thought: "We were too busy saving ourselves; no one saw it go. All those years, all that history, and no one was even looking. It's just..." There are no words.

But "come with me," the Doctor says, leading her by the hand away from the fiery spectacle of destruction outside of the plate glass windows.

In the next shot, Rose emerges from the TARDIS. Rose's fallen face in close-up begins to come round as we hear a baby cry, strangers laugh...and then Rose and Nine stand in the midst of a crowd, still points of observation in a rapidly moving world. She observes the mundane surroundings anew, with a wiser eye, with a new sense of value for the everyday.

Nine: "You think it'll last forever, people and cars and concrete. But it won't. One day it's all gone. Even the sky." The melancholy mood is broken, however, when Rose announces that she smells chips. "Only got five billion years until the shops close," she jokes.

This pattern: the secret information from the divine messenger (he's called a "Time Lord," after all), the otherworldly forces of good and evil at work, the Doctor's intervention, the restoration of normalcy (which comes to feel like paradise in retrospect), and the meting out of punishment, appears repeatedly throughout *Doctor Who*. The figure who has witnessed all possible ends—has even met his own end many times—gives us the whiff of death we need to understand our present world in a new way. *Doctor Who* is an apocalyptic narrative, a revelation.

As Martha Jones soliloquies in "The Last of the Time Lords,"
I traveled across the world, from the ruins of New York to the fusion mills of China. Right across the radiation pits of Europe. And everywhere I went, I saw people just like you living as slaves. But if Martha Jones became a legend, then that's wrong because my name isn't important. There's someone else. The man who sent me out there, the man who told me to walk the earth. And his name is The Doctor. He has saved your lives so many times and you never even knew he was there. He never stops, he never stays, he never asks to be thanked. But I've seen him, I know him. I love him. And I know what he can do.

Remember, "apokalypsis" means to reveal something, the lifting of a veil. Our veils are all around us all the time; we shroud ourselves and cloak ourselves in order to cope with a constantly shifting and often very scary world. But what apocalyptic narratives in the most traditional sense do is stage the moment of revelation—the lifting of the veil—over and over.

Fiction allows us to have this sense of privileged information—that one day, the world WILL end and we WILL die—and then come back to the "real" world with open eyes. The experience of the end, even if vicarious, makes us realize what's important, and appreciate the earth anew.

That's the hope: that the temporary experience of the end of the world will wake us up, remind us that our own time here is finite, and let us go forth to live lives rich with experience and meaning, however we define it. As the Eleventh Doctor puts it in "The Big Bang," "We're all stories in the end. Just make it a good one, eh?"

Notes
1 See Elaine Pagels, *Revelations: Visions, Prophecy, and Politics in the Book of Revelation*, (New York: Penguin Books, 2013).
2 Jon R. Stone, "Apocalyptic Fiction: Revelatory Elements within Post-War American Films," *Reel Revelations*, John Walliss and Lee Quimby, eds., (Sheffield, UK: Sheffield Phoenix Press, 2010), 58.
3 Walter Benjamin, *Illuminations*, Harry Zohn, trans., (New York, Schocken, 2007), 94.
4 Frank Kermode, *The Sense of an Ending: Studies in the Theory of Fiction*, (New York: Oxford University Press, 2000), 47.
5 Kermode, 4.
6 *Ibid.*, 90.
7 Benjamin, 101.

Finding Fandom

Erika Ensign

When I attended DePaul's *Celebration of Doctor Who*, I did a panel on *Doctor Who* fandom. I wrote a lovely opening statement for that panel. Sadly, the exact text is now lost to the ages. However, in January of 2015, I still had those notes. And it's a good thing I did because I was honored to guest-host the very fine *Reality Bomb* podcast. I needed a closing essay for that episode, so I reworked my *DW* fandom opening statement into an audio essay, which you can hear on *Reality Bomb* Episode 019. Here is the text I read from, which is now the closest thing I have to the words I spoke from the stage back in 2013:

I'm here today... well, because Graeme isn't. But that's not the only reason. When you try to think about all the events and decisions that lead to something happening, it can be mind-boggling. But sometimes, just sometimes, you can trace a thread back. My thread, the one that led me here, weaves primarily through one fabric. That fabric is *Doctor Who* fandom.

Now I know that's something every one of you knows something about. You wouldn't be listening to a *Doctor Who* podcast if you weren't a part of *Doctor Who* fandom—no matter how peripherally. Heck, there wouldn't *be* a Reality Bomb podcast, or any other *Doctor Who* podcast for that matter, if it wasn't for the fandom.

Doctor Who fandom is an endlessly fascinating topic to me because it has endless facets. Everyone's fandom-story is different, just as everyone's experience with the show itself is different. *I* can say with absolutely no exaggeration that discovering the world of *Doctor Who* fandom was the most important thing that's ever happened to me.

My story starts with social media. (Well, technically it starts with me becoming a *Doctor Who* fan at age 5, but fast forward about 30 years and let's get back to that social media thing.) I am a late-adopter. For years I thought Facebook was stupid, and I simply could not understand what Twitter was or how it worked. My little sister told me social media was great and I'd love it. I really should have listened to her. She's a librarian after all. Always trust librarians.

Eventually I capitulated, and boy howdy am I glad I did. Twitter brought me to the *Nerdist* podcast, hosted by Chris Hardwick—an enthusiastic *Doctor Who* fan. He brought me to Kyle Anderson, who writes *Doctor Who* articles for Nerdist.com and now has his own *Doctor Who* podcast, the excellent *Doctor Who the Writers' Room*. Both Chris and Kyle were interviewed on a podcast called *Radio Free Skaro*. At the time I thought: "An entire podcast devoted just to *Doctor Who*!?" It blew my mind! (Little did I know that, even at the time, there were dozens of them.)

Through *Radio Free Skaro*, I discovered a far-flung family I never knew I had. *Doctor Who* fandom has tons of different and wonderful and special and creative corners. Mine is the world of *Doctor Who* podcasting. The podcasters took me in and made me feel so welcome (in a very Twittery sort of way) that I couldn't believe I hadn't known these people all my life.

They convinced shy little me to come to conventions—alone—something I was very nearly too timid to do. They encouraged me to blog about *Doctor Who*—and whatever else I wanted. They helped me start my own shared *Doctor Who* podcast, *Verity!* And one fellow in particular, a host of that very first *Doctor Who* podcast I found, Steven Schapansky—one of the Three Who Rule from *Radio Free Skaro*, he made me feel welcome and then some. Steven and I got married in February of 2013. AT A *DOCTOR WHO* CONVENTION. Yes, that's right. The Gallifrey One convention in LA will be our destination anniversary weekend for as long as that convention continues. And I wouldn't have it any other way.

Since then, I've moved from the United States to Canada to live with Steven in Edmonton. *Doctor Who* fandom brought me out of my shell and then all the way across an international border. And, despite leaving so much behind to move to a new place, I have more friends than ever; I just don't see them in person terribly often.

Podcasting was not only my gateway into *Doctor Who* fandom, it's how I celebrate it. And I'm thrilled to be able to celebrate it here. Podcasting has brought me into contact with so many fans, each with a wonderful story about how they found *Doctor Who* and how they interact with it. For some people, fandom means chatting about the latest episode around the water-cooler (or Twitter-cooler). For some it means knitting-circles, creating scarves and question-mark sweater-vests. For some it means creating art or stories while safely tucked in their own home space. The list goes on and on.

For me, it means creating podcasts I'm proud of, guest-hosting podcasts I'm also proud of, keeping in touch with friends and family whom I truly care about, and living a life in which I couldn't be happier. Thank you, *Doctor Who*. Thank you, podcasting. Thank you, fandom.

The Adventures of Sarah Jane Smith

Sherry Ginn

Sarah Jane Smith is an investigative reporter when we first meet her in the episode "The Time Warrior," and she is quite suspicious of the Doctor during the course of this episode, thinking that *he* might be behind the mysterious events which are occurring in both the present and the past. Sarah Jane proved to be a new type of companion for the Third Doctor, one who, although impressed by his brilliance and *joie de vivre*, nevertheless insisted that he never condescend to her or treat her differently simply because she was female. The way in which her character was presented was contested by those in charge of the series. Terrance Dicks, for example, did not want to address feminism, preferring instead that Sarah Jane's character continue the traditional pattern with respect to the Doctor's companions, i.e., the damsel-in-distress who can scream loudly and wait to be rescued by the Doctor (Chapman 7). Barry Letts was willing to allow a new type of companion to emerge, yielding to the social and political realities of the 1970s. Elisabeth Sladen characterized Sarah Jane as impulsive; ready for anything new; everything very obvious; and, righteous indignation. Sladen's portrayal of Sarah Jane, in both the 1970s and the 2000s, was true to her vision of the character.

From their first meeting, Sarah Jane refused to prepare coffee for the Doctor, to allow him to protect or coddle her, and to remain on the sidelines when the action commenced. Based upon both her beliefs and her actions, Sarah Jane would be labeled a feminist, someone who believes that women and men should be considered equal: socially, economically, and legally. According to Margaret Matlin, a feminist "is a person whose beliefs, values, and attitudes reflect a high regard for women as human beings." Sarah Jane embodied the new woman, the woman arising out of the Women's Liberation Movement of the 1960s, referred to today as the second-wave of the women's movement, or liberal feminism, feminists who believe women should be given equal access with men to educational and vocational opportunities. Sarah Jane's youth and education would coincide with such liberal feminism, and she served as one of the first feminist role models for young men and women watching *Doctor Who* during the 1970s, including this speaker.

As "The Time Warrior" proceeds, Sarah Jane insists upon being in the thick in the action and refuses to stay behind when told that she should not attempt to rescue the Doctor because she is a girl. Later when working in the kitchen at Irongron's castle, the better to drug him and his men, Sarah Jane tells Meg, the cook, that she is not afraid of men; that women are equal to men and they should not be subjected to slavery just because they are women. These statements are very much in keeping with 1970s feminist philosophy and continue to inform the viewer as to the type of person the new companion will be. Thus, in our first meeting with her, Sarah Jane shows us that she is inquisitive, is willing to help out, will not take 'no' for an answer, and will stand up for herself and what she believes is right. We also see that her impulsivity can lead to danger and that she possesses the arrogance of youth. And, I contend that these are some of the same characteristics that we see in the new companions, those beginning with Rose Tyler, although the writers and the show-runners still do not seem to quite "get it right." Perhaps that is because the Doctors are male and the writers and directors are mostly male, and we can only speculate about what would happen if the Doctor regenerated as a female.

References

Chapman, James. *Inside the Tardis: The Worlds of* Doctor Who. London: I. B. Taurus, 2006. Print.

Ginn, Sherry. "Spoiled for Another Life: Sarah Jane Smith's Adventures with and Without Doctor Who." In Gillian Leitch (Ed.), Doctor Who *in Time And Space*: *Essays on Themes, Characters, History and Fandom, 1963-2012* (pp. 242-252). Jefferson, NC: McFarland and Company, Inc, 2013. Print.

Matlin, Margaret W. *The Psychology of Women*, 3rd ed. Ft. Worth, TX: Harcourt Brace, 1996. Print.

"The Time Warrior." *Doctor Who*. Dir. Alan Bromly. Perf. Jon Pertwee, Elisabeth Sladen. BBC Video. Originally broadcast 15 December 1973–5 January 1974. DVD.

Companions Against Global Warming: A Case of Public Humanities Engagement

Ashley Hinck

Part of what many of us love so much about *Doctor Who* is the complicated ethical questions, fascinating moral situations, and provocative claims about humanity (Crome; Decker; Lewis & Smithka). Indeed, each speaker on this "Philosophy and *Doctor Who*" panel has demonstrated that *Doctor Who* offers a sophisticated, rich, and interesting philosophy. What I would like to add to this discussion is an example and explanation of how that philosophy gets moved from a fictional television show to the real world. To do this, I want to talk about two key terms that can help us think through how philosophy gets moved from *Doctor Who* to the real world—that will be Part 1 of my presentation. In Part 2, I want to offer a case study of when that happened—when philosophy was successfully moved from *Doctor Who* to the real world. The case study is a high school lunch-time club that I formed during fall 2012 in which high school students created their own *Doctor Who* fan activism campaign about global warming.

When we think about how philosophy gets moved from the fictional TV to the real world, we're focusing our attention on the kind of philosophies that direct our actions or tell us how to live—these are ethics, or what I call ethical frameworks (Hinck, 2016). *Doctor Who* ethical frameworks can be thought of as the lessons or moral themes of the shows. To articulate a *Doctor Who* ethical framework, we might ask, What does it mean for the Doctor to protect the earth? What is the role of the companion? What makes the Doctor's enemies evil? What makes the Doctor good? What trade-offs does the Doctor accept? What does the Doctor seek to protect? Clearly, there are many ethical frameworks in *Doctor Who* that can be applied in many different ways to real world politics. Rhetoric invites fans to see a particular ethical framework and apply that ethical framework to a current issue in a particular way.

Rhetoric can be thought of as communication about public issues discourse or public talk. It's all of the political speeches, pamphlets, commercials, billboards and other public communication that fills our lives. Rhetoric helps us coordinate action about these public issues—this is where we persuade other citizens to vote a certain way or volunteer at a particular event or donate money to a particular charity. In relationship to ethical frameworks, rhetoric is what can invite other fans to apply ethical frameworks in the same way. We can find lots of different ethical frameworks in Doctor Who and apply them in lots of different ways. Rhetoric is what persuades us to use the same ethical framework applied in the same way and to take whatever activist action is requested—whether that's voting in an election, signing a petition, donating money, or joining a protest rally. Rhetoric takes the philosophy of Doctor Who and brings it into the real world for a whole group of people.

So, ethical framework and rhetoric help us understand how philosophies from Doctor Who can be moved from a fictional TV show to the real world. Now, we can take a look at a case study of when that happened. During the fall semester of 2012, I worked with a group of students at a local alternative high school to develop a fan activism project. The project was funded by the University of Wisconsin Madison's Public Humanities Exchange grant. The students chose the text (Doctor Who), identified an ethical framework, and applied it to global warming. Then, they created their own rhetoric, in the form of blog entries, that invited other Doctor Who fans to take action too. They titled the blog: Companions Against Global Warming. If you're interested, you can read the blog posts at cvsgw.wordpress.com. Their rhetoric made a number of sophisticated arguments that connected Doctor Who ethical frameworks to civic action, including the following: The Union of Concerned Scientists is our Torchwood 5; Global warming is such a large threat to Earth that it's the equivalent of all of the doctor's enemies joining forces; Global warming scientists are like allies of the Doctor; the Doctor isn't going to save us; we have to be our own companions. Across each of these arguments, students invited other Doctor Who fans to apply a Doctor Who ethical framework to global warming activism. Through rhetoric, Doctor Who's philosophy became relevant to global warming.

In conclusion, I'd like to point to a couple of implications. This project demonstrates the richness of the intersection between rhetoric and media studies. If rhetoric is making things matter to other people, then Doctor Who can provide the resources and community relations necessary for that public action. Doctor Who's philosophy is rich and significant. Indeed, it offers great potential for social change because of its rich philosophy.

References

Crome, A. (2013). *Time and Relative Dimensions in Faith: Religion and Doctor Who.* Darton Longman & Todd. Retrieved from http://www.myilibrary.com?id=549461

Decker, K. S. (2013). *Who is Who?: the philosophy of Doctor Who.* London; New York: I.B. Tauris.

Hinck, A. (2016). Ethical frameworks and ethical modalities: Theorizing communication and citizenship in a fluid world. *Communication Theory, 26*(1), 1–20.

Lewis, C., & Smithka, P. J. (Eds.). (2010). *Doctor Who and philosophy: bigger on the inside.* Chicago: Open Court.

Lewis, C., & Smithka, P. J. (Eds.). (2015). *More Doctor Who and philosophy: regeneration time.* Chicago: Open Court.

The DNA of *Doctor Who*

Derek Kompare

Every long-running media story or setting (what the industry also calls a "franchise"; see Derek Johnson's excellent new analysis of the concept) carries the DNA of its origins through every iteration. Consider:

* Sherlock Holmes – Rooted in 19th century urbanism, Victorian morality, ascendent forensic science and criminology, pop fiction
* *Star Trek* – A product of the Sixties: the Cold War, the space race, changing geopolitics, the civil rights movement, and even the counterculture, all tempered with a strain of militarism and the flying fists of mid-60s action-adventure TV
* *Star Wars* – A soup of Seventies neo-mysticism, mythology, Tolkien, movie brat cinephilia, and early Silicon Valley technophilia

No matter what happens down the line, that original formula is still there, passed on, if also modified along the way. Each of these particular franchises currently has major iterations in imminent release and/or production, and all of them still very much bear these original marks (even *Sherlock* and *Elementary*, which each somehow manage to successfully transfer Doyle's Victorian London to the 21st century London and New York, respectively).

In the case of *Doctor Who*, while its original manifestation is still primary, it has had three more alterations significant enough to affect the current series. Like other strands of DNA introduced and passed on in other living things, these aspects will always be part of whatever *Doctor Who* will be in the future (more or less, as we'll see).

First, and fundamental, is the series' origins in the BBC of the early 1960s, which launched its function as a national institution. Famously conceived as Saturday family tea-time fare meant to bridge the afternoon into the evening, with the ostensible function of being broadly "educational" as well, *Doctor Who* in its first 17 seasons (1963-80) represents the cultural assurances of public service broadcasting in its prime. While it still adjusted to changing styles and producers over this time—the differences between, say, "The Daleks' Master Plan" (1965-66) and "Spearhead From Space" (1970), broadcast exactly four years apart, are much starker than the differences between the similarly spaced "Planet of the Dead" (2009) and "The Bells of Saint John" (2013)—the series still functioned primarily as a national broadcast institution, alongside many others from the BBC of the 1960s and 1970s.

This sensibility is clear throughout this span. The Doctor is an emphatically English (not quite British yet) agent of disorder: he may not do things the "right" way, but he always gets the "right" result. Established history can't be altered, but humanity (i.e., England) will persist far into the future. Those Troughton-era "bases under siege" survive and face down real monsters. Jon Pertwee transforms the Doctor into an English action hero on English soil, sometimes facing down reactionary and destructive national powers, and ultimate Doctor Tom Baker channels the classic cool of Englishmen from Oscar Wilde to David Bowie as the unflappable eccentric.

Times change, though. Around the time producer John Nathan-Turner (known by fans as JNT) assumes the reins in 1980, *Doctor Who* gradually shifts from being a national institution to a cult institution. The series, like so many other pre-Thatcher British institutions at the time, finds itself increasingly marginalized and abandoned by the new establishment. It was literally displaced from its institutional home on Saturdays at this time and aired instead in the middle of the week for most of its last decade.

At the same time, however, it began to be fervently embraced by a newly organized and rapidly expanding (thanks to international distribution) fandom. With the mainstream turning away, *Doctor Who*, led by JNT, embraced its cult status. The producer and his cast made regular appearances at conventions around the world. The series both ran from its past (in storytelling style) and towards it (in increasing use of old monsters and continuity). The Eighties Doctors symbolized this turn away from comfortable hegemony and towards brash marginality: Peter Davison's Fifth Doctor may have the most obviously "English" wardrobe of all, but is nonetheless seen as a crazed outsider in many of his stories. Colin Baker's Sixth Doctor brandishes his contrarian aesthetic and demeanor like a knife. Sylvester McCoy's Seventh Doctor clowns like Chaplin to mask a brooding, deceptive heart. By the time

McCoy's Doctor had picked up his trademark question-mark umbrella in 1987, the series made its last turn down Cult Alley, because that seemed all that was left to go. Accordingly, Doctor Who closed out with some of the most unusual, bracing, and divisive stories in its history, including "The Happiness Patrol" (1988), "The Greatest Show in the Galaxy" (1988), and "Ghost Light" (1989).

With no more TV series in production, and almost no interest from the BBC (aside from the aborted attempt to relaunch the series in 1996), the "cult" essentially assumes ownership of Doctor Who in the 1990s. While known as the "wilderness years," these are more precisely its "indie rock" years, when fan writers, greatly inspired by the tone and style of the McCoy era (but drawing concepts and characters from the series' entire history, as well as tropes in Eighties and Nineties SF and politics) wrote and edited licensed novels "too broad and deep for the small screen" (as the original Virgin tagline put it).

The Virgin and BBC novels were Doctor Who at its most experimental: with darker themes, complex plots and characters, and long-running narrative arcs. This was also Doctor Who at its most "adult," although in retrospect (from the viewpoint of one of those "adult" fans of the books at that time), and despite some stunning additions to the saga (such as Paul Cornell's *Timewyrm: Revelation* [1991], Kate *Orman's The Left-Handed Hummingbird* [1993], Gareth Roberts' *The English Way of Death* [1996], Ben Aaronovitch and Kate Orman's *So Vile A Sin* [1997], Lawrence Miles' *Alien Bodies* [1997], and Lance Parkin's *The Infinity Doctors* [1998]), it was, on the whole, more the sort of earnest, slightly callow "adult" material that only those in their smitten twenties could produce. In 1999, inspired in part by the success of the novels at keeping Doctor Who alive and kicking, fan-led Big Finish Productions began releasing full-cast audio dramas (with stories featuring, by 2012, regular appearances by all five of the living classic series Doctors, and almost all of their companions) which faithfully recreated the sensibility of the TV series while retaining some of the more experimental innovations inspired by the novels. Big Finish has released some of Doctor Who's most original and compelling adventures, with Colin Baker's unfairly-maligned portrayal of the Sixth Doctor particularly rehabilitated in stories like Rob Shearman's *The Holy Terror* (2000) and *Jubilee* (2003), Jac Rayner's *Doctor Who and the Pirates* (2003), and Gareth Roberts and Clayton Hickman's *The One Doctor* (2001).

And then, seemingly out of the blue in 2005, the BBC takes *Doctor Who* back to television, reclaiming it as a national institution in the classic mold. However, now the model national institution isn't reassuringly English, but rather pitched as a global media franchise, the flagship of a solidly entrepreneurial BBC. While the "wilderness years" DNA clearly influenced the new iteration's respective showrunners (Russell T Davies, who actually wrote one of the Virgin novels, and Steven Moffat) and many of its writers, and has been tacitly acknowledged by long-term fans, publicly it's been elided, as if the show disappeared "sometime in the 1980s" and miraculously reappeared in 2005. Thus, the DNA of the 1990s is effectively hidden in the 2000s-10s, though its influence persists.

Doctor Who is now both populist and cult, a combination that couldn't have existed back in the 20th century. It's unabashedly promotional, clamoring for attention across multiple media and product platforms in a very crowded media marketplace. Davies and Moffat have been incessant MCs, propelling a global hype machine because they have to be. On-screen, the staid pacing of the classic series and meditations of the novels and audios have been replaced with a slick, thrill-ride ethos. The new series Doctors are younger, extroverted, and more than a bit narcissistic, "clever boys" needing and seeking attention in a way that never mattered as much before. Plots—in particular, under Moffat—have emphasized time travel, alternate realities, and long-running narrative arcs, as well as a much broader emotional spectrum than was ever seen previously on screen.

All that said, the flexibility of the concept—a strange, seemingly immortal being has adventures in time and space in a small blue box—has certainly been proven time and again. Unlike Holmes, *Star Trek*, or *Star Wars*, who remain tied to stricter confines of character, tone, and setting (countless parodies notwithstanding), *Doctor Who* can continue to regenerate. Every time it does, however, it will continue to carry the DNA of its previous incarnations.

From: https://dkompare.wordpress.com/2013/05/01/the-dna-of-doctor-who/

Doctor Who: The Grand Narrative and Postmodern TV

Michele Leigh

"Myth is not defined by the object of its message, but by the way in which it utters this message."
— Roland Barthes, *Myth Today*

When *Doctor Who* was reprised with great success by Russell T Davies in 2005, it built upon the 26 odd seasons of storylines from the original series, but also took liberties with, rewrote, or completely ignored previous plot lines in favor of creating alternative storylines. Earlier in 1965, the creators of *Doctor Who*, playfully labeled the second serial of season three "The Myth Makers," thus acknowledging their and the show's part in creating a new master narrative, a new set of myths revolving around a hero/anti-hero and his traveling companions. The creators/writers of the contemporary rendition of *Doctor Who* (2005-present) have continued the tradition of myth-making. This paper explores the connection between myth-making and post-modern narrative television in the 2005 reboot; particularly interesting is the way the show divulges the myth of the Great Time War and its myriad of mini-myths.

In their most basic form, myths are stories that relate historic events, that explain the origins and/or destruction of a people. These myths tend to be linear in structure and often feature a hero who must experience some tribulation in order to uncover the truth. In the case of Doctor Who, the great battle between the Time Lords and the Daleks falls squarely within that rubric. While the Doctor may stray from his calling, historically, the Time Lords have a policy of non-interference and neutrality, while they are tasked with observing history as it was, is and could be. According to the 10th Doctor, rather than seeing time as a series of cause/effect relationships, Time Lords experience time "from a non-linear, non-subjective viewpoint, it's more like a big ball of wibbly-wobbly, timey-wimey... stuff" ("Blink"). The Time Lords have a unique non-linear perception of time that is particularly well suited to postmodern television.

This begs the question, what is postmodern television? Isn't all television postmodern? Within a strict timeline, yes, perhaps all television is postmodern. I am more concerned how, within post-modernity, our concept of narrative shifts from, as Jean Francois Lyotard would say, "totalizing universal truths," to embracing chaos, uncertainty, and contradiction as structural elements of narrative. According to Lyotard "narrative function is losing its functors, its great hero, its great dangers, its great voyages, its great goal. It is being dispersed in clouds of narrative language[...] Where, after the metanarratives, can legitimacy reside?" Lyotard sees power shifting to the individual, localized narrative that focuses on a singular event. With this in mind, we can consider all episodic television postmodern, but how do we account for serialized television?

In response to Lyotard, John Stephens and Robyn McCallum provide a redefinition of metanarrative that might prove more useful when talking about serialized television. Stephens notes that metanarrative "is a global or totalizing cultural narrative, a schema which orders and explains knowledge and experience" — in other words, it is a story *about* a story, encompassing and explaining other "little stories" within conceptual models that make the stories into a whole. While one could argue that television sitcoms perhaps have historically focused on the individual, singular event played out each week, serialized television shows buck that trend and are more in line with Stephen's narrative model. Prime-time television has been propagated by shows that build on this model: *Twin Peaks, The X-Files*, the various incarnations of *Star Trek, Doctor Who*, and *Lost*.

In her essay "Narrative Form in American Network Television," Jane Feuer observes that "Television is not very well described by models of narrative analysis based on linearity and resolution" (101). While the sitcom, which relies to some extent on each episode existing within its own world, defies linearity and grand myth-making, the serial might imply the opposite. Feuer draws upon scholars like John Ellis and expands the notion of seriality to ALL television "in the sense that 'the series implies the form of the dilemma rather than that of resolution and closure'" (160). The lack of linearity in serialized television is further complicated by television shows that deal with time travel like, *Quantum Leap, Doctor Who* and more recently, *Continuum* and *Travelers*. Any form of time travel necessarily disrupts all notions of linearity and complicates our notions of narrative, especially when the time travel involves righting some wrong done in the past or altering the timeline in some way.

In the reprised version of *Doctor Who*, the Doctor is a modern day Odysseus, traveling through time and space in search of a home and family that no longer exist. Throughout the first series, the 9th Doctor (Christopher Eccleston) alludes to a catastrophic event that happened off screen while the show was on hiatus (between 1996 and 2005), what we later learn is the Last Great Time War. In his article "Mythic Identity in Doctor Who" David Rafer suggests that "The Doctor assumes various archetypes from the scientist-hero, Trickster, wanderer, wise old man, and young fool. He functions on multiple levels and is thus the multifaceted mythic hero whose transforming archetype defends civilization whilst continually running away from it, fights for order but exists in chaos." This 9th Doctor not only marks the reboot, he also signifies a stark shift in the way the Doctors are portrayed. No longer the eccentric scholar type, Eccleston's Doctor is a leather jacket wearing street tough, hardened by his experiences, he bears an unbelievable sadness, but above all he is angry, angry with the universe and with himself.

At the end of that season the 9th Doctor regenerates and while David Tennant's version of the 10th Doctor sits more heavily on the eccentric scale, he is still burdened and often overwhelmed by his sadness and anger, the source of which we discover in bits and pieces throughout the 10th Doctor's tenure, he is responsible for end of The Great Time War—the complete destruction of the Daleks and the Time Lords [see "The Satan Pit" (2006), "The Sound of the Drums" (2007), "Journey's End" (2008)]. With each incarnation of the Doctor, we find out more details about the Great Time War and his role in the loss of so many lives. In the two-part story "The End of Time" (2009-2010), which includes a prophecy, a time-lock, several companions and a regeneration, the 10th Doctor battles the only other remaining Time Lord, his 'frenemy,' The Master (John Simm). The Master has been 'programmed' by Rassilon, President of the Time Lords, to be their savior (from The Doctor) and thus the Master tries to control humanity as part of his plan to alter time and restore the Time Lords in what Rassilon calls "the end of Time itself!" The Master fails and the end of time does not happen quite when/as Rassilon had imagined it, in fact, it isn't until "The Day of the Doctor" (2013) that we learn of the fate of the Time Lords and Gallifrey. The decision to end the Time War turns out to be too difficult for the War Doctor (John Hurt) to bear and he is helped out by the 10th Doctor and the 11th Doctor (Matt Smith). In the end, the three Doctors decide to freeze Gallifrey in time and store it in a pocket universe for all time rather than be responsible for its utter destruction. Though, because of the disruptions in time, the Doctor's earlier selves will not remember that Gallifrey was saved and will go on bearing the guilt and anger.

Doctor Who establishes a fluid mythology for the Doctor and the characters with whom he interacts, one that offers no real resolution or closure. In his 1977 book *Movies and Mythologies,* Peter Harcourt notes "mythology can be seen as a distortion of history." The Last Great Time War allows for both distortions and incongruities within the series as a whole, due to the ripple effect of The Doctors' actions. The current television show uses the 'little narratives'/episodes to subvert the overall master narrative, interrogating the problems and potentials that arise from this subversion. More significantly, this postmodern myth becomes important in the way the myth is revealed, it becomes a nodal point for modern day anxiety about reality, history, time and ultimately truth. Postmodernity offers a lens through which to read and make sense of time travel shows like *Doctor Who,* and, in doing so, perhaps we develop coping mechanisms for living in an age when facts are questioned, histories debated and reality presented in terms of "alternative facts."

References

Baudrillard, Jean. 1994. *Simulacra and Simulation*. Ann Arbor: University of Michigan Press.

Butler, David, Ed. 2007. *Time and Relative Dissertations in Space: Critical Perspectives on Doctor Who*. Manchester: Manchester University Press.

Feuer, Jane. 2011. "Narrative Form in American Network Television." In *Critical Visions in Film Theory: Classic and Contemporary Readings*, edited by Timothy Corrigan, Patricia White, and Meta Mazaj. Boston: Bedford/St. Martin's.

Harcourt, Peter. 1977. *Movies and Mythologies: Towards a National Cinema*. Toronto, Canadian Broadcasting Corporation.

Joyrich, Lynne. 2006. *Re-viewing Reception: Television, Gender, and Postmodern Culture*. Bloomington, IN: Indiana University Press.

Lyotard, Jean-Francois. 1979. "The Postmodern Condition: A Report on Knowledge." The Postmodern Condition by Jean-Francois Lyotard. Accessed March 02, 2013. https://www.marxists.org/reference/subject/philosophy/works/fr/lyotard.htm.

Moffat, Stephen, writer. 2007. "Blink." In *Doctor Who*, produced by R. T. Davies, directed by H. Macdonald. BBC Broadcasting.

Rafer, David. 2007. "Mythic Identity in Doctor Who." In *Time and Relative Dissertations in Space: Critical Perspectives on Doctor Who*. David Butler, Ed. Manchester: Manchester University Press.

Stephens, John and Robyn McCallum. 1998. *Retelling Stories, Framing Culture: Traditional Story and Metanarratives in Children's Literature*. New York: Garland Publishing.

Thumim, Janet. 2004. *Inventing Television Culture: Men, Women and the Box*. Oxford: Oxford University Press.

Reflections of an Academic Fan

Gillian I Leitch

I started watching *Doctor Who* when I was about eight or nine years old, when TVOntario started airing the program on Saturday evening before *Saturday Night at the Movies*. I am not sure what drew me to the show initially, but I was already an active consumer of Science Fiction. *Star Trek* was a regular in reruns, and a lot of other shows and movies had grabbed my attention. I enjoyed (and still do) the creation of new worlds, cultures, and ideas that were a part of science fiction. But *Doctor Who* was different. For a start, it was very British, and with an English mother this was familiar and understood. It used history which fascinated me [spoiler alert – I am now a historian] and it was funny. And of course, there were the cliff-hangers. Having to wait for the next episode to see what happens was a great thrill. I continued to watch the series, and when we moved west I watched it on PBS on Saturday nights. And as fun as the cliff hangers were, there was a bit of a thrill watching the whole story all at once, and late at night which made me feel a bit 'naughty' as my parents were long in bed. An added bonus.

Doctor Who watching was not a solitary endeavor; my brother watched it with me, but I was really not sure who else did. It seemed like a bit of an odd show, and because it was on late at night, well, it did not seem that popular. And then I noticed an advertisement for a local fan club (a part of the Doctor Who Information Network – DWIN for short), so my brother and I went to an art glass studio in the west end of Edmonton and watched "Pyramid of Mars" with a bunch of fans. It was a revelation—other people watched the show! And it was fun experiencing the Doctor with a group of interested people. I had entered the world of fandom. I subsequently discovered that there were books, magazines, and things like buttons and toys, and so forth. What fun!

I attended my first convention "TimeFest" in Spokane, WA in 1986. It was here that I began to understand that there were many levels to *Doctor Who* and I was able to insert myself into an even wider network of fans and creators. I met the actors from the show—John Levene, Ian Marter, Katy Manning, Nicholas Courtney, and Anthony Ainley, and also the producer John Nathan-Turner. I was able to ask them questions about the program's production, their roles, their careers and of course I got their autographs. Learning more about the process of production added layers to my enjoyment of the series.

And then the series was canceled. I consider this the winter of my fandom. PBS continued to air the show for a few more years, so I was able to videotape all of the existing shows for future enjoyment. I am really not one who reads science fiction, so I was not connected to all the novelizations. And the fan club had faded away. When my local PBS station stopped showing *Doctor Who* the videotapes were all that I had left.

When it was announced that Fox was going to produce a television movie of *Doctor Who*, I like many fans, was very optimistic. The 1996 movie was a disappointment on many levels. Sure it was the Doctor, but it didn't feel like it, and he was awfully 'American' even with the English accent. And the movie led to nothing. I was comforted by the others who were as equally ticked off as I was. The videotapes continued to be my only real source of *Who*.

I was working on my Ph.D. in History when the series returned. It came as a great shock and joy when I found out that *Doctor Who* was coming back, and as a co-production with the Canadian Broadcasting Corporation. It was a bit like winning the lottery. I didn't even need cable! The first episode "Rose" was good, and I was pleased with the casting of the Doctor. Christopher Eccleston had captured the character just right. Little did I know, the rebirth of the series would lead to a new avenue of research in my academic life. One of my fellow historians was also active in popular culture and thought it would be a good idea for me to present a paper on *Doctor Who* at the Popular Culture Association conference, seeing as I had seen the new series, and had seen most of the episodes of the old series. I was in a position to provide historical context, and as a Canadian (the US hadn't aired the episodes of the series at that point) I had privileged access.

It was an interesting academic question – putting the new series in context, comparing it to the old series, and identifying the important similarities and differences. So I presented my first paper on *Doctor Who,* and I was hooked. I have now presented almost every year at the conference on the series, and have edited two books on *Doctor Who* and one on time travel in television. I straddle two worlds with the series. On the one hand, I am a fan of the series, and watch it for entertainment, on the other, I also study *Doctor Who,* and each episode is fodder for my writing.

In examining the series I still can identify why I started watching the series in the first place and can say that a lot of what initially caught my attention continues to do so. I enjoy the portrayal of different worlds, the new ideas, and the expression of values and ideals through science fiction. Even though the actors, producers, and writers change with time, the essentials are preserved. The Doctor is still the enigmatic, somewhat moody, quirky, alien who travels about in time and space.

Looking Back at the Influential Season Five

Rob Levy

When it aired in 1967-68 Season Five of *Doctor Who* marked not only the beginning of Patrick Troughton's second season as The Doctor but also saw a change in the dynamic of the program that would eventually become a blueprint for the show's success in the next century when Steven Moffat and his production team would use the iconography from that season to transform the contemporary series in the Matt Smith era.

Troughton's 'cosmic hobo' portrayal in Season Four did not warm the hearts of fans, thus Troughton was given more free reign with the character and decided to tone down the over the top comedy in favor of a more fleshed out persona, which saw the Doctor becoming more calculating and manipulative. The humor was still there, however. As the season progressed it was obvious that the 2nd Doctor was more willing to maneuver situations and people in order to see a resolution that worked to his advantage.

This move did two things: first, it allowed Troughton to grow into the character as he saw fit while expanding his range as a performer. Second, for producers Peter Bryant and Innes Lloyd, Season Five was yet another attempt to reinvigorate the show and chart a new course for it that veered away from the course set in the William Hartnell era. In 1967 Bryant and his team desired a change of pace for the show in order to avoid stagnation and possible cancellation.

As a result, Season Five found the producers throwing some serious drama into the mix while also ratcheting up the tension created from the last two stories of Season Four, "The Faceless Ones" and the epic season finale "Evil of the Daleks." Thus these two stories saw *Doctor Who* further shed its swinging '60s image in favor of darker SF tinged with horror and an added sense of peril, which transitioned nicely into the new season.

No one knew it at the time, but by transforming *Doctor Who* from the purely children's show of its infancy into a more traditional SF show, they were, in fact, laying the foundation for not only the very survival of the program but also for the show's return over four decades later as a worldwide phenomenon. Decades later Moffat's production team also found itself inheriting many of the same criticisms the producers had in 1967-68; that the show was too horrific, violent and adult themed.

The deepening of the production in 1967-68 was also very controversial. Many critics of the time believed the show's change was too violent and scary (a tag that would haunt the show throughout its history). However, the creative team was onto something groundbreaking and refused to relent.

They still got their children's audience, however now they put them behind the couch much more frequently. Upon hindsight making Season Five more adult, more terrifying and bigger in scope helped it thrive by freshening the stale air. It also was a step towards making the show a more legitimate SF adventure program. In many ways, Moffat's squad has applied the same actions to terrorize his contemporary audience.

Season Five, dubbed the *Monster Season*, began on September 2nd of 1967 and ran through June 1st of 1968. Everything about it was ambitious. Many classic elements of the *Doctor Who* that are seen today were first introduced during this season. This includes the skillful use of recurring guest characters, the introduction of UNIT, the sonic screwdriver and the idea that a season is a collection of several 'event' episodes which pit The Doctor against baddies who initially seem to have gotten the best of him. There was also a strategically placed sense of mystery surrounding just who The Doctor was. This aspect of his character was pivotal in making the season work. The aura around the main character that was cemented in Season Five went along way in helping shape the essence of the Matt Smith's interpretation of The Doctor.

In Season Five there were two companions in the TARDIS for the entire season and both were allowed some breathing room for development as characters, something fans would see happening again in the Matt Smith era. These companions Victoria, Jamie, and Zoë. They came from different time periods yet nonetheless were given a heftier load to do in stories which allowed the producers to focus the action around the Doctor and not completely on him, an aspect the program had gotten away from since the Hartnell Doctor.

Four decades later it would be impossible for the Ponds to work as companions in the new series if the dynamic of The Doctor and Jamie and Victoria and later Zoë had not worked so well. Although this concept was also tried again later in the classic series during the 1970s and 80s, these attempts would miss their mark in establishing a chemistry that connected with audiences.

Both Season Five of the classic series and the Matt Smith years rely on elements of horror and fantasy in their stories. There has always been some horror in *Doctor Who,* but Smith's seasons are the closest we have come to seeing the all-out assault on our psyche that played out in Season Five.

It was designed from the ground up to startle and scare. From the cramped, airtight terror of "Tomb Of The Cybermen" to the claustrophobic angst of "The Wheel In Space," one cannot help but be scared. In between, there were the terrifying Ice Warriors, a megalomaniac named Salamander and an omniscient entity called The Great Intelligence.

Since very little survives of Troughton's first series, most interpretations of him in the role of The Doctor stem from what exists of the monster season, and why not? He's amazing in it. He clashes with a wide array of villains, baddies, and menaces, all the while treating the whole business as if it were a silly romp. Upon first glance, he seems like an odd and unassuming man of science but when things get deadly he turns on a dime to defeat the nemesis of the week.

It is this duality of character that has endured from Troughton's Doctor and Season Five. During this season he brought more mystery to the character while peppering it with an uneasy aspect that we may not really know what he is up to.

Another interesting thing about The Monster Season was that this idea that The Doctor's role as both a wandering traveler and as an involved participant in the order of the universe. We see this theme intensified later under Smith's watch as The Doctor clearly knows his actions have consequences and he is not afraid to be aggressive in manipulating events to his own end.

Another way to understand the magnitude of Season Five is to look at the monsters of that season. Although some of them debuted previously it was not until Season Five that The Cybermen established themselves as a bonafide baddie. This happened again in the new era as the somewhat watered down Cybermen of the Davies era were brought back with much more horrific effect over the last three seasons, leading up to their reimagining from writer Neil Gaiman in the latter part of Season Seven.

Salamander from "The Enemy Of The World" was your run in the mill dictator hellbent on domination. Troughton played him and The Doctor in that story and was clearly having fun. Salamander is indicative of the kind of delusional madman that would emerge time and time again in the classic series and now and again during the new one as well.

Another highlight of Season Five which will serve as benchmarks for contemporary *Doctor Who* is the introduction of the Ice Warriors. We cannot help but feel the peril that befalls the Second Doctor and his companions when he meets them. Although the Ice Warriors were used again after they debuted in Season Five they were never as menacing in subsequent appearances. This is changed for their return in Season Seven.

Moffat greenlit Mark Gatiss' Season Seven Ice Warriors story fully aware of just how much they made people scream when they debuted in Season Five. When the titans of Mars met Victoria in "The Ice Warriors" it was an iconic moment for the show that would transcend decades to become a measuring stick of sorts for how scared the female companions were when they met evil aliens.

Just as Season Five of the Classic Series opened with the epic "Tomb of The Cybermen," Season Seven opened with an epic opener that played out like and epic film. This idea of starting the season off with a bang really originated with the Monster Season.

The pacing of this landmark season was relentless. Each story built off of elements of its predecessors, creating a crescendo that built as the season continues. This is an element that has carried over into the new show.

The core theme of Season Five is the aforementioned idea that The Doctor is one mysterious man who will stop at nothing when battling a large universe filled with evil. We see this theme in the new series in the Eccleston and Tennant eras but intensified in Season Five and Season Six of Matt Smith's tenure. With Season Seven this theme is arguably a driving theme for the show.

As the central character The Doctor changes throughout Season Five. Troughton's Doctor morphs before our eyes (much in the way the McCoy Doctor did much later) from an imp-like clown to an astute, clever, cunning and devious professor. In the monster season, Troughton changes his emotions, going from being funny and whimsical to blunt, brutal and confrontational. The Second Doctor, as seen in Season Five, had no problems with doing what he saw as being right. As that season progresses Troughton's seemingly jumbled logic manifests itself into an agenda of fighting injustice and evil. This agenda becomes more apparent as the season progresses. By mid-season the cosmic hobo is gone and replaced with a clever fellow whose guile is often masked by perceptions of eccentricity and a very clever smirk. Beneath the quirkiness, however, is a wise and devious Time Lord capable of extraordinary things.

The Eleventh Doctor Matt Smith is on record as saying that a lot of his performance is based on Patrick Troughton's portrayal of the 2nd Doctor. In preparing for the role Smith watched a lot of what remains of Season Five, particularly "Tomb of The Cybermen," and mined elements of the Second Doctor for the role. In fact, every Doctor since Peter Davison has cited Troughton's performance in Season Five as a reference point for them shaping their portrayals.

When you watch Smith in the role you do see a lot of Trougthonish behavior, most notably the sense of charm that masks a manipulative and enigmatic figure that, like the 2nd Doctor, emphasizes the themes of one man fighting evil in the galaxy throughout space and time. There also the idea that no matter what happens The Doctor is somehow one or two steps ahead of his adversaries.

Both actors share a sense of subtle wisdom in their performance brought out through mannerisms and facial expressions. Each of these incarnations possesses a proclivity for mischief, curiosity and a sense of purpose. Their individual Doctors also share a sense of urgency in their movement and mannerisms. They both wring their hands and walk at a very brisk pace, often accompanied by rapid-fire technobabble.

With the third full season of The Eleventh Doctor, many of the plot points touched upon in Season Five have been utilized. Most noticeably with The Cybermen, Ice Warriors and the return of The Great Intelligence.

Patrick Troughton's fingerprints are also smudged into Smith's performance. He definitely has copped the 2nd Doctor's charm and smirk and made it his own. He's also taken the concept of muddled logic to a whole new level. He also has added texture to Troughton's cagism as he developed an identity for The Doctor.

Physically, he's taken the suspenders, bow tie and fondness for headwear (fezzes, a derby etc) from the Second Doctor. He's also perfected the idea of The Doctor as a mad genius, introduced much more subtly in Season Five and fleshed it out in his portrayal.

Undoubtedly Steven Moffat needed no help in making his characters for the new series, but one sees the same heroism and curiosity of Jamie McCrimmon in Rory Williams and one can, at times, easily see the intelligence of Zoë Herriott and the terror of Victoria Waterfield in Amy Pond. Separated by four decades you can see the same reaction to Victoria's encounter with the Ice Warriors in how Amy faces the Weeping Angels.

Perhaps the greatest Whovian plot device ever, The Sonic Screwdriver originated in near the end of Season Five in "Fury From The Deep." Originally used to open locks, it has become so much more. In fact, the Sonic Screwdriver has become synonymous with the program now. The screwdriver has become a staple of most episodes and in many instances is central to an aspect of the show.

Season Five is also an interesting thing in that it capped off the season with a new twist, a rescreening of "Evil of The Daleks." After Zoë joined the TARDIS the Doctor showed her the events of that story as a warning of the issues that may come with traveling in time and space. At the time a repeat was unheard of so the fact that they did that really ramped up the program's stature and production values.

In many ways, screening of that episode was a predecessor of the mini-episodes and web content we see today. It was something the first time the show went outside of its normal formatted structure to emphasize plot and build character development.

The 40 episodes commissioned for that season were tightly produced, well acted and relied on imagination, horror, and effect to jar the audience. As a result, the season set a standard of excellence that is still felt today as the cast and current production team strive to make every story an enriching piece of creative television. These stories were:

"Tomb Of The Cybermen"
An archaeological expedition on Telos uncovers a deadly secret in one of the most terrifying masterpieces of classic *Doctor Who*. The Doctor faces The Cybermen in closed quarters and stops at nothing to defeat them.

"The Abominable Snowmen"
The Yeti debut here in this gripping six-part story. Set in the Himalayas, the visiting Doctor and his companions get into trouble immediate

when The Doctor returns to a Tibetan monastery. Part murder mystery, part cosmic battle, and completely frightening this story made it clear that this was a season of scary proceedings.

"The Ice Warriors"
These Martian Warriors debuted here. Set in the year 3000, The Doctor must save the world from alien invasion. This six-parter was criticized for its violence.

"Enemy of the World"
Patrick Troughton plays The Doctor and the evil dictator Salamander. The story is a bit odd for the season, but Troughton is amazing in it. Salamander is a mad despot determined to take over the world. To make things worse he has a climate control device to help him do this.

"The Web of Fear"
The Yeti returns, but this time London is under invasion. This is the story that sets up UNIT and introduces us to The Brigadier. The episode is highly regarded for its location filming and use of shadows.

"Fury From The Deep"
This undersea adventure marks the first appearance of the Sonic screwdriver. The story has some very scary monuments of fright in it. Set in the North Sea it has an ecological theme but also makes a commentary on corporations. A theme used to a lesser extent last season in *The Almost People* and *Gangers*. Fed up with the dangers of traveling in the TARDIS Victoria leaves.

"The Wheel In Space"
This story has a new companion named Zoë. We see the return of The Cybermats, (previously seen in "Tomb of The Cybermen" and Smith's "Closing Time"). The Doctor schemes and plots his way through the story, ultimately destroying the Cyberfleet, a plotline reused throughout the years and again by Smith in Season Six, once more.

Looking back, you would be hard pressed not to find a timey-wimey symmetry between *Doctor Who's* Monster Season and Matt Smith's tenure on the show. The program we love now would simply not exist if it did not embody aspects of this classic season in some way.

Tragically a great deal of this season is now lost, but what does remain serves as a reminder of just how brilliant and relevant this season remains today. Despite this, its legacy remains because it has become an inspiration and blueprint for the 11th Doctor's production team.

*Note this paper was written before Season 7 of the new series. Its tense has been edited to reflect its proper age.

Seductive, Sexy, and Culturally Significant: Captain Jack's Continuing Role in the *Whoniverse*

Lynnette Porter

When Captain Jack Harkness (John Barrowman) burst into *Doctor Who* during "The Empty Child" in 2005, no one suspected that the flirtatious, time-traveling con man would become as "immortal" in popular culture as he soon would become in the series. When he meets the Tenth Doctor (Christopher Eccleston) and companion Rose Tyler (Billie Piper), he becomes smitten with them, and the audience likewise falls for him. After all, who wouldn't be seduced during the London Blitz by (at least vicariously) dancing and drinking champagne atop an invisible spacecraft tethered to Big Ben? By the end of the reboot's first season, the Doctor had made Jack a better man, one willing to sacrifice himself to save not only the Doctor (whom he kisses farewell) and Rose, but all humanity. Just as Captain Jack had already escaped death several times before he encountered the Doctor and Rose—he explains that he once was saved from execution and then slept with both his executioners, who turned out to be a lovely couple—his self-sacrifice is "rewarded" with immortality (and a lengthy stay trapped on Earth without the technology to leave).

This granting of immortality in *Doctor Who* both ensured a future reunion or two between the Doctor and Jack and paved the way for spin-off series *Torchwood*. The original episodes were broadcast between 2006 and 2008, with the critically acclaimed mini-series *Children of Earth* apparently concluding the series on the BBC in July 2009. However, like the immortal Captain Jack, *Torchwood* would not die. Because of a surprising partnership between the BBC and U.S. cable network Starz, the longer mini-series *Miracle Day* brought what remained of the decimated post-*Children of Earth* Torchwood to the U.S. and implied a possible later continuation of *Torchwood* with an American cast. That plan did not come to fruition, and *Torchwood* as a television series has been comatose ever since. That does not mean that it is officially dead. Series creator Russell T Davies said in a 2012 interview that *Torchwood* survives "in limbo" and could return in a decade or two (Connelly), and *Torchwood* star Eve Myles hopes for one more chance to film *Torchwood* to provide the fans with closure (Jeffery). After all the cult favorite's changes, from alien-visits-Earth-for-sex plots in the early episodes to devastatingly hardcore drama in *Children of Earth* to the misguided, difficult-to-follow *Miracle Day*, the television series awaits a possible resurrection as something new. But not Captain Jack. He is far more proactive as a survivor.

Although novels, radio plays, and audio books starring the *Torchwood* cast helped fans get their *Torchwood* fix between new episodes, the first wave of non-television stories largely ended with the conclusion of *Miracle Day*. However, Captain Jack just keeps coming back to life in different media. Aided by co-authors Carole E. Barrowman and John Barrowman, Captain Jack returned in the book *Torchwood: Exodus Code* in 2012. By 2015, Big Finish began producing a series of *Torchwood* audio plays, with the first, *The Conspiracy*, starring John Barrowman as Captain Jack; by autumn 2016, twelve titles featuring the original *Torchwood* cast members had been released. Also in 2016, Titan began publishing a new *Torchwood* comic book series, created by John Barrowman, Carole E. Barrowman, and Antonio Fuso. During San Diego Comic-Con 2016, John Barrowman announced that he was in talks to bring *Torchwood* back to television, in part by using the new comic book series as a Kickstarter campaign to indicate interest in a *Torchwood* reboot. Many fans agree with Barrowman that "we need Captain Jack back on the screens" (Fullerton).

The larger question is why this character, in particular, gained the public's attention, has held it for more than a decade, and earned a dedicated fandom eager to follow the dashing Jack from medium to medium. Of course, part of the answer is John Barrowman, a larger-than-life character himself. He gleefully joined the *Doctor Who* family first as a fan and later as an actor. In addition, he sings and dances his way across the U.K. and U.S. as a one-man variety show, unabashedly dons costumes during fan conventions, and often acts what other men his age might term "silly." This *joie de vivre* is contagious and empowering for his audiences. Like the title of his first autobiography and his signature song at his concerts, *I Am What I Am*, John Barrowman is unafraid to let the world see just who he is, and that confidence helps make him a role model for his fans, as well as Captain Jack's.

Possibly the greatest service that Captain Jack continues to provide fans is openness about his sexual orientation (originally described as omnisexual, but depicted as bisexual on television). Just as Barrowman is an advocate for LGBTQ equality and proudly and very publicly shares home movies, photos, and anecdotes of his life with husband Scott Gill, so has Captain Jack openly had a not-long term-enough relationship with fellow *Torchwood* operative Ianto Jones (Gareth David-Lloyd). The intimacy of that relationship was less common on television in 2006-2009, and the "realness" of a couple's early seductions, playfulness, occasional doubts or disagreements, and the final poignancy of dying together make the Jack-Ianto pairing memorable long after *Children of Earth* ends their love story.

In many ways, the fans will not let Ianto stay dead, either. The desire for more Jack-Ianto stories has resulted in the Big Finish audio drama *Broken* (2016), which allows listeners to time travel back to the early days in the *Torchwood* television series when Jack is only Ianto's boss and takes Ianto for granted. The bleak audio story dramatically highlights how Jack and Ianto begin to see each other more clearly, paving the way for their eventual coupledom.

Years after this love story came to its televisionary end, Jack and Ianto as a couple and, in particular, Captain Jack as a cultural icon are still role models for many young people facing societal discrimination or familial disappointment or disapproval because they are not heterosexual. While *Torchwood* was still on the BBC, the U.K.'s Channel 4 LBG Teens website used Captain Jack as an example in the "Am I gay or bisexual?" section that provides information to teens questioning their sexual identity: "It might not seem like a big deal that Captain Jack is bisexual in *Torchwood* . . . However, ten years ago the idea of openly gay and bisexual characters in television programmes aimed at teenagers was unthinkable." In a 2013 interview with the *Radio Times*, Barrowman reflected on the continuing cultural significance of Captain Jack: "You've got these young teens in school being bullied because of the sexuality that they are just discovering. They write to me all the time to say that Captain Jack helped them be strong and positive about themselves, rather than hiding and being embarrassed. It was a great, great thing to have a hero who really doesn't give a shit who he kisses" (Holmes).

Although Barrowman and Captain Jack continue to entertain their fans in multiple media, both the actor who keeps bringing Jack Harkness back to life and sexy adventurer Jack deliver far more than just a good time. They continue to raise awareness of LGBTQ characters and the need for social acceptance and legal equality for the LGBTQ community. Although television immortality is nice, their real-world legacy empowers audiences and helps effect cultural change. That's the type of immortality in which the *Who*niverse should take PRIDE.

References

Broken. Big Finish. Dir. Scott Handcock. Writ. Joseph Lidster. July 2016. CD.

Channel 4. LGB Teens. "Am I Gay or Bisexual?" 2007. Web. 6 Sep. 2016. https:// web.archive.org/web/20070323124427/http://www.channel4.com/health/microsites/ L/lgb_teens/boys/are-you-gay.html

Connelly, Brendon. "Davies Says Torchwood 'In Limbo,' Could Be Back in 'Ten or Twenty Years.'" 30 Oct. 2012. Web. 7 Sep. 2015. http://www.bleedingcool.com/ 2012/10/30/ davies-says-torchwood-in-limbo-could-be-back-in-ten-or-twenty-years/

"The Empty Child." *Torchwood*. Dir. James Hawes. Writ. Steven Moffat. 21 May 2005. BBC. Television.

Fullerton, Huw. "John Barrowman Is In Talks to Get Torchwood Back on TV." *Radio Times*. 24 July 2016. Web. 6 Sep. 2016. http://www.radiotimes.com/news/ 2016-07-24/john-barrowman-is-in-talks-to-get-torchwood-back-on-tv

Holmes, Jonathan. "John Barrowman: 'I Would Love to Play Captain Jack Again.'" *Radio Times*. 19 Oct. 2013. Web. 6 Sep. 2016. http://www.radiotimes.com/news/ 2013-10-19/john-barrowman-i-would-love-to-play-captain-jack-again

Jeffery, Morgan. "Torchwood Star Eve Myles: 'The Fans Deserve Closure.'" *Digital Spy*. 26 Jan. 2012. Web. 7 Sep. 2015. http://www.digitalspy.com/british-tv/s8/ torchwood/news/a362247/torchwood-star-eve-myles-the-fans-deserve-closure.html#ixzz3kh8ZBF4n

Reflections on Two Panels

Kathryn Sullivan

I was on two panels at "A Celebration of *Doctor Who*" on May 4th, 2013. The 9 am panel was "The Long Appeal of *Doctor Who*" with my fellow panelists Erika Ensign, Mary Robinette Kowal, Jody Lynn Nye, Sherry Ginn, and Gillian Leitch. The noon panel was "*Doctor Who* and Gender" and I shared the stage with Carole Barrowman, Tara O'Shea, Lynnette Porter, Sherry Ginn and Scott Paeth.

Panel discussions are always free-wheeling and often go in unpredictable directions. The only notes I brought with me for the panels were a list of significant characters and their roles in *Doctor Who* and sections of my essay, "The Fanzine Factor" from *Chicks Dig Time Lords* so I wouldn't forget important names and dates. The following will combine thoughts I had from both panels as some points overlap.

The Long Appeal

The appeal of *Doctor Who* can be different for each person. I started watching the show as an adult in the 1980s, with an already wide viewing background of a lot of different science fiction shows. Some shows were cheesy, some attempted to be technical, and for many of them, the special effects could range from basic to fantastic. *Doctor Who* appealed to me on several levels. The writing was very good, with stories that could change genre from month to month. The main character was a type of hero I hadn't seen in American shows. His response to problems wasn't the usual one with violence. Tom Baker's Doctor, the one I first saw, either used jelly babies or the sonic screwdriver. I found that refreshingly charming.

The Doctor usually tries to find other solutions to problems. Terrence Dicks started the "never cruel or cowardly" description, and that has suited most of the Doctors. The idea of him relying mostly on his wits and a sonic screwdriver rather than fists or guns is still quite different from many science fiction shows.

Another appeal was that Tom Baker (and the previous Doctors) wasn't the "standard handsome" leading man that was the norm on American shows. He wasn't Captain Kirk with a new love interest every week. In *Doctor Who,* the stories focused on the Doctor and his friends traveling together and having adventures in time and space.

For the American audience already used to intellectual leading characters such as Mr. Spock in *Star Trek* and Illya Kuryakin in *The Man from U.N.C.L.E.* here was a leading character who combined the best aspects of both. Traveling with the Doctor meant you were safe. Sure, you could be shot at by Daleks and other aliens or captured by amorous aliens (poor Peri), but the Doctor was (mostly) a traveling companion, not a threat in himself to any female.

Now this makes sense when you look back at the origins of the show as a family drama in the UK. But I think it helped with the long appeal of the show. Because there was no romance or "sex appeal" imposed by the writers, the viewer could add their own impression. The Doctor could be heterosexual (suggested by the fact of a granddaughter), or he could be asexual. Fan fiction of the Classic and Wilderness years ranged through all sorts of speculations. Some fan-written stories had the Doctor finding romance with one of his companions, while others added a new character (often closely resembling the author).

That all changed with the new series, but I can't help but wonder. Would the show have lasted as long as it did if the Doctor had started at the very beginning with something like the 10th Doctor and Rose's romance? Or the Eleventh Doctor's tendency to fall in love/get engaged every week? I feel the new series' takes on the Doctor worked as a change of pace for a long-lived show, but I'm glad Capaldi's Doctor is perhaps back to friendship with the people he travels with.

Gender

I tend to look at the exploration of gender in *Doctor Who* recently as attempts to correct the rewriting of history. We saw the rewriting in the dismissal of female companions as 'always twisting their ankle' or 'screaming.' Yet when you go back and watch the Classic episodes you see companions advancing the story, helping the Doctor, saving others while the Doctor worked at solving another part of the problem. In *Doctor Who*, there were women prime ministers, captains of ships, leaders of planets and soldiers long before the acceptance of similar gender roles appeared in American SF shows.

We saw the rewriting of history similarly in the continual refrain that women didn't like *Doctor Who*, had never liked it until the 2005 series. Yet, when you look at the footage of conventions back in the

PBS years, the photographs of the audience, when you examine the names of writers of fanzine stories, con-runners, fan artists, you find women participating just as much as men, at least in North America. I saw many times during the Wilderness Years, in the days when most of the fan community was in rec.arts.drwho, when at least every other month, someone would say, "there's no women here," completely ignoring the presence of women like Dr. Siobahn Morgan, who ran the Doctor Who FAQ at nitro9 (nowadays http://nitro9.earth.uni.edu/doctor/faq.html) and who every month posted a link to that website and updates. Every other month women posting would have to out themselves, to say, yes, they were still there, as readers and viewers, writers of fanzine stories, con-runners, con-attendees, and costumers. All fans still.

Fans sometimes have short memories. Fandoms come and go. A show can be popular for one season or for many, but the fandom for it can fade away not long after the show ends. As fans dropped out during the hiatus, history was rewritten to leave out the missing fans as if they had never been there. That's why, with a show that lasted for fifty years, it helped to have a celebration to document prior history.

Schedule for A Celebration of *Doctor Who*

9:00–9:55
The Long Appeal of Doctor Who
>   Erika Ensign, Sherry Ginn, Mary Robinette Kowal, Gillian Leitch, Jody Lynn
>   Nye, Kathryn Sullivan

10:00–10:55
Doctor Who and Philosophy
>   Gerry Canavan, Ann Hetzel Gunkel, Ashley Hinck, Derek Kompare, Scott
>   Paeth, Philip Sandifer

11:00–11:55
Doctor Who Aesthetics
>   Piers Britton, Tammy Garrison, Derek Kompare, Robert Levy, Philip
>   Sandifer, Lynne M. Thomas

12:00–12:55
Doctor Who and Gender
>   Carole Barrowman, Sherry Ginn, Tara O'Shea, Scott Paeth, Lynnette Porter,
>   Kathryn Sullivan

1:00–1:55
Doctor Who Fandom
>   Carole Barrowman, Erika Ensign, Tammy Garrison, Jennifer Adams Kelley,
>   Gillian Leitch, Lynne M. Thomas

2:00–2:55
Doctor Who and Narrative
>   Cary Elza, Jennifer Adams Kelley, Michele Leigh, Jody Lynn Nye, Tara
>   O'Shea, Mary Robinette Kowal

3:00–3:45   Dalek (with live commentary by Robert Shearman)
4:00–5:00   Robert Shearman Keynote and Q&A

Screening Schedule
Selection 1: Exploring the TARDIS
9:00–9:50   The Edge of Destruction
10:00–10:25   The Mind Robber (Episode 1)
10:30–11:20   The Doctor's Wife

Selection 2: Anniversaries
11:25–1:10   The Three Doctors
1:15–2:00   School Reunion
2:05–2:30   An Unearthly Child (Episode 1)

Selection 3: Surprise Screening
2:30–3:00   My Own Private Wolfgang (100, Big Finish)

Music provided by
The Well-Tempered Schism

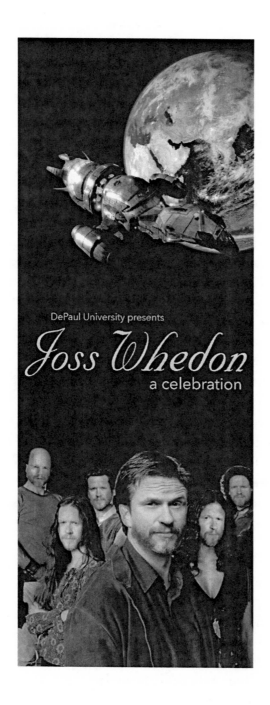

DePaul University presents

Joss Whedon
a celebration

Introduction

Paul Booth

The second annual DePaul Pop Culture Convention was never really meant to be; that is, 2013's *Celebration of Doctor Who* was intended to be just a one-off experience. But as 2014 rolled along and we started to hear from people that attended or spoke at the *Doctor Who* event, it seemed like a good idea to reopen the files and start anew with a different theme.

Looking back, there were a lot of anniversaries in 2014 that we could have celebrated, but I was drawn in particular not to an anniversary but to an auteur: Joss Whedon. It had been just over a decade since *Firefly* had ended and it was still a major part of cult media. *Buffy* had also ended just over a decade previously, and *Angel's* final season ended in 2004. So while there wasn't a strict "anniversary" theme for the Whedon event, there were a lot of discussions and articles popping up online about his most popular shows. (Plus, we were in a period between *Avengers* and *Avengers: Age of Ultron* so there was a lot of cinematic buzz as well.)

Finding a keynote speaker for the *Celebration of Joss Whedon* proved challenging as well, and I think we lucked out when Cheryl Cain agreed to speak! (It would have been nice to have Joss himself attend, but as I found out when I asked, he was filming *Age of Ultron* outside the States.) Cheryl wrote the *Firefly* episode "War Stories"—a fabulous episode—and offered both a thoughtful discussion of the making of *Firefly* in her keynote talk, as well as a very-well attended writer's workshop that presented tips and hints for aspiring screenwriters.

We also had a remarkable workshop with Mat Irvine, one of the special effects supervisors on the Classic *Doctor Who* series during the later Tom Baker and Peter Davison eras. Mat happened to be in town during the event and I asked if he wanted to participate; he was eager to share his stories of working on the original series as well as building (and later restoring) the Doctor's robotic dog K9. (Mat also spoke to one of my classes which was exhilarating!).

In contrast to the first Pop Culture Conference, the *Celebration of Joss Whedon* held multiple panels at the same times as well as screenings and workshops—we packed a lot into the nine-hour day (perhaps too much). Panels included a compelling one on Gender in the works of Joss Whedon, and about which our panelists debated the feminist overtones of shows like *Buffy the Vampire Slayer*. Other panels included focusing on the Religion and Ethics in Whedon's work, the Mythological, Cultural, and Narratological Roots of Whedon, a discussion about teaching Whedon's works as well as a special Student's Perspectives on Whedon from students who had taken classes on Joss Whedon. We had panels from fans about Problematic Portrayals in Whedon's work and panels showcasing fan work from Columbia University's *Water Cooler* student magazine.

We also took a number of steps for this event to develop some procedures and ideas that are still in place today; for instance, we instituted an anti-harassment policy that still is in place today. The use of this policy has led to a number of interesting and eventful conversations, some positive and some not. In short, we didn't have one in place for the 2013 event because we didn't anticipate much need for one; it simply wasn't on our radar. This is perhaps because of the discrepancy between academic conferences and fan conventions— something that, as I've noted in the introduction, became a deliberate focus of the Pop Culture Conference. While many fan conventions have instituted anti-harassment policies (as well they should), it is still relatively rare for academic conferences to have them, perhaps because the conferences are often considered professional events (many professors are required to attend some, and they, in part, work as professional development) and so are viewed differently than how fans may view conventions. (At the same time, I think there is a need for anti-harassment policies at conferences anyway—some academics can be offensive as well.)

Well, they're important, and it was important to us that we make sure attendees at the Pop Culture Conference feel safe and that there would be places to turn if they didn't.

I did field one panicked email from a professor who was interested in attending, but then saw the policy—he was worried that something had happened to prompt the use of it. (I was also contacted by the *Chicago Tribune* with a similar question, was there a reason why the policy was in place?). To the professor, I responded that it wasn't in *response* it was *proactive*. It wasn't trying to stem something that happened but to prevent things from happening in the first place. There may be a fundamental misunderstanding about the use of anti-harassment policies; hopefully this will change as they become more common.

The cover of the program for the event also prompted some reactions. I hired Jeremy Kanne, a graphic designer whom I'm friends with, to make the cover, and he rather brilliantly (in my opinion) created an iconic and unique image, indelibly linked to the conference in my mind: Whedon's face superimposed on the bodies of all the major characters from *Firefly*. It is haunting and it is brilliant; it will never be surpassed.

I'm honestly not sure why so few of the speakers from the Whedon event submitted papers for this book; I suspect it was just long enough ago that what they had discussed are lost in the mists of time. I hope you enjoy the papers that did come in, and I'm happy to update with more if any future submissions are sent.

Writer Keynote

Cheryl Cain

I was so honored when Paul asked me to talk at the Joss Whedon event in 2014. I have had the pleasure of working with Joss in production on *Buffy the Vampire Slayer* and as a writer on *Firefly*. As a writer, I can't imagine a better mentor to have learned from than Joss. I am so impressed by not only his ability to deliver pithy and memorable lines on the page, but also his ability to construct believable characters and compelling storylines. There is no one like him out there.

So I was thrilled to come and talk at the DePaul Pop Culture Conference about my experiences working in the Whedonverse. I knew that I would have a good time talking about being a writer and how we came up with our stories and how we created emotional moments that connected our audiences with our characters. But I was also happy that I ended up not just speaking at the conference but also doing a lot of listening there as well in the many breakout sessions.

While I know a lot of conferences are out there to talk about how to become a writer, I haven't been that exposed to ones that evaluate a whole body of work and what does that body mean to our culture as a whole. This was a new experience for me to see what happens at the end of the story when it is out in the world, rather than trying to craft the story to give it birth. It was so interesting to see how the various students and teachers deconstructed Joss's many stories and were able to find common themes to explore. While many series have a central theme to them, like redemption, and they certainly try to have themes for each episode; they don't always think about how those themes relate to our current culture and how they affect that culture. If they did, I would worry that those stories would become too self-aware and awkward versus having those themes explored through the characters and their choices. But what I learned at the conference is that they can affect our culture.

Stories, whether told in print, on the television or on the big screen nowadays live so much longer than in just the moment that they are read or viewed. Stories have so much more effect on our culture than in times past when they were more of a singular experience. The internet has allowed audiences to do so much more. They can comment on a show, they can create fiction around that show; they can become in some ways a part of the show. And that has taken these individual shows to a higher level that influences our culture in more ways than I realized, and we need people to evaluate that and figure out how that affects us as a people. And that is what this conference and the people who study these stories do.

Before I even worked on *Buffy the Vampire Slayer*, I enjoyed watching the show. For me as a woman, it made me feel like I could be strong and vanquish my enemies. That while I might not be fighting vampires, I still needed to learn how to be strong and fight for what I wanted. It inspired me. I can still remember as a child watching TV shows that had strong female leads that showed me that I could be anything I wanted to be, if I was willing to fight for it. While other shows taught me how to be a better friend, how to fight for what I thought was right in the workplace and gave me a desire to see the world. And one of my favorite reasons to watch a show was to escape life and to recharge through the power of these stories. I still get a thrill anytime I hear the *Star Wars* music. That music is tied to a world that made me fall in love with stories and inspired me to want to tell them myself. This conference reminded me what a cool thing it is to not only be a writer but also to be a fan.

And what a great way to showcase the importance of these stories through this conference that brings together not only academics who study the importance of these stories and the writers who wrote them, but also the fans that enjoy them. I thought I was going to be there to share stories and help the audience understand better on how they were created, but instead I was excited that I also learned something there as well.

As television writers, we are so consumed with creating the world of our characters, crafting memorable scripts and then seeing them produced that we forget what happens once those stories are launched. I mean, we hope that fans enjoy them, are touched by them, but we don't always think about how these scripts link to the larger world of stories and character archetypes. We're so focused on how to construct these stories that we don't think about the fact that there are tons of people deconstructing these stories to find universal themes afterward.

And that is what I enjoyed about this conference. I listened to speakers talk about the mythological influences seen in Joss's work. I heard debates on how ethics played a role in these stories and how religious themes are explored. Most writers spend years learning their craft, but when we go to break a story, we don't usually talk in the language of mythology or how ethics plays a role. We talk about the world and how these characters are going to grow in it through the stories we send them on.

But how wonderful that, in a way, we are tapping into the collective unconscious when we tell these stories. That we're playing out larger themes that are universal and human and that when a student or teacher goes to deconstruct a story that they're finding these common themes that sometimes we're not even aware that we're inserting into our tales. And how cool is that? I so appreciate this conference reminding me of that and as a writer, it further helps me to create deeper and more relatable stories.

Neither Shiny Nor Afraid: *Firefly*'s Mal Reynolds as Chandlerian Hero

Gordon Dymowski

In his essay "The Simple Art of Murder," Raymond Chandler starts with a basic assumption: "Fiction in any form has always intended to be realistic." Although he focuses on mystery/crime fiction, in particular, much of his discussion focuses on both the nature of fiction and the quality of its hero, regardless of genre.

In fact, it was Chandler himself who created the archetypal "knight errant" prevalent in hard-boiled fiction. It's an often-quoted passage that bears repeating:

> ...down these mean streets a man must go who is not himself mean, who is neither tarnished nor afraid. The detective in this kind of story must be such a man. He is the hero, he is everything. He must be a complete man and a common man and yet an unusual man.

These are qualities that find themselves in many heroes of modern fiction, and this essay will argue that they can be found in an unlikely place: Mal Reynolds, war hero turned scavenger, captain of the *Serenity* in Joss Whedon's *Firefly*. Although he integrates elements from disparate genres (like Westerns, science fiction, and *Manga*) into the series, this essay will argue that Whedon establishes Mal Reynolds as a Chandlerian hard-boiled protagonist the series pilot *Serenity,* and this essay will show how that plays out throughout the course of the pilot.

(This essay is going to be a superficial examination, preferring to encourage further scholarship into parallels between Chandler's work and Whedon's *Firefly* as a whole. There are also some parallels between Mal Reynolds and other Chandler-influenced protagonists like Robert B. Parker's Spenser...but for now, this essay will have an intentionally limited scope.)

One of the key aspects of *Firefly* is how it approaches world building: a more structured, potentially corrupt "Alliance" contrasted with a more "free" planet with a mix of Eastern and Western culture. Although there is an obvious conflict established in the beginning of the pilot with the Battle of Serenity Hill, *Firefly* establishes a future that Chandler would describe as

...not a very fragrant world, but it is the world you live in...

Through this world, we meet Mal Reynolds – a man who initially believes that he and his fellow Browncoats are *"too pretty to die"* but six years later, becomes a man focused on *"doing the job."* In fact, one of the key aspects of Mal's character that reflects Chandler is that

He talks as the man of his age talks, that is, with rude wit, a lively sense of the grotesque, a disgust for sham, and a contempt for pettiness...He must be, to use a rather weathered phrase, a man of honour, by ' instinct, by inevitability, without thought of it, and certainly without saying it.

Throughout the *Firefly* pilot, Mal Reynolds (like other characters) speaks in a very unusual rhythm, sounding more like the traditional frontier cowboy than a science fiction captain. Starting with Mal informing Bendis that they were *"just too pretty for God to let us die,* Mal Reynolds' way of speaking demonstrates a strong sense of the absurd – too many to quote (and this article will outline further examples), but anyone who can describe their most recent score as *"protein in all the colors of the rainbow"* demands being heard. It's also through dialogue that Mal Reynolds demonstrates and codifies his sense of honor, coming to a head when he informs Patience after the final shootout with her men, when he tells her, *"...Let me make this abundantly clear: I do the job. And then I get paid...go run your little world."*

In other matters, we can see how Mal Reynolds may regard relationships. Chandler writes:

I do not care much about his private life; he is neither a eunuch nor a satyr; I think he might seduce a duchess and I am quite sure he would not spoil a virgin; if he is a man of honour in one thing, he is that in all things.

When we meet Mal Reynolds in Serenity, he keeps himself at arm's length with his crew: his more formal military-style relationship with Zoe (and resulting tension with Wash); a slightly more fraternal relationship with Kaylee (who calls Mal "nice," and Mal's response is that he's a *"mean old man."* We see some tension between Mal with both Shepherd Book and Jayne. With Book, there is a more general disregard of the former's spiritual beliefs (Book: *"Mind if I say grace?"* Mal: *"Only if you say it out loud"*). However, while Mal has a tense yet mutually respectful relationship with Jayne, especially in the latter's possible betrayal of Mal to the federal officer onboard Serenity. It's only with Inara that we see any indication of Mal Reynolds being interested in more romantic/sexual matters, as their relationship progresses from banter (*"How's business?"* *"None of yours"*) to a more protective and potentially caring one (witness the "moment" as Mal Reynolds pauses after urging Inara to leave with others during a Reaver attack on Whitefall).

But perhaps the one piece of dialogue that reinforces the idea of Mal Reynolds as a Chandlerian hero is his final exchange with Simon Tam. After Simon wonders aloud why Mal won't kill him in his sleep, the captain answers in a short speech that seems ripped out of one of Chandler's novels:

> You don't know me, son, so let me explain this to you once: if I ever kill you, you'll be awake. You'll be facing me, and you'll be armed.

At this point, we witness the initial arc of Mal Reynolds' character – a man looking to gain redemption after a bitter defeat. A captain looking to stay free and incorruptible within a potentially corrupt system – a system that allows for the manipulation and possible torture of young people (outlined by Simon's story of his sister, River) to a more organized, sanitized way of living (symbolized by the Alliance). It is through this arc that "Serenity" – the pilot for *Firefly* – allows Mal Reynolds to symbolize one of the key aspects of Raymond Chandler's ideal hero, and why *Firefly* has encouraged a strong following, for as Chandler stated,

> In everything that can be called art there is a quality of redemption. It may be pure tragedy, if it is high tragedy, and it may be pity and irony, and it may be the raucous laughter of the strong man.

Marry, Kill, or Shag? Love Affairs with Characters in the Whedonverses

Sherry Ginn

My name is Sherry Ginn. I am the author of *Power and Control in the Television Worlds of Joss Whedon* and co-editor with Heather M. Porter and Alyson Buckman, of *Confounding Purpose, Confusing Identity: Examinations of Reality and Fantasy in Joss Whedon's Dollhouse.* My favorite Whedon series is *Firefly* (what else?), and I am also a huge fan of *Farscape, Doctor Who,* and *Babylon 5.* I thought I would tell you about my favorite and least favorite characters in the Whedonverses in a hopefully humorous way.

I went to a panel at Dragon*Con a couple of years ago featuring Jane Espenson. Someone in the audience asked her, with respect to working with Ronald Moore on *Battlestar Galactica,* Joss Whedon on *Firefly* and *Dollhouse,* and Russell T Davies on *Torchwood Miracle Day,* which of them she would marry, kill, and shag? So I thought I would do that for this panel. [BTW, she said, kill Moore, shag Whedon, and marry Davies.]

If I had my choice of which characters in the Whedonverses to kill it would be Angel and Paul Ballard. Ballard was a creepy stalker. I never found him to be a sympathetic character. Angel was just too broody and self-centered to live (before and after he was turned). Maybe Xander as well; he was just mean and rotten to his friends. Ward would also be added to this list because he was a psychopath and a traitor.

Who would I marry? That is really easy. I would marry Giles, who is witty, handsome, nurturing, very intelligent, and not scared of strong women. I would also choose Wesley for the same reasons, but only the Wesley of *Angel* because he has matured and actually grown "into himself" on that series. I might also choose Coulson. I love his sense of humor. He is attractive and he has a job that would take him away from home often, which is actually a good way (IMHO) of keeping the spark alive.

Who would I shag? That is too easy—definitely Spike and definitely Jayne. Those bad boys, you just know that they would know how to please a woman. And, Hawkeye: those eyes are dreamy and those arms could hold a woman quite nicely.

As you can see, all of my choices are male because I am a heterosexual female. However, I am not afraid to admit that I can appreciate a well-written and, dare I say, strong female character. So if I were to choose among the female characters, my choices would be as follows.

Just like I would be attracted to the best-looking, sexiest men as sexual partners, I would do the same for the women. The sexiest women in the Whedonverses are Zoe (those arms), Cordelia (those legs), November (those curves and eyes), and Black Widow (the whole package).

Hands down, I would want to marry Kaylee. She is such a sweetheart. She is not afraid to speak her mind, has a great sense of humor, and she could keep my car running as well as all of the household appliances, thereby saving us money.

My kill list would have to include Dawn, as she was way too whiny. Joss Whedon and crew really slipped up there, casting an older actress to play the part of a girl who was supposed to be much younger. What kid these days does not know about sex?

I want to add another category to the "kill, shag, marry" list and that is, which characters would I want to have at my back. Really who would not want Zoe, Jayne, Coulson, May, Black Widow and Hawkeye. That sounds like a great team. I wonder what we can call ourselves. Whedonites (Whedon + Dynamite)? Whedonombs (Whedon + Bombs)? I'll get back to you about that.

Damaged Goods: Broken Women/Killing Machines

Michele Leigh

Joss Whedon has had a successful career that has spanned a variety of media outlets from comics, to the internet, film, and television. As a writer/director, Whedon has been both praised and condemned for the portrayal of women in his work. To say the least, Whedon's women are complicated.

This paper does not purport to evaluate the success or failure of Whedon's female portrayals, rather it offers up musings on one type of woman, found frequently in Whedon's work – the woman who has been tampered with, damaged physically and/or psychologically. The tampering is often at the hand of science or sanctioned by some government or corporate interest. The woman, who because of some trauma in her past, has lost or repressed part of herself, usually her memory. She is broken in some way and this damage is connected to her becoming a lethal weapon, a killing machine. This female character pops up in many of Whedon's works from *Firefly* (2002-2003) and *Serenity* (2005), to *Dollhouse* (2009-2010), and to *Agents of S.H.I.E.L.D.* (2013-present). In *Firefly*, we see the character of an adolescent girl, River Tam (Summer Glau) damaged because the school for gifted children she attended was actually using her as a science experiment in an effort to create the perfect weapon for a totalitarian regime. In *Dollhouse*, Caroline Farrell (Eliza Dushku), a college student/political activist finds, or rather looses herself in a Los Angeles Dollhouse (part of the Rossum Corporation), where her memories are wiped clean and she becomes Echo, a doll who can be imprinted with a new identity and new memories and rented out to the highest bidder. Whedon takes a different approach with the character of Skye Johnson (Chloe Bennet), a computer hacker trying to investigate the actions of the military group S.H.I.E.L.D., when she is pulled in to become part of the very system she is trying to bring down. Skye's trauma, perhaps much less violent than the other two women, stems from the fact that she was abandoned by her parents as a child and in trying to find them, it is revealed that she has been under surveillance because she is inhuman/alien, given experimental alien blood to save her life and later transformed into

Quake, a being who can use vibrations to cause earthquakes and destruction, and thus becomes a tool of the very organization she was originally investigating.

While all three women navigate and cope with their trauma in unique ways, River Tam offers an interesting example of how Whedon uses the physically, emotionally and/or psychologically damaged woman, and how she functions in the growing landscape of anti-feminist rhetoric and the fight over legal control over women's bodies. I am particularly interested in the role of trauma on the female psyche and the effect it has for women's ability to navigate a culture dominated by male aggression.

In his article "'I am a leaf of the wind': Cultural trauma and mobility on Joss Whedon's *Firefly*," Matthew Hill explores the significance of the communal cultural trauma experienced by Americans after 9/11 on Whedon's sci-fi western television show. For Hill, the crew of *Firefly* and Malcolm "Mal" Reynolds (Nathan Fillion) stand in for a traumatized America. Mal, who fought on the side of the Independents in the War of Unification, experienced his defining moment, his greatest trauma during the battle and subsequent defeat at Serenity Valley. The trauma Mal experienced weighs on him, follows him (there are multiple references in various episodes to the loss, to brown coats and Independents). It had become so ingrained in his psyche that he even named his ship Serenity. Hill goes on to note that unlike other post-9/11 narratives which hunker down and reinforce ideas of American greatness, *Firefly* manifests its trauma in the form of mobility as a way to escape hegemony rather than retribution.

In River, at once the most vulnerable and the most dangerous character on the ship Serenity, the collective cultural trauma, the overwhelming power of the Alliance, is literally written on her body.1 The viewer's first introduction to River is itself born of trauma. As many including Hill have noted, River is in essence born a second time on Serenity when Mal opens the cryo chamber to reveal a naked River in the fetal position, not yet ready to enter back into the world (her re-entry was forced by Mal who opened the cryo chamber a week before the due date.) Her re-entry into the world is fraught with violence, everyone shouting, Kaylee getting shot, the federal agent apprehended and tied up, and everywhere the threat of more potential violence, capture and return to the Alliance. As if that were not enough to scar a young girl for life, the episode "Safe" and the film Serenity further explain just how the trauma was inscribed on her body.

"Safe" provides a little background into Simon and River's past, in both the lead-in to the show and the show itself. The voice over and opening shots for this episode are different from those that aired before it. For the first time, when we are introduced to River, we see flashes of River in a chair with machines hooked to her head, a needle, and blood. Throughout the episode snippets of the past are interspersed with the main story about selling cattle, Shepherd Book (Ron Glass) getting shot, Simon and River getting kidnapped, and River's psychic ability almost getting her burned at the stake. This episode shows us the cute, super intelligent, and precocious child River was before she was sent to the Alliance Academy. The episode begins in the Tam home, cozy and warm, the scene in muted earth tones, browns and reds. In an effort to distract Simon from his homework, which she points out is wrong because the problem in the book is "fallacious," River pops up from behind the sofa. She distracts him by saying (perhaps a bit of foreshadowing) "We are going to have to resort to cannibalism," and then concocts an imaginative and elaborate scenario where they are trapped by Independent troops and must get back to their Alliance platoon before their father enters to read by the fire. On the surface this scene presents us with the ideal image of family, home, and safety; however, the communal cultural trauma that Hill mentioned is manifest in River's play, only River because of her age is prey to the political hegemony that Mal and crew avoid. Later in the episode, in the midst of some nonsensical comments, we get clues as to the dark extent of River's trauma—"You can't just shove needles in my eye and ask me what I see" and "a body can be drained of blood in 8.5 seconds." River has a moment of lucidity as she and Simon joke and reminisce over hodgeberries and their childhood. She admits she does remember, too much, the memories are confused sometimes with made up things and with secrets. She knows she was broken and what it took for Simon to save her. River struggles with her trauma, she struggles to get control of her mind, her memories, her body.

It isn't until *Serenity* that River's story is more fully fleshed out, as it were. In many ways, the film is River's tale, as much as it ties up loose ends from the television show. What unfolds through the film are the horrors of River's transformation from an innocent little girl to a lethal weapon, a killing machine. In her sleep they have poked and prodded her, they have messed with her subconscious, they have implanted information, in essence, they have rewritten her neurological coding in an effort to remove what was River Tam and to give birth to a Frankensteinian monster that they could control and use for their benefit. The kink in the Alliance's plan for River comes not just from Simon, who frees her from the Academy, but also from River herself, not just in the coded letters she wrote to Simon in "Safe," but also in her dreams and flashbacks where she pushes back, she resists their hegemonic control. For instance, in the first scene in the schoolroom, when the teacher asks the children why the Independents would choose to fight the Alliance. River speaks out that they are tired of meddling, they don't want to be told what to think, in their homes and in their heads, she attempts to hold on to some part of herself before the teacher/technician plunges the needle into her skull yet again.

After River's escape, the Alliance goes to great lengths to retrieve 'their property.' In addition to having the Alliance ships and soldiers all on the look out for 'the weapon,' they hire the Operative (Chiwetel Ejiofor) to hunt her down and return her, no matter the cost (in terms of human lives—that cost was high.) On the run from the Alliance and the Operative, River leads the crew into what seems like a suicide mission through Reaver territory to find a deserted planet named Miranda. The truth of what happened in Miranda is one of the many secrets that were rattling around in River's brain, a horrible secret that could weaken the Alliance—that they were responsible for creating the Reavers, truly despicable, monstrous, pillaging, cannibals. The push to solving the mystery of Miranda was again River subconsciously resisting, pushing back, fighting the loss of control over her brain. River's final act of resistance comes in the final scene while fighting off the Reavers. When Simon gets shot and his life is in danger, River, who until then was a frightened little girl, cowering in the corner, finally takes control of her faculties and single-handedly destroys the remaining Reavers. Unlike the previous time she was triggered into a killing spree, here she makes the decision to fight, she controls her actions, and they are graceful and fluid, a thing of beauty amid all the horror.

River, like Echo and Skye who will follow her, must find herself, in the face of trauma and horror. She must resist being the property of the corporate/military state, she must take control of her own body. While Hill's argument about *Firefly* and the character of Mal, in particular, being a reaction to, a working out of the cultural trauma of

9/11 is compelling, I find River's reaction to trauma more interesting. In addition to ideas of retribution and a resurgence of the myth of American greatness, after 9/11 there was also a knee-jerk attempt to restore order through hyper-masculinized/politicized attempts at protection, from others, from ourselves. The results of which ranged from the creation of an extreme surveillance to the rise of populist racism and renewed attempts protect women from themselves through state control over women's bodies. Whedon's broken women, like River Tam, overcome their trauma and manage to resist the power structures that try to own and control them.

Notes
1 I will be talking about the show in episode order not airing order.

References
Hill, Matthew. "'I am a leaf of the wind': Cultural Trauma and mobility on Joss Whedon's *Firefly*." *Extrapolation*. 50.3 (2009): 485-511.

"Men were deceivers ever": Of Shakespeare and Superheroes

Walter Metz

In the past few years, the seemingly disparate careers of Joss Whedon and Kenneth Branagh have crossed tracks. Famous for tackling the Olivier canon of Shakespeare and cinema masterworks—*Henry V* (1989) and *Hamlet* (1996)—Branagh directed one of the Marvel superhero movies, *Thor* in 2011. Known for his geeky science-fiction frippery—*Buffy the Vampire Slayer* (1997-2003) and superhero movies *du jour*—Joss Whedon, as if inspired to return the favor and wander into Branagh's domain, in 2012 directed a digital video version of *Much Ado About Nothing*, set in contemporary Los Angeles. The choice of play seems intentionally directed toward Branagh, as his *Much Ado About Nothing* (1993) represents one of the high points in Shakespearean comedy on film.

What are we to make of this crossing of the tracks of two seemingly different artists? For one thing, this recent work indicates that the boundaries between high and low culture are not as stable as literary critics would have us believe. Via casting, Branagh's cinematic stunts have been trying to teach us this for decades. By filling the role of the traveling actor in *Hamlet* (1996) with Charlton Heston, king of the classical Hollywood epic, Branagh suggests that the world of Hollywood action does not lie that far from Shakespearean Elsinore. In turn, by casting eminent Shakespearean Anthony Hopkins (a terrifically devious Claudius in Tony Richardson's 1968 version of *Hamlet*) as the father of the gods in Thor, Branagh brings Shakespearean gravitas to the world of comic book fisticuffs and hammer smashing.

Whedon's foray into *Much Ado About Nothing* allows us to revisit some foundational assumptions in genre theory. In *Henry V*, before they are to fight and most likely die at the Battle of Agincourt, Shakespeare has one representative from each of the British kingdoms spar about their ethnic identity. The comic relief grounds the tragedy of war in its proper location, human emotion.

The best of Whedon's work—*Dr. Horrible's Sing-Along Blog* (2008), for example—uses comedy to similarly put into focus the hopeless fate of humans in a cold, indifferent world. Dr. Horrible learns at the end that the only way he can become the super-villain that he so longs to be is to kill all he loves in the world. This is the stuff of the Theater of the Absurd, and one of the reasons why Shakespeare is the fount from which the tragicomedy of works such as *Waiting for Godot* springs. Dr. Horrible is the Samuel Beckett of contemporary American popular culture. This seems far afield from Branagh's light and energetic *Much Ado About Nothing*, filled with actors of tremendous charisma and vitality: Denzel Washington, Michael Keaton, and the like. However, Whedon is engaged in his own casting interventions: trooper Nathan Fillion's Dogberry stands not far behind his Captain Hammer, "corporate tool."

Eclipsing Branagh's earnest version, Whedon's take on *Much Ado About Nothing* delivers a sophisticated understanding of the cultural history of comedy. I want to explore one such strain: by reworking Roman New Comedies, themselves derived from their Greek precedents, Shakespeare reinvented a language for understanding the funny ways in which men and women relate to one another. The cinema thrives in visualizing these theatrical mechanisms, especially in the genre of romantic comedy. In an attempt to keep his film contemporary and relevant, Whedon relies on the conventions of the Hollywood romantic comedy to emphasize the New Comedy roots of *Much Ado About Nothing*. In particular, Whedon's film resonates with *The Graduate* (Mike Nichols, 1967), one of the masterpieces of the genre.

Whedon begins his film with the preparations for a party at the suburban home of Leonato (Clark Gregg). The film uncovers the ways in which the tropes of festival theater—parties will celebrate the end of strife by etching out time for music and lovemaking—inflect modern narrative. From Katherine Mansfield's "The Garden Party" (1922) to Virginia Woolf's *Mrs. Dalloway* (1925), the anticipation of a party undergirds much representation of familial celebration. *The Graduate* also begins with a party, one that Benjamin Braddock (Dustin Hoffman) desperately wants to escape because it represents the values of his parents' corrupt generation: "I've got one word for you, Ben… plastics!"

In *Much Ado about Nothing*, the younger generation does not reject its elders as directly; instead, Shakespeare positions the young and the middle-aged as reinforcing foils. Despite its status as a subplot, the "will-they-or-won't-they" dynamics of Benedick and Beatrice have captivated audiences for hundreds of years. These purported minor characters have provided the template for much film and television, ranging from the screwball antics of 1930s film lovers to Sam and Diane on *Cheers* (NBC, 1982-1993).

Because their friends have played a trick on them, both Beatrice and Benedick believe that the other has fallen in love with them. After the funniest moments in Whedon's film, when first Benedick (Alexis Denisof) and then Beatrice (Amy Acker) do cartwheels trying to spy on their friends' conversations to see what their soul mate has confessed about them, Benedick retreats to the outdoor grounds to figure out whether he actually loves Beatrice as much as his friends have indicated she loves him. Beatrice walks outside of the house and inelegantly swats at a fly.

Under the pretense that it is time to come inside and eat, Beatrice stands before an equally ridiculous Benedick, who is flexing and stretching his muscles in order to impress her. A shot from behind Benedick reveals him gloating: "You take pleasure in the message?" A cut reframes Benedick in the foreground, with a perplexed Beatrice framed in the background by his prone body. *The Graduate* is rife with such framings of men and women, the most famous of which is the seduction scene with Ben and Mrs. Robinson (Anne Bancroft). Mrs. Robinson in the foreground raises her leg, framing Ben in the background as he queries, "Mrs. Robinson, are you trying to seduce me?"

Whedon's most inventive sequence in *Much Ado About Nothing* dovetails with *The Graduate* to profound effect. The villainous Don John (Sean Maher) plots to mislead Claudio (Fran Kranz) such that he will accuse his fiancée, Hero (Jillian Morgese) of infidelity, thus ruining the returning warriors' celebration of domestic harmony. The morning of the wedding, while people are recovering from the debauchery the night before, Claudio swims in the backyard suburban swimming pool. He surfaces wearing a ridiculous snorkeling apparatus on his face. Don John and his cronies, Borachio (Spencer Treat Clark) and Conrade (Riki Lindhome), surface around him. Pretending they mistake him for Benedick, they plant the notion in Claudio's mind that another man has already been making love to Hero. Their treachery accomplished, they leave the pool. Claudio storms out of the water, angrily drying himself off, while shouting at Benedick at the horrors of the domestic world.

A similar alienation subtends the swimming pool scene in *The Graduate*. In the midst of a destructive affair with Mrs. Robinson, his parents' friend, Ben tries to avoid the other adults as much as he can. However, on his birthday, his Dad (William Daniels) forces him to try out the scuba gear he has bought for his son. With no other recourse, Ben dons the apparatus, but then sinks inert to the bottom of the pool, retreating to a world where he does not have to confront the hypocrisy of his parents' generation. The centripetal force of *The Graduate*, a gravitational pressure on Ben forcing him into isolation at the bottom of the pool, is answered by the centrifuge that is *Much Ado About Nothing*. The youthful Claudio, Whedon's film's Benjamin, is propelled out of the pool by the machinations of Don John and his henchmen. He flies into a rage, falsely confronting the innocent Hero, ending the chances of their marriage, and threatening to rip apart the friends and family that surround him.

In this way, the populist Josh Whedon uses the language of the Hollywood romantic comedy to reinvent *Much Ado About Nothing*. However, the genre play does not stay contained within the world of comedy. The film is also the place at which Branagh and Whedon—surely two of the most significant filmmakers in contemporary popular American cinema, known for their action cinema—meet. Shakespeare reassures:

"Sigh no more, ladies, sigh no more,
Men were deceivers ever,-
One foot in sea and one on shore,
To one thing constant never."

Deceivers indeed, this Branagh and Whedon dynamic duo. But of what significance? A messenger asks Beatrice about Benedick, whom, sit-com style, she believes she hates but really loves as no other can be loved: "I can see he's not in your good books." Beatrice responds with fire: "No, and if he were I would burn my library." At first glance, Branagh may burn the library's comic book section, and Whedon the Shakespearean folios with the fiery romantic comedy of *The Graduate*, but after the smoke clears, a new bookshelf hitherto unseen emerges, and our cinema is much the better for it.

"He Saved the World A Lot"

Eleanor Pye

Understanding Pop Culture can be a tricky task. What are the norms in today's society? How does that differ from what is expected? For example, everyone has his or her own list of favorite TV shows or movies. Whether it includes series that are currently on the air or those that hold a special place in your heart; those programs usually balance on that fine line between shows that a lot of people enjoy and others consisting of guilty pleasures. Today's rules indicate that there are no rules. Professionals behind-the-scenes as well as notable actors are moving across the media platforms. One cannot deny the cultural significance of the work of Joss Whedon, creator, writer, producer, and/ or director of critical and audience favorites. Whedon has paved the way in the current and future landscapes for media creators.

It is from the perspective of both creator and fan that Whedon tackles projects. This is reciprocated multi-fold by the devoted fan response to Whedon-based projects; most notably being the series *Firefly* which faced a quick demise on network TV in the fall of 2002. Although the series was cancelled after being bounced around the programming schedule and airing just ten episodes, its life did not end there. *Firefly* rose from the ashes due to fan response to the show (and its creator).

In a time when social media did not yet exist, fans took to online messaging boards, sharing their love for *Firefly* and refusing the let the story die with the series. When *Firefly* was released on DVD in 2003, sales went through the roof, as fans wanted to enjoy the series for themselves as well as share it with family and friends. Universal Pictures, the studio behind *Firefly*, took notice of both the online chatter and the sales profits. Soon, they were in talks with Whedon and his team to develop a movie to wrap up some of the stories within the TV series. The film, *Serenity*, was released in September 2005.

As with some of Joss Whedon's other projects, a story does not simply fade away once a television series is cancelled or the final frame of film is shot. Joss Whedon's affection for the graphic novel (and its comic book origins) helped bring these characters to a new life and a new medium. Joss soon turned his own fandom into a new avenue for storytelling, a pattern that repeats itself over and over again! Those *Firefly* side stories that never were explored on TV or within the film came to life in print as either short series or as a single-issue comic. *Buffy the Vampire Slayer*, the television series that enjoyed a successful run for seven seasons from 1997 to 2003, continues to generate new "seasons" in comic book form. While the actors may have all moved to other projects, the "Scooby Gang" characters continue on and entertain a new generation of slayers—uh, readers.

Television, film, and print; all are successful businesses within the media industry. However, another platform was being pioneered within the Whedonverse: the internet. When an industry-wide writer's strike abruptly curtailed the 2007 television season, Joss Whedon developed a self-funded side project with his friends, all of whom were out of work due to the strike. *Dr. Horrible's Sing-Along Blog* was released in three parts, for free, on the internet in July 2008. After a short period of time, the episodes became available for purchase through iTunes as well as a bonus material-packed DVD, both of which were well received. The project itself was lauded as innovative and won a number of awards, including a Creative Arts Emmy.

"An Emmy? But it didn't debut on TV?" That's true, and while the current entertainment landscape boasts critically acclaimed and award-winning original series from services such as Netflix, Amazon, and Hulu, in 2008, that simply did not exist. However, after the success of *Dr. Horrible*, you can be sure the industry was taking notice. Once again, the landscape began to change.

Joss Whedon was propelled to a new level of recognition when he agreed to bring Marvel's *The Avengers* and its subsequent sequel to the big screen. He serves as executive producer for the Marvel's *Agents of S.H.I.E.L.D.* television series on ABC. Yet, he stays true to his passions. His very next project after *The Avengers* was a modern-day film version of Shakespeare's play *Much Ado About Nothing*. Why? Because Whedon and his friends would gather at this house regularly and perform read-throughs of Shakespeare's work. So, why not make it into a film? And that is exactly what he did: bring in all his friends— actors who have worked with him over the years and those from behind the camera—and shoot the film on location, at his house.

Whedon continues to pursue his passions, challenging himself to work on the projects that bring him joy, that appeal to him as a fan, regardless of the medium. He does not conform to the confines of that which may be familiar or would guarantee success. He tests his limits with each new project and holds true to those core beliefs that makes each of his projects just a little bit special – a Whedon project. I would say it is a brand, but that minimizes its elegance and its rich storytelling. Rather, to many, a Whedon project is something that will make you pay attention, think a little, and, quite often, get you even a little bit angry. Why? Because life is not always fair, and the good guy doesn't always win. Whedon understands that and that is how he constructs his works.

The title of this piece is "He Saved the World A Lot." It is borrowed from the epitaph on "Buffy's" (temporary) tombstone in *Buffy the Vampire Slayer*. Has Joss Whedon literally saved the world? No. But he has made the entertainment industry into a richer landscape, full of complex stories and well-rounded characters while fostering an inclusive community of fans who treasure being treasured.

"Get a Pic! Do a Blog!": Multimodality in the Joss Whedon Classroom

Jason Lawton Winslade

In 2004, one year after *Buffy the Vampire Slayer* had left the airwaves and as *Angel* was finishing up its final season, I proposed a course at DePaul University for first-year students entitled "Reading the Vampire Slayer." This was one of many multidisciplinary courses in the First Year Program known as Focal Point Seminars, intended to introduce students to various perspectives and methodologies on a single topic, be that a person, place, event, text or idea. At the time, "Buffy studies" was still in its early years, with the first scholarly anthology on the show only a few years old, coinciding with the inception of *Slayage*, the International Journal of Buffy Studies in 2001. I had an article in that premiere issue of *Slayage*, focusing on witchcraft and popular culture, which to this day is still my most frequently cited scholarly work, despite its incomplete and simplistic approach to the show (I followed up in 2013 with a much more in-depth essay on the show's witchcraft trope in the *Joss Whedon and Religion* anthology from McFarland Press). So I had some grounding in the field, such as it was. But that first year of teaching the course, I had no idea what to expect. Many students had never even heard of the show and thought the course was on vampires. The majority of the students were women and only a few were deeply familiar with the subject matter.

I continued to teach the course over the next eight years or so, garnering some attention from the local press (whose research consisted of reading the course catalog – no one ever spoke to me) and usually filling the class with at least a half to three-quarters of the students familiar and eager to discuss the show. Of course, as streaming technology evolved, we moved from focusing on DVDs to Netflix. And as the distance from the show's ending increased, that familiarity unexpectedly also increased, as more and more students were introduced to the show by their parents or older siblings. Even more surprisingly, growing numbers of male students registered for the course, perhaps due in part to Whedon's enormous success as director of Marvel's *Avengers* film, to the point that the male students outnumbered the female, and to my gratification, were just as eager to discuss the feminist ideas behind Whedon's work. Ultimately, in 2012, I expanded the course to include Whedon's other works, like *Firefly*, *Dollhouse* and *Doctor Horrible's Sing-Along Blog*, coinciding with the shift in the field from "Buffy Studies" to "Whedon Studies," reflected in the transformed description of *Slayage* as a journal of Whedon Studies.

In teaching the course, I was continually challenged to make an increasingly dated television program relevant to millennial students. However, as the many scholarly fans of Whedon's works can attest, his shows are a gift that keeps on giving in terms of media representation of issues surrounding gender, morality, the individual and community, and philosophies of life, violence, power, death, and everything in between. Yet I was still concerned about my approach. In a 2010 essay, entitled "'Have You Tried Not Being a Slayer?' Performing Buffy Fandom in the Classroom," I explored the impact of students' fandom (and my own) on their experience of the course, engaging students in conversations specifically addressing their fandom and observing the instances in which their fandom inhibited their success in the course and where it enhanced their learning. Once again, this exploration coincided with developments in the field that questioned the role fandom played in scholarly analyses of Whedon's shows, and indeed, how that fandom impacted the legitimacy of the field itself. In my other scholarly work examining alternative spiritual practice, I found this concern reflected a much broader discourse in academia skeptical of researchers who are immersed in a "cult" following, whether of an alternative religion or of a television show.

As a result of this debate, I was worried, as I stated then, that I was" simply creating a more critical consumer and [was] not doing enough to encourage students to become cultural producers" (22). But as the class progressed, I learned that the best way for students to absorb, examine and question these ideas was through producing their own work. At the time I published that article, the First Year Writing program at DePaul had begun to incorporate electronic portfolios into their classes as not only a repository for students' work throughout the term but as a holistic, rhetorical presentation of students' achievements in the given course, including a significant reflective component that often was intended to directly address that course's goals and learning outcomes. Thus, a significant aspect of teaching writing under this new paradigm was an emphasis on visual rhetoric and presentation. Concurrently, faculty were encouraged to incorporate multimodal assignments into their curriculum. Initially presented as a supplement to or "remix" of an already completed written assignment, these multimodal projects, in my Whedon class particularly, came to take on their own independent life and have called for their own brand of pedagogy. Indeed, my thought for my students was that since the primary sources for their research were entirely media-based, that the main way they could contribute to the discourse about that media was to make their own.

I took Henry Jenkins' call for the creation and development of participatory culture as my lead, in which "fans envision a world where all of us can participate in the creation and circulation of central cultural myths" (256). I also wanted to create a foundation for multimodal discourse that students could apply beyond the Whedon classroom. I subscribed to Takyoshi and Selfe's assertion that "in an increasingly technological world, students need to be experienced and skilled not only in reading (consuming) texts employing multiple modalities, but also in composing in multiple modalities, if they hope to communicate successfully within the digital communication networks that characterize workplaces, schools, civic life, and span traditional cultural, national, and geopolitical borders" (3). And even though students would occasionally show some initial resistance to these projects, when they realized that this was just a more rigorous form of what they already do—posting, tweeting, creating gifs and vids, etc—the projects developed organically. And of course, the sophistication of these projects grew over time as social media itself evolved. Some projects utilized apps and skills familiar to students: for instance, a fake movie trailer or homemade music video using clips from shows (a genre that itself has received scholarly attention in Buffy Studies), creating fictional online blogs for characters (something *Buffy* did itself in its final season), or even reframing the events of a show in a newspaper format to demonstrate the values of that fictional culture, as one student did with the 'verse of *Firefly*. Several students went further with artistic projects, such as a coloring book that addressed issues of gender performance on *Buffy* (prefiguring the sale of adult coloring books that are just now being sold as official merchandise from Dark Horse, the comics company that produced the *Buffy* and *Firefly* comics).

Some students chose to focus on their digital media skills, such as two students who created online quizzes similar to the popular Buzzfeed-type quizzes. One student created a kind of morality test to see which *Dollhouse* character a participant might be like. Another student used a similar format, focusing on Willow from *Buffy*, to ask the question, "what's your sexuality," but then critiquing the format itself by having every result be the same: "a quiz can't tell you how you identify!" Another student created a Tumblr page for Whedonverse cosplay examples and making it public for anyone's contributions. Two years after the class, the page is still receiving posts from Whedon fans. In the case of all the successful projects, students created multimodal work that was the culmination of research and theorizing, not the other way around.

Often in my classes, students gain invaluable insight on their claims by creating a multimodal project. In what was probably the best instance of superb multimodal work that enhanced and supported written work while standing on its own as a salient piece of academic work, one student went above and beyond by filming a video that was a lip-synched performance of "I'll Never Tell," the number sung and danced by Xander and Anya in the musical episode of *Buffy*. This student adeptly filmed herself performing both roles in split screen, dressed in "feminine" garb for the Anya role and more "masculine" costume for the male role, including a backwards baseball hat. The accompanying paper addressed how the relationship of Xander and Anya on the program critiques heteronormativity, presenting it in its romanticized form and then showing its failures. Here the student directly addresses criticism of the show that frames the Xander and Anya relationship as "anti-feminist" when in fact, she argues, it highlights the shortcomings of traditional patriarchal gender roles. By embodying both roles in her video, re-enacting a performance from the show that itself was meant as a metacommentary on the Hollywood musical number for straight couples, the student emphasizes the show's questioning of traditional heteronormative relationships and offers a decidedly queer critique of the form itself.

These projects demonstrate the ways that students not only are inspired by the work of Joss Whedon as fans, but how their participation in cultural creation enhances and enriches their scholarly work. At the Joss Whedon Symposium at DePaul University, I was able to introduce some of these students and their work to the broader academic community and giving them an opportunity to engage with other scholars who value multimodality and media study as much as they do. I believe these projects and their use in academic discourse make a strong argument for the inclusion of material like that of Joss Whedon's work into college level classes. And that the further use and development of multimodal projects, media literacy, and visual rhetoric is essential in the 21st-century liberal arts education. It may not always be Buffy, but we can hope to make use of such strong cultural products in our classrooms for many years to come.

References

Jenkins, Henry. *Convergence Culture: Where Old and New Media Collide.* New York: New York University Press, 2006. Print.

Takayoshi, Pamela and Cynthia L. Selfe. "Thinking About Multimodality." *Multimodal Composition: Resources for Teachers.* Ed. Cynthia Selfe. Cresskill, NJ: Hampton Press, Inc. 2007. 1-12. Print.

Winslade, Jason Lawton. "'Have You Tried Not Being a Slayer?' Performing Buffy Fandom in the Classroom." *Buffy in the Classroom: Essays on Teaching with the Vampire Slayer.* Eds. Jodie A. Kreider and Meghan K. Winchell. Jefferson, NC: MacFarland and Company, 2010. 21-34. Print.

Schedule for Joss Whedon: A Celebration

11:00–12:00

Religion and Ethics in Whedon

Scott Paeth, Gerry Canavan, Jonathon Lundy, Katie Wilson, Candace West

Fan Works on Whedon

Conner Good, Chloé Campbell, Katie L. Ramos, video by eilowyn

12:00–1:00

Whedon's Characters: Villains, Heroes, and Everypeople

Sherry Ginn, Rachel Eells, Damian Serbu, Megan Connor, Patrick Smith, Steven Silver

Fans Weigh In: Problematic Portrayals in Whedon

Anne Peterson, Michi Trota, Jennifer Cross, Gordon Dymowski

1:00–2:00

Keynote Speaker

Cheryl Cain

2:00–3:00

Writers Workshop

Cheryl Cain

Whedon and Fandom

Lynne M.Thomas, Allison McCracken, Thom Gaughan, Steven Silver

3:00–4:00

Props Workshop

Matt Irvine

Teaching and the Academic Study of Whedon

Jason Winslade, Sharon Ross, Tanya Cochran, Ian Peters

4:00–5:00

Gender in Whedon

Amber Davisson, Tamy Burnet, Cary Elza, Alysa Hornick, Michele Leigh

Mythological, Cultural, and Narrative Roots of Whedon

Walter Metz, Kristen Micek, Courtney Neal, Simone Becque, Michael Nelson, Eleanor Pye

Student's Perspectives on Whedon

Jason Winslade, Sara Birchler, Caleb Bunselmeyer, Nikki Kaplan, Kennedy Odulio-Papa, Sloane Smith, Vanina Valadez

Screening Schedule

9:00–11:00 *Cabin in the Woods*—Introduction by Walter Metz

9:00–10:00 *Buffy the Vampire Slayer*: "The Wish"—Introduction by Allison McCracken

9:00–10:00 *Angel*: "Smile Time"—Introduction by Michi Trota

10:00–11:00 *Dollhouse*: "The Attic"—Introduction by Amber Davisson

10:00–11:00 *Buffy the Vampire Slayer*: "Hush"—Introduction by Eleanor Pye

11:00–12:00 *Buffy the Vampire Slayer*: "Once More With Feeling"—Introduction by Ian Peters

12:00–12:50 *Firefly*: "War Stories"—Introduction by Cheryl Cain

1:00–2:00 *Buffy the Vampire Slayer*: "The Zeppo"—Introduction by Katie Wilson

1:00–2:00 *Firefly*: "Jaynestown"—Introduction by Scott Paeth

2:00–4:00 *Much Ado About Nothing*—Introdution by Walter Metz

5:00–6:00 *Dr. Horrible's Sing-Along Blog*—Introduction by Jef Burnham

5:00–6:00 *Angel*: "Apocalypse Nowish"—Introduction by Amber Davisson

5:00–6:00 *Dollhouse*: "Echo (Unaired Pilot)"—Introduction by Paul Booth

Depaul University's
Celebration Of
SUPERNATURAL

Introduction

Paul Booth

The third annual DePaul Pop Culture Conference, held on 09 May 2015, focused on television show *Supernatural* in honor of its 10th anniversary. It also was the conference that broke all records—more people attended, more people presented, more papers submitted, more money raised for charity. It was a highlight of the year and continues to be something people ask me about. It was the first year for many new initiatives for the conference—the first year I had a research assistant to help with planning (Jess Glass did an amazing job), the first year we made tee-shirts for the event, the first year we broke $1000 in raising money (for Random Acts), the first year we made a real social media push, and the first year that a real scandal happened behind the scenes.

Once the second Pop Culture Conference on Joss Whedon happened, I knew we had to start an annual event; before the *Supernatural* event, we didn't even have a web page! We came up with the name DePaul Pop Culture Conference in order to start to brand ourselves—to have some sort of consistent theme throughout the years. I realized that in order to have any sort of consistency, we'd need to have some stable elements from year to year. It also helped to preserve my sanity so I wouldn't have to remake everything again every time!

The Celebration of Supernatural featured one of the most popular speakers for our Keynote – Robbie Thompson, one of the then-current producers/writers of *Supernatural*. Robbie is the author of the 200th-anniversary episode "Fan Fiction"—a musical episode that we screened at the conclusion of the conference as a sing-a-long—and one of the most respected writers on the show. Robbie was extraordinarily kind in giving his time and energy to the conference—not only did he answer questions during the entirety of his Keynote, he spent the next hour afterward answer additional questions from the audience and mingling with the attendees. The line for autographs stretched out the door and he pleasantly chatted with everyone the entire time. His energy and enthusiasm helped fuel an incredibly busy day filled with panels, screenings, workshops, sing-a-longs, a costume contest, and bake sale.

We featured two additional workshop speakers at *The*

Celebration of Supernatural—television critic Maureen Ryan and Writer/Internet star Mark Oshiro. Maureen gave a fantastic workshop talk on writing television criticism (the pointers of which I've taken into some of my classes) and Mark answered questions about his web series Mark Watches and Mark Reads. There were also podcasting workshops and a live taping of the *Water Cooler* podcast from Columbia College.

For the two previous Celebrations, most of the speakers were people that I knew or had reached out to, and most of the attendees were people from the community. I knew I wanted to expand and make the event larger to reach more people and approach more topics. Over fifty people submitted abstracts for the conference and we had an incredibly packed day with panels focused on Genre and *Supernatural*, the Family in *Supernatural*, Monsters and Demons in *Supernatural*, Race in *Supernatural*, Social Issues in *Supernatural*, Problematic Tropes in *Supernatural*, Fandom and *Supernatural*, Meta-episodes in *Supernatural*, and Gender in *Supernatural*, among many others. We decided to go back to the "celebration" aspect of the Pop Culture Conference to give a more cohesive focus for the event, and this helped spur submissions as well. One panel that was particularly well-attended was the "Writing about *Supernatural*" panel, which featured fans, academics, and professional critics all in discussion about the ways that *Supernatural* can be written about. Speakers on this panel included Katherine Larsen, Lynn Zubernis, Mika Kennedy, Maureen Ryan, and Leah Wilson (from BenBella Books).

The Celebration of Supernatural was also the first time there was a slight scandal that emerged during the planning. Those of you in *Supernatural* fandom will be aware of some very passionate feelings about different characters, their relationships and friendships, and their explorations. Different groups of fans may feel differently about these characters than other groups, and I received a number of email messages throughout the lead-up to the conference asking me to monitor different speakers and panels about the content of some of the fan works. Some of the messages were quite dramatic (and we actually asked for extra Public Safety officers to be present, although no threats were made) and pointed towards some of the fervid feelings about the show.

At the same time, it really demonstrates the need for more cross-collaboration between academics and fans, of the type that the Pop Culture Conference engenders. Such antagonistic discourse isn't limited to fandom (academics sure can be mean), so having a productive discussion about the topics in a safe and welcoming environment can be helpful. It turned out to be a lot of emails for naught—nothing happened and everyone seemed to have a pleasant experience.

Working with Jess Glass as a research assistant was phenomenal, and I'm so happy that we were able to award her with a surprise gift from Random Acts, the chosen charity for our event. Random Acts is a non-profit dedicated to acts of kindness. They attempt to inspire acts of kindness around the world both big and small. Through a silent auction, tee-shirt sales, a bake sale, and individual donations, we were able to raise over $1300 for the charity, which is remarkable given that we had an attendance of just over 300 people. As an example of their mission, they contacted me before the conference to find a suitable person to give an act of kindness to—I nominated Jess, who had helped me with putting the conference together. Right before our Keynote talk, Jess was surprised by Random Acts with a brand-new computer!

A Celebration of Supernatural was special in so many ways, and I'm so proud of the work that was accomplished. Please enjoy a selection of the pieces that were presented at *The Celebration of Supernatural*.

Keynote

Robbie Thompson

Look, Dr. Paul Booth is a madman.

Why else would he invite a former college dropout (me) to be the keynote speaker for the Pop Culture Celebration of *Supernatural*, held at the prestigious DePaul University, no less? Why would he ask the writer (also me) of one of IMDb's lowest rated episodes of the series, "*Bitten*," to poison the minds of his impressionable students? We may never know this maniac's true motives, but I am so grateful and honored that he asked me to come to this fantastic event and that he gave me the opportunity to meet some of the most wonderful humans in the world.

How did this come to pass, you ask?

Well, a few years ago, I met Dr. Lynn Zubernis through the delightful web of awesomeness that is the *Supernatural* Fandom. Dr. Zubernis has written several wonderful books on the phenomena of *Supernatural* (the phenomenal TV show, not the phenomenon) and was asked to attend DePaul's event. In discussing the day's festivities, Dr. Booth also asked if Dr. Zubernis knew of anyone from the show who might be available to speak at the event. I can only assume Dr. Zubernis asked everyone she knew affiliated with the show, as well as strangers, neighbors and small children, only to learn they all had scheduling conflicts and could not attend. She must have then been unfortunately forced to settle on asking foolish me if I would be interested in attending the Celebration.

Over email, Dr. Booth told me about the event. Each year, his program focused on a different pillar of the pop culture community, such as *Doctor Who* and Joss Whedon. *Supernatural* was turning ten years old (they grow up so fast, it seems like just yesterday the show was taking its first steps), and he and his program were planning a celebration and critical examination of the greatest show in the history of shows (in this or any other dimension). I was intrigued, and hey, who doesn't love Chicago?

But also, I was terrified.

See, I am not a public speaker.

I'm more accustomed to talking to myself while walking around my neighborhood, working out dialogue and scenes out loud, all the while hiding this "delightful" behavior by wearing my headphones, pretending I'm "taking a call." Anyone who walked by me during the five years I was lucky enough to be a writer on *Supernatural* must have thought I had a pretty passionate relationship with the characters of one of the longest running sci-fi show's in history (spoiler alert: it's <u>still</u> going, and will never stop. Never! If you are reading this in the year 2021, I hope the boys finally made it into outer space! Won't someone let them touch the stars already?! Please!)

Fortunately for me, and my writerly (not a word) nerves, Dr. Booth, like all great teachers, is a fantastic communicator. He was kind and patient enough to explain that my responsibilities would be less about giving a speech and more about communicating and interacting with the attendees, taking the form of a Question and Answer session, followed by a talk with his students about the process of writing and working in episodic television. I was relieved if not still mildly terrified. I agreed to attend and we put it in on the books as the kids say (do kids say that? I'm a dinosaur.)

And so, the weekend came at last, and I flew out to Chicago (my wife missed me terribly or so I'm told). The night before the event, I finally met Dr. Booth in person, and found him even smarter and more handsome in person. He had set up a meet and greet dinner that evening where I was fortunate to meet his brilliant wife, Kate, (who would have missed him terribly too if he had left her behind in Los Angeles) as well as several professors, academics, critics and students, all of whom walked me through their upcoming presentations, panels and discussions that they would be conducting for the event.

I was floored.

When I was in college, in the Jurassic Era, studying pop culture was not celebrated. In fact, it was looked down upon, I'm sad to say. This always disappointed me. I'm a lifelong student of pop culture, and when I was at the two colleges I attended (don't worry, I only dropped out of one. Thanks, Mom!) I wanted to understand the effect pop culture was having on me, and the world (in that order). At the time, there weren't enough teachers like Dr. Booth and programs like DePaul's.

Fortunately, times have changed. There are also fewer dinosaurs walking around.

During that evening, I learned there are many brilliant, incisive and passionate emerging voices in what has become one of the fastest growing fields of research and analysis in academia. These are voices filled with incredible insight, productive criticism and a keen eye for the future and the impact the pop culture we consume has on all of us. I met Ph.D. candidates, television critics, undergraduate students, overgraduate students, and fans. All of whom taught me so much in a short amount of time about their fields of expertise, their dissertations and their thoughts, feelings, and analyses of a little show called *Supernatural.* They were all vastly smarter than the person writing this, and I left filled with excitement, knowledge, and pizza.

The next day (after calling my wife to tell her I missed her), I met students and fans of the show, many of whom had come in from out of town to be a part of the event. DePaul's Celebrations are unique because they combine academic attendees as well as fans, and in that combo, there is so much overlap. It was pretty clear within five minutes of attending the event that we are all students, academics, and fans.

In short, I felt at home.

Everyone, and I do mean everyone (insert Gary Oldman .gif here) had great questions. I did my best to rise to their level. They lifted me up when I fell. The Q and A, expertly moderated by Dr. Booth, flew by and was over before I knew it. We then moved into the "talking about writing" section, where again, everyone had great questions, illuminating insights and funny stories to share.

I even met a few folks that loved "Bitten."

In conclusion, if a maniac like Dr. Booth reaches out and asks you to attend one of DePaul's Pop Culture Conferences, or if you're a student at DePaul or just in town for this special weekend—go, go learn something.

I did, and I remain grateful to this day.

Saving People: *Supernatural* and Social Issues

Laurena Aker

"If you're possessed by an urge to do a drug or to harm yourself, or to beat yourself down, then you have to beat those demons as we try to do on *"Supernatural."*
– Jared Padalecki, March 12, 2015 from the launch of his first "Always Keep Fighting" campaign

Supernatural is the longest, continuously running science fiction show in the history of American television. If you ask any of its millions of loyal fans what the show is about, most likely you won't be regaled with stories of mythological monsters or apocalyptical battles. Instead, you'll be told that *Supernatural* is about the bond between two brothers, Sam and Dean. It's about how the love of family gives you the strength and courage to keep fighting, even against insurmountable odds. It's also about heroes who never stop trying to do the right thing, even though they are flawed and deeply scarred from life's traumas.

"Sam and Dean are always dealing with something greater than themselves, and I've sort of learned from the two of them that they get through it with each other, and with help and with support." – Jared Padalecki

Similar to the lessons that Jared learned from portraying Sam for so many years, *Supernatural* has helped fans feel less alone when dealing with life's struggles. Sam and Dean's bravery inspires, their love envelops, and their redemptions provide hope to fans as they face or recover from life's challenges. The first half of the brothers' motto "Saving People" applies as much to real life as it does to the show, as cast members and fans internalize the show's messages according to their own life situation.

DePaul University's "*Supernatural* and Social Issues" panel (May 2015) explored how the show has both represented and impacted society's problems, with each of the four panel members focusing on a different issue. My discussion called attention to how the nurturing environment of the "SPN Family" (as the fandom considers itself), the show's inspirational characters and its altruistic themes empower people to change their lives in ways they never imagined possible. Being a part of *Supernatural*'s odds-defying success and longevity emboldens cast and fans to change careers, reach out to help others, or have the confidence to improve, or in extreme cases value, their own life. Far beyond the typical impact of being part of a show or joining a fandom, if open to its influence, *Supernatural* redirects the course of people's lives.

Exploration of creative talent is part of any fandom. It is common for fans to express their thoughts about shows, movies, books or music through photography, art or prose. Several chapters in my book, *Fan Phenomena: The Twilight Saga*, specifically address the concept of fandoms as incubators for creative awakening in light of *Twilight*'s measureable impact on women's writing and the publishing industry. What seems to distinguish *Supernatural*, however, is that people move beyond creative experimentation. Instead, their discovery of *Supernatural* feels like a "life event," prompting long-term, life-altering changes. There are countless stories of the show inspiring fans and cast to extend themselves and take risks which dramatically change the direction of their lives. For example, I unexpectedly transitioned from corporate career and family roles to independent author. My writing was motivated by a need to not only analyze the intricate complexities of the show, but also to express the deep emotions it elicited. The decision to commit to a writing *career*, however, was grounded in the show's message that ordinary people are destined for higher callings. The *opportunities* to become a full-time author all came from the immediate acceptance and welcoming embrace of fellow professionals within the SPN Family.

Similarly, cast members have also felt *Supernatural*'s bubble of empowerment, crediting changes in their lives to the impact of *Supernatural*'s extremely close fandom. For example, Gil McKinney admitted that the musical aspirations he abandoned earlier in his life were rekindled when fans supported his performances at convention concerts. The safe, accepting environment of the SPN Family audience allowed him to both rediscover and enjoy his latent singing talent, inspiring him to uproot his life and move across the country to investigate a Broadway career. Richard Speight, Jr. perfected his improvisational skills, becoming a stand-up comedian and show emcee hosting twenty *Supernatural* conventions each year. Another *Supernatural* alum, Rob Benedict, whose life was literally saved by co-stars when he fell victim to a stroke during one of those conventions, has been added to the convention's standard playbill with his band, Louden Swain. Working together, "Rich and Rob" are turning their convention experiences into a new web series, *Kings of Con*. There are many other stories from actors such as Osric Chau, Briana Buckmaster and Kim Rhodes, who only appeared in a few episodes of the series but have found their lives immeasurably altered by the support of the SPN Family both at conventions and through social media.

The farthest reaching examples of *Supernatural's* impact may be cast members becoming leaders of charitable causes. First, to recognize the power of the fandom, Misha Collins created a new charity, Random Acts, to channel the good that can be done by an organized, enthusiastic group of people. Jared Padalecki then timidly began the "Always Keep Fighting" campaign in March, 2015. Reassured and strengthened by his faith in the SPN Family, he acknowledged his own intense struggle with depression and losses to suicide. A year and five successful awareness campaigns later, he has grown into a public voice and international symbol of courage on this issue. Co-star Jensen Ackles subsequently joined Jared to create a related charitable fund and collaborated with Misha to launch a 24-hour global crisis helpline staffed entirely by *Supernatural* fans.

Do the show's themes of hope, resilience, and heroism, or its example of two insignificant individuals saving humanity, stir people to bold action? For eleven years, fans have witnessed the unending strength and forgiveness that Sam and Dean draw from their brotherly bond. The extraordinarily close friendship between Jared, Jensen and their families recreates that atmosphere of safety and unconditional acceptance in real life, as they enthusiastically act as patriarchs of the SPN Family. That sense of security, what the show calls "having your back," fosters personal and professional growth as people feel they will be supported if they step outside the previously defined boundaries of their abilities.

Supernatural's record-breaking time on the air has also provided stability to its fans. Its presence feels permanent and trustworthy; its messages have time to penetrate psyches and affect change. Younger fans have literally grown up with the show, while older fans have passed into new life stages under the protective watch of Sam and Dean's heroism. Charitable, community, social and professional organizations, projects or endeavors have time to take root and grow to maturity. Misha's G.I.S.H.W.H.E.S. (international fundraising scavenger hunt for Random Acts), for example, doubled in size in its first three years and promises to be the largest ever this year with tens of thousands of participants (2016 is its fifth year).

"Saving People" is more than a tagline to *Supernatural*'s cast and fans. It's become a way of life. As a community, a family, *Supernatural* creates a supportive environment bolstered with the encouraging example of the philanthropic and family ideals of its stars. With the series' renewal being nearly assured each year, its total impact on the world's social issues has yet to be realized. All indications are that the SPN Family is just getting started.

References

Prudom, L. (2015, March 12). *'Supernatural' Star Jared Padalecki Talks Depression and Why You Should 'Always Keep Fighting.'* Retrieved from Variety.com: http://variety.com/2015/tv/people-news/jared-padalecki-always-keep-fighting-depression-suicide-twloha-1201451708/

Subversive and Recursive: Vampires in *Supernatural*

Candace R. Benefiel

In season one of *Supernatural*, Dean Winchester famously remarked, "Demons, I get. People are crazy" ("The Benders," S1.E15). Aside from that endorsement of the unpredictability of human actions, he was reinforcing the idea that the various supernatural beings with which he and his brother would interact over the next 12 seasons (and counting) would behave along set lines. A demon, or a leviathan, or a vampire will act according to their nature, and by consulting the "lore" to determine a creature's capabilities and weaknesses, hunters will be able to vanquish them, even if the victory comes at a price. In most cases, the lore of *Supernatural* mimics the accepted mythology of monsters in contemporary Western culture and folklore. And yet, by establishing the parameters of a creature within the universe of the show, the writers can manipulate the characteristics of any given monster to put it at odds with a current interpretation.

In the case of the vampire, the writers of *Supernatural* have chosen to adopt the older, and more monstrous, version of the mythology. Vampires, they posit, are evil. They are cold and soulless beings without regard for family or other social ties. This stands in opposition to some iterations of the vampire in recent popular culture, and this is nowhere more apparent than in the episode "Live Free or Twihard" (S6.E5). Investigating the mysterious disappearance of a young woman, Sam and Dean discover she is a fan of a trendy teen vampire romance series and has been carrying on an online flirtation with someone who claims to be a vampire. (That the character names of the girl and her lover are Kristen and Robert, and that they bear more than a passing resemblance to the lead actors in the Twilight movies, only underlines the point of the episode.) Robert, it turns out, is, in fact, a vampire, although he shares few characteristics with the romanticized creature mortal Kristen is expecting. In fact, he is bait, set out to trap innocent teenage girls into vampirism. Once they are captured, they are turned, brutally, and put to work corresponding with other young girls, pretending to be the sensitive, brooding-but-essentially-good vampires they expect from their reading. The actual leader of the vampire nest is a fat, oily, unattractive and casually violent vampire who takes great delight in the popularity of fictional vampires that make easy prey of these unsuspecting teenagers. At the time when this episode first aired in 2010, the vast popularity of *Twilight*, *True Blood*, and other vampire narratives made the *Supernatural* episode a subversive reading of the vampire trope, with its emphasis on the treacherous and (literally) bloodthirsty nature of the nest. Complicating the portrayal is the subplot that Dean has been attacked by the nest leader, and is gradually succumbing to vampirism himself. This is most clearly illustrated when Dean, having previously commented on the creepiness of a romance cover that depicts a vampire watching over his sleeping love interest, finds himself in almost the same pose, as he visits the home of Lisa, a woman he has been dating. The uneasiness of the scene is accentuated by the knowledge that Dean is fighting against his newly awoken vampiric instinct to attack (and most likely kill) his sleeping lover. That he manages to restrain himself does give the scene a glimmer of romanticism, but the threat emphasizes the dangerous nature of the monster within him.

Yet even *Supernatural* is unable to resist the rehabilitation of at least one vampire. When Dean spends a time in Purgatory, he befriends another lost soul, the vampire Benny Lafitte. Appearing in several episodes, Benny is shown as a loyal friend to Dean, and upon escaping from Purgatory, they remain in contact, forming a small support group for each other. When (in "Citizen Fang," S8.E9) Benny appears to have attacked innocent people, Dean defends his friend, over the doubts of his brother Sam, and is gradually proven correct, as Benny is being set up by another vampire. With the character of Benny, *Supernatural* subverts its own rules, to make a sympathetic vampire who struggles against his nature. In later appearances, Dean first abandons Benny, who is having a hard time sticking to bagged blood ("Torn and Frayed" S8.E10), and then, when Sam is trapped in Purgatory, Dean asks Benny to voluntarily go back to find Sam a way out ("Taxi Driver" S8.E19). Benny agrees to this, and rescues Sam, but sacrifices himself, preferring to remain in Purgatory rather than return to a world where he fits with neither the vampires nor the humans. While Dean "leaves the door open" for Benny's return by refusing to burn his bones, it is understood that this is unlikely. At this point, even Sam agrees that Benny is not a typical vampire. He has redeemed himself through his selfless actions. Benny's final appearance (to date) is in the episode "The Werther

Project" (S10.E19). When Dean is possessed by a malevolent entity, he hallucinates that he is back in Purgatory, where he once again encounters Benny. Although Dean quickly decides that Benny is a figment of his delusion, the image of his friend is very compelling, and he listens to what the false Benny has to say. And that is an effort to persuade Dean that suicide is his best choice. Dean, though tempted, realizes that the real Benny would never advise him to take that path, or allow it if he tried.

Benny, even in this false incarnation, is a redeemed character, and worthy of the trust Dean places in him.

There are other vampires in *Supernatural*, to be sure, but in general, they show the same patterns of recursion to an older, harsher mythology that contrasts with the more palatable vampires of most recent narratives. Boris, the master vampire from "Live Free or Twihard," is not a redeemable or attractive character, and can be seen both as a throwback to earlier vampires, and as a subversion of the more recent tropes. Benny, in an opposing sense, is redeemed in ways that Boris never seeks to be, and subverts the *Supernatural* universe's rule that monsters will follow their nature, wherever it leads them.

The Family in *Supernatural*

Allison Broesder

On the surface, *Supernatural* is a show about two men fighting monsters, facing demons, and chasing after everything that goes bump in the night. It's meant to be a horror show that scares, that thrills, and gives us insights into the things that frighten us. It deals with larger than life situations—like the Apocalypse and demon deals and soullessness. It seems far removed from the mundane—and yet as we delve deeper into this show, we can see that at its heart the motto, "saving people, hunting things, family business" rings true. This show, deep down, is a family show masquerading as a horror show - and through that guise it can teach us things about family that the average family show can't: the true value of family.

First, let's look at the average family show.

Most family shows on television, right from their inceptions, centered on the home life. Shows like *Leave it to Beaver, Happy Days*, and *Father Knows Best* all center on the family and home life. They're comprised of scenes surrounding the nightly meal, of dad coming home from work and kicking off his shoes while mom makes that meal or takes care of the home. Children are a central focus. The nuclear family is often upheld as a key and crucial pillar of our society. Some shows are more unconventional in their presentation of family—from *All In the Family* to *Gilmore Girls* to *Modern Family*—and yet they, too, focus on a home situation and the every day that comes with ordinary struggles. Things like homework for the kids, bills for the parents, and any strife —either real or blown out of proportion—between the married couple are explored and resolved in half an hour segments each week. For family shows, the worst thing that happens is anything that threatens the equilibrium of that family life. Those threats can range from something quite ordinary like a leaking pipe that disrupts the everyday routine to the serious difficulties surrounding a character's disease or injury from an outside attacker. In the end, the stability is often restored and the nature of the family remains intact—a mom, a dad, kids, and perhaps extended family there to lend a hand.

Supernatural, on the other hand, is perceived as being much bigger than these stories—escapism that allows its viewers to transcend the mundane and everyday into the extraordinary. Demian and Barnes point this facet out to Dean at the end of "The Real Ghostbusters." Demian tells Dean, "All right. In real life, he sells stereo equipment. I fix copiers. Our lives suck. But to be Sam and Dean, to wake up every morning and save the world. To have a brother who would die for you. Well, who wouldn't want that?" It's one reason that the show isn't classified as a family show. It's gory, messy at times, full of rougher language than most family show fare, violent, and filled with fantastical creatures. Angels, demons, vampires and many other beings are featured each week as the Winchesters face a plethora of these entities throughout the series run. The Apocalypse itself looms large for two seasons as Lucifer is preparing to break free from his Cage and then unleash his power on the earth to subdue it to his will. Viewers watch as the Four Horsemen of the Apocalypse ride ahead to make way for him — and the Winchesters fight back to stop it. The fantasy elements of the show draw us in, capture our imaginations, and allow us to explore mythical and Biblical lore in new and fascinating ways. And yet, the kernel at all of these stories remains that of family.

But how?

Let's look at the first incident that takes place on the show. In the Pilot, we watch a typical family show scene take place. There, a mom, a dad, and two boys are preparing for bed. The baby is kissed goodnight and placed into his crib, the older boy is gleefully hoisted by his father and lovingly embraced. They turn in for the night, and quiet falls over the house. This is the nuclear family prior to the invasion coming to destroy their equilibrium. As Azazel comes to their house, he destroys that nuclear family with one sweeping action. We watch in horror as John goes to his wife to see why she screamed only to find her on the ceiling, bleeding. Just as he gets his youngest son from the crib, she bursts into flames and they are no longer a nuclear family. They have been destroyed — and its repercussions shape the remainder of the show.

In this aftermath, we learn throughout the series that John went after the creature that destroyed their family with revenge on his mind. It is this single purpose that shapes both Sam and Dean into the men we meet in the Pilot and follow throughout the series. Their unconventional family and upbringing shaped not only their views of their own family but of family in general. To them, family became sacred. It is the raison d'etre they use every day to hunt, to follow through long past Azazel's defeat, and even now in season ten against the Mark of Cain. Family is the very backbone of that motto, and they live it through each day. Dean also told Sam in Wendigo, "I mean, our family's so screwed to hell, maybe we can help some others. Makes things a little bit more bearable. And I'll tell you what else helps. Killing as many evil sons-of-bitches as I possibly can." For them, protecting family—even if it is other people's—is crucial to dealing with what happened to theirs. If another family can be spared the anguish they endured, then it is worth it. Through saving these people, these families, they can then save their own and prove the worth of family itself.

Even so, we see Sam and Dean build a new family to replace the nuclear family destroyed in the Pilot. They do this again and again as we see them build networks with other Hunters. Bobby, Ellen and Jo, Ash, Kevin, Charlie, and others are to fill in the gaps they lack. They're to be their family that they fight for and try to save. In many ways, this hunter network is more like the *Supernatural* version of the blended families we see on shows like *Modern Family*. There's nothing conventional or traditional about the family they create. None of these people are blood relatives. And yet, Sam and Dean will call them family again and again as they face their big struggles. In "The Curious Case of Dean Winchester," Bobby is ready to refuse the help the brothers offer —and then Dean tells him, "You don't stop being a soldier 'cause you got wounded in battle. Okay? No matter what shape you're in, bottom line is, you're family." Bobby tells Dean "Family don't end with blood, boy," giving the show its second motto surrounding family. Family is something that is built and rebuilt and cherished. It is something that each brother values in their own way. Each person they choose to adopt becomes another branch of their family tree.

And yet, that family status is not simply given easily, either. For Sam and Dean to accept someone into their family, they must prove their worth. Bobby proved it countless times throughout Sam and Dean's childhood and then again as the mentor they turned to for many years. Ellen and Jo proved it when they could set aside the painful circumstances surrounding Bill Harvelle's death and forgive them for their father's sin. Kevin proved it when he remained diligent on the Tablet—even if he protested and fought toe to toe. It's that tenacity that perhaps earned his family status the most. Charlie earned it by accepting their truth and helping them to take down Dick Roman. While those like Kevin, Charlie, Bobby, and Ellen and Jo are accepted into the

Winchester Family tree, others are cast out.

We see it in cases such as Gordon and Samuel Campbell. One is a blood relative and the other is not. At the start, Gordon Walker is considered worthy to be part of their patchwork family—at least by Dean. In Gordon, Dean sees a father figure to latch onto after smarting from John's loss. He seems someone of like mind, someone as driven as John had once been, and someone that Dean can talk to about things he can't with Sam. It isn't until Gordon's willing to kill the innocent nest—proven by Sam's own abduction and return without being harmed—that Dean reconsiders. At this stage, Gordon is cast aside and rejected from the Winchester family tree. Similarly, Sam—although Soulless at the time—chooses to accept Samuel into their family. He sees him as a mentor or at least knowledge and useful to hunting. He accepts the man at his word and is willing to do what he wants in order to keep killing creatures. Soulless Sam does so for a year, building a network not only with Samuel but with the rest of the Campbell branch of the family.

And yet, as the brothers start to work together and Dean starts to doubt Samuel or his intentions, we start to see rejection. Dean doesn't trust him, and when it is finally exposed that Samuel isn't only running a hunting operation, he's also working for Crowley, a Winchester enemy and demon, both brothers turn on Samuel. He's turned them over to Crowley in exchange for his own daughter's restoration—the nuclear family destruction being reversed in part. It, too, fails and when the Winchesters meet him again after escaping Crowley's clutches they find him further corrupted by another creature that ends up killing him.

What Sam and Dean and *Supernatural* itself teaches us about family through these lessons is just how precious it is. It is something to be valued, protected, treasured, and above all held sacred. It is not easy, it is not something that just happens, and it is never to be taken for granted. Family isn't always going to be the happy or pleasant picture seen in other family shows filled with the everyday or the mundane issues that daily life throws at us all. Instead, it is going to be a daily fight to not only overcome the outside forces threatening to destroy its fabric—as it so often does for Sam and Dean—but to hold together the bonds that family forges and hang on tight. *Supernatural*, as a family show, gives us insight into how important family is in so many ways.

This importance also translates well to the fan base that follows it. We see it in the fandom moniker #SPNFamily and the community that follows the show. Fellow fans build communities, not unlike the Winchesters and their hunting communities. While not everyone is blood, everyone seems to adhere to Bobby's statement that "Family don't end with blood," and replacing the hunting part of the unofficial tag line of the series with other terms such as support. Fans refer to each other as family—and while it may not always be smooth or easy, they've come to build networks that endure and grow stronger because of the inspiration from *Supernatural* itself.

Supernatural may be considered a genre show by so many outside the fan base - but those who watch beneath the surface know the truth. *Supernatural* is a family show—one that gives us an understanding into its real value, its true struggles, and its true and rich rewards. It gives us the chance to see how family could be or should be —that while worrying about daily tribulations may be our reality, we can be more and should do more not only for each other as a family but for the world around us. It makes family transcend the home life and it makes family the focal point for which fans rally around each week.

To quote Chuck, "In the end, they chose family—and isn't that the whole point?"

And yet, family status isn't simply given away. We see it in cases such as Samuel Campbell and Gordon Walker. One is a blood relative, the other is not. Gordon Walker is accepted at first—by Dean at least. He's a father figure to help Dean soothe John's loss. Gordon seems like minded, and someone Dean can relate to in a way he can't with Sam. It isn't until he moves to kill the innocent vampire nest that Dean reconsiders. Gordon is brutally rejected, cast out from the Winchester family. Samuel Campbell, their maternal grandfather, becomes an unusual mentor to Soulless Sam. It is Dean that can't trust him, and once the true nature of his hunting operation is revealed—and his subsequent double cross that handed them over to Crowley—that we see both Winchesters reject Samuel from their family for good.

Hunting the Mother Monster

Amber Davisson

In the first episode of *Supernatural*, Sam and Dean hunt a Woman in White. Legend says that this type of ghost comes into being when a woman who has been wronged by her lover kills her children by drowning them and then commits suicide. The resulting ghost kidnaps and kills unfaithful men while haunting the earth in a restless search for her lost children. In the inaugural episode of the show, Sam and Dean defeat this particular Woman in White by forcing her to revisit her home and face the children she drowned. The first episode of *Supernatural* is just one of many in the series where the hunters are confronted with a monster whose monstrosity is tied to her motherhood. In the *Supernatural* universe, Mother Monsters are everywhere.

Edward Ingebretsen, in the book *At Stake: Monsters and the Rhetoric of Fear in Public Culture*, argues that monsters serve a disciplining function in public life. A monster is a symbol of the humanity that is lost when someone crosses the boundaries of appropriate behavior. Motherhood has long been a popular subject matter within the monster movie genre. Most mothering takes place behind closed doors, and it is difficult for society to monitor or regulate. Monster movies often point to the anxiety society has about the things mothers could be doing in spaces where no one is there to police them. The prevalence of mother monsters in horror is both emblematic of our fear of the damage mothers may do in private and serves as a warning to young women about what society expects of them. The mother monsters in *Supernatural* point to the fact that our fear of mothers has a strong gender component.

Women are socially constructed as highly emotional creatures, and the hormones associated with pregnancy, childbirth, and bonding are often used as a plot device to create characters whose emotions make them completely unreasonable. Eve, the mother of all, is the archetype of the over loving and over protective mother. She does not see her children as monstrous. Crowley's mother Rowena is the opposite. She is a bad mother who has never properly bonded with her child and now engages in emotional manipulation. While we often see monsters on the show that are smart or calculating. These mother monsters are portrayed as crazy, deranged, and overly emotional. These are two extreme cases of motherhood gone awry; in other episodes, we see characters like Amy Pond who turn monstrous when they need to feed their children or the Amazon women who only care about making more daughters. In each case, it is the emotions tied to motherhood that push these women into monstrosity. The message is clear, mothers are dangerous

To balance out the images of mother monsters, the show offers a maternal figure in the character of Dean Winchester. Scholars Julia Wright (2008) and Bronwen Calvert (2011) have argued that while Mary Winchester looms in the background as the matriarch of the family, Dean has taken on the role of the mother in the day-to-day hunting. In many episodes, Dean provides the maternal affection and caring that is lacking in Sam's life. While these arguments are interesting and valid, it is also worth pointing out that one of the few good mothers on the show is male and reads highly masculine. It is as if the characteristics of a mother are safest when they are divorced from the perceived over emotional behavior of a woman.

From the first episode of *Supernatural*, motherhood has been constructed as potentially dangerous and often monstrous. In this way, the things that need hunting and killing in the *Supernatural* universe are very much a reflection of the things we fear in this universe.

References
Calvert, Bronwen. 2011. "The Representation of Women in Supernatural." In Stacey Abbott and David Lavery (Eds) *TV Goes to Hell: An Unofficial Road Map of Supernatural* Ontario: ECW Press: 90-104.
Ingebretsen, Edward.2001. *At stake: Monsters and the rhetoric of fear in public culture.* University of Chicago Press.
Wright, Julia M. 2008. "Latchkey hero: masculinity, class and the gothic in Eric Kripke's Supernatural." *Genders* 47.

No One Cares That You're Broken: Dean Winchester as an Adult Child of an Alcoholic in Seasons 1-7

Rachel Dean

Dean's emotional and psychological problems can be shown to stem largely from John's alcohol abuse. Within the *Supernatural* canon, oblique references have been made to John Winchester's alcoholism. That he abused alcohol is clear, as well as Bobby "the town drunk" Singer (5x15), but the impact that it has on Dean is clear when compared to the 13 attributes of an adult child of an alcoholic. This makes him one of the few characters on television whose mental health issues are clearly shown to have a source in the alcoholism of a parent.

According to Janet Geringer Woititz's book, *Adult Children of Alcoholics*, the thirteen common traits are the following:

1. Adult Children of Alcoholics guess what normal behavior is.

2. Adult Children of Alcoholics have difficulty following a project through from beginning to end.

3. Adult Children of Alcoholics lie when it would be just as easy to tell the truth.

4. Adult Children of Alcoholics judge themselves without mercy.

5. Adult Children of Alcoholics have difficulty having fun.

6. Adult Children of Alcoholics take themselves very seriously.

7. Adult Children of Alcoholics have difficulty with intimate relationships.

8. Adult Children of Alcoholics overreact to changes over which they have no control.

9. Adult Children of Alcoholics constantly seek approval and affirmation.

10. Adult Children of Alcoholics feel that they are different from other people.

11. Adult Children of Alcoholics are either super responsible or super irresponsible.

12. Adult Children of Alcoholics are extremely loyal, even in the face of evidence that the loyalty is undeserved.

13. Adult Children of Alcoholics tend to lock themselves into a course of action without giving serious consideration to alternative behaviors or possible consequences. This impulsively leads to confusion, self-loathing and loss of control over their environment. In addition, they spend an excessive amount of energy cleaning up the mess.

(pages 37, 44, 47, 56, 61, 63, 73, 74, 77, 82, 84 from the 1983 expanded edition)

The most obvious traits which Dean has are 4, 6, 7, 8, 9, 10, 11, 12 and 13, with some evidence for 1, 3 and 5.

4. Dean is his own harshest critic, constantly judging himself for all manner of things, such as breaking in Hell, torturing people and so on, all coming to a head in 7x04, where he is put on trial for his actions. Dean's own guilt causes this trial and sentences him to death, without mercy.

6. Dean's level of personal responsibility is extreme. In 7x05, Sam asks what is wrong with Dean, who replies, flippantly, that something is always eating him, that it's just who he is. "Something happens, I feel responsible, all right? The Lindbergh baby, that's on me. Unemployment, my bad." Under the bravado and humour, it reveals a lot about Dean. He has been responsible for his brother's life since the age of four. Before that, he took it upon himself to console his mother after his parents fought (5x16). He took care of his father, taking on the role of nurturer in the family. Parentification, taking on the role and responsibility of a parent, is very common amongst children of alcoholics.

7. Until Lisa, Dean has never had a long-term romantic relationship in the canon of the show. He is shown to be extremely sexual, however, there is little emotional intimacy between Dean and his sexual partners. Dean has difficulty connecting to another person, which prevents him from entering long-term relationships.

Beyond that, Dean has shown a complete lack of being able to make and retain friends of serious nature. His relationships can be considered more as acquaintances or familial. Those who break the mould (Jo, Bobby, Ellen and Castiel) become family and that is the reason Dean is able to justify his affection. By calling them family, Dean is able to transcend the feeling that he doesn't deserve their love and friendship and allows himself to become attached to them.

8. When Sam dies in 2x21, Dean literally sells his soul to Hell. This constitutes something of an overreaction. This overreaction is in

response to growing up in an uncertain environment. Dean grew up not knowing whether his father would return and if he did return, how he would act towards him. John was a strict and mercurial father and his drinking would have likely exacerbated these tendencies. That, in turn, affected Dean and the way he reacts to things. Growing up in an environment like that, the only way Dean could have any mastery over his life was through maintaining strict control over everything that he could.

9. With Dean's chronically low self-esteem, he cannot obtain self-affirmation, so he seeks it in other people. His interactions with John are proof of that. He is "Daddy's little brunt instrument" (3x10), and allows himself to be used to achieve John's goals, to the extent that he is the one to kill Azazel (2x22), the culmination of over two decades worth of ambition for John. While Dean's reasoning for hunting and destroying evil creatures is different than John's, there is definitely an element of impressing his father, gaining his approval in his continuation of "the family business" (1x02). Beyond that, Dean's interaction with Gordon in 2x03, has an element of wanting to impress the other man, for Gordon to approve of the work he's done. With his father gone, Dean seeks out another older male whose approval he can try to gain.

10. Many ACoAs feel that they are different from other people, because they are. Other people did not have to take on adult responsibilities as children or deal with inconsistent parenting styles or deal with emotional and/or physical abuse. It leads to feeling profoundly alienated and alone. In Dean's case, it is even more severe, since he is one of the few people who has seen what is lurking behind the veil of the normal world, leading to serious isolation and loneliness. In 1x06, Dean says that while Sam is a "freak," so is he. Dean believes he is weird and unable to function in normal society, with normal people. In addition, he fully believes that he is incapable of this. In 1x08, Dean claims that he would "blow his brains out" if he had to live a normal suburban life, no matter how much he is shown to actually desire it (3x10).

11. Dean tends towards the super responsible end of the spectrum. He has been responsible for caring for his brother since the moment John thrust him into his arms and sent them out of the burning house in Lawrence. In 1x18 and 3x08, flashbacks have shown that Dean was caring for his brother for days at a time while their father went on

hunts when he was far too young for that type of responsibility. Beyond that, Dean was shown comforting his mother as a small child (5x16), cleaning up the emotional wreckage his father had wrought even before the fire. Dean feels the need to save everyone, but especially his brother. He takes all the bad things that happen to his family and even to strangers and internalizes it, becoming guilt.

12. Dean is the epitome of providing undeserved and unwavering loyalty. He was loyal to his father, sticking with him and by his side when Sam left for university. And he is loyal to a fault with Sam. Which is turned against him in season six. Despite his concerns over Soulless Sam's conduct, he still trusts him enough to have his back, until after Sam allows him to be turned by a vampire in 6x05. Dean's loyalty is so strong and blinding that he got turned into a vampire because he couldn't fully comprehend how wrong Sam is.

Following that, Dean was loyal to Castiel, even when the evidence against Cas was mounting. Bobby and Sam voiced their concerns about Castiel's behaviour, but Dean could not bring himself to believe it. Castiel's actions were out-of-character for him, which means that Dean did not learn his lesson from Soulless!Sam. Cas had earned Dean's trust ("He has gone to the mat cut and bleeding for us so many freakin' times," 6x20). For ACoAs, once trust has been awarded or earned, it is not easily revoked. Cas even comments on Dean's inability to lose faith in him ("And the worst part was Dean, trying so hard to be loyal, with every instinct telling him otherwise," 6x20). Because they trust so completely, true betrayal stings deep and season seven shows how badly Castiel's betrayal has broken Dean. He remarks that what Cas did was one of the first things he couldn't shake off, "You know, whatever it was. It might take me some time, but... I always could. What Cas did... I just can't...I don't know why" (7x17).

13. An impulsive, poorly thought-out plan after being crushed by grief to sell his soul in exchange for Sam's life led to a full year of this for Dean (season 3). Dean resigns himself to his situation, allowing the loss of control to take over his life and given the events of 3x10, led to self-loathing (he shoots a demonized version of himself in his dream, which comes back to taunt him. An extremely literal demonstration of his self-loathing). After Dean finally admits that he doesn't want to die and go to Hell, Sam and he spend the rest of the season trying to find a way out of his deal.

Beyond those, the most common characteristics of ACoAs, there are several interesting things that show how deeply Dean was scarred by being raised by an alcoholic. The title of this essay, "No one cares that you're broken," a line delivered by Dean to Cas in 7x22, demanding that he "clean up [his] mess." However, it's a great way to describe Dean and how he expects people feel about him. No one has ever cared that he is broken. His father didn't, even though Dean lost his mother at four. Dean was conscripted into the roles of guardian to Sam and warrior against the supernatural from an early age. Bobby tried to care for him and to provide some normal childhood activities, however, a few attempts to provide some normalcy is not sufficient. Bobby may have exacerbated the problem, considering his own rampant alcoholism, and wavering expectations of Dean. When Dean was staying with him, clearly sometimes he was expected to be a normal child and he was likely expected to be an adult and a hunter at other times. Shifting and inconsistent expectations lead to several of the issues listed above.

Neither of Dean's parental figures ever took it upon themselves to recognize the pain and psychological problems Dean has endured throughout his life. Not until season seven does Bobby even suggest that Dean talk about his pain, breaking from his tradition of encouraging Dean to deal with his pain through repression and alcohol abuse. By then it is far too late, Dean fully believes that he no one cares that he is broken and that he doesn't deserve to be cared about.

Another symptom of John's alcoholism is in Dean's own relationship with alcohol. By season seven, Dean is an alcoholic. Sam comments on Dean's inability to get drunk, calling it akin to "drinking a vitamin" (7x18). The amount of alcohol Dean needs to get drunk is considerable and he seems to enjoy drinking for the first time in years (maybe since 2x15). When he drinks, by season seven, it's because he needs it to function. In seasons one and two, Dean's use of alcohol is overindulgent, but not a necessity. By season four, he drinks heavily when he cannot cope with things emotionally, as in 4x16 when he is torturing Allistair. In 5x11, he admits to drinking 50-60 drinks a week, if only to get to sleep (as he confesses this to a hallucination, one can presume this to be accurate). He is heavily dependent on alcohol between seasons five and six, but by season seven, this has moved to full-fledged addiction. Possibly part of why he can't shrug off Castiel's betrayal 7x17 is that alcohol is no longer helping him cope. He needs it to be level, so no longer provides him to with mental escape and emotional coping mechanism.

Dean using alcohol to cope is, in part, because he has never been taught appropriate coping mechanisms. In 5x11, he references that the way he deals with emotions and what he considers to be normal is to repress them, using alcohol. He doesn't have the tools to cope with his emotions, so he patterns his actions on those he saw in his father and adopted father, to drink and suppress his emotions. Without any idea how to cope with emotions and inhabiting a world where high alcohol consumption is normalized behaviour, his own addiction is not surprising.

But why does this all matter? Dean's a fictitious character after all. When taken as whole, Dean Winchester represents one of the very best portrayals on television of what happens to a child who is raised by an alcoholic. For many ACoAs, there is a level of serious brokenness, trauma and consistent psychological pain and unhealthiness associated with it. *Supernatural* confronts the psychological pain of ACoAs without flinching or sugar-coating it. It's unique and fascinating in this aspect. While it is painful to watch Dean falling into alcoholism, it is one of the most compelling, well-acted, subtle and honest portrayals of an ACoA.

Remarks upon the Fan/Producer Relationship in *Supernatural*, May 2015

Laura Felschow

I'd like to briefly touch upon two things today. I first researched the relationship between *Supernatural* fans and producers during season four, and as many of us know the show has since then created a number of episodes commenting on or utilizing the show's fandom. It was this narrative strategy of meta humor and metacommentary that finally brought *Supernatural* notice in the mainstream press. Before episodes like "The Monster at the End of this Book" (4x18), "Sympathy for the Devil" (5x01), "The Real Ghostbusters" (5x09), or "Fan Fiction" (10x05), *Supernatural* was struggling to get respect even on its own network. But by mining fandom, commenting both on dedicated viewers and on themselves as actors, writers, directors, and producers, *Supernatural* suddenly found itself a hot topic not just in online circles of cult fandom but on the cover of mainstream magazines like *Entertainment Weekly* and *TV Guide*. *Supernatural* was engaging with its fandom in a way that no television program had ever consistently done before.

But what of it? *Supernatural* has battered that fourth wall between itself and its fandom, but this move has not marked a real shift in how the industry overall interacts with or listens to fans. If anything, the people behind the scenes making television programs and films have *retreated* from direct engagement with fandom. In the early 2000s before the rise of Twitter, showrunners like Ron Moore, Rob Thomas, and Damon Lindelof & Carlton Cuse were regularly engaging with fans on message boards, podcasts, etc. These days, most showrunners, staff writers, and other production personnel may be visible on social media, but often declare that they care less than ever about what fans think. Meanwhile, other showrunners who once engaged with fans online – such as Damon Lindelof, Kurt Sutter, and just this week, Joss Whedon – have now abandoned social media. For every Bryan Fuller, there are a dozen showrunners turning a deaf ear to the voices of fans. *House of Cards* showrunner Beau Willimon has even gone so far as to say that with changes in distribution in the network era wherein entire seasons are released at once, there is no pressing need to take fans' opinions into account.1

Actors and actresses seem to be picking up the slack. Seeing social media as a direct line to the youth market, the producers of teen dramas on ABC Family2 and The CW ask their casts to engage directly with fans on a regular basis via Facebook, Twitter, Tumblr, Instagram, Vine, and more, as well as live tweeting their own show or holding post-episode Q&As online. But these practices seem to reify the distinction between actor and fan, person of interest and interested person.

Supernatural's Misha Collins is someone who has attempted to blur those boundaries, engaging in fandom in a manner that displays interest in fandom and its behavior just as much as fandom is interested in him and the show. What interests me here is this move wherein actors or actresses turn the attention directed at them, back onto fandom. Orlando Jones of *Sleepy Hollow*, a *Supernatural* fan himself, has taken fan engagement further in this direction.3

Jones has tweeted out requests for links to fanfic and posts links to favorite stories of his own, creates YouTube videos of himself reading fan comments, reblogs fandom posts on his Tumblr, and has even participated in Tumblr-sponsored in-person fan discussion sessions. Demonstrating that he knows the target imagined audience for *Sleepy Hollow*, Jones has reached out to *Supernatural* fans as well by live tweeting *Supernatural* episodes and promoting fandom crossover with the hashtag #SuperSleepy. He purposely cultivated a strong relationship with *Sleepy*'s fandom by attempting to treat fans as creative individuals in their own right whose voices deserved to be respected. With the announcement that Jones will be leaving *Sleepy Hollow* in season three, the Twitterverse exploded with emotion.

Outside of *Supernatural*, Orlando Jones is among an incredibly small cadre of actors who view fandom as a creative community of its own. This brings me to my second point of interest and more firmly back in the realm of *Supernatural* and the topic of fan/producer power dynamics.

For those unfamiliar, *Supernatural* actors Richard Speight Jr. and Rob Benedict are currently utilizing IndieGoGo to crowdsource funding for their own comedy project, *Kings of Con*. In *Kings of Con*, Speight and Benedict use their experiences at *Supernatural* conventions as the narrative basis for their show, portraying two actors who are "super famous" for 13 weekends out of the year when they attend the conventions for a show in which they were guest stars. In essence, these actors are taking their relationship with fandom and building a show around it...while asking that same fandom to provide the funding for said project. The campaign, which ends today (May 9th, 2015), has already raised more than double its original goal of $100,000.

Putting this in conversation with Louisa Stein's discussion of the fan movement to create *Wayward Daughters*, these two campaigns nicely illustrate the different power structures at play when it comes to the fan/producer relationship. Speight and Benedict, even as character actors on television that have somewhat limited power within the industry overall, still have the power to repurpose fandom for their own gain. Meanwhile, those in fandom who want *Wayward Daughters* to become a reality can only keep asking, keep talking about it, and will more than likely not be heard or recognized by the execs at the CW. Fans can fund *Kings of Con*, but lack the infrastructure and the right to actually create the project that they *really* want to see.

Notes

1 Grant, Drew. "TV Writers and Showrunners Increasingly 'Mute' Fans." *The New York Observer*. 20 November 2014. <http://observer.com/2014/11/tv-writers-and-showrunners-increasingly-mute-the-fans/>.

2 Re-branded in 2016 as Freeform.

3 Both Suzanne Scott and Bertha Chin have now presented conference papers on the topic of Orlando Jones & fandom; While Scott's paper is not available online at this time, Chin's paper is available here: https://onoffscreen.wordpress.com/2015/07/06/orlando-jones-needs-to-gtfo-of-our-fandom-supernatural-conventions-and-gate-keeping/

Supernatural: Celebrating Mass Culture with a Little Help from Popular Culture

Monica Flegel

My two favorite definitions of mass and popular culture get at the heart of what culture looks like in contemporary, industrialized mass society: specifically, that most of us don't get to produce the cultural products we consume; instead, mass culture is produced for us by those who do not necessarily share our ideologies, our subject positions, and our specific interests. Mass culture has to appeal to a large number of people and in so doing, its aim is, as the great Jan Radway elucidated, to be "minimally acceptable" to a "huge audience" (285). Now, it's questionable whether or not SPN has a huge audience, but I'd guess that keeping 2 million viewers happy on a regular basis is still something of a conundrum for the writers. While all those viewers may tune in weekly for SPN, chances are, as Radway points out, that we are not all happy with what we see—instead, the persistence of the show speaks instead to the "existence of an ongoing, still only partially met, need" (286).

This is where fanfiction comes in. Fanfiction, traditionally, is not mass culture, it's popular culture: made by the people, for the people. John Fiske describes popular culture as "the art of making do" (4), and I feel that for many of us, fan fiction does just that: it helps us take a mass culture product, like *Supernatural*, and make it into something that can work for us. The reality is that while *Supernatural* constructs itself, within the show universe, as a small, boutique-y, indie product, one that has only a small number of passionate fans who are very much engaged, in reality, the 2 million fans our show has tuning in want very different things from our show. Even those of us who seemingly want the same thing, such as an intense focus on Sam and Dean and their brotherly relationship, still have conflicting views on that relationship, with some of us preferring them angry and miserable, and others wanting the brothers to get some good therapy and learn to talk honestly with each other so they can develop into full, healthy human beings. Others believe that the show will be a failure if Dean and Castiel don't become a couple, and still, others will argue, with anyone who will listen, that any hint of romance will destroy the integrity of the story.

140

Supernatural can't give us what we all want: its continuation speaks to "an ongoing, still only partially met need," one that we complement and supplement with fanfiction and online meta that allows us to "make do" with those aspects of the show that most please and inspire us. As Dean says in "Fan Fiction," "you have your version of the show, and I have mine." But my question is: is that enough? Theorists of popular culture believe that the division between mass culture and popular culture is disappearing: as the barriers break down between fans and producers (happening more and more on Twitter and other platforms), and as fans increasingly take up the tools to create mass culture on a scale that they previously could not, will we see the gap between what some of us want and what the writers/show can provide decreasing? The idea that fans themselves might influence the direction of mass culture has long been a desirable dream for many fan culture theorists; the thinking was that increased fan engagement in the production of mass culture would mean that the ideologies and interests of the less powerful can be made manifest in the culture we all consume.

I used to believe this, but now that I see fan pressure having success in terms of influencing mass culture, I am beginning to wonder if this is a good thing. I wonder whether or not the desire to please fans will steer writers away from the stories they want to tell. I wonder whether or not more vocal groups of fans will be able to make their head-canon *become* canon. And I wonder what we lose in the process. For me, what has always been lovely about fanfiction is that it is *not* the show – it is a space for "what if?" and for darker, sometimes more perverse, and often unfeasible storylines to be worked out, played with, and explored. I *like* the distinction between fiction and fanfiction, and I am curious as to how the boundaries and differences between the two will transform as we see the world of cultural production and consumption changing. *Supernatural* has been at the forefront of this discussion – it is open in its engagement with fans and fan texts, and perhaps more than any other show, lays bare the complexities of negotiating story-telling and fan desire. Even if I sometimes find myself concerned about some of the doors it has opened, I respect and value the risks that *Supernatural* has taken in this regard, and believe that, ultimately, it will stand as a testament to the changing relationship between writers and fans in a digital world.

References

Fiske, John. *Reading the Popular*. New York: Routledge, 1989.

Radway, Janice. 1984. *Reading the Romance: Women, Patriarchy and popular literature*. Chapel Hill: North Carolina University Press.

Naturalizing *Supernatural*: Revisited

Joseph Graves, Jr.

"In the beginning God created the heavens and the earth. And the earth was waste and void; and darkness was upon the face of the deep..."
Genesis 1—2.

Well, this last season of *Supernatural* revealed to us that the "darkness" was actually God's sister! Can't say I saw that one coming. We also learned that God's creation (our universe) could not exist without light and dark. I can say that I did see that one coming. Is this yet another example of *Supernatural* naturalizing itself? Astrophysicists have observed for some time that the galaxies in our universe seem to be doing something really weird. That is, they are rotating at a speed that the gravity generated by their observable matter shouldn't be able to hold them together. In other words, they should have torn themselves apart a long time ago. Thus astrophysicists have hypothesized that there must be something else, which they dubbed "dark matter." Dark matter does not interact with electromagnetic force, hence the reason we can't see it. Furthermore, dark matter seems to outweigh light matter at a ratio of six to one.

Is this physical reality a metaphor explaining why Chuck (the light) could not defeat Amara (the darkness) without the help of his archangels (Lucifer, in particular)? Was not Amara locked away by the mark of Cain and hence undetectable, just as dark matter is in the physical universe? These are questions only the writers can answer, but this does seem to be another example of the plot devices I discussed in my 2013 essay "Naturalizing *Supernatural.*" That essay focused on the conflation of naturalism and supernaturalism in the series storyline, particularly in the originally planned seasons 1 - 5. Those seasons were organized around "The War in Heaven." This central plot device is based upon ancient Judeo-Christian lore. The "war in heaven" is not fully described in either the Old or New Testament. It is alluded to in Ezekiel 28:1-19, Isaiah 14:12-15, Luke 10:18; 2 Peter 2:4, Jude 6; and Revelation 12:3-4, 7-9; as well in the apocryphal texts of Enoch 1 and 2. This war is central to Christian theology, in that it plays a key role in explaining both how evil and humans come into the world. After all, if God is omnipotent, omniscient, and good; how could he have created a world in which so much evil and misery prevails? Naturalists, of course, claim that it was we who created "God" precisely to give a rationale for our own immoral and evil acts.

In some sense, Sam and Dean Winchester struggle throughout the first five seasons with whether God and his angels are "good." Indeed, in season two we find Dean Winchester still unconvinced that God and angels exist (Season 2: Ep. 13: Houses of the Holy). In this episode, a vengeful spirit claiming to be an angel is convincing good people to kill others based on information from God. Sam begins to believe that this is really an angel, while Dean is skeptical. Dean eventually demonstrates to Sam that the vengeful spirit is not an angel, but is left wondering how the spirit had foreknowledge of events, specifically which individuals should be killed to save the lives of others. Dean and Sam only truly become believers in angels after they met Castiel in season four (Season 4: Ep. 1: Lazarus Rising.) Yet despite their knowledge of the existence of angels, heaven, and god, they insist on circumventing God's plan, which is revealed to them via the prophet Chuck (who we later learn was God in disguise...and yes I figured that out before it was revealed last season) the Archangel Michael, and others of the heavenly host (Archangel Gabriel, Zachariah, Joshua, etc.). This raises the question of whether the Winchester's defiance was the result of them believing that their reason, derived from a natural structure, the brain, was superior to the supernatural design of God? Last season partially answers that question. We find out that God had begun to question his own plan. This explained why he decided to take some time off, reflect on what humans had accomplished and failed to accomplish. God spent some time appreciating various aspects of human culture. By definition, culture was created by the free will that God had given humans, and not directly by God. Late in the season, we find Chuck barring his soul to Metatron, while listening to the blues. God states that it was this music that inspired him during his absence from heaven. Finally, after Amara had defeated Chuck, it was Dean Winchester's willingness to sacrifice himself and his logical discourse to Amara that saved the day. This is a yet another example of the ongoing tension between the natural and the supernatural in this series.

After the conclusion of season 11, we are left with some interesting questions. How will Dean adjust to the resurrection of his mother (Mary Winchester)? Did Sam survive the bullet fired by Lady Antonia Bevell (London chapter of The Men of Letters)? Will the

English Men of Letters succeed in exterminating the Winchesters? Will Chuck and Amara allow such a thing to proceed? Where is Lucifer in all of this? Clearly, the writers have much material to work with going forward, and there does not seem to be any clear resolution of the natural/supernatural conundrum at the core of this series anywhere in sight.

Love, Death, And Codependence: The Family in *Supernatural*

Patricia L. Grosse

The "SPN Family" exceeds the usual boundaries between television shows and fandoms. The fans of *Supernatural* tend to feel very connected to the stars of the show in a loving way, and it seems that the stars and creators of the series return this love in return. There is a beautiful symmetry to this relationship between fan and show, often discussed at fan conventions and on online forums and certainly poked fun of in bonus content the series puts out online as well as within several episodes show itself: Season Four's "The Monster at the End of this Book," Season Five's "The Real Ghostbusters," Season Seven's "The French Mistake," and Season Seven's "Time for a Wedding" all bring different aspects of the relationship between fandom and media into the series.

In the panel, "Love, Death, and Codependence: The Family in Supernatural, at the 2015 *Celebration of Supernatural,* I discussed the fluid conception of family the show's main characters, Sam and Dean Winchester, hold. As this talk was meant to engender discussion with the panelists and audience, it is not as in-depth as a conference paper might be. I have revised it in such a way as to, hopefully, represent the porousness of academic and fandom relationships to each other and to the media they center upon. As I remark at the beginning of my talk, I wear my fandom on my sleeve and am proud to have been a part of this *Celebration.*

I've been a fan of *Supernatural* since I started graduate school about six years ago—it's always on TNT and when I decided to start running there it was. I'd seen a few episodes when it initially began running on the CW back in 2005, but did not find in the brothers' awkward relationship anything to relate to. I found much to admire during those early forays into running—the difference being that I had begun a Ph.D. program in philosophy with a specific focus on the philosophy of embodiment and love, and I could see in the show shining examples of the dangers and wonder of both topics. I recall the scene that hooked me as I ran along at Planet Fitness—Castiel unfurling his wings in the Fourth Season premiere, "Lazarus Rising." What kept me running was the friendship that developed between Castiel and Dean, a friendship that is portrayed as a familial one.

"Family" in the show can be extended to anyone in the purview of the brother's lives. In Dark Dynasty, this week's episode, Charlie is called on to help Dean due to her love of the pair ("They're like brothers to me," she says). If she is, in fact, dead as the trailer for next week implies we will have the result of a truly furious Dean.1 In the previous episode, "Angel Heart," Castiel is drawn to help the wayward daughter of Jimmy Novak, his vessel, because she's family (but not really, but close enough). The "good guys" of *Supernatural* can be clearly seen as characters that never give up on family.

While the relationship between the brothers is the most important in the show, it seems that everyone the two are close to for what seems to any amount of time (dies) become family in a matter-of-fact way: the boys (*especially* Dean) bond rather easily with Castiel, Kevin, Garth, Charlie, etc. This easy attachment is a likely psychological effect of the death of their mother and the distance of their father. The bond between Sam and Dean becomes closer and closer throughout the series, and, as is mentioned frequently in the show, more and more codependent. They are not OK with losing each other and go back and forth with who is the most irresponsible in their attempts to get their family back.

With these guiding thoughts, I want to ask three questions that may drive our discussion:

1) It is my contention that the death of Sam back in Season Two's "All Hell Breaks Loose" and Dean's subsequent deal with the Crossroads Demon broke Dean in a fundamental way, more than even Hell would later on. How does this "break" draw itself throughout the seasons and affect Dean's future relationships and ability to grieve those losses?

2) I'm inclined to believe that the very fact of these complicated relationships that these two alpha males have with each other and nearly every nice-enough person they come across speaks to something in the audience—Dean has room to cry and therefore opens a space for masculinity and emotion to coexist. How does the notion of family as portrayed in this show appeal to the fan base of the show?

3) There are two lines of character development that seem to be contradictory: On the one hand, the loss of loved ones outside

the pair seems to become less and less devastating as time goes on. By the time Kevin dies (he is one among many in the great cascade of dead tertiary family members), they have already lost too much. On the other hand, even the angel Gadreel, who killed Kevin last season, is considered with a certain sympathy by the end of the season, a sympathy which has a touch of the closeness that drives the show's main characters. How do we hold these seemingly opposing truths simultaneously?

Notes

1 I was correct in this assumption: Dean slaughtered the entire Styne family in the follow-up episode, "The Prisoner." The murder of the last member of the family, Cyrus Styne, who was presented in a more sympathetic light, represented the brutalizing effect of the Mark of Cain on Dean's psyche—pre-Mark Dean would have likely spared the boy.

"That's some meta madness": *Supernatural,* the Politics of "Like," and Raising Hell in the Ivory Tower

Mika Kennedy

Hi, my name is Mika, and I just finished my second year as a Ph.D. student in English. I think I'm the requisite black sheep of this panel, in the sense that I'm not all that familiar with fan studies, and despite the title of this panel, I actually don't write about *Supernatural,* I just fic within it. But I *do* teach composition, argumentation, and experimental fiction. I came into this conference thinking about two things in particular: a fan cultures panel at an experimental form conference at the University of Michigan last fall, and Peter Elbow's 1993 article on writing pedagogy, titled "Ranking, Evaluating, and Liking: Sorting out Three Forms of Judgment." Over the past few decades we've seen the increasing visibility and professional viability of fan studies; so my object here is not to demonstrate or debate the legitimacy of the field, but to now turn our attention to where and how fandom or fan studies might productively intersect with other fields, and how it might attend to some of the growing pains encountered by many of our newer critical disciplines.

Last October, I attended a fan culture panel at the University of Michigan. To me, it was significant in that it wasn't about explaining the baroque curiosity that is fan culture. Rather, it asked how including fandom can do productive work for the academy. Because whatever wank fandom stirs up, it's also institutionalized a lot of useful practices like trigger warnings, providing a space for people to engage a text, and increasing intersectional fluency via online discourse. That is, the panel focused on fandom/fan studies' potential service to and incorporation into the academy. Good stuff! But I think that while, for instance, those practices I listed earlier are elements of fan culture, they are not the actual vitality of it.

Let's put it this way. If you're a literary scholar, your overall project is to use texts to speak to some significance beyond that text; style, genre, sociopolitical bents, cultural moments, whatever. Clearly, things like *Supernatural* can do that work. I have to confess my personal reticence when it comes to *Supernatural* and this form of engagement, however. Not because there's anything wrong with it; there generally isn't, but because that's really not what I want my relationship to *Supernatural* to be. Sometimes I slip up, and then you get me wanting to do Bergsonian readings of S6, or like, let's talk about S7's trenchant critique of Midwestern politics, you know, occupational hazard. But one of the vital things about fandom, separate from other literary studies, is that it's not always about this, often *not* about reaching out to some wider scheme, or societal fabric. It also grasps inward, and affords a relationship that allows you to say, oh man, let's talk about what must be going through Sam's head right now, or oh goodness, that is really going to upset Castiel, because x/y/z. It's about taking the residents of a text as people with whom one can empathize, rather than only as tropes or literary figments. There's an intimacy there that you traditionally steer clear of when you're assembling a literary critique. Often for good reason, but I'd argue that there's also productive potential in pedagogy of play, alongside more traditional forms.

For instance, that Peter Elbow article I mentioned is about returning a similar empathy to the writing classroom, and learning how to "like" and engage peer and student writing *before* launching into the usual practices of peer editing and critique. He argues that pedagogies that encourage intimate engagement first make students more invested in their practice and product and better able to offer the same to their peers. Given the rise of the material turn in literary studies, and relatedly the increasing focus on the embodied reader, the moment seems right to bring fandom and fan studies into this conversation, too. Where can we return the fannishness of fan practice to academic practice? And in addition to speaking to fandom/fan shows as objects of traditional analysis, or as a set of productive disciplinary practices, is there also room to consider them as a source for alternative pedagogical and literary methodologies? How might this work on the ground?

While acknowledging the limitations of "liking," I suggest there remain untapped productive potentials in recuperating "liking" as well, not in place of but alongside and in partnership with present forms. Better student writers; better pedagogical practice; a better academy. I think these are important intersections to consider because it's usually not professional to like things, and as a result, professionalism implies the performance of critical distance. But where does that end and respectability politics begin? And what is the point of bringing fandom into the Ivory Tower if it means checking "like" at the door? (Or at least, making sure your "like" is dressed in business casual.)

Men, Masculinity, and Melodrama:
Supernatural at Its Finest

Bridget Kies

I am not someone who can claim to be a fan of *Supernatural* since the pilot. In fact, I'd never heard of the series until an academic conference on fan fiction in 2010, when Berit Åström of Umeå University gave a paper on mpreg (male pregnancy stories). Berit described the intimate bond between Sam and Dean Winchester, as well as actors Jared Padalecki and Jensen Ackles, as contributing to various kinds of fanfiction about the series. Shortly after, I read Catherine Tosenberger's now legendary (in academic circles, anyway) essay on the popularity of "Wincest." I thought the series, the actors' names, the fanfiction, and the fans themselves all sounded weird, but this made me want to check it out.

Supernatural quickly became the centerpiece of my research, which looks at representations of masculinity on television and in fan communities. I began watching the series from the beginning. I acquired new accounts at LiveJournal, PhotoBucket, Tumblr, and Twitter to access fan fiction and other fan-created works, and to make new friends in the *Supernatural* fandom. I was struck by the way the series made use of melodrama by allowing brave, strong men to express their inner pain. How profoundly I admired the series occurred to me when I watched the fourth season episode, "Heaven and Hell." As a tearful Dean confessed to Sam that he had tortured souls in Hell, I actually touched my television set and told him I'd never stop loving him.

This anecdote speaks to what has been *Supernatural*'s major appeal for many fans: its careful combination of melodrama and action. *Supernatural* is not the first example of film or television to tap into this kind of genre-mixing. The films of James Dean, for instance, are often examined as being examples of "male melodramas" because of the centrality of emotional conflict between James Dean's characters and others (especially family members) and his inner turmoil. Similarly, *Supernatural* depicts the stories of tough men: they shoot guns, sleep in dirty motels, drive a muscle car, and aren't afraid to put their lives in danger. Yet the typical episode concludes with Sam and Dean—later extended to other central characters—ruminating on their feelings about something. The network that broadcasts the series, the CW, usually targets its programming to young women, and these more emotionally tolling moments are intended to balance out the heavy action and gore to give the audience the fullest picture of the Winchesters are real, complex humans.

The action scenes, while exciting, also speak to the ways in which the series combines styles for different audiences. My first publication on the series was a chapter in Lynn Zubernis and Katherine Larsen's book *Supernatural: Fan Phenomena.* In my essay, "The Monstrous Male Body," I looked at how the narrative often feminizes the male body as a form of torture. For instance, Dean describes his torture in Hell by Alistair as tantamount to rape. At the beginning of season seven, the angel Castiel, whose gender is never fully clear, harbors the souls from Purgatory inside his body in a form of supernatural pregnancy. While not every viewer may pick up on these parallels, I suspect many do; *Supernatural* fans are smart about interpreting their canon. Even for those who don't, the idea that bodies are subject to torture and external forces certainly positions Sam and Dean as more fragile than they may seem to be on the outside.

My research eventually migrated away from readings of the canon itself and to readings of fan works. My second project looked at werewolf and shapeshifter stories, often called "ABO" for alpha/beta/omega, the different kinds of werewolves. In many ways, these stories get at some of the same ideas that I discussed in "The Monstrous Male Body," but because fan writers are free from the constraints of broadcast television, they can push the bodily boundaries even further. When I first began reading these stories, I confess I thought they were simply excuses to write strange animal sex. But the more I read, the more I understood that fans were taking the idea of the grotesque feminized body from the series and giving it a happy ending. In many stories, Sam and Dean (or Jared and Jensen) come to appreciate that their bodies can shift between animal and human or give birth to children. While a television series requires that the narrative problem never fully be resolved in order to produce more episodes, these stories offer resolutions in the form of happy endings.

As my research has evolved, so too has *Supernatural.* It is common for long-running television series to cycle characters in and out as actors migrate to other projects, but I found the introduction of so many recurring characters less interesting than the intimate, isolated world of the early seasons. My research found a new direction looking at historical television series, and I had less time to devote to *Supernatural*. Many of the fan communities in which I had participated were abandoned as fans moved to other social media platforms or other fandoms altogether. After several intense years, I found myself presenting a paper at the Fan Studies Network conference declaring my "break-up" with *Supernatural*. I'm still fascinated by the series' enduring popularity. Because of it, the CW has begun broadcasting more series that combine action and melodrama, and in that way, *Supernatural* has had a lasting effect on the network. I didn't exactly lie when I told Dean that nothing he could do would ever make me stop loving him. As one of the first series I ever published about, *Supernatural* occupies a special position in my academic CV. And as the first still-broadcast series for which I participated in certain fan communities, a series that took me through a move across three states and five years of my life, *Supernatural* will always a very special place in my heart.

Supernatural: The Little Show That Could

Lisa Macklem

Supernatural, fans will tell you, is a very special show. It has certainly been blessed both by passionate and dedicated fans and by luck. As it enters its twelfth season, *Supernatural* becomes the longest running North American fantasy show in history. The highest season average for ratings, according to Nielsen was 3.81 million viewers, and that was in the first season. In the eleventh season, the average has dropped to 1.78 million. Why is *Supernatural* still on the air when shows with higher ratings are regularly cancelled? This is where the luck kicks in.

Supernatural came on the air in 2005 at a time when genre television was seeing a rise in popularity. Fans and sci-fi "nerds" and "geeks" were beginning to be seen in a more favorable light and gaining in hegemonic cache in both society and industry. Being a fan was being facilitated by the rise in digital communications and access. Television was looking for new ways to monetize in an increasingly digital and competitive marketplace. All of these factors have facilitated a unique dialogue to spring up between fans and producers of *Supernatural*. The manifestations of this dialogue can be seen within the television show itself. Producers are able to step away from genre expectations and rely on fans' knowledge base to push creative boundaries. Yet, an increased sense of entitlement and the pressure to please the fans at all costs may also lead to a chill on creativity.

Part of *Supernatural*'s good fortune has to do with the network that it is on, and that is also related to the way television viewing has changed over the lifetime of the show. In *Supernatural*'s first season, it aired on the WB network, but by the second season, Warner Brothers and CBS became partners in the CW, aiming programming at younger audiences, with the commitment to fantasy and, later, comics programming. This also meant that the network was more proactive than other networks when it came to interacting with viewers and fans. Most recently (June 2016), this has translated into the CW negotiating shorter release windows of their programs with Netflix, thereby making the programs available sooner for fans who no longer subscribe to more traditional modes of entertainment (Littleton). The CW was also one of the first networks to look to Twitter to gauge audience engagement and to count DVR 3-day and 7-day viewing ratings.

In early seasons, fans were flattered by acknowledgement of their concerns and even existence. Fan fiction and the thank you to Kripke paid for by and from the fans in *The Hollywood Reporter* at the end of his tenure, as well as attendance at multiple fan conventions were ways that fans paid homage and celebrated the text. The fans promised Kripke that "On whatever road you travel next, know that your fans will gladly shut their cakeholes and ride shotgun with you" (Superwiki "Eric Kripke") Of course, fans are just as likely not to shut their cakeholes and be vocal backseat drivers. Sandvoss posits that what often draws fans to a particular show is that they identify with a particular character, thus seeing themselves within the text (832). Inclusion in the text itself, as well as a sensitivity to reception, such as getting rid of characters who were not well-received, were recognition of fans by production. However, this hierarchy is being challenged by an increased sense of entitlement by fans. In part, this is a result of what Jenkins, Ford, and Green describe as spreadable media. According to Jenkins, Ford, and Green, "Audiences are making their presence felt by actively shaping media flows, and producers,... are waking up to the commercial need to actively listen and respond to them" (2). Jenkins, Ford, and Green also stress the importance of the changes in technologies and "the social logics and cultural practices that have enabled and popularized these new platforms, logics that explain why sharing has become such a common practice, not just how" (emphasis in original, 3).

There is ample evidence within the text of *Supernatural* to conclude that fans do have an influence on the final product. However, not all interactions have been positive. There were a series of tweets from writer Adam Glass who was challenged over the depiction of gay characters on the show that also indicates that fans' interactions may have a chilling effect on the writers' creativity, and this may cause the dialogue between fans and producers to be muted or cut off entirely, closing the communication channel to production. If the relationship becomes an adversarial one in which nothing the producers say is accepted at face value as either true or sincere by the fans, the producers may be less likely to try to engage in that dialogue.

It is clear that fans have been invited into the creative process. June Deery states that: [v]iewers may now join a community of critical readers whose attention to the show's production and to the program as artifact may, in fact, alter the ontological status of the show-as-perceived-by-viewers, producing a postmodern self-reflexivity – what Umberto Eco has termed "neo-television" – even when this self-consciousness was not embedded in the show by its producers. (175)

Supernatural is a perfect example of a show whose fans enjoy this new access to production and are also embedded within it through the inclusion of fan conventions and meta episodes like "The French Mistake" that actually incorporates the filming of the show. When producers can engage their fans in such an immersive way, producers can almost ensure the economic survival of their creation. The other benefits of the relationship from the producers' point of view may be an increased ability to be more artistically creative as demonstrated by the use of humor and fourth wall breaking by *Supernatural*. However, in giving fans a greater say, this might also result in a creative chill for the producers when fans object vociferously to elements such as the women characters or the relationship as they perceive it between Dean and Castiel. As in any relationship, as both sides, fan and producer, get to know each other better, expectations are raised and disappointed. The changing economic landscape of television production and the increasing use of the digital environment will continue to influence the power hierarchy between these two groups. To date, *Supernatural* has been able to maximize this relationship both in terms of economics and cultural production, whether this will continue in the changing landscape remains to be seen.

In the most recent season, the writers have addressed some of the fans most pressing concerns. Fans have wanted to know since season five whether Chuck was definitely God, and where Dean's amulet went, and why the amulet didn't light up around Chuck as it was supposed to. Writer Robbie Thompson recently remarked that "History and continuity are wonderful tools to help build and sustain the world of shows and comics. I think it's important to know the history in order to help move the narrative forward, but also so that, when you do make changes in order to tell a new story, you know what you're changing and how to change it so it isn't disruptive to the overall experience and for long time fans. It's a tough balance, and I have different feelings about it as a writer than I do as a fan."

Supernatural is still the little show that could. It maintains that fine balance between fans, writers, and producers and pushes the boundaries of what defines a successful television show. Entering its twelfth season, the show has given no indication that this will be the last. As long as the network and fans remain behind this show, it seems likely that it will continue, especially as changes to traditional network television continue as well.

References

Deery, June. "TV.com: Participatory Viewing on the Web." *The Journal of Popular Culture* 37.2 (2003): 161-183. Print.

Jenkins, Henry, Sam Ford, and Joshua Green. *Spreadable Media: Creating Value and Meaning in a Networked Culture.* New York: New York University Press, 2013. Print.

Littleton, Cynthia. "Netflix, CW Near Deal That Accelerates Streaming Window as HULU Ends In-Season Pact." *Variety.* (20 June 2016). http://variety.com/2016/tv/news/netflix-cw-output-deal-the-flash-hulu-1201799176/. Web.

Sandvoss, Cornel. "One-Dimensional Fan." *American Behavioral Scientist.* 48.7 (March 2005): 822-39. Web. 10 June 2013.

Supernatural: Season 1-8. Exec. Prod. Eric Kripke et al. Warner Brothers, 2013. Blu-Ray.

Superwiki. *Supernatural Wiki.* Est June 2006. http://www.supernaturalwiki.com/index.php?title=Super-wiki

Thompson, Robbie. In Matt O'Keefe, "C2E2: Robbie Thompson on Supernatural, Spidey and Fandom" March 16, 2016. *The Beat.* http://www.comicsbeat.com/c2e2-robbie-thompson-on-supernatural-spidey-and-fandom/. Web.

Supernatural Blurs the Lines between Femininity and Masculinity

Christina Maenpaa

There might be few female characters featured on the CW's
Supernatural, but there is plenty of femininity. Although the series is
draped in hypermasculinity, the heroes' performance of the feminine
makes up for the lack of female characters. The hypermasculinity is
contextualized by muscle cars, rock music, knives, pretty women, and
guns; yet, *Supernatural* stretches the definition of the masculine
presenting relentless displays of vulnerability. These moments of
vulnerability and powerlessness define the femininity. *Supernatural*
allows their men to be feminine. From the series' inception, the
Winchesters have been placed in the feminine position where they are
often objectified to create humorous moments. But, the feminine is also
working to emphasize the moments of moral ascent and descent. For
instance, focusing on Dean, a moment of moral ascent happens when he
is placed in a feminine position of powerlessness after being beaten by
Lucifer. Dean's powerlessness motivates Sam to overcome Lucifer's
possession long enough to jump into hell's cage and end the apocalypse
("Swan Song" 5.22). In contrast, a moment of moral descent occurs with
the absence of femininity and the presence of hypermasculinity that
leads Dean, with the help of the male character Crowley, to an
acceptance of evil that transcends him into a demon ("Black" 10.01).
The coexistence of the brothers' feminine and masculine performances
suggests a collapse of the dichotomy.

We Have Always Been Here

Dawn Xiana Moon

In the early days of the internet, back when we were on Prodigy or CompuServe and email addresses were long strings of numbers with a comma in between, I was wrestling with Q on starships and leading away missions on far-away planets. I drank Romulan ale in Ten Forward, flirted with fellow Starfleet officers, and launched photon torpedoes at Klingons. I was in middle school.

My father was an aerospace engineer; he raised us on a steady diet of *Star Trek* and *Star Wars*. He handed me Isaac Asimov books in elementary school and I read them, wondering why I didn't have a robot nanny or automatic food-making gadgets. To this day, I find the background engine hum from *Star Trek: The Next Generation* comforting; Picard and crew feel like extended family members. So it's no surprise that shortly after I convinced my father to give me internet access, I'd worked my way to second-in-command of the CompuServe *Star Trek* trivia and sim organization. I and others around the country adventured in our virtual world with no scripts and few rules - years later I tried *Dungeons and Dragons* and found the dice and massive rulebooks too restrictive; in Fleet 74 we typed our characters' interactions without graphics or the weight of character sheets and charisma stats. To a 13-year-old, it was glorious.

All that to say: I've always been a nerd. And proudly so. But growing up I rarely saw people that looked like me onscreen - sure, we had Sulu and Psylocke, but Asian characters were few and far between. (I didn't realize until I was an adult that *X-Men*'s Jubilee was supposed to be Chinese.) Geek culture was a microcosm of my life; I moved from Singapore to the US at the age of five, to a school district where the only Asians were myself and my brother, and a friend and his younger brother. Asian-Americans rarely appeared in media at all. And when we did, we were invariably the martial arts master, the submissive woman, the uber-nerd/scientist, or the Dragon Lady seductress. Characters wore our ethnicity like a costume—Psylocke shed her British skin for a vague and undefined Asian one purely so the creators could make her stand out. And with her new, generically Asian self, she thought of herself as more sexual. I didn't relate to any of this. My heroes were characters like Princess Leia and *Babylon 5*'s Delenn, forces of personality who were fully themselves and didn't need rescuing. If they were sexy—and in retrospect they were—it wasn't because they were trying. Like my role-playing character, they commanded armies. And it wasn't just the female characters I admired—I saw myself in Luke Skywalker and Captain Kirk.

Living in a world where people who look like you are functionally non-existent yields odd fruit. Bryan Lee O'Malley of *Scott Pilgrim* fame talks about how he never realized that he'd whitewashed himself out of his own story until seeing the comic in movie form and realizing that no one looked like him. When I wrote stories myself, my Mary Sue characters were uniformly white. As I've talked with other Asian-Americans, I've realized that I wasn't the only one—many of us did the same thing.

So if I and others of color are able to imagine ourselves as white —and not just able, but do by default—what's the problem? We lose out on so much when we only give voice to a white, wealthy, Western, male point of view. It's a generalization, but the old stalwarts of science fiction—people like Arthur C. Clarke and Isaac Asimov—were primarily writers of ideas. They weren't as concerned with characterization. One of the things I've noticed and enjoyed as more diverse writers—women, people of color, LGTBQ+ folk—have been gaining more notoriety in the science fiction world is that we're seeing more fully-developed characters, more writing with heart, more creative stories that explore cultures and new perspectives. The overall state of science fiction writing is more literary than it's ever been, and we're entering stories and points of view that we've never seen in the genre. Homogeneity is boring—as audiences, we tire of the same stories told from the same perspectives. In art, specificity makes subjects more interesting, and lately, we've been reaping the benefits of diversity in our narratives.

Stories help us understand each other. They teach us what's important, what we should value. They teach us who we are; they give us our history and connect past, present, and future. They allow us to enter into others' realities. Without *Will and Grace*, would our culture be as comfortable with homosexuality? Without Anne Frank's diary, would we sympathize as strongly with Jews in World War II? There's a reason that one of the first things that governments do in war is create propaganda dehumanizing their enemies—a person you've been told enough times is less than human is a person you will eventually view—and treat—as less than human. But luckily, the reverse is also true.

I have a two-year-old niece who is just starting to watch television and movies—I've been on a (currently successful) mission to turn her into a geek, just as my father did with me. She recognizes Darth Vader, and I'm teaching her to speak a few phrases in Klingon. How wonderful it would be for her to grow up in an America where actors onscreen reflect her daily reality. How wonderful it would be for her to grow up in an America where writers tell stories that reflect multiple aspects of her life. How wonderful it would be for us all to understand each other just a little better while enjoying good art.

Notes on Collaborative Authorship, Getting Medieval, and Dean Winchester's Pie

Kristin Noone

"Hey, see if they've got any pie. Bring me some pie. I love me some pie."
—Dean Winchester, "All Hell Breaks Loose: Part One"

I have been thinking a great deal about pie. Specifically, Dean Winchester's love of pie, medieval pies—and the different forms they can take, from a kind of edible grab-bag for traditionally working-class consumption to, at the other end of the spectrum, extravagant confections with live blackbirds baked in for a feast—and the extended metaphor of consumption and collaboration and affection one might construct from a pastry edifice. I hope to sketch out, in an early-draft and open-ended fashion, some notes toward a new—though in some ways quite old—means of thinking about authorship and fan works and writing, a way in which we are all pie-makers, and Dean Winchester loves what we make.

Authorship in the Middle Ages, Nicholas Watson writes in *The Idea of the Vernacular*, might be construed as "the search for truth as a collaborative project that does not end with the completion of a text but merely moves into a new phase"; in other words, a "fluid and reciprocal relationship with the world" (13). Authors participated in "an intellectually and morally authoritative tradition, within which one might fill several roles, copying, modifying, or translating as well as composing"—roles which might find productive corollaries with fic writers, translators, betas (draft-readers and trusted editors), and which might shift or combine in multiple diverse forms. Medieval writers often knew their intended audience intimately, being dependent on commissions from patrons and persons in positions of power; thus, these writers saw themselves not as isolated genius figures but as participants in what Watson refers to as "ongoing conversation" (13). Chaucer and Gower, for instance, both present themselves as entrants into a tradition of interpretive commentary and remaking—especially in the vernacular—asserting their right to be worthy partners. Many other authors, as Thomas Usk does, apologize for "rude and boisterous language"; we might conclude, as Watson does, that popular writing in the Middle Ages exists not in a single definitive form but as a flowing series of modification and adaptation (10).

I am not contending here that medieval conceptions of authorship can be traced linearly down to twenty-first-century participatory culture; authorship and copyright as we know it can be traced no further than eighteenth-century discussions of intellectual ownership and author's rights. I am suggesting, however, that an understanding of that pendulum swing might provide greater historical grounding and comprehension of the compassion and empathy present in that form of gift economy. As Watson notes, in the Middle Ages "writers gain authority less by their originality than by their contribution to an ongoing tradition," and participate in acts of transformation—translation, rewriting, marginalia—in the service of a truth defined as "conformity with the moral structure of reality *plus the ability to improve the reader*" (12; emphasis added). I am interested in the ways in which this very old attention to the collaborative nature of meaning-making—that act of reciprocity with the world, as John Lydgate invites readers into conversation in the *Troy Book* and Sir Thomas Malory requests that readers pray for his deliverance from prison—seems to re-emerge in the transformative works and gift economy of participatory and fan culture, exploring new modes of authorship intimately tied to empathy, love, desire, and community networks.

In *Fic*, her magisterial study of fanfiction's prehistory and ever-mutable landscape, Anne Jamison observes that transformative fandom culture, in particular the production of fan texts, despite "radically new implications and subversions...represents the swinging back of the pendulum to that older way of thinking" (xiv), a means of considering texts as shared resources that function in a gift economy, a world in which authors and artists create works without expectation of remuneration. Similarly, Kristina Busse and Karen Hellekson have explored the function of fandom as resistance site, site of criticism and (re)interpretation of dominant narratives, but also a place of intimate encounters, designed to be shared: a communal experience of textual interaction. Writing specifically of the *Supernatural* fandom, Katherine Larson and Lynn Zubernis read fandom as an idealized (if imperfect and subject to internal politics) gift economy (17), which recalls earlier medieval models of the gift economy, that fantasy of lords bestowing arm-rings and titles in acts of ideal inexhaustible expectation-less generosity. As D. Vance Smith comments on the medieval romance "Sir Launfal," this world is always a form of fantastic play: imagining inexhaustible capacity for gift-giving through literature. Fandom, with its gift exchanges, works freely offered to readers, and practices of comment and kindness, might be viewed—in general preliminary terms—as another attempt to imagine this fantastic compassionate space: a world in which any acts may be possible, sometimes with tentacles. Acts of fandom authorship, like acts of medieval authorship, are therefore always about generosity and consumption; but active, aware, engaged, and (for the most part) compassionate if critical consumption.

And consumption leads us into baking ovens, and hence to pie. Specifically, to the domestic history of the pie: a medieval mainstay, covering the extremes from a working-man's lunch to fantastic, fancy flights of extravagance, the ordinary and the extraordinary, or *Supernatural.*

"The pie," C. Anne Wilson explains in *Food and Drink in Britain from the Stone Age to the Nineteenth Century,* "was a development of the Roman idea of setting meat inside a flour and oil paste as it cooked. In northern Europe, where butter and lard were the common cooking fats, pastry began to be made which was strong and plastic enough to be molded into a free-standing container; and thus the pie was invented"; the name was bestowed from the *pie* or *magpie,* collector of miscellaneous objects which would be reflected in the eclectic potential mixture of ingredients (253). The pie serves, I venture here, as an apt, if somewhat fanciful, metaphor for the act of authorship and the collective nature of creating narrative, both in the Middle Ages and in fandom culture. Pies might cater to any tastes, hot or cold, simple or extravagant, sweet or savory: one might find a simple seasoning of pepper and salt, or turkey pies sealed with butter, or "minced small with beef marrow, orange and lemon candied peel, spices, rosewater, orange juice," or, more elaborately, filled with "six young rooks" or prepared with a "filling of figs, raisins, apples, and pears, all ground up and cooked with wine and sugar to which was added boiled fish with spices…the mixture was placed in its pastry coffin and planted on top with stoned prunes and quartered dates." (136) Whatever one's taste, medieval and early modern pies provided satisfactory consumption; they might be straightforward (prepared in the vernacular, perhaps) or decadent and exploratory and only appreciated by a select audience (themes also found in various subgenres of fanfiction). Whatever a consumer might seek, a pie (or a fanfic) will exist to fulfill their wildest — or humblest—desires.

Which brings us back, inevitably, to Dean Winchester and pie.

Dean's love of pie, in a show that actively engages with folklore, Americana, and its own fan base, is not accidental; Dean is a creature who enjoys consuming (alcohol, burgers, pie), and the folkloric history of the pie is a rich and flavorful one. I would like to propose here, in an early and tentative and perhaps unbaked fashion, that we—as fellow consumers, authors, academics, scholar-fans, and fan-scholars—might pay closer attention to the show's edible metaphors, and explore the ways in which these investigations not only enrich our own writing but invite us to taste older ingredients of writing, collaborative authorship, and acts of generosity and community in our contemporary fandom work.

References
Jamison, Anne. *Fic: Why Fanfiction Is Taking Over the World*. Dallas: Smart Pop, 2013. Print.
Smith, D. Vance. *Arts of Possession: The Middle English Household Imaginary*. Minneapolis: University of Minnesota Press, 2003. Print.
Watson, Nicholas, and Jocelyn Wogan-Browne, Ruth Evans, Andrew Taylor. *The Idea of the Vernacular, an Anthology of Middle English Literary Theory 1280-1520*. University Park: Penn State Press, 1999. Print.
Wilson, C. Anne. *Food and Drink in Britain from the Stone Age to the Nineteenth Century*. Chicago: Chicago Review Press, 1991. Print.
Zubernis, Lynn, and Katherine Larson. *Fandom At The Crossroads: Celebration, Shame and Fan/Producer Relationships*. Cambridge: Cambridge Scholars Publishing, 2012. Print.

From the Back Porch to DePaul: *Supernatural*, Fannish Impulses, and the Cultural Economy

Jenny Roth

I'm here today because about nine years ago, my co-author Monica and I spent a lot of time on the back porch talking about this great new show, *Supernatural.* We read the fanfiction and commented on it, and we discussed the merits of Sam vs. Dean because, at that time, we were on opposite sides of the fence. Those fan moments grew into a laugh that we might do research on *Supernatural*, which eventually became a reality, and then the basis of many years of our collaborative work in fan studies, cyberfeminism, new media studies, and law and culture.

When I thought about how I could celebrate *Supernatural* as part of this panel, and talk about the impact of its fans, I considered how my own career, and the trajectories of various undergrad and grad students have been caught up, sometimes completely unknowingly, in the case of many assistants, in the web of *Supernatural* and its fandom.

Following on the work of Matt Hills, Henry Jenkins, Abigail de Kosnik and others, I and Monica recognize fan culture as part of a much larger cultural economy. We have often argued that fan fiction should be remunerative if that's what a particular author wants; we've critiqued how the internal policing of fan norms around publication often fall uneasily in line with gender norms that hold women back and, ironically, keep women silenced; and we've tried to break down some of the dominant binaries that contribute to the construction of fandoms by using evidence that illustrates there is no clear-cut divide between 'us fans' and 'them others' / between 'legitimate' authors and 'hobbyists' / between writing for pleasure and writing as labour / between fan culture and culture, among others.

Here, I'd like to move beyond the question of fan fiction and remuneration, though, to think about how fan culture and cultural production, actually happen in a lot of different ways, in a lot of different spaces—this Celebration being one of them. How it might be useful to think about fans as working from within and affecting many different cultural spaces, depending on each of our locations? In this way, fan culture is caught up in the cultural economy much beyond the production of texts that may or may not be published, or the continued support of a particular program via free advertising and a large, devoted, consumer base, or the sale of fan art. Fans connect to the cultural economy in ways that are quite nuanced and can be unforeseen.

I thought of our example: our fan discussions on the back porch lead to a fan studies project for which we received funding over a number of years. With that funding, we provided scholarships and salaries to undergraduate and postgraduate students—some of whom had never watched *Supernatural*. Some of those students have gone on to do their Doctorates, and have been successful themselves in obtaining funding for their own research—widely divergent from the field of fan studies, and *Supernatural*—in part because they could show a track record of scholarships and successful research work.

One of those Doctoral students travelled to do her work in another country, contributing to economies overseas; others attend Canadian Universities where their fees contribute to the Universities' budgets, which in turn fund employees, Faculty, and support staff. In the course of our own research, we also contributed to the North American economy with payments to airlines, hotels, conferences, restaurants, producers of merchandise, and fan conventions, at minimum.

One line of argument that often appears in discussions about fandom and cultural production is that fandoms are somehow 'separate' from wider culture; they are 'outside of' the mechanisms of traditional producer-consumer relations. In order to better understand the web of cultural and economic production that fandoms spin, it might be useful to consider how *Supernatural* fandom, in particular, has contributed to the lives of people who are not *Supernatural* fans, in ways that have very little to do with the inner circles of the fandom. We are part of a much larger cultural economy and processes of cultural reproduction beyond the question of whether or not fan fiction should be remunerative. In order to recognize the impact that fans have, we may need to broaden the scope of what we consider to be 'fan works' and their effects in order to fully recognize that fans ourselves are diverse, and work in many different ways and different spaces, but that what binds us together, is that when we love something, like *Supernatural*, it will work its way, somehow, into what we produce.

Presentation at *Supernatural* Conference

Margaret Selinger

Before I say anything today, I want to thank Professor Booth for allowing me to be a part of this Celebration. As you can probably guess, I am not an academic. In fact, I'm not even entirely sure that at this point I would call myself a fan, although I certainly have in the past. One of the reasons for my on again/off again relationship with *Supernatural* is the way that teenage female fans, like myself, have been represented on the show. I'm going to say three things about that representation this year. One of them is critical, one is complimentary, and one may be a tad controversial.

First off, the critical. When *Supernatural* first introduced fans as characters in season 5, they (we) were played primarily for laughs, at least when they were female. In Becky's first appearance, she claims she "doesn't appreciate being mocked," but when she returns for the con episode later that season, that is exactly what happens. Her sexual interest in Sam is portrayed as over-the-top, and her only creative response to the show is explicit Wincest fanfic, which is presented as equally ridiculous. The male fans we meet also start off as purely comical, with Damien and Barnes spending the episode LARP-ing, wearing Sam and Dean costumes, and lowering their voices to imitate theirs, despite the fact that *Supernatural* to them is a book, and they would have no idea what the characters should sound like. Even Chuck, although not a fan, is shown in a similar light. He recounts his failures with women, is terrified of speaking in public, and is unable to get Becky's attention.

By the end of the episode, Becky has transferred her sexual obsession onto Chuck, calling herself "the yin to his proud yang." Chuck's yang is proud because he, like Damien and Barnes, has fought a monster, attaining a trace of what the episode presents as ideal masculinity, the monster-killing prowess of Sam and Dean. Throughout the episode, the men have tried to achieve or imitate that kind of masculinity, and the women have been attracted to it. This particular version of ideal masculinity is, in effect, what inspires both sets of fans, drawing them to the story.

The ideal masculinity portrayed in the most recent episode

concerning fans, season 10's "Fan Fiction," is remarkably different--as are the fans who are attracted to it. The fans in this version are teenage girls, high school students like me, and they care about the boy's emotional vulnerability far more than they care about their ability to defeat monsters. Marie thus sings a tribute to Dean's "single man tear," and when she praises Sam's heroism, she calls him her "sweet, brave, selfless Sam," a far cry from how Becky strokes Sam's chest and marvels at how "firm" it is. Their investment in the books is not about desiring the boys sexually; in fact, they dismiss the idea of being attracted to the Sam and Dean they see in front of them, explaining that they are too old. They are completely about the story, both the preservation of it and the continuation of it through the musical that they wrote, their fanfiction.

Back in Season Five, the only fanfiction discussed was Becky's explicit incestuous story, which puzzles and disgusts poor Sam and Dean, and even Becky giggles when she talks about writing it. In Season Ten, although the "you know they're brothers, right?" gag about Wincest appears again, and I'll come back to that in a moment, fan production is treated with remarkable frankness and even respect-- arguably as much respect as is given to everything that's happened in the show itself since the original creator Eric Kripke left. (I'm thinking here of the moment when Dean describes the entire plot of the show since season 6, only to have it be dismissed by Marie as "the worst fanfiction [she's] ever heard.") Jokes may be made about robots and ninjas in the musical's "experimental" second act, but what we actually see of the musical consists of several brief songs and one moment of true pathos, when the actors playing the Winchester family line up on stage and sing an acoustic version of "Carry On Wayward Son." The fans' creation is not mocked; it has real emotional power.

As you may have guessed, that was the complementary portion of our program. To conclude, I'd like to focus on something that even this most flattering of episodes continues to present as controversial: slash fic. In Season Five's convention episode, slash fic is not discussed, but the hints of Wincest remain, especially when it's revealed that Damien and Barnes are a same-sex couple, much to Dean's consternation. Because Chuck's novels had not yet introduced Castiel as a character, "Destiel" fanfiction was not available as a topic. By season 10, this has changed, and although Wincest is old news to Dean, Destiel is a new and horrifying discovery. Dean is alarmed to see the two actresses who portray him and Cas acting romantically, demanding to know "is that in the show?" It is not. As in the show, the Destiel romance is confined to subtext only.

It's clear that the creators of this episode want to give their approval to slash. At the end of the episode, Dean even encourages Castiel's actress to "put as much sub into that text as you possibly can" and in a callback to the earlier conversation with Marie about Wincest, says that the actresses "should stand as close as she (Marie) wants you to." But this approval is only given to subtext. The word "subtext" is itself used multiple times by Marie to describe what she is doing. The show ignores the fact that almost all fanwork takes this subtext, which is all the show gives, and makes it the canon. The romantic relationships are not subtext, but text. That is what makes those works "transformative" to use another word the episode deploys. Now, I am not here to sing the praises of slash, and slashfic as a genre. There many issues of racism, misogyny, and biphobia to be discussed in that community. But the fact remains that for many queer fans, fanfiction is how they represent themselves because all they get from the show is subtext. This episode's almost literally paternalistic embrace of fanfic is only achieved by ignoring what Lev Grossman calls "a powerful critique, almost punk-like anger, being expressed" by fanfiction because as he says "a lot of times you'll read these stories and it'll be like 'What if *Star Trek* had an openly gay character on the bridge?' And, of course, the point is that they don't, and they wouldn't, because they don't have the balls, or they are beholden to their advertisers."

To whom, I wonder, is *Supernatural* beholden? It's not the CW. They also air "The 100," which proudly boasts a bisexual protagonist. Perhaps it isn't external pressure holding them back, but a desire to continue with what works. This subtext strategy has, after all, been a been a crucial element of the show over the past 10 years, especially with the addition of Misha Collins in season 4. And, given how proudly they discuss this strategy during the one-hundredth episode, it seems unlikely things will change. "Fan Fiction" may be, as writer Robbie Thompson said, a love letter to the fans. But it is also, at least in part, a love letter from the show to its own queerbaiting.

SPN Survivors

Karla Truxall

"You never know when a moment and a few sincere words can have an impact on a life."
– Zig Ziglar

For me, Jared Padalecki's Always Keep Fighting movement started at a *Supernatural* convention in October 2013 when a young fan asked Jared and Jensen about suicide. That moment forever changed my life. In fact, I wrote an open letter to that brave fan a year later and chose to read it as my opening remarks in the "Saving People: *Supernatural* and Social Issues" panel:

Dear Brave SPN Fan,   written November 2014

On October 27th, 2013 you and I were at the Westin Hotel in Rosemont, IL to see Jared Padalecki and Jensen Ackles at Creation Entertainment's Salute to *Supernatural* convention (ChiCon). You were in line on the left side of the stage to ask a question. In fact, you asked the LAST question of Jared and Jensen's panel that day. You asked if Jared and Jensen thought Sam and Dean would ever give up on life. Would they ever feel so overwhelmed to consider suicide?

My heart broke when I heard your question and tears immediately started to roll down my cheeks as I reached for my husband's hand. I worried for a moment how the boys would handle your question. Jensen was very somber and remained silent as he deferred to Jared. Jared's answer was beautiful. He told you, "Getting rid of yourself is never the answer. Keep on fighting the fight." Jared went on to talk about how when he's struggling, he's learned to take the focus off himself and his problems, and look for ways he can help someone else. By doing this, you help yourself by helping others.

I tried to find you after the panel but I was on the other side of the room and there were simply too many people between us. On that day, I wanted to find you, give you a hug, and encourage you any way I could through my tears. Today, I still want to find you and hug you, but I also want to thank you and praise you for your courage because YOU and that moment at ChiCon have forever changed my life!

I lost my nephew to suicide and his death ripped a hole through my heart and knocked me off my feet with such force, I've really struggled with how to move forward. My homework assignment from my counselor is to look for opportunities to talk about my nephew and to talk about suicide. I thanked Jared in the autograph line for his genuine, heartfelt answer to your question. I also found the courage over the next several months to reach out to others who were at ChiCon and talk about your suicide question and my suicide loss.

In the process of reaching out to others, I discovered there were people all around me who were suffering in silence, and that they too, just needed a little help on how to move forward. I realized I needed to take my loss, my journey, and pay it forward to help others within the SPN Family. And so . . . I created SPN Survivors.

I want you to know I think about you A LOT and I will never forget you! I wonder what impact Jared's answer has had on you over the last year. I want to know you are OK.

You are Awesome! You are Brave! And you inspired me to take the necessary steps I needed to move forward in my journey, and to help others along the way. I would be honored if you would contact me.

With Much Love,
~ Karla

Within six months of that moment at ChiCon 2013, the concept of SPN Survivors was born. It came to life as a website, Twitter and Facebook account the following October. In the weeks that followed, every *Supernatural* cast member and fan I spoke to about SPN Survivors was so encouraging and supportive of my vision that I knew I was on the right path.

That path was further validated when Jared launched his first

Always Keep Fighting (AKF) campaign one week before SPN Survivors had its first suicide prevention table at Vegas Con in March 2015. The excitement surrounding the AKF movement, the heartfelt stories shared in Vegas, and the outpouring of love and support from the SPN Family inspired me to create our Battle Buddies - specially chosen stuffed animals with words of encouragement from several SPN cast members printed on a custom designed bandana. Our Battle Buddies' mission is to encourage you, give you a reason to smile, and remind YOU to Always Keep Fighting for better days ahead *because* #You Matter!

SPN Survivors celebrated its 1st Anniversary at ChiCon 2015 with the launch of our Battle Buddies, which sold out before Jared and Jensen even took the stage. The stories shared and the tears shed with us at our table in the vendor's room that weekend hold a special place in my heart. We went home feeling inspired to look for opportunities to share our Battle Buddies with those who need them most. We have since partnered with a local hospital and school district to provide our Battle Buddies to kids and teens struggling by no fault of their own and need help.

Today SPN Survivors is a non-profit organization whose mission is to reach out, offer support, and bring people together through education and awareness while shining a spotlight on suicide prevention, self-care, Mental Health First Aid, and local, state and national resources. I am in awe when I look back and see how far we've come.

Ultimately, Zig Ziglar was right. "A moment and a few sincere words" had a huge impact on my life. It led to the birth of a non-profit organization dedicated to its motto: Helping People, Saving Lives, The Family Business! I hope SPN Survivors provides many moments that impact lives for years to come.

DePaul University "A Celebration of *Supernatural*": *Supernatural* Fandom Panel Notes

Leah Wilson

I want to use my couple of minutes today to talk a little bit about *Supernatural* fanworks and transgression.

There's a narrative in our culture—one I think we saw a lot, fairly recently, in the coverage of *Fifty Shades of Grey* and its origins as *Twilight* fanfiction—of fanworks as transgressive 1) legally, as I believe someone else on the panel will be discussing, and 2) morally. In both cases, the transgressor is, of course, the fan, and the transgressee is the copyright holder.

I don't really truck with either of those, but they also aren't what I want to talk about here. I want to look at fanworks as transgressive in a different way—as crossing other kinds of boundaries, and in the process forcing us to rethink them. Especially, if necessarily briefly: 1) moral boundaries; 2) gender and sexuality boundaries; 3) the boundaries of stories; and 4) the boundaries between creator and fan.

I believe all of these things happen in fandom and through fanwork creation generally, but I think you see it more clearly and intensely in *Supernatural* fandom.

The reason, I think, is first, because *Supernatural*, as a universe, is deeply concerned with transgression. Boundaries in *Supernatural* are especially porous, even more so than most small-s supernatural science fiction and fantasy shows. The show's original incarnation was designed around Sam and Dean crossing geographical boundaries of states as they traveled across the country, hunting things and saving people; since then, they've traveled between more figurative states—like life and death. Heaven and hell and purgatory are all places you can go to and come back from.

The second reason is that the show's writers have embraced regular violation of the fourth wall—from meta episodes like "Changing Channels," where the Trickster traps Sam and Dean in a series of television shows, and "The French Mistake," where Sam and Dean end up in our world, in Jared Padalecki and Jensen Ackles' shoes, to the always-popular Becky the Wincest fanfiction writer and the "Fan Fiction" musical episode.

So—those four kind of boundaries I mentioned earlier: moral boundaries, gender and sexuality boundaries, story boundaries, and the boundary between creator and fan.

Supernatural fanfiction, from the beginning, has played a little more fast and loose with mainstream **moral boundaries** than the average fandom—or not more, but in a way that's more widespread. Until Castiel came along, I think you could comfortably say there were two main fanfiction pairings in *Supernatural* fanfiction: Wincest, featuring Sam and Dean—which is, you know, incest—and J2 RPF, or real person fiction, featuring Jared and Jensen.

I actually find the explosion of RPF in Supernatural—maybe in part driven by the potential squickiness, for some readers, of Wincest—to be even more fascinating here. It blurs the boundaries between character and actor—in the case of some fics, where the actors playact their characters, literally. And it also makes the actors, real people, *into* characters, in the case of Alternate Universe or AU fic.

(Though in another way, J2 turns the basic dynamic between the two actors in public appearances into, as English professor Anne Jamison noted of *Twilight* in her book *Fic*, "one massive erotic romance prompt." "Jared Padalecki" and "Jensen Ackles" are treated not as themselves so much as character archetypes.)

Second: *Supernatural* fanfiction also plays a lot with **gender and sexuality boundaries**—it's the first place I know I saw things like gender- or sex-swap, where a character is either temporarily or from birth a different sex and/or gender, and ABO, or Alpha Beta Omega fic (which I'll let you look up for yourself if you aren't already familiar with it), which in some of its most interesting incarnations (to me) plays a lot with the concept of gender.

(And since my time is short, I'll just say you can read more about the way *Supernatural* fanfiction plays with gender and sexuality in Emily Turner's essay "Scary Just Got Sexy" in *In the Hunt*; her concept of transgression in *Supernatural* were a big influence in my discussion today overall.)

Third: *Supernatural* fanfiction plays with the **boundaries of stories**. *Supernatural* itself does this, as it takes traditional myths, from the Woman in White to the Bible, and reinvents them. And fanfiction always does this, borrowing bits and pieces of someone else's story. But

Supernatural fanfiction seems to do this even more vociferously than average. Aside from *maybe Harry Potter*, I don't think I've seen another fandom with more crossover fics—and with *Supernatural* it's often the characters that crossover, not, as with *Harry Potter*, the universe. I mean, the fact that there's something called "SuperWhoLock" at all— that's *Supernatural, Doctor Who*, and *Sherlock*—I think says a lot about how permeable and frequently violated those boundaries between stories are.

And fourth and finally (I promise): *Supernatural* fanfiction, with the apparently eager assistance of *Supernatural*'s writers, blurs the **boundaries between creator and fan**.

This is a boundary that is often taken for granted—you are a professional, you create canon, or you are a fan. The distinction between those two was never *actually* all that clear—if you look at the midcentury science fiction community, for instance, you can see how frequently writers crossed back and forth, and a lot of professional writers got their start in, for example, early *Star Trek* fic zines, the same way we're hearing about fanfiction and popular fanfiction writers being published today.

In *Fic*, Amber Benson—who played a vampire in a couple of *Supernatural* episodes—tells a great story about her friend Javi, who created *The Middleman*, mourned it being pulled off the air . . . and then wrote a fanfic crossover online between the show and *Doctor Who* as a way of continuing it. He is both creator and fan—and frustrated by his show's cancellation, unable to "legally" create more stories in the world he invented, used the same outlet frustrated fans do.

It feels a little bit, sometimes, like the writers of *Supernatural* are playing a game of transgression chicken with fans—re-appropriating fan spaces the same way fans re-appropriate the show.

And that, I think, is probably the most interesting fanfiction transgression of all: the writers writing, in effect, Real Person Fanfiction about *Supernatural* fans.

Writing About *Supernatural*

Lynn S. Zubernis

Writing about Supernatural should be just about the easiest thing in the world for me – after all, it seems sometimes that's pretty much the only thing I write about! Yet it has not always been easy, largely because of my own struggle to figure out just who I am when I write about the Show. A fangirl? A professor? A blogger? Fans analyse a text (including a television show) differently than someone writing literary criticism or an episode review or a psychological analysis. Fans write with passion and emotion and excitement and 'squee,' viewing the characters we love as human beings instead of literary tropes or marketing tools. Journalists and academics are more dispassionate, writing in a different 'voice.'

My dilemma? I am, often simultaneously, all of the above. I'm anything but dispassionate when it comes to *Supernatural,* but I'm accustomed to writing textbooks and research articles for professional journals (and more recently, episode reviews for a website). Integrating those disparate voices has proved challenging over my past decade of writing about *Supernatural.*

When Kathy Larsen and I first began writing about the Show we'd fallen for, we didn't want to check our fangirl credentials at the door just because we were professors writing about a media text. We wanted to share our squee alongside our analytical observations about fandom and *Supernatural.* Critical distance? Not exactly. We wanted to immerse ourselves in the Supernatural fandom and look at it from the inside instead of from outside by wielding an intimidating magnifying glass. After all, everything behaves differently as soon as the glass is in place, and your vision is inevitably distorted. *Fangasm: Supernatural Fangirls* turned out to be more the story of two best friends on a road trip through fandom than an academic book (we published that one as *Fandom At The Crossroads*), and that turned out to be a good decision – we wanted other fans to see themselves in the story, and to feel validated, and they did.

Our dilemma about what sort of book to write and for which audience was a struggle, however. The question of audience is one that any writer must grapple with, no matter the forum. Our books on

Supernatural are written for both academics and fans, but each skews one way or the other. We split our work into two books, one more academic and one not, because publishers couldn't figure out who was the audience for the original book. A hybrid book seemed impossible to them: How do you write dispassionately about something you're passionate about? It was a good question. In *Fangasm*, it played out in a series of questions we had to keep asking ourselves. How do you carry on an intelligent conversation with Jared Padalecki when you're in his trailer and he's taking off his clothes? How do you talk seriously to Misha Collins when you've just been commenting to each other about his backside as he bent over to retrieve his bags getting out of the van in front of us? What we finally realized is that ultimately, we don't need to be dispassionate. No one else is. We all love our fields; we all have our favorite texts. No one has to justify their passion for Henry James in academia, after all. It's more a balancing act. One which requires some smoothly engineered (most of the time…) code switching.

When I write for the Fangasmthebook blog on Wordpress, that's a different audience all together with different expectations. I'm not a journalist; nobody pays me to blog and there are no advertisements on the blog to serve as hit incentives. It's a fan blog where I can share fannish things — con adventures, photos, interviews, *Supernatural* episode reviews, personal opinions. That is also different from what I write on the *Fangasm* Twitter or Tumblr or facebook. Sometimes it's challenging to switch back and forth between platforms because they each attract a different type of fan, and fans form different sorts of communities on each. It's the kind of complication that makes writing about fannish things fascinating, though.

I would be remiss not to mention yet another type of writing about *Supernatural* — writing fanfiction. One of the themes of *Fangasm Supernatural Fangirls* was exploring the internalized shame that fans still feel sometimes. Shame about being fans (perhaps especially fangirls), about creating fanworks and writing fanfiction, about being passionate about something as "silly" as a television show. And yet, what we found in our research and wrote about in *Fangasm* is that there are all sorts of benefits that fans (again, perhaps especially female fans) gain from fandom. Validation, emotional expression, friendship, creative expression, self-discovery. It's all there, and why should we be ashamed of that?

As one attendee at the Celebration of *Supernatural* said: "Just embrace it. I write stories, and I post stories. That's pretty impressive!"

Damn, right it is. When I write and post fanfiction, the audience changes once again. The norms broaden, with fantasy and imagination valued over canon and factual accuracy. There is no publisher to please, and the editor is a fellow fan who volunteers to 'beta.' Perhaps most importantly, I write with anonymity, using a pseudonym as is the norm of most online fan communities. That anonymity, while sometimes used to bully or police, can also grant a freedom that allows a level of self-expression not available on other platforms. I can ship or not ship, yank Sam and Dean and Cas out of canon and throw them into another universe, change characters' genders if I want. I can explore things that the Show itself never could. I can write for myself. Of course, fanfic writers are as concerned about readers as any writers, so an awareness of audience remains. But as much as I treasure the positive comments and kudos, that isn't my primary motivation when I write fic.

I guess I really am embracing it.

Schedule for A Celebration of Supernatural

9:00–10:00

What Came Before: Genre and *Supernatural*
Ian Peters, Gordon Dymowski, Kate Kulzick

Love, Death, and Codependence: The Family in *Supernatural*
Katie Wilson, Allison Broesder, Patricia Grosse

10:00–11:00

Workshop: Television Criticism
Maureen Ryan

Panel: Hunting Things: Monsters in Supernatural
Amber Davisson, Candace R. Benefiel, Courtney Neal, Patrick Smith

Breaking the Fourth Wall: Meta *Supernatural*
KT Torrey, Thom Gaughan, Linda Howell, Lisa Schmidt

11:00–12:00

Q&A Session
Mark Oshiro

Saving People: *Supernatural* and Social Issues.
Laurena Aker, Karla Truxall, Rachel Dean, Galen Foresman

12:30–1:30

Keynote
Robbie Thompson

2:00-3:00

Workshop: Writing Television
Robbie Thompson

Workshop: Podcasting
Kate Kulzick, Jon Clarke

Problematic Tropes in and of *Supernatural*
Jennifer Cross, Kate Lansky, Mark Oshiro, Anne Petersen, Erin Tipton

Exploring Fandom in *Supernatural*
Rebecca Tushnet, Melissa Bruce, Monica Flegel, Lisa Macklem, Jen Roth, Leah Wilson

3:00-4:00
Live Podcast Recording
Water Cooler (Julian Axelrod and Freddy-May Abisama)
Men and Women: Gender in *Supernatural*
Bridget Kies, Stephanie Graves, Rhonda Nicol, Tina Maenpaa
Writing about *Supernatural*
Kathy Larsen, Mika Kennedy, Maureen Ryan, Leah Wilson,
Lynn Zubernis

4:00-5:00
Morality and Religion in *Supernatural*
Scott Paeth, Kian Bergstrom, Anne Casey, Galen Foresman, Shelby
Mongan
It Goes Both Ways: Fans and Producers
Laura Felschow, Kristin Noone, Margaret Selinger, Louisa Stein

5:00-6:00
Masquerade
Judges: Kathy Larsen, Mark Oshiro, Lynn Zubernis

Screening Schedule
9:00–10:00: "Changing Channels."
10:30–11:15: "A Very Supernatural Christmas"
11:00–12:00: "Fan Fiction."
11:15–12:00: "Frontierland"
12:30–1:30: "Pac-Man Fever."
1:45–2:30: "Larp and the Real Girl"
2:30–3:15: "In the Beginning"
3:15–4:00: "The Usual Suspects"
4:00–4:45: "The End"
4:00–5:00: "The French Mistake"

A CELEBRATION OF STAR TREK 2016 DEPAUL UNIVERSITY

Introduction

Paul Booth

May 07, 2016 saw over 200 *Star Trek* fans and scholars come together for a one-day celebration of the program, in honor of its 50th anniversary. DePaul University's Media and Cinema Studies program (along with the American Studies program, the Digital Communication and Media Arts program, and the School of Cinematic Arts) hosted the event, with speakers Brannon Braga (writer and executive producer of more than 300 episodes of the *Star Trek* series—for over 13 years he worked on *The Next Generation, Voyager,* and *Enterprise,* and wrote the films *Generations* and *First Contact*), Lisa Klink (a writer who started her career in the world of *Star Trek,* writing for *Deep Space Nine* and *Voyager*) and academic Dr. Lincoln Geraghty (author of *American Science Film and Television, Living with Star Trek,* and *Cult Collectors*).

The well-attended keynote panels at "A Celebration of *Star Trek*" brought new insight into this fifty-year-old program. Brannon spent an hour with a question and answer session, thoughtfully discussing aspects of his time on the show. He answered questions about the production process, his involvement with the films, and some of his inspirations, among others. Lisa discussed both her time writing for the two *Star Trek* series *Deep Space Nine* and *Voyager,* as well as giving particular tips as to becoming a writer in Hollywood. Lincoln discussed the enduring myths of *Star Trek* and how it encapsulated—and continues to encapsulate—American culture.

A Celebration of Star Trek was the first time that we had three keynote speakers—with such a diverse pool of talent, there could have been hundreds more!—and in many ways, it highlighted the key feature that makes the Pop Culture Conference special. Each of these Keynote events was very well attended, and fans, students, academics, and community members all experienced the event together. We all asked questions together, sat together, chatted together, and bonded over our shared love of *Star Trek.*

Another well-attended and engaging lecture at the event was the Leonard Nimoy Tribute by sociology professors John and Maria Jose Tenuto. Their moving discussion of Mr. Nimoy's contributions to *Star Trek* and other popular culture texts brought new insights to the icon.

The Tenuto's are well-known for their thoughtful work on *Star Trek*, and I'm pleased to offer one of their more academic papers in this book.

In addition, each year raises money for a particular charity, usually nominated by one of the Keynote speakers. "A Celebration of *Star Trek*" raised over $1200 for Chimp Haven, a group dedicated to rehabilitation and resettlement of chimpanzees. The money was raised in a variety of ways—a silent auction, a bake sale, tee-shirt sales, and individual donations.

I was particularly honored to work with two graduate students on the conference—early preparations and scholarship by Mariah Cowan helped bring over 50 speakers to speak on two dozen or so panels, including: IDIC: Philosophy and *Star Trek*; The Federation: Politics and *Star Trek;* Through the Wormhole: Reevaluating *DS9*; History of the Klingon Empire; The Cultural Impact of *Star Trek;* Trekkies, Trekkers, and Beyond: Fandom of *Star Trek;* Learn Klingon; *Star Trek* and Gender; LLAP: The Future According to *Star Trek*; Canon, Fanon, and In-Between: *Star Trek* Fan Works; Generations of *Trek*: Film, TV, and the Evolution of Star Trek; Debating the Future: Otherness and Privilege in *Star Trek*; Klingon: A Case Study of Conlangs in Mass Media; Beam Me Up: *Star Trek* Performance; The Future is Here: Science and Technology in *Star Trek*; Klingon Christmas Carol; Teaching Trek: Pedagogy and *Star Trek;* Queer Identities in Cosplay and Fandom. Mariah's research was extraordinary!

I'd be remiss, though, if I didn't extol the virtues of Laura Bluett, my research assistant who helped put the whole event together. She not only helped with organization of the conference and the planning of the panels, but designed the art, logos, and program; helped run the charity event; designed the tee shirts (and even Ubered down to campus with them in big boxes); helped moved tables and chairs; ran the Keynote overflow; and came up with vendor ideas. This conference wouldn't at all have succeeded if not for Laura.

One fun and unique panel held at the end of the day was the Fantasy Draft Crew! panel, where panelists used a fantasy-football-style draft to bring different members of *Star Trek* crews together and have discussions about how they might react in hypothetical situations. Crews ranged from one where aliens ruled the ship to one that swapped gender dynamics, illustrating the same ratio as *The Next Generation*'s male to female crew but in reverse.

We also featured a special Board Game room, run by Bonus

Round Café, a new board game café opening in Chicago. Bonus Round brought a variety of games, including many *Star Trek* themed games, that attendees at the conference enjoyed. Throughout the day we saw children and adults playing games and getting into the conference spirit.

The Pop Culture Conference has proven to be an exciting one-day event that brings different groups of people together to share their love and appreciation (and criticism) of a piece of media. It includes both academics and fans as panel speakers to attempt to create links between fandom and academia—two groups that engage in very similar practices, even if they do so in different ways. Panels are slightly more intellectual than the average panel at a fan convention and they are slightly more engaging that those at scholarly conferences—the Pop Culture Conference aims for thoughtful discussion rather than reading scholarly papers.

I hope you enjoy reading some of the pieces that were presented at *The Celebration of Star Trek*.

Portions of this piece were originally published in the Fall/Winter 2016 Astrosociological Insights Newsletter.

Producer Keynote

Brannon Braga

I was always distrustful of the term "pop culture." It sounded insignificant, short-lived, a low-calorie snack consumed quickly and without thinking, like popcorn. I'd spent most of my adult life contributing to so-called pop culture, and I felt accosted by the phrase and all the vapidity it implied. Fortunately, my experience at the DePaul Pop Culture Conference changed my view entirely.

When I was invited to be the keynote speaker at the 2016 symposium, I was certain they'd made a terrible mistake. What business did I have talking at a prestigious university? I didn't even have a college degree! But the topic that year was a celebration of *Star Trek*, and who better to discuss that popular TV show than someone who made a few hundred episodes. I wasn't sure what to expect, but I figured it would be something like a *Star Trek* convention in a fancier setting.

Boy, was I wrong. There were tables stacked with academic books on *Star Trek* for sale, all of them covering a wide range of esoteric and detailed topics. The economics of *Star Trek*, the ethics of *Star Trek*, the sociological impact of *Star Trek*, and countless others. I'd never seen these books, much less imagined their existence. And there were the distinguished panel discussions: The Science and Technology of *Star Trek*, the Pedagogy of Trek, *Star Trek* and a Culture of Inclusivity, Otherness and Privilege in the *Star Trek* Universe, Gender and *Star Trek*, Klingon Culture and History, and so on. This was no ordinary *Star Trek* convention.

During my talk, students and professors asked penetrating questions about my work that I'd never considered and could barely answer. These were passionate, serious-minded students, teachers, and fans who were clearly impacted by material I had written. They were engaged on a level I'd never seen before. Or had I...?

I began to have a deeper appreciation for those goofy *Star Trek* conventions. They weren't just nerd-fests. They were places where thousands of people from around the planet could go to connect with one another, all of them thoroughly knowledgeable about the *Star Trek* universe, a shared history of sorts, a truly global mythology. There was nothing on Earth quite like it; one could argue that it was pop culture at its all-embracing peak.

When I first started working on *Star Trek: The Next Generation* in 1990, I never imagined that, over 20 years later, I would be standing at a podium in De Paul University experiencing these revelations. Only then did I realize how pop culture could inspire people, change the course of personal and professional lives, and send forward-thinking, positive ideas into the world. If nothing else, a cultural phenomenon like *Star Trek* could bring families together for an hour or so to enjoy a good story that explored uniquely humanistic issues.

I'm grateful for Paul Booth's invitation to the DePaul Pop Culture Conference. This wonderful program is not just popcorn, but a hearty and healthy 10-course meal. I had been so busy cooking up pop culture that I never took the time to eat. Thanks for giving me a seat at the table.

Writer Keynote

Lisa Klink

I'm really pleased to be part of *A Celebration of Star Trek*, because *Trek* has done a lot for me. The first time I ever got paid for writing anything was for an episode of *Deep Space Nine* called "Hippocratic Oath." More on that later. Based on that episode, I was hired on staff at *Voyager*, where I stayed for the next three years. It was a terrific place to start. The producers and crew had been working on *Trek* for years and knew what they were doing. Even better, the writing offices were on the Paramount lot, where the show was filming, so I could walk over to the set whenever I wanted. I've worked on other shows that filmed in Canada or New Zealand, which makes that a little more difficult.

Now let me take you back in time, back to where this all started: 1990, my junior year of college. I was an English major and hadn't quite figured out what I wanted to do with it, maybe journalism, maybe law school. I loved movies, so I took an introduction to film class. Why not? Then they brought in a speaker who changed my life: Thom Mount, a successful Hollywood producer who had worked on movies like *Bull Durham* and *Natural Born Killers*. He screened his new movie for us: *Frankenstein Unbound*. It was a truly terrible film. But that wasn't the point. This was the first time I had encountered anyone who worked in Hollywood, an honest-to-God grown-up who made movies for a living. It had never hit me before that this was a career option. Now I knew what I wanted to do. So after graduation, I hopped in my car and drove to Los Angeles. I was going to direct action movies. James Cameron was my hero. *Terminator 2* had just come out and it blew me away. I remember sitting in the theater and thinking, "I want to do that!"

So I came to Hollywood and got a job working for a director: Kathryn Bigelow, who was the only woman directing action movies at the time. I read scripts for her, which was a fantastic education for a writer. For each script, I had to decide not only whether it was a good or bad, but why. Kathryn was directing a movie called "Strange Days" at the time, and I had the chance to watch her work. Which made me realize that I didn't want to be a director after all. It was constant, barely controlled chaos, with people firing questions at her all the time. Writing, by myself in a quiet room, was more my speed. So I wrote an action movie. Which did not come out well at all.

Then I went to a writing panel at a *Star Trek* convention. Brannon Braga was on that panel. So was Ron Moore. They were on *Next Generation*, and they said that they accepted spec scripts. If I sent them an episode, they'd read it. Probably not those two guys in particular, but somebody would. This was amazing. No other show did that, and nobody does it now. I liked *Next Generation*, so I wrote an episode. It came out a whole lot better than the screenplay.

So I sent in my script. Fortunately, I was unaware that they received something like 5,000 a month. Writing that script showed me that I liked writing for television. I actually work better within certain boundaries, like the world of a particular show. With an original screenplay, I had the entire universe to choose from. Every detail had so many options. I found it paralyzing. I want a couple of walls to bounce off. TV was a better fit.

Eventually, some *Deep Space Nine* intern read my script and liked it enough to pass along to the producers. They didn't buy that script, but invited me in to pitch story ideas for the show. Great. I went in, pitched my heart out, and didn't sell anything. I went in three more times, still didn't sell anything. But they kept inviting me back, so I kept trying, and finally pitched the story that would become "Hippocratic Oath."

I want to take you through the development of that episode, from pitch to shooting, and how it changed along the way. I'm assuming a basic familiarity with the show and characters, but please ask questions if I've lost you.

When I was thinking about ideas, I wanted to do a Bashir story. The character hadn't been developed much, and I think I identified with him because he was the young, idealistic, fresh out of med school kid. Anytime you're developing ideas for a character, think about his particular weak points. What would be the biggest challenge for this guy, not necessarily for other characters, but a real test for him. Indiana Jones is afraid of snakes – throw him in a pit of snakes. So I had the idea of throwing Bashir into a nasty alien jail, where he had to fight and kill and compromise his identity as a healer to survive.

I had this entire, detailed story worked out when I went in to pitch. Out of my whole story, they picked out three words: Bashir in jail. They started riffing on it, using movie shorthand: what if it was more like *The Great Escape* or *Stalag 17*? The showrunner, Ira Behr, brought up *Bridge On the River Kwai*, with Bashir as Alec Guinness' character, being captured by bad guys and forced to work for them, then getting personally invested in it. Then someone else suggested using O'Brien as the William Holden character, trying to stop the work that he was doing. That made it really interesting. Bashir and O'Brien were very different people who had developed this odd kind of friendship. O'Brien had come over from *Next Generation*. He was the seasoned, get your hands dirty engineer who had worked his way up from ensign, and been on the front lines for plenty of battles. At first, Bashir had kind of followed him around like a puppy, wanting to be friends until he wore down the guy's resistance and they formed a real friendship. So what would happen if they found themselves on opposite sides of a conflict? I love stories like that, where our heroes disagree, and neither of them is entirely right or entirely wrong. *DS9* was really good at exploring those gray areas.

So I went home and watched *Bridge on the River Kwai*, then the staff broke the episode together. This involves everyone sitting in a room, talking out the story and coming up with what happens in each scene, with somebody taking notes on a white board. This gets transcribed into an outline, which the writer uses to generate the first draft. So the story started off with Bashir and O'Brien getting captured by a group of Jem'Hadar, who'd been established as a race of very fierce, tough soldiers working for the Dominion, who were the evil empire of the delta quadrant. We knew that the Dominion were controlling them by keeping them addicted to a drug called ketracel white. When the leader of this group of Jem'Hadar, called Goran'agar, learns that Bashir is a doctor, he pulls him aside and tells him that being on this planet has somehow broken his addiction to the drug. He brought his men here, but the same thing isn't happening to them. He orders Bashir to figure out why, and how to duplicate the effect. Bashir realizes that Goran'agar isn't like other Jem'Hadar they've encountered. He wants to break free of the Dominion and think for himself. He doesn't want to be a killer anymore. Which makes Bashir genuinely want to help him. But when he tells all this to O'Brien, he's skeptical. He thinks Goran'agar is manipulating Bashir. From his point of view, as a soldier, they cannot help the enemy in any way. It's their duty to escape. That's all.

The two of them are separated and O'Brien does manage to escape. He jury rigs a weapon and traps in the jungle and goes all MacGyver on their ass. Then he comes back for Bashir – "Let's go." But Bashir thinks he might have a possible cure. He can't leave now. They argue, and Bashir pulls rank, which really messes with their dynamic. O'Brien has always been the senior guy sharing the wisdom of his experience with young Bashir. But technically, Bashir outranks him. O'Brien makes the decision to ignore this, and destroys the potential cure. "Nothing keeping you here now. Let's go." Goran'agar catches them, then lets them go. What he told Bashir was true – he doesn't want to be a killer anymore. O'Brien misjudged him. But there's no chance for a cure now. The other Jem'Hadar are now in drug withdrawal and in full revolt, and all they can do is run for it. Our heroes get away, but now they have this unresolved conflict between them.

On a serialized show like *Scandal*, this would continue to affect their friendship in future episodes. But *Deep Space Nine*, like all the *Trek* shows, had mostly stand-alone episodes. The idea being that viewers could watch them in any order and not get lost. So you had to essentially hit the reset button at the end of every episode. In "Hippocratic Oath," there was a final scene with Bashir and O'Brien heading back to the station. They talk about what happened, and don't really resolve it. Both still think they were right. Then Bashir mentions that tonight is supposed to be their weekly darts game. O'Brien says it's okay, he doesn't feel much like playing either. They're quiet, and Bashir says, "Maybe next week." And that's it. Back to normal. It's a little frustrating, but those were the rules of this show. I did say I liked restrictions, right?

When you write for television, you also have to consider practical concerns like schedule and budget. You can't hire ten guest stars and build five new sets for one episode. You want to use the existing sets as much as possible, which is tough when the story takes place on an alien planet. That's why a lot of the episodes involving away missions have a B story back on the station or ship. In this case, we had a B story about Worf, who had just joined the show, adjusting to life on the station. He ends up interfering with an undercover investigation of Odo's and learns his lesson about how the strict rules of Starfleet don't always work in a "frontier outpost" like *DS9*.

The staff gave me some notes, mostly about adding depth, particularly with the Jem'Hadar leader, Goran'agar. We needed to really understand why Bashir felt compelled to help him. They also told me to ratchet up the potential threat from the other Jem'Hadar soldiers who were increasingly suffering withdrawal from this drug. I did another draft, then the staff took over rewrites. I was very lucky to have Ron Moore rewriting me. He added a lot, including a great speech by Goran'agar about the Founders, who were at the very top of the Dominion hierarchy. To the Jem'Hadar, the Founders were like gods, who required them to sacrifice themselves in battle, but with no promise of reward. Now we really want Bashir to save this guy. Ron also built a nice parallel relationship with Goran'agar and his second in command and friend, who disagreed about what to do with these humans, trust them to help us or just kill them.

And some little things changed over the next few drafts: names of Jem'Hadar characters, adding lines of dialogue here and there to clarify something or remind the viewer what happened back in act one. I was really happy with the finished product. And I will never forget walking onto the soundstage where they'd built the jungle set, with the crashed shuttlecraft, and there was a Jem'Hadar in full makeup. I had typed some words into my computer, and now they'd come to life. It was pretty awesome.

I spent the next three seasons on *Voyager*, going through the same process on every script and getting a little better at it every time. I went on to work on other shows and got the opportunity to do some really cool stuff, like writing the *Borg Encounter: 4D* ride. I wrote an episode of an animated show: *Buzz Lightyear of Star Command*, and two issues of the *Batman* for DC Comics. Now I write novels. I find it really interesting to work in different formats and learn the different rules. It always comes down to telling a good story: characters I care about trying to accomplish a meaningful goal, with lots of obstacles that challenge them to overcome their own weaknesses to get what they want.

Living the *Star Trek* Future: Nichelle Nichols and the Implicit Religion of *Star Trek: The Original Series*

Laura Ammon

I am a cultural historian of religions. I ask questions about the complex, delicate, highly symbiotic relationship between 'religion' and 'culture' which are themselves complex, intersected, and diverse. I have lately been working on a project that asks about the role that space plays in the implicit religion of *Star Trek*, from *The Original Series* to the recent movie re-boots. Implicit religion is a way of exploring religious commitments in explicitly secular forms by focusing on the ways that those things are treated as sacred, holy, and human. *ST* is a future world clearly connected to our planet, its inhabitants, cities, and populations with a solution for many of our challenges. In the *ST* future, there is no hunger, poverty, homelessness, economic disparity (no economics at all actually) within the Federation. It is the world as perhaps at least some wish it would be, a way the world ought to be (equal, just, with a place for everyone and everyone in their place). It is a possible future, possibly humanity's best future. *ST* appeals to our desire for a realization of the promises of modernity, the resolution of hunger, racism, sexism, ableism, poverty, and the end of disease, and a world united and collaborating with other worlds. In *ST* it appears bigotry is vanquished and overall humans (and other beings) behave in rational ways. It is the modernist dream realized, the future we can achieve with the triumph of technology and science which is often treated as a sacred narrative promising human transcendence. The *ST* universe creates a mythology governed by science, rationality, and technology. *ST:TOS* was born at a moment when the US was engaged in finding our way into space, broadening our horizons and the presence of women and people of color on the bridge of the Enterprise was powerful.

The *ST:TOS* was a forerunner in imagining a future that was multiracial and multicultural, and was, for the 1960s at least, radical. *Star Trek* also presents a secular vision of the future, without religious conflict and seemingly without religious practice or devotion (at least for the members of the crew). The values and vision of a peaceful future society that appreciates Infinite Diversity in Infinite Combinations have spawned a kind of religious vision of the future of its own, valuing science, technology and human capabilities for conquering social ills. This is the genius of *Star Trek*. It is a mythology of our future, the story of US, our best modern selves.

Nichelle Nichols was one of the first black women on a TV series and the first black woman in space (at least on TV). And she was a powerful first. Her iconic status in the world of television led to her role in the development of the US space program. The popularity of *ST:TOS*, led Nasa to ask Ms. Nichols to help them recruit African Americans and women for the space shuttle program. She stepped off the bridge of the Enterprise and into NASA where she was an enthusiastic space program ambassador. She recruited astronauts that participated in the space program through the 1980s into the 1990s. Just to name a few she recruited Guion Bluford, the first African-American astronaut, and Sally Ride, the first US woman astronaut.* She also recruited Judith Resnik and Ronald McNair, who both perished on the Space Shuttle Challenger in 1986. One of Ms. Nichol's recruits is Mae Jeminson, an astronaut and a medical doctor, who points to Lieutenant Uhura from the original *Star Trek* cast as an inspiration for her chosen career track. Jemison was the first African-American woman to travel in space aboard the space shuttle Endeavour. (As a side note, Mae Jemison was a guest on *ST:TNG* sixth-season episode "Second Chances" which aired on May 24, 1993.) Dr. Jemison has developed an NGO—the 100-year starship program—which aspires to interstellar travel in the next 100 years. She proposes a starship that can journey from earth to Alpha Centauri, a mere 4.3 light years away, or 25 trillion miles (so close and yet so far away). While scholars have treated *Star Trek* fandom as a serious phenomenon since at least the early 1990s, Jemison's willingness to credit *Star Trek* as the inspiration for her career choice demonstrates some of the power of fictional visions of the future to influence representation in the present and the nontrivial importance of representation for women and underrepresented minorities on present-day earth. Nichelle Nichols changed the world, both through her work as an actor and her work with the space program.

I want to read a piece from Jemison's 100-year starship website, because it so exemplifies the mythology and values of *ST*, demonstrating another angle of the implicit religious content of the *ST* worldview.

We exist to make the capability of human travel beyond our solar system a reality within the next 100 years. We unreservedly dedicate ourselves to identifying and pushing the radical leaps in knowledge and technology needed to achieve interstellar flight, while pioneering and transforming breakthrough applications that enhance the quality of life for all on Earth. We actively seek to include the broadest swath of people and human experience in understanding, shaping and implementing this global aspiration." (https://100yss.org/mission/purpose)

These are *ST*'s values and Ms. Nichols embodies those values both in her creation of the character of Lt. Uhura and as an evangelist for the space program. She inspired a generation of people of color to reach for the space program and apply those values to programs such as the 100 Year Starship. The story of *ST* is the story of us as explorers, it is one of conquering our own limitations and fears, of "Boldly going where no one has gone before" and providing role models and a mythology to support the dream of space.

In August 2015 Nichelle Nichols flew on SOPHIA—Stratospheric Observatory for Infrared Astronomy—to observe the NASA astronomy program in action (http://www.space.com/30805-star-trek-nichelle-nichols-sofia-observatory.html). At 83 she is still a pioneer and active NASA supporter. While *ST:TOS* can be a bit dated, in some ways it is more radical in its vision for female characters than its 21st-century reboot. While Benjamin Sisko was the first African American captain in the *ST* universe in 1993, this was 5 years after Colin Powell was appointed Chair of the Joint Chiefs of Staff in 1989. The first woman commander on a ship at sea was appointed in 1988 and Captain Janeway launched into space in 1995. By the 1990s *ST* had lost at least some of its cutting edge. And while it is a challenge for any show to come close to *ST Voyager* for beating the Bechtel test (every episode in season 5 passed!) the roles for women and people of color have not been as influential or radical as *ST:TOS*. Nonetheless, the most recent ST doesn't have the same kind of gender power that *ST:TOS* brought. I think the recent film reboots do important work for the US psyche and processing 9/11 and the subsequent wars as I have argued elsewhere, but *ST:TOS* changed the world for women and people of color, creating an inclusive mythology of an interracial future that we have at least in some part realized. Nichelle Nichols has advocated for *ST*'s view of the future as OUR future, a future in space that we are all building and getting closer to with every NASA mission and Mae Jemison's 100-year Starship expands that future. *Star Trek* functions as a mythology and provides a religious outlook, with an underlying ideology and worldview. *ST* is a kind of religious story, a future realized. Now we are floating in the stars, women, and men, going boldly where no one has gone before.

The first woman in space was Valentina Tereshkova in June of 1963 (Sally Ride went to space 20 years!! later).

"Homo Sapiens Only": *Star Trek* and the Unhuman

Nathanael Bassett

Abstract

As a cultural institution, *Star Trek* advanced the notion of diversity by using an allegorical future where multiethnic crews could work together to explore outer space. Yet the aliens they encountered often looked somewhat human, and aside from cultural conflicts, these aliens are largely relatable and comprehensible. In the best cases, they adopt the Starfleet banner and act like typical Federation citizens (humans). Only when the truly bizarre is encountered do we see a real tension with a cosmic Other. Non-humanoid species may be corporeal or otherwise, space-dwelling or preternatural. Their sapience emerges only when they chose to be relatable to humans. Yet this unhuman-ness resides not only in the strangeness of aliens, but the strangeness of ourselves.

How do we conceive of a thing which is by definition beyond our conception? The characters of *Star Trek* managed to reconcile the truly strange, and managed to understand the true Other not without horror, but in spite of it.

In *Star Trek VI: The Undiscovered Country*, Jim Kirk and his crew invite a group of Klingon diplomats to dinner onboard the Enterprise, a starship so often paired against such foes. During the course of conversation, Commander Chekov claims the Federation believes "all planets have a sovereign claim to inalienable human rights." To which Azetbur, daughter of the Klingon Chancellor responds, "Inalien... If only you could hear yourselves? 'Human rights.' Why the very name is racist. The Federation is no more than a 'homo sapiens' only club" (Meyer, et al. 1991).

Due to budget limitations, *Star Trek* and most other science fiction tend to portray the alien in film as almost exclusively humanoid - bipedal, average height 5'6," and usually with odd skull features, ornaments or coloring that denotes their non-humanness. But occasionally, *Star Trek* depicts beings who challenge human comprehension, similar to Lovecraft's terror of "starfish" aliens. These are fundamentally different entities. As Trig writes,

> the inclusion of the "un" in unhuman aligns the concept with the notion of the uncanny. Like the uncanny, my account of the unhuman accents the gesture of repression that is synonymous with the uncanny, especially in its Freudian guise. With the unhuman, something comes back to haunt the human without it being fully integrated into humanity... the unhuman is tied up with notions of alienage... (116).

Trig is arguing for a phenomenology not exclusive to humans, since we often presume a human materiality. Phenomenology should not be anthropocentric, and this is where speculative realism enters the picture. Harman unveils a Heideggerian root to ontologies of objects, by arguing that things "withdraw from human view into a dark subterranean reality that never becomes present to practical action any more than it does to theoretical awareness" (1). This place evokes Morton's conception of a "coral reef" of phenomena and things that have always been here with a strange life of their own, underneath Heideggerian Dasein's trip through Angst, beneath Husserl's phenomenology, and below Kant's discovery of transcendental space and time behind thought itself. Bogst believes rejecting correlationalism while embracing multiple other correlations results in some form of centrism, or trading our anthropocentrism for something else. Speculative realism must be applied. Why not apply it to speculative fiction like *Star Trek*?

This search for a decentralized look at human-nonhuman relations is also similar to actor network theory and Latour's discussion of hybrids, another form of cyborg resulting from our historical interdependence on and with things. In any of these cases, investigating alien materiality places our attention in contexts entirely elsewhere from human experience. In *Star Trek*, encounters with aliens force us to ask things like "what is it like to be a non-corporeal entity?" Or, like Shaviro's "what is it like to be a rock," what would it be like to be a Horta, an alien which seems very much like a rock? These questions are repeated in encounters where we see an initial horror and confusion, then attempts to communicate, and finally, a reconciliation between the human and non-human. But the unhuman is not just present in elaborate costumes, but within ourselves.

Trig writes that horror as an affective response is necessary when "experiencing oneself as other." Horror is about transformations between our being and that of the unhuman. "Only in the disjunction between the experience of oneself as human and the realization that this same entity is fundamentally beyond humanity is the possibility of an unhuman phenomenology conceivable" (119). Massumi follows idea in an exploration of the nonhuman at the heart of the human. Instinct is "the instrumentality of intelligence wrapped into reflex" (1) The supernormal is a force of "affective propulsion" where instinctual forces are totally embodying. This is how the cuckoo bird functions — it invades the nest of another bird by preying on the maternal instincts so effectively that the host's chicks are neglected and can be pushed from the nest without incident. Massumi writes that "animal becoming is most human. It is in becoming animal that the human recurs to what is nonhuman at the heart of what moves it. This makes it surpassingly human." *The Next Generation* episode "Genesis" adopts instinct and becoming with the natural guise of horror. A medical treatment gone awry causes the crew to "devolve" into various monstrosities. The normally clean and bright decks of the Enterprise-D become dark. Crew quarters turn into exotic, primeval environments. Those affected by this disease exhibit strong instinctual behaviors - predatory mating, obsessively soaking in a bath, weaving webs and skittish movements that mirror the strangeness of their changing appearance. A "becoming" (Deleuze & Guattari) takes over, as crew hierarchy falls apart and new, primitive ecologies reemerge across decks. Data notes that most of the crew are scattered through the ship: "However, there are several large concentrations in the arboretum and the aquatic lab." Commander Riker being reduced to an *Australopithecine* is the strongest sign of this, as he goes from being unable to command others and focus on the simplest thoughts, to dumbly pounding on Picard's fishtank.

Citing Lapoujade's assertion that "at the heart of the human is nothing human," Masumi is arguing for instinct without horror, something that comes up in Manning's work on artfulness and intuition. The "memory of the future" we create is part of a process of always becoming - we have never arrived at the future, it is always emerging (or again, becoming) - as is the case in *The Next Generation* episode "Emergence." The Enterprise-D itself births a lifeform which must use holographic characters as projections of its desires and wishes to communicate with the crew. Engaging with uncertain beings and scenarios via intuition is often promoted by Starfleet officers. La Forge tells Data in "The Defector" that while intuition interferes with rationality, it's necessary because "you just can't rely on the plain and simple facts. Sometimes they lie."

This uncertainty is a final element to how *Star Trek* engages with the unhuman. Episodes like "Schisms" (*TNG*), "Phantasms" (*TNG*) and "Realm of Fear" (*TNG*) use doubt to describe how characters are unable to rely on their own perceptions when engaging with the unhuman. In "Schisms," Riker wakes after going to bed moments earlier. He is in disbelief when told that the entire night has passed. The collective foggy memory of crew members abducted to a subspace torture chamber must be pieced back together though hazy feelings. Psychoanalysis gets a nod in "Phantasms," where Data subconsciously perceives interphasic organisms feeding on their cellular cohesion, but coexisting with the crew through another realm. Data's nightmares are the only clue to saving the ship.

Uncertainty also emerges through this psychoanalytic frame. "Realm of Fear" uses Reginald Barclay's neuroses and his terror over teleporting to describe the difficulty in communicating uncertainty. When he tells others about how he sees something while using the transporter, no one believes him. He becomes afraid of not only those creatures, but of "transporter psychosis," that he is driving himself crazy. The experience of "oneself as the other" (Trigg) is also seen in other episodes with psychological layers, such as Riker's experience in a psychiatric facility in "Frame of Mind," O'Brien's implanted memories of prison in "Hard Time," or Bashir's exploration of his subconscious in "Distant Voices." Their experience with psychologists (or, perhaps "alienists") reveals the self-as-other and the need for an honest embrace of that strangeness.

All of these scenarios are resolved are resolved because the crew acknowledges horror and strangeness. Beneath horror is ignorance: "what is this thing, how can it hurt me?" Starfleet is full of people who defy John Gray's argument that science and technology evolves, but never "civilization" or people. Despite Quark's comments in *Deep Space Nine's* "The Siege of AR-558," the humans are idealized explorers who are never overwhelmed by the horrific otherness of things they encounter. Instead, they acknowledge "Infinite Diversity in Infinite Combinations" and attempt to respect life in all its forms, from the Horta to the Crystalline Entity. The former is a being responsible for the death of all life from multiple planets. Despite the lack of communication, Picard's crew attempt to respect this unhuman thing's place in the ecology of their fictional universe. Ignorance is only improvable after it has been acknowledged.

Horror may be a default mode of encountering the unhuman, but *Star Trek's* optimism those encounters as resolvable through the sincerity and willingness of Starfleet to accept the strange, embrace and learn from the unhuman, and ultimately treat the alien as worthy of "inalienable" rights. We should be so gracious, with the alien all around us (Bogost) and even inside ourselves. We do not need to go to space to encounter the strange, and *Star Trek* shows us that our responses are not limited to horror.

References

Bogost, I. (2012). *Alien Phenomenology, or, What It's Like to Be a Thing*. Minneapolis: University of Minnesota Press.

Deleuze, G., & Guattari, F. (1987). A Thousand Plateaus: Capitalism and Schizophrenia. *Minneapolis: University of Minnesota Press*.

Harman, G. (2002). *Tool-Being: Heidegger and the Metaphysics of Objects*. Chicago: Open Court.

Latour, B. (1993). *We Have Never Been Modern*. (C. Porter, Trans.). Cambridge, MA: Harvard University Press.

Lovecraft, H. P. (2005). *At the Mountains of Madness: The Definitive Edition*. Modern Library.

Gray, J. (2013). *The Silence of Animals: On Progress and Other Modern Myths*. Macmillan.

Masumi, B. (2015) The Supernormal Animal. In Grusin, R. (Eds.) *The Nonhuman Turn*. Minneapolis: University of Minnesota Press.

Manning, E. (2015) Artfulness. In Grusin, R. (Eds.) *The Nonhuman Turn*. Minneapolis: University of Minnesota Press.

Meyer, N. (Director), Meyer, N., Nimoy, L., & Narita, H. (Writers), & Winter, R., & Nimoy, L. (Producers). (1991). Star Trek VI: *The Undiscovered Country* [Motion picture on Netflix]. United States: Paramount Pictures.

Morton, T. (2015). *They Are Here*. In Grusin, R. (Eds.) *The Nonhuman Turn*. Minneapolis: University of Minnesota Press.

Shaviro, S. (2015) Consequences of Panpsychism. In Grusin, R. (Eds.) *The Nonhuman Turn*. Minneapolis: University of Minnesota Press.

Trigg, D. (2013). "The Horror of Darkness" Toward an Unhuman Phenomenology. *Speculations a Journal of Speculative Realism*, (4), 113–121.

The Future, According to *Trek*

Allison Broesder

Stories that capture essential truths about their times, culture and the human condition become timeless. They are passed on from one generation to the next. Aesop's Fables, Grimm's Fairytales, and classic literature such as *To Kill a Mockingbird, The Lord of the Rings,* and *Frankenstein* are prime examples. Television, as a medium, is no different. Some shows have the ability to harness truth about their time in such a way that they transcend it. They become classic examples of screenwriting's ability to examine our complexities. They can explore our past, present, and future, giving us pause to consider just where it is we have been and where we are going. Some shows can become beacons of hope, giving us glimpses into a bright and fantastical future. *Star Trek* has done this since its debut in the 1960s and continues to do so with each incarnation or reboot it launches. It continues to grasp truths that resonate, exemplify what is the best about us and show us a future that is not only bright but worth fighting for. The show may have been billed as a western set in space, but *Star Trek* captures so much more about what it means to be human and to strive for a better tomorrow.

The casting done on the original series alone exemplifies so much of the stories we see told in its short three season run. To cast a range of different people with different backgrounds, races, religions, and histories in the 1960s was truly a bold move. The regular cast comprised of an African American woman, an Asian man, and two Jewish men. It is a groundbreaking gathering of people showing that we are a stronger people and world for embracing diversity rather than shunning or oppressing it. Their characters reflected much of this thinking, allowing *Star Trek* to prove that we are better together than segregated.

These characters worked together on screen through their undeniable chemistry and proved over and over again that not only could people of varying backgrounds work together for a greater and common good, they could do so with true affection, courage, and loyalty. The fact that a member of their crew was not even human mattered little to the group—despite all of Bones's grousing. Often, it seemed that any attempt by others outside the Enterprise to latch onto Spock's half-blood status caused the group to close ranks and come to his defense—often a revolutionary and dangerous concept of the 1960s landscape. No one questioned if Uhura could do her job at communications, and Sulu often navigated the Enterprise with clear expertise. The notion that their races or genders made any difference hardly ever makes the discussion. The fact that we also are shown the first interracial kiss in television history is evidence of Star Trek's ability to push the envelope all the while forcing us to face society's shifting sands.

Not only do the characters capture a brighter and more diverse future, the structure of their universe does so brilliantly. The concept of the Federation, modeled clearly on the existing UN, allows for Kirk, Spock, and the crew of the Enterprise to interact with many other cultures, races, planets, and species. It allows them to stand on a foundation centered on peace—even if it doesn't always work out that way. The attempts to show that each race and each planet that joins the Federation has a voice of their own proves that they are trying to build a better galaxy and a better future through diplomatic and peaceful measures as a first line of defense rather than turning to violence. Those who are members have voices and places within its structure and while the system is not perfect—as the UN itself is not perfect—it is the attempt at trying to build this kind of foundation that makes *Star Trek* a beacon of hope that we can someday perhaps work through our own difficulties, conflicts, and struggles without resorting to war as a first response.

These aspects of the show and franchise are captured in key original series episodes. "Mirror, Mirror," "Let that Be Your Last Battlefield," and "The Mark of Gideon" all show us varying aspects of *Star Trek*'s ability to endure and transcend its time period. It shows how we can hope for a better future, a better understanding of ourselves, and a better connection amongst our diverse world. "Mirror, Mirror" shows the Federation as it would be if run as a dictatorship. To ascend, one must kill their superior, and violence as the first response, not the last resort. It shows a darker side of ourselves through the doppelgangers presented and reminds us that this lurks out there if we don't do anything to stop its accession. This is the darkness that threatens us all—as it is in us all in varying degrees. It is the very nature that we must recognize and stand against in order to strive for that brighter future presented by the show.

"Let That Be Your Last Battlefield" tackles race relations head on. When they take a wounded refugee aboard, they discover that his most striking feature is to have one-half of his face black and the other half white. He is being chased and seeks political asylum. When the crew of the Enterprise is confronted by his pursuer, they note that his face has the same appearance—simply reversed. Both hate each other so much and are after one another for crimes committed by their respective races. The episode is a clear chastisement on racist beliefs, pointing towards the notion that we must and can rise above such thoughts if we are to survive as a species in the future. It is this episode that perhaps allows *Star Trek* to truly build a foundation that shows we can perhaps set aside such notions and build a better future for all and not simply for the few.

"The Mark of Gideon," shows us one of the best ethical debates the series has ever had. It asks us about health care, about the needs of the many and of the few, and begs us to understand what it means to live in such a clearly overpopulated world. It challenges the concept that finding a cure to any and all diseases is to be seen as a good thing—and it makes us think long and hard about what living without any diseases may mean in the long run for a human population. Its exploration of these subjects gives us pause as we unravel the mystery Kirk is faced with as he is alone on his ship with but one woman—used to contract the very virus they need to weed the population and cease the suffering of crammed living spaces with little to no hope of relief.

Finally, the "Errand of Mercy," posits a question about war. The Federation and Klingon Empire are both drawn to a neutral planet, Organia, to negotiate terms. Both sides are hot-blooded and ready to battle one another over the rights to either annex or maintain the independence of Organia. The people of the planet are peaceful and make no attempts to resist the oncoming Klingon annexation. Even when Kirk and Spock attempt to push them to fight back, it is for naught. Even after the Klingon Commander "kills" hundreds of its citizens, they refuse to resist. Kirk and the Commander are pushed to the brink, needing to fight one another and their ships to undergo a battle—one for the citizens Klingons have killed and the other for the right to advance the Empire. The leader of Organia is stunned that Kirk would be willing to wage a war—that he's debating in favor of doing so despite the fact that it will eventually end in peace and that millions will have been killed in the process when they could have avoided that by negotiating peace in the first place. The examination in the episode pushes us to consider—to wonder about a future that may not see war as the first step to solving a nation's problem. It asks us to examine our needs to wage war—why we do, the costs it incurs, and the fallout from its cessation. It is this message that allows Star Trek to transcend its genre and medium, making key arguments for our betterment and a brighter future.

The original series movies also point to so much of these same debates and issues. The *Wrath of Khan, Search for Spock*, and *Voyage Home* as a trilogy prove that we can rise above any challenge, face down our fears with human hearts, and fight back to save our futures—even from ourselves. The ethical debate of the Genesis project asks us to question how far we should go with our science, the loss and resurrection of Spock asks us to search our own hearts and answer the question, "Is it the needs of the many or of the few?" and the *Voyage Home* asks us to see beyond our own folly before it is far too late to stop the measure—even if the movie itself bends time and space to save the day. It is what makes them endure as classics and allows them to pass from one generation to the next.

Not only do these episodes and movies exemplify the various debates, challenges, and revolutionary ideas that make the series endure well into its fiftieth year, the show's technology and health systems do much of the same. Much of the technology introduced in the original series has been replicated in some method in the real world. Pick up a cell phone, go to a doctor and get a temperature taken, or take in the wonder that is the International Space Station, and it is as if the science fiction of *Star Trek* has become reality. While other aspects such as warp drive and starships are still light years removed from reality, the fact that any of their technology has become firm reality proves that there is a future that can be bold and bright.

Star Trek proves to us that we can go boldly where no one has gone before—be it in our ethical debates, our technology, or acceptance of others, or our ability to find peace even amongst the most dangerous times. It proves that it can stand the test of time as a story-telling vehicle that can transform itself from *Original Series* to *Next Gen* to *Voyager* and beyond. It continues to make us answer difficult questions—ones that are as pertinent today as they were in the 1960s, and it truly proves to us that we can and will live long and prosper if only we can continue to seek those answers for as long as it shall take.

Empathy, the Prime Directive, and Respect for Others: From *Star Trek* to the Everyday

Vivian Chin

Live Long and Prosper! Although LLAP may seem more like a form of farewell than an opening, it is possible to repurpose moments from *Star Trek* and its offshoots to suit one's needs. May you live long and prosper can serve as a friendly greeting with a special meaning to insiders. Although orthodox fans might wish to maintain a more literal approach, others can still find themselves in accord with the title of a study of the television serial, *Living with Star Trek*, when bits of shows resurface, possibly misremembered, prompted by the quotidian and serving as insights regarding everyday life.

Of the many iterations of *Star Trek*, the original series and *The Next Generation* provide viewers with ways to experience valuable life lessons regarding empathy, respect for difference, and possibly anti-colonial politics. Cognitive psychologists have posited that theory of mind, or the functioning of mirror neurons to engage empathy, is more likely to occur through literary fiction than through popular fiction. However, *Star Trek* can also produce empathetic responses via its representation of non-humanoid life forms. Although a fear and hatred of difference may appear in narratives involving the Ferenghi, the Romulins, and other unfriendly beings; and a decidedly anti-Communist perspective may manifest in narratives of the Borg, the cast of the original *Star Trek* embodied the zeitgeist of the later 1960s with its uncommonly racially diverse cast. And while some female characters may resemble the extreme body proportions of a Barbie doll, others are less beholden to such physical standards of femininity. From the mother Horta to accelerated humanoids, from excessively cerebral evildoers to those who speak in an untranslatable allegory, *Star Trek* shows us that those who are unmistakable Other are worthy of respect and empathy.

The writer of the blog *Neurologism* re-imagines *Star Trek* and produces silly connections between *Star Trek* and mirror neurons, creating captions for familiar characters. Counselor Deanna Troi remarks, "Captain, I'm detecting high levels of mirror neuron activity!" Data, in confusion, asks, "I can haz mirror neurons?," and Spock as a voice of reason, states, "Mirror neurons? Highly illogical." *Star Trek*,

mirror neurons, theory of mind, and empathy are thus in the ether—
with humor and to broaden interest in neuroscience.

Two characters serve as empathic role models, Gem and Deanna
Troi. Regarding Gem, McCoy explains, "Complete empathy. She must
be a totally functional empath. Her nervous system actually connected
to yours to counteract the worst of your symptoms and with her
strength, she virtually sustained your body's physical reactions," thus
healing Kirk. While Gem is mute, Deanna Troi and her cleavage can
speak, suggesting an evolution of the empath that still conforms to
gendered expectations that properly socialized women will be sensitive
to the needs of others often to the point of self-sacrifice.

While the Prime Directive may serve as a plot device bound to
the butterfly effect, it can also appear to take an anti-colonial stance.
Film, Television and the Psychology of the Social Dream notes this
position. "The prime directive conveys a not-so-subtle anti-colonialist
and anti-imperialist message to be sure, but it can also be interpreted as
a warning to countries to think twice before using force on recalcitrant
adversaries" (40). Thus its politics can be both empathetic and pre-
emptively defensive.

Popular culture can maintain a certain interpretive flexibility
because of the ways that the audience can interact with the text. Lincoln
Geraghty comments in *Living with Star Trek* that pop culture at times
presents a utopian future "…the fictional text is becoming more and
more of a template for how fans might achieve that utopia and [...] its
binary nature as an open and closed text is becoming increasingly
contested in the work of those who study its devoted audience" (6).
Geraghty cites the scholar George Lipsitz regarding the power of pop
culture. "Television in particular performs as a 'therapeutic voice
ministering to the open wounds of the psyche' through its vocabulary
of emotion and empathy…" (6). A viewer can connect to a text and find
healing.

An episode of healing transpires in "name of show." Through a
mind meld with Spock, we hear the mother Horta lament, "The end of
life…" and despite this creatures low tech abject appearance, we can
empathize with her condition and fear of genocide. Protesting his call to
heal the Horta, Bones complains, "I'm a doctor, not a bricklayer!" This
complaint echoes his remark, "I'm a doctor, not a coal miner" in a
different episode. Dr. McCoy denigrates laborers but goes on to
perform work that he at first considers dirty and beneath him. His

consideration for the wounded or sick surpasses his elitism. Viewers can learn to approach distasteful yet helpful tasks with empathy to serve those in need.

The fast-moving people of "Wink of an Eye" inhabit a different time zone, and despite being scantily clothed, suggest the possibility of empathy for people who function "differently" in time, such as people who are considered "slow" or even people with executive function challenges.

A deep understanding of multiculturalism eventually manifests when Captain Picard finally understands the power of narrative and urges an alien to "Give me more about Darmok." Viewers are invited to consider how metaphors are us, how mythologies and allegory shape our understanding, "Darmok on the ocean, A metaphor for being alone, isolated, Darmok on the ocean" he intones, at last comprehending the necessity to have empathy for an unfamiliar culture through its narrative framework.

In everyday reality, when one finds oneself in a situation of competitive intellectualism, one might recall the mean beings with the big brains who showed no empathy and as a result, received a harsh lecture on humanity from Captain Kirk. How one might remember or misremember this episode, being able to imagine offensive people as inhumane aliens can be both entertaining and empowering, with the demand for empathy ever present.

While some may wonder if claims regarding mirror neurons constitute pseudoscience, or hold that such neurons only exist in primates, Vittorio Gallese and Michele Guerra, assert in "Embodying Movies: Embodied Simulation and and Film Studies," that ""After two decades of research it is established that a similar mirror mechanism is also present in the human brain" (184).

Empathy and respect are necessary to human coexistence. In order to seek out new ways of practicing empathy, we may remember and rewrite episodes of *Star Trek* to fit our needs. The future of cultural studies includes cognitive science, neurobiology, and a consideration of the embodied cognition possible in viewing such an anachronistic yet enduring medium as television. Let us boldly go to a place of better understanding of the functioning and power of empathy.

References

Gallese, Vitorio and Michele Guerra. (2012). "Embodying Movies: Embodied Simulation and Film Studies. *Cinema : Journal of Philosophy and the Moving Image,* 3: 183-210.

Geraghty, Lincoln. (2007). *Living with Star Trek.* I.B. Taurus.

John, Yohan. (2013). "Do mirror neurons explain understanding, or is it the other way round?" *Neurologism.* March 2013. Web. https://neurologism.com/2013/03/

Kidd, David Comer and Emanuele Castalano. (2013). "Reading Literary Fiction Improves Theory of Mind." *Science* 18 Oct 2013:Vol. 342, Issue 6156, pp. 377-380.

Rieber, Robert A. and Robert J. Kelly. (2014). *Film, Television and the Psychology of the Social Dream.* Springer.

Star Trek, "The Devil in the Dark." Season 1, Episode 25.

Star Trek, "The Empath." Season 3, Episode 12.

Star Trek. "Wink of an Eye." Season 3, Episode 13.

Star Trek: The Next Generation. "Darmok." Season 5, Episode 2.

"*Trek* Fandom Always Wins!": The Literary Legacy of *Star Trek*

Cait Coker

Fan Studies has often given *Star Trek* credit for being the moment when fandom changed: when women entered into the science fiction convention scene in droves, when fans began writing and circulating vast quantities of fanfiction, when the relationships between content producers and fans evolved to become more than just a straightforward hierarchy. Because of its longevity through various incarnations, *Star Trek* fandom has never died, nor has its fannish activity paused; rather, each generation of fans has contributed to a vast literary legacy through print and digital media—one that has even spawned the Tumblr tag "Trek fandom always wins!" While TOS episodes themselves have contributed to numerous popular fannish tropes seen elsewhere (including sex pollen, telepathic bonds/soulmates, and "fuck or die" scenarios), and yes, the slash genre's identification of K/S, we should consider other elements of fannish publishing such as the franchise's unusual interplay between fanfiction, media tie-in novels, and actual *Star Trek* canon (from character names to a number of high-profile fans-turned-pro writers, such as Jean Lorrah, Peter David, and Ronald D. Moore); the transition from print zines to listservs, online archives, and locked fan communities; and finally, how the fandom in many ways served as *the* model of fannish literary activity for five decades.

The earliest fanzines appeared while the show was still on the air; notable titles include *Inside Star Trek* (July 1968-1979) and *Spockanalia* (September 1967-June 1970). Material from both those publications and others would be reprinted in the licensed compilation *Star Trek Lives! Personal Notes and Anecdotes*, edited by Jacqueline Lichtenberg, Sondra Marshak and Joan Winston and published in 1975. Amongst other things, the book includes what the *Oxford English Dictionary* identifies as the first time the term "fan fiction" is printed in its current usage (the term, in use since the 1930s, originally signified only fiction by a fan of SFF, rather than amateur, derivative, or transformative works).

However, *Star Trek Lives!* was rather controversial, consisting as it did of the work of Big Name Fans; many readers felt it was neither indicative of the fannish scene, nor that the editors should have been legitimized in this way. The book discusses several notable fanfics, including the shared-universe *Kraith* series (1970-1980) by Lichtenberg and the epic hurt-comfort novel *Spock Enslaved!* (1974), and includes sometimes lengthy quotes, but no full stories. This would change with the publication of *Star Trek: The New Voyages I* (1976) and *II* (1978), a pair of anthologies edited by Sondra Marshak and Myrna Culbreath that included nine fan stories apiece with introductions by Trek actors and writers. Other officially licensed collections of fan writing would not appear until 1998 with the yearly *Strange New Worlds* anthologies; they ceased publication in 2007 and were only revived in 2016.

Meanwhile, the official series of novels initially drew heavily on fan writers who began to turn pro. Jean Lorrah wrote several fan novels, including *The Night of the Twin Moons* (1976) which was reprinted several times because of its popularity, and then went on to write several licensed volumes, including *The Vulcan Academy Murders* (1982) and *The IDIC Epidemic* (1988). A particularly interesting contribution came from Barbara Hambly, now best known for her numerous volumes of mysteries. In her novel *Ishmael* (1985), a time-traveling and amnesiac Spock finds himself in 1860s Seattle and taken in by Aaron Stempel—the antagonist (played by Mark Lenard, better known to fans as Sarek of Vulcan!) of the television show *Here Come the Brides* (1968-1970). In addition to providing an ending for that show—also cancelled—it featured numerous quiet cameos via character description from other genre favorites, such as the Fourth Doctor (described as carrying a flute in the pocket of his coat), a certain scruffy space smuggler (Han Solo from *Star Wars*), a man in black (Paladin from *Have Gun Will Travel*), and trail-hands from Virginia City (Little Joe and Hoss Cartwright from *Bonanza*). The novel was accepted and already printed before anyone noticed the characters from the other shows; luckily, rights for *Here Come the Brides* belonged to the same company, and it went on the market without a problem.

Numerous print zines of fan works appeared well into the 1990s and into the early 2000s, with novels and serials devoted both *TOS* and the other series. As the Internet became more widely available, online fannish communities created numerous listservs, websites, and online archives for fan fiction. The release of the 2009 *Star Trek* Reboot spawned yet another generation of fandom, this one almost completely online (I have found only two print zines with Reboot characters, both of which are also crossovers with the *Lord of the Rings* movieverse). Interestingly, there was a great deal of cross-generation interaction: "Fact finder" communities emerged for younger fans who had questions about the older canon and fanon, and older fans happily answered questions, recommended specific episodes, or pointed them to other useful resources. Further, fan zines as a medium and literature of their own are finally being recognized by academia in general and academic libraries in particular, with numerous projects currently motion at both Texas A&M University and the University of Iowa to catalog, digitize, and preserve our fannish heritage. At the same time, the Organization for Transformative Works has founded the academic journal *Transformative Works and Cultures* to discuss fan works more generally, and AO3, or *Archive of Our Own*, as a massive online archive of fan writing and art. For its Fiftieth Anniversary, the literary legacy of *Star Trek* is both assured and growing.

The Persistence of Scholarly Interest in *Star Trek*

Bruce E. Drushel

It is not surprising that *Star Trek* is the subject of much media attention in 2016, given that the original television series debuted on NBC-TV on a September evening fifty years before, or that much of that attention would focus on its longevity as a franchise. Few fictional creations of television and film aside from James Bond and *Doctor Who* can claim such sustained popular interest. More surprising has been the interest expressed by scholars and other serious writers, which seems if anything to be increasing in both variety and depth. Particularly compelling is the absence of both purely historical interests in the franchise's texts and condescension toward its fans. Instead, authors regard the franchise as very much alive, with relevance to contemporary concerns and as multifaceted in both its appeal to audiences and to the fields of knowledge to which it speaks.

Literary Criticism

The sheer number of stories produced by *Star Trek*'s five live-action television series, 13 films, animated series, and countless novels and fan fiction tales provide ample fodder for literary critics. Roughly speaking, the film and television stories number about 700 and the officially licensed novels, short stories, audio books, and e-books nearly 800, in addition to an uncountable number of fan fiction stories. Among the approaches have been its comedic form and individualism (Richards) and the functions of its iconic characters to explore such issues as human rights, masculinity, militarism, and colonialism (Harrison) as well as the cultural conditions that allow for queer readings by audiences of nominally heterosexual (or asexual) bodies.

Race & Ethnicity

Its pioneering multicultural bridge crew established the reputation of the original *Star Trek* as inclusive and utopian in an era of racial and ethnic division in the U.S. Even so, a number of academic studies have called into question the fulsomeness of producers' commitment to racial equality. Among them, Bernardi has acknowledged *Star Trek*'s involvement in a liberal-humanist project embracing, not just race, but also Cold War philosophy and pacifism. But it also accuses the series' producers of inconsistencies, contradictions, and even facilitation of racist practice in pursuit of its diversity creed. A second study by Pounds compares treatment of race and ethnicity in *Star Trek* and *Star Trek: The Next Generation*, noting the differences in approaches taken but also the different contexts undergirding race relations in Hollywood and broader society in 1967 and 1987.

Gender & Sexuality

At least as controversial have been the *Star Trek* franchise's representations of women and sexual minorities. While critics have praised the television series and films for populating both starship crews and alien cultures with women in titular positions of leadership, the characters frequently are valued for excellence in traits associated with male-defined women, including nurturing, subservience, and conventional femininity. *Star Trek: Voyager* particularly has been singled out for women in such prominent roles as captain and chief engineer, though it also featured a waif-like alien whose chief function was to augment the holographic doctor's interpersonal skills and an emotionally-stunted Borg female who dressed in form-fitting "cat" suits. Palmer observed that the original series' most prominent female cast member, Lieutenant Uhura, outranked most of the crew of the *U.S.S. Enterprise* yet was almost never placed in positions of authority, even in the later films.

If their limited roles tended to perpetuate a second-class status for women in the Star Trek universe, the absence of identifiably lesbian, gay, bisexual, transgender characters completely erased queerness from it. Accounts from those associated with the franchise depict a production environment that was, at best, insensitive to queer fans and members of the cast and crew (including actor George Takei and writer David Gerrold) and, at worst, hostile to them (Drushel). Studies of Star Trek point to characters who can be read queerly; however, many of these (e.g., Q, Kivas Fajo, the Genaii) have been antagonists or, in the case of *Star Trek: The Next Generation's* Traveler or *Star Trek: Deep Space Nine's* Garak, suspicious in either past or motive.

Fandom

Of course, an early area of interest by scholars was *Star Trek*'s fan culture, which began with pleas to the network not to cancel the original series in the late-1960s, became more active when bereft fans began sharing their own stories after *Star Trek* was cancelled in 1969, grew with the rise of conventions in the 1970s and 1980s, and moved into uncharted territory with the distribution online of fanfiction and fan-produced episodes on video. A key study by Lamb and Veith introduced many in the scholarly community to "slash" fiction, in which a mostly straight, female community shares homoerotic versions of the relationships among canonical *Star Trek* characters, including Captain Kirk and Mr. Spock. Another explores a variant of fan video, so-called "vidding," in which previously unrealized subtext is foregrounded by the synchronization of key scenes with evocative music (Coppa). Seminal work in the study of fan fiction came from Henry Jenkins, who dismissed the characterization of fans as social misfits and mindless consumers and legitimized their appropriation of franchise characters and themes as "texual poaching." Jenkins is among those arguing for fans as active, rather than passive, audiences who force primary texts to accommodate their alternative interests.

 Star Trek was among the charter group of cultural artifact to be the subject of Intellect Publishing's *Fan Phenomenon* book series. In the introductory chapter, Drushel argues for *Star Trek* as an exemplar of media-based fandom. Subsequent chapters in his anthology address *Star Trek* fandom in its various forms, including the late-career metamorphosis of actor George Takei into in-demand speaker, social media icon, and conscience of the LGBT rights movement, the fraught relationship of a "satellite" fan to more intense expressions of attachment to its stories and characters, parodies of fandom, and the impact on fan culture of the recent "rebooting" of the franchise.

Religion, Ethics, & Philosophy

Character relationships in serial texts that evolve over time frequently are revealing of the inner perspectives those characters and, to audiences and critics alike, may suggest tenets of familiar creeds and philosophies. Jindra is among those scholars who find religion in *Star Trek*, born in fandom's regularized practices, canon, and hierarchy. He also believes the traditional ridicule and persecution fans of the franchise have experienced have resonances for adherents to many religious organizations.

 Likewise, the imaged world of *Star Trek* has evolved in a way that parallels the changing values of our lived experience, including issues of self-determination, equality, and proxy warfare. In their book, *The Ethics of Star Trek*, Barad and Robertson relate the lessons of Star Trek to the teachings of the world's great philosophers on such subjects as good and evil, right and wrong, and power and corruption. More broadly, McCrone has used texts from *Star Trek* to argue against what he calls the "Myth of Irrationality," or the Western belief that human creativity and emotional behavior arise from deep wells of irrationality.

Politics

Political scientists, too, have mined the cultural phenomenon of *Star Trek*. Jutta Weldes has argued the franchise's films and series are potent examples of the prospect for popular culture texts to inform and influence state action, just as the broader culture is imagined to do. Weldes also makes the case for connections between iconic science fiction texts like *Star Trek* and issues in the realms politics and diplomacy, including imperialism, resistance, representation, and anti-collectivism.

Science

Star Trek has been remarkably prescient in anticipating technologies that eventually came into common usage or whose future development is highly plausible. From tablet computers to solid-state memory to tiny wireless communication devices to needleless injections, the writers for the *Star Trek* franchise were, more often than not, on target. And the science underlying such prospective developments as faster-than-light travel and matter-energy-transportation, if not conclusive, at least is compelling. In his forward to *The Physics of Star Trek*, no less than Stephen Hawking wrote, "The physics that underlies *Star Trek* is sure worth investigating. To confine our attention to terrestrial matters would be to limit the human spirit." (Krauss, xiii). In some cases, technologies in common usage in series' episodes have spurred scientists to speculate on the science that might enable them. Though 3D printing crudely approximates *Star Trek*'s pattern replicators, Drum and Gordon for instance have proposed diatoms, a type of single-celled algae, as the foundation for the more sophisticated replication abilities *Star Trek*'s writers anticipate.

Conclusion

It would be facile to conclude this piece simply with the statement that the films, television episodes, and books of *Star Trek* are more than the simple escapist tales non-*aficionados* presume them to be. It would be more accurate and of greater credit to the creative forces behind *Star Trek* to say that they offer a unique example of iconic popular culture texts that raise questions worthy of systematic inquiry and are written in such a compelling fashion as to encourage investigation and produce pleasure in reading accounts of it.

References

Barad, Judith A. and Robertson, Ed. (2001). *The Ethics of Star Trek*. New York, NY: Perennial.

Bernardi, Daniel. (1998). *Star Trek and History: Race-ing Toward a White Future*. New Brunswick, NJ: Rutgers University Press.

Coppa, Francesca. (2008). Women, Star Trek, and the early development of fannish vidding. *Transformative Works and Cultures 1*.

Drum, Ryan.W. and Gordon, Richard. (2003). Star Trek replicators and diatom nanotechnology. *Trends in Biotechnology 21* (8), pp. 325-328.

Drushel, Bruce E. (2012). If art imitated reality: George Takei, coming out, and the insufferably straight Star Trek universe. In Pullen, Christopher (ed.). *LGBT Transnational Identity and the Media*. New York, NY: Palgrave MacMillan (273-289).

Drushel, Bruce E. (2013). *Fan Phenomenon: Star Trek*. Bristol, UK: Intellect Books.

Harrison, Taylor. (1996). *Enterprise Zones: Critical Positions on Star Trek*. Boulder, CO: Westview Press.

Jenkins III, Henry. (1988). Star Trek rerun, reread, rewritten: Fan writing as textual poaching. *Critical Studies in Mass Communication 5* (2), pp. 85-107.

Jindra, Michael. (1994). Star Trek fandom as a religious phenomenon. *Sociology of Religion 55* (1), pp. 27-51.

Krauss, Lawrence M. (2007). *The Physics of Star Trek*. New York: Basic Books.

Lamb, Patricia Frazer and Veith, Diana L. (1986). Romantic myth, transcendence, and Star Trek zines. In Palumbo, Donald (ed.), *Erotic Universe: Sexuality and Fantastic Literature*. Westport, CT: Praeger, pp. 235-55.

McCrone, John. (1994). *The Myth of Irrationality: The Science of the Mind From Plato to Star Trek*. New York, NY: Carroll & Graf Publishers.

Palmer, Dale. (2014). Redefinig the masculine hegemony: Gender and sexual politics in *Star Trek*. In Eiss, Harry (ed.). *Electric Sheep Slouching Towards Bethlehem: Speculative Fiction in a Post Modern World*. Cambridge, UK: Cambridge Scholars Publishing (99-110).

Pounds, Michael C. (1999). *Race in space*. Lanham, MD: Scarecrow Press.

Richards, Thomas. (1997). *The Meaning of Star Trek*. New York, NY: Doubleday.

Weldes, Jutta. (1999). Going cultural: Star Trek, state action, and popular culture. *Millennium-Journal of International Studies*, 28 (1), pp.117-134.

Weldes, Jutta. (2003). *To Seek Out New Worlds: Exploring Links Between Science Fiction and World Politics*. New York, NY: Palgrave MacMillan.

Star Trek: Deep Space Nine and Gene Roddenberry's Philosophy

Gordon Dymowski

Star Trek has always been considered an outlet for Gene Roddenberry's humanistic philosophy and desire to write stories that reflect upon the "human condition." Through *The Original Series* in 1966 and *The Next Generation* in 1987, Gene Roddenberry attempted to express his philosophy with mixed results. (For more details about *ST:TNG's* growing pains, readers are directed to the documentary *Chaos on the Bridge*).

However, despite Roddenberry's death in 1991, the production team made plans (with Roddenberry's approval) to move ahead on *Star Trek: Deep Space Nine*. Set on a space station around a newly-liberated planet near a wormhole, the show received initial criticism for "not being Trek enough." However, looking at some of the concepts within the show—and some of the themes it worked through—reveals that despite any direct involvement from Roddenberry, *Star Trek: Deep Space Nine* is the Trek spinoff that best reflects Roddenberry's philosophy.

As Roddenberry once remarked,

Star Trek was an attempt to say that humanity will reach maturity and wisdom on the day that it begins not just to tolerate, but take a special delight in differences in ideas and differences in life forms. [...] If we cannot learn to actually enjoy those small differences, to take a positive delight in those small differences between our own kind, here on this planet, then we do not deserve to go out into space and meet the diversity that is almost certainly out there.

Part of what gives *Deep Space Nine* its particular resonance is that diversity is treated in a very non-binary matter. For the first two seasons, *Deep Space Nine* resembled more of the "frontier town" Western trope of storytelling than *Star Trek's* usual focus of exploration and the loneliness of command. (Let's call it the "Horatio Hornblower" trope, for lack of a better term). By focusing on alien cultures needing to get along, rather than the usual good human/bad alien dichotomy (or even the more overt Cold War parallels between the Federation and the

Klingons), *Deep Space Nine* was able to explore diversity—and the impact of cultures upon individuals - than its more allegory-filled cousins.

Much of that diversity even reached into the cast, as *Star Trek: Deep Space Nine* featured an African-American male as its lead character. As the story begins, Benjamin Sisko has lost his wife, his ship, and much more due to the Battle of Wolf 359 ("The Best of Both Worlds"). Ironically, Sisko is then asked by Jean-Luc Picard—the man who Sisko holds responsible for his wife's loss—to run Deep Space Nine, formerly a Cardassian space-station overlooking Bajor called *Terok Nor.* Sisko's mission is to transition Bajor into Federation membership—a very daunting task, as dialogue in the first episode "Emissary" makes clear:

Commander Benjamin Sisko: Is it going to happen?

Capt. Picard: Not easily. The ruling parties are at each other's throats. Factions that were united against the Cardassians have resumed old conflicts.

Commander Benjamin Sisko: Sounds like they're not ready.

Capt. Picard: Your job is to do everything, short of violating the Prime Directive, to make sure that they are.

As the story progresses, Sisko learns that he is also considered the "Emissary" of the Prophets, figures in Bajoran spirituality. Throughout the series, Sisko's efforts to work through matters of state reflect Roddenberry's desire to tell stories about "social issues." Many *Deep Space Nine* stories not only work through general politics, but often focus on much shaper issues, whether around homelessness (the two-part "Past Tense"), war crimes from different perspectives ("Duet"), racism ("Far Beyond the Stars"), and even the bonds between fathers and sons ("The Visitor").

Through it all, at a time when portrayals of African-Americans were becoming more prevalent, Benjamin Sisko was a strong portrayal of a man with a very difficult mission, yet still found balance for family, baseball, and yet had the "loneliness of command." Unlike other *Star Trek* spin-offs, there was a genuine humanity in the commander, and who often struggled with his decisions (such as "In the Pale Moonlight").....

Another aspect of Roddenberry's philosophy that *Deep Space Nine* echoes is its willingness to question the status quo....even to the point of deconstructing the Federation itself. As the series progresses, we are introduced to the Maquis—a group of colonists amongst planets along the Federation/Cardasian border that oppose Federation policy. (Granted, they were introduced as a lead-in to *Star Trek: Voyager*, but they're *still* a critical concept. Eventually, the Federation finds that on the other side of the Bajoran wormhole is the Dominion, a near-dictatorship led by a shape-shifting race that was once persecuted, but who has now acquired dominance through genetically-created soldiers and diplomats. (Odo, the Security Chief of Deep Space Nine, is a member of this race...and is also very conflicted about his status). In the fourth season two-parter "Homefront/Paradise Lost," martial law is declared on Earth after it is suspected that Changelings (the alien race behind the Dominion) have infiltrated positions of power.

And this was five years before 9/11.

Religion and spirituality were usually taboo and/or rationalized on other spinoffs, but in *Deep Space Nine*, it was treated with great deference and respect. Despite knowledge that the "Prophets" were aliens, Sisko went out of his way to reiterate that Bajoran culture was very spiritual in nature, and refused to insult their culture. Even when it would have been advantageous for Sisko to use his status as Emissary, he chose not to...and many *Deep Space Nine* scripts avoid the usual tropes around "gods" (namely, they are gods, aliens, technology and/or children) that *Star Trek* series tended to rely on for storytelling.

One final aspect of Roddenberry's philosophy that *Deep Space Nine* reflects is that the series explores diversity within alien cultures. Klingon culture is given ample room to breathe in the series, moving away from the strictly samurai-like culture promoted in *The Next Generation*. Rom and Quark—the two Ferengi who run the bar—share widely different motivations: Quark is purely about greed while Rom has more noble intentions....there are way too many examples, but thankfully, *Deep Space Nine* provides plenty of opportunities for a Roddenberry-esque exploration of cultures.

As the first *Star Trek* property without Roddenberry's direct involvement, it is particularly ironic that *Deep Space Nine* is the show that most directly reflects his worldview. Unlike its starship-centric cousins, *Deep Space Nine* provided a unique look into community—and the greater social condition—which would have made Gene Roddenberry *very* proud.

Contesting the Boundaries of Fandom: Gender and *Star Trek Into Darkness*

Jaime Hartless and Sarah M. Corse

Our talk today is drawn from a project we are working on that examines the construction of the *Star Trek* fandom with particular attention to how identity claims are contested around gender. Our first analysis, entitled "Sci-Fi and Skimpy Outfits: Making Boundaries and Staking Claims to *Star Trek Into Darkness*," was published in the recent edited volume *Fan Girls in and Media: Creating Characters, Consuming Culture*.1 In it, we address a serious problem that afflicts many Sci-Fi and Fantasy fandoms—namely the domination of these spaces by men and the consequential exclusion of women. There have been countless think pieces on this subject in recent years, including articles exploring how women are accused of being 'Fake Geek Girls'2 when they express sincere interest in Sci-Fi franchises, analyses of how these franchises fail to provide a sufficient number of dynamic female characters3, and exposes of the harassment women face when they enter male-dominated fan industries4 (e.g., the harassment of female programmers and video game critics during Gamergate) and male-centered fandom communities5 (e.g., the exploitation and harassment of women at conventions like Comic Con.)

Our research focuses on the marginalization of women within the *Star Trek* fandom, specifically addressing how the reboot of the series has failed to update its treatment of women. We take as our central focus a controversy surrounding the recent film *Star Trek Into Darkness*, wherein Dr. Carol Marcus, played by actress Alice Eve, is needlessly objectified—forced to strip down to her underwear for reasons tangential to the plot, then ogled by Captain Kirk (and by extension the viewer). This brief interlude was amplified by the film's marketing team and highlighted in multiple trailers and TV spots.

This representation of Dr. Marcus was criticized, prompting screenwriter Damon Lindelof to issue an apology via Twitter, saying to his fans through multiple Tweets, "I copped to the fact that we should have done a better job of not being gratuitous in our representation of a barely clothed actress" before qualifying his apology with a justification that "We also had Kirk shirtless in underpants in both movies. Do not

222

want to make light of something that some construe as 'misogynistic' [sic]...What I'm saying is I hear you, I take responsibility and will be more mindful in the future." He and director J.J. Abrams later went on to apologize and explain their narrative choices in a variety different forums, acknowledging the controversy while ultimately explaining it away as a faithful representation of Captain Kirk's womanizing and justifying it on the grounds that there was comparable male nudity.

We were less interested in the reactions of the creators, however, than we were in how Sci-Fi fans understood the controversy. Through examining the comment feeds of news coverage of the incident, we found that Damon Lindelof's apology was received very negatively by many (male) Sci-Fi fans, who interpreted it as a concession to "political correctness," using authenticity6 claims to dismiss feminist critiques of female representation in the franchise. Framing themselves as the 'true' and most 'authentic' Star Trek fans, these predominantly male fans asserted that critics of the Alice Eve underwear scene misunderstand what Trek is really about, referencing *The Original Series* where female objectification was a normal and taken for granted aspect of the franchise. Trapped in a political context where feminist critiques are already not taken seriously,7 women who objected to this sexist representation struggled to have their criticisms recognized as legitimate.

When we analyzed the boundary work8 of fans in response to the Lindelof apology, we found two primary strategies in use. The first relies on inclusionary claims of authenticity that insist 'true fans' of *Star Trek* liked the Alice Eve scene. Such claims make boundaries on the basis of (1) displays of expertise such as references to the history of the *Star Trek* oeuvre from *The Original Series* onward, (2) assumptions that the 'true fandom' is homogenous and made up of heterosexual males, and (3) by claims that *STID* must be driven by market decisions based on the assumed fandom. The inclusionary claims are exemplified by commenters from *Entertainment Weekly* and the *National Post*, respectively, who say, in response to articles about the Lindelof apology that the scene is "[N]othing outside of the norm if you're familiar with *Star Trek* shows" and "[T]he issue here is that the people complaining likely have no idea who the character is and do not follow *Star Trek* lore." A later comment from the *ET* website similarly glosses over the debate, saying, "no one sensible cares." On *ComicBookMovie.com* a poster makes his understanding of the homogeneity of the male heterosexual fandom explicit: "yeah, apologize to the 10 women who saw this movie…" (ellipse in original) and two posts later "How many female Star Trek fans are there to piss off anyway? This is a 98% male franchise, of course we appreciate hot women in this. There was no need for an apology." On the same forum, another poster makes the third point with "Abrams know how to make a blockbuster…scantily clad ladies."

The second and complementary strategy is an exclusionary one focusing on the reviled 'others' who exist outside of the boundary of true fandom and who are presumed to have originated the critique of the scene. Posts on the *ET* website include ones naming "insecure females" as "the ones who feel offended, & therefore do the complaining," ones targeting feminism (i.e., "Is there anything good Feminism doesn't seek to destroy?"), and at least one blaming "fat girls" specifically (i.e., "'*Star Trek*': Damon Lindelof apologizes to fat girls for showing Alice Eve in her underwear. Corrected it for you"). Together, these two strategies demonstrate both the construction of symbolic boundaries[9] around communities of taste *and* the conflation of such symbolic boundaries with social boundaries[10], such as gender and sexuality.

Please see Corse and Hartless for a more complete analysis and description of data and methods.

Notes

1 Corse, Sarah and Jaime Hartless. 2015. "'Sci-Fi and Skimpy Outfits': Making Boundaries and Staking Claims to *Star Trek: Into Darkness*." Pp. 1-20 in *Fan Girls and the Media: Creating Characters, Consuming Culture*, edited by Adrienne Trier-Bieniek. Lanham, MD: Rowman and Littlefield.

2 Romano, Aja. 2012. "Sexist Rants Against 'Fake Geek Girls' Hit New Low." *The Daily Dot*. Last modified, November 13. http://www.dailydot.com/news/tony-harris-peacock-fake-geek-girls-cosplayers/.

3 Rose, Steve. 2015. "*Ex Machina* and Sci-Fi's Obsession with Sexy Female Robots." *The Guardian*. Last modified, January 15. https://www.theguardian.com/film/2015/jan/15/ex-machina-sexy-female-robots-scifi-film-obsession.

4 Curry, Colleen. 2014. "Violent Threats Against Women Are Getting Even Worse in the Gamergate Controversy." *Vice News*. Last modified, October 15. https://news.vice.com/article/violent-threats-against-women-are-getting-even-worse-in-the-gamergate-controversy

5 Pantozzi, Jill. 2013. "When Professionals Aren't: The Pax East Tomb Raider Cosplay Harassment Story," *The Mary Sue*. Last modified, March 28. http://www.themarysue.com/pax-tomb-raider-cosplay/

6 Fine, Gary Alan. 2003. "Crafting Authenticity." *Theory and Society* 32 (2): 153-180.

7 McRobbie, Angela. 2004 "Postfeminism and Popular Culture." *Feminist Media Studies* 4 (3): 255-264.

8 Lamont, Michele. 1992. *Money, Morals, and Manners.* Chicago: University of Chicago Press.

9 Lamont, Michele and Virag Molnar. 2002. "The Study Of Boundaries in the Social Sciences." *Annual Review Of Sociology* 28: 167-195

10 Tilly, Charles 2004. "Social Boundary Mechanisms." *Philosophy of the Social Sciences* 34 (2): 211-236.

Horta, Humpbacks, and the Encounter at Farpoint: On *Star Trek*'s Inclusion of Animals

Timothy Harvie

Gene Roddenberry's vision of the *Star Trek* universe was one where humanity overcame the violence and prejudices that have plagued much of its history and unified in a vision of equity, exploration, and a just society. *Star Trek* has consistently been at the forefront of addressing important social issues. These include issues of race, American identity, torture, the relationship between religion and society, the ethics of war, and dialogical approaches to diplomacy. One area that has received less formal attention is how *Star Trek* includes other animals in its ethical purview. While this aspect of *Trek*'s vision has been less central to the impact of this cultural phenomenon, it has been consistently addressed across multiple series. This was seen early in *Star Trek: The Next Generation* (*TNG*), when it was revealed that the food replicators addressed not only the pragmatic issue of food and prolonged space travel, but it had a moral rationale as well. In the episode, "Lonely Among Us," Commander Riker says to the Antican ambassador, "We no longer enslave animals for food purposes." In giving a moral rationale acclaimed Trek screenwriter, D.C. Fontana, intended to offer ethical insight into Starfleet's ethics. Other animals are not simply products of human consumption, but beings whose moral relevance makes demands on human interactions with them. This concern for other animal species is illustrated at key moments throughout *Star Trek*'s illustrious history. I will briefly address three instances where *Star Trek* put forward innovative ethical discussions regarding other animals: the Horta, Humpback whales, and the creatures at Farpoint Station.

In *The Original Series* (*TOS*) episode, "The Devil in the Dark," Kirk, Spock, and McCoy reach a human mining colony where a creature has killed several of the human workers. It is soon discovered that human industrial practice has placed this species at risk. The Horta, a mother who is the last of its kind, is defending her eggs which are in jeopardy from the mining activities carried out by humans to meet energy needs. Kirk labels the Horta a "monster" when he learns of the deaths of some miners. It is after the Horta removes and hides a key mechanical piece that Kirk calls her a "creature"1 and shows disdain for the leader of the miner's ongoing use of the monstrous nomenclature. After wounding the Horta, Kirk attempts to communicate. The creature moves forward when Kirk speaks and recoils like a wounded animal when Kirk raises his phaser. In this scene, Kirk is expanding his consciousness as to what constitutes morally relevant life.

However, it is only with Spock's mind meld that the viewer fully understands the full thrust of the episode's message. Through Spock's turning the pain and psychological state of the Horta into words, the Horta speaks. "The thousands of … devils. Eternity ends, chamber of the ages, the altar of tomorrow. Murderers. Stop them. Kill, strike back. Monsters." With these words, we understand who is to be identified as the devil in the dark and who is truly monstrous. The devil is not the Horta, but humans who encroach upon the natural habitat of the animal and jeopardize its existence through need for industry. The devil is we who treat animals and nature as we see fit in our quest for expansion and consumption of materials. The Horta and the miners strike a deal which is profitable for both. At this point in *Star Trek*'s development, there is still no need to curb industry profitable to humans and the animal can be used to aid human expansion.

These themes are taken further with the fourth motion picture in the *Star Trek* movie franchise: *The Voyage Home*. The instrumentalist conclusion of "The Devil in the Dark," where the humans concede to co-existing with the Horta provided it remains profitable, is challenged with Spock's logic. The Vulcan says to Kirk, "To hunt a species to extinction is not logical." Spock counters the instrumentalist narrative that humanity constructs for its unfettered use of other species. For it to be illogical to hunt a species to extinction there are two possibilities. First, human use of the species is no longer possible after extinction and so it is illogical for humanity to harm itself and limit the benefit it may receive from an animal. Second, it could be illogical because the moral value of another species of animal is derived from its benefit for humans. It seems that Spock has the latter in mind when he says to Kirk, "Admiral, if we were to assume these whales were ours to do with as we pleased, we would be as guilty as those who caused their extinction." Here Spock argues against an act saving the Humpback whales if it is simply to use this species as an instrument for human benefit. Contrary to Immanuel Kant, Spock argues that animals have direct value by virtue of their own existence, and not merely indirect value by virtue of their benefit to humans.2

Finally, in the pilot episode of *TNG* the new crew is forced to stand as proxy in a mock courtroom by the omnipotent Q who is putting humanity on trial. The challenge Q puts before Picard is the mystery of Farpoint station which appears to inquire how the Bandi colony can power such a place with limited technology. It is only at the conclusion of the episode that viewers are exposed to the possibility that humans are being tested not only on their cognitive potential, but also their moral potential. As the space animal (Picard refers to it as a "creature") attacks the colony, Groppler Zorn implores Picard to do away with it as it is killing his people. Picard simply asks whether it has reason to do so. The Bandi were using the wounded creature's ability to convert energy to matter in order to advance the industrial capabilities of the humanoids. Picard declares that this is not a good enough reason to advance the suffering of the animal. The final test comes from Q who presses the Captain, "Save yourself it may attack you now...make phasers and photon torpedoes." At the conclusion the audience realizes that humanity is judged not only on its ability to solve puzzles, but even more how it responds to a wounded animal and the threats of its mate.

In these examples, we see *Star Trek*'s expanding moral inclusivity regarding other animals. In moving from an instrumentalist approach to other animals to recognition of their dignity independent of humanity, *Star Trek* continues to challenge one of the more pressing moral questions of our day: how are we to treat other animal species? *Star Trek*, in its various iterations, challenges its audience to consider the potential of the moral dignity of other animals and our relationship to them. In a world that has lost half of its vertebrate wildlife in the last forty years due to human activity, *Star Trek* challenges us to change our approach to other animal species.3 Let us make it so.

Notes

When Star Trek refers to a "creature" it generally invokes the notion of an animal. When beings with greater communicative powers with hominoids are intended the language used is typically "entity" or "being."

2 Immanuel Kant, "Metaphysics of Morals (1797)" in *Practical Philosophy* ed. Mary J. Gregor (Cambridge: Cambridge University Press, 1996), 563-564.

3 *Living Planet Report 2014: Species and Spaces, People and Places.* no. 1, World Wildlife Federation International, 1-180.

Idealism in *Star Trek*

Jody Lynn Nye

I saw my first episode of *Star Trek* when I was ten. I fell in love with it immediately, because it was so much better than the other major science fiction program of the day, *Lost in Space*, and far less scary for a ten-year-old than the *Twilight Zone* and *Outer Limits*, or any of the cheesy black-and-white movies that aired on weekend television. The characters seemed like real people, well rounded, with real concerns and personalities that I could come to admire.

I've always considered science fiction to be the literature of hope because it postulates that we as a species will survive and go on to greater discoveries. As Captain James T. Kirk so majestically states as the Alexander Courage music begins every episode of the original series, "To seek out new life and new civilizations. To boldly go where no man has gone before." The words still give me chills. The ideals of the Federation are given to us up front. They also appear throughout the episodes. The Prime Directive, ordering the Federation not to interfere in the culture of another people, was its most important. Although it came later, the Enterprise is described as an exploration vehicle, not a warship. In positions of trust and authority, for the first time on nationwide television, a mixed-race crew of command officers, together on the bridge. *Star Trek*'s mission is to serve as an example of how we could be, instead of how we are. Sure, there were limitations. Sure, Kirk broke the Prime Directive more often than we saw him supporting it, but it made him hesitate. Good rules are more... guidelines than fiats.

Certainly, it's idealistic, unlike so much science fiction or other literature, but how is that a bad thing? Yes, it was and continues to be a product of its time—most minorities are invisible, but it tried. Faces that had not been present on other programs were here on this one. Roddenberry's casting choices were deliberate. A black woman, a trusted and respected officer, in the midst of a period where prejudice against people who looked like her was open and violent. A Japanese man, when living memory could bring forth images of the unjust west-coast internment camps. A Russian, America's worst enemy in a Cold War that had children cowering under their desks in what would be a fruitless effort in the case of the nuclear war everyone thought was minutes away. And an alien—well, if we're going to go to the stars, we have to embrace non-humans. And when you come to the libraries full of fan fiction that *Trek* engendered, you see that writers felt free to add their own ideas because *Trek*'s universe was open. It pushed the limits of how society should function, a meritocracy based on competence and compassion. I greatly prefer the optimism of Star Trek to much that has come afterward, with its dark palettes and endless pessimism about our survival and ability to cooperate. *Trek* was not mindlessly optimistic—the difficulties between races, for example, was something that they treated seriously—but they approached the subjects with an eye toward mutual survival and prosperity. The very symbol that Starfleet personnel wore on their chests, the IDIC, infinite diversity in infinite combination, is a worthy mission statement. It affected how I approach my own writing. The long view allows us to speculate on where we can go. Shutting down opposition stunts both sides of an argument. Having an example of optimism and idealism is a good model for looking forward to the future.

The Narrateme of *Star Trek Voyager*

John Tenuto, edited by Maria Jose Tenuto

"Stories can be whimsical, frightening or melancholy or many other things. But noble stories are the ones that can most affect our lives. May I have your permission to tell others this story?"
- Eudana, "Prime Factors" *Star Trek Voyager*

Introduction: Now, Voyager

There is a tendency for modern peoples to equate myth with both antiquity and false situations. It is ubiquitous, this thinking of myths as only the narratives of Zeus or Demeter. It is also problematic, this description of false situations or statistics as "myth." For example, "googling" the word *myth* nets numerous websites comparing truth to fiction. Yet, myths are neither irrelevant nor fictitious. Myths are stories that answer "enduring and fundamental human questions" (Leonard and McClure 1). While often utilizing fictitious situations and characters, myths speak truths that are beyond time or region. Because of this ability to speak to fundamental human truths, myths have a universal quality.

Many mythologists recognize at least some value in a temporally divorced and culturally comparative study of mythology. Joseph Campbell's monomyth is a good example of this. Myths have universal themes and character emerge from commonly shared archetypes for Campbell, yet he allows that like dreams, the actual sequence of the narrative may be different. The themes are what are really universal for Campbell who teaches that "myth is the public dream and the dream is the private myth" (*The Power of Myth*). Predating Campbell, and contrasting with him, is Vladimir Propp whose syntagmatic study of Russian narratives are the exemplar of his *Morphology of a Folktale*. Propp identifies the 31 narrateme, or sequential narrative steps, found in most Russian fairy tales, despite where or when they were authored (25-65). For Propp, because the study of myth is much like the study of science, his almost mathematical theory is predicated on his thesis that "the sequence of these functions is always identical" (22). For Campbell, it is about universal characters and themes. For Propp, it is about universal narrative steps or structure. Utilizing narrateme, this paper will demonstrate how Propp's syntagmatic structures are expressed in

231

the modern myth of *Star Trek Voyager*, especially its premiere two-hour episode "Caretaker." Despite the centuries, Russian folktales and this science fiction television program have much in common structurally. Myths are indeed beyond time and region, and by showing the commonalities between *Star Trek Voyager* of the 1990's and 2000's with Russian narratives of antiquity, this thesis shall be expressed.

The 31 Narrateme of *Star Trek Voyager*: "Caretaker" Thought of Syntagmatically

Propp identifies 31 narrateme, or narrative steps which form a sequence expressed in the one hundred Russian folktales he studied. These narrateme are also expressed with the premiere episode of *Star Trek Voyager*, titled "Caretaker." This episode was shown on January 16, 1995, to an estimated audience of nearly 14 million people. Written by Jeri Taylor and Michael Piller, the episode was the first show on the new network UPN and the first of 168 episodes (Startrek.com). It is one of the most watched episodes of the series and introduces each of the characters and the show's premise. The show recently celebrated its 20th anniversary. Amazingly, the episode expresses each of Propp's 31 narrateme, in the exact proper sequence.

The first of Propp's narrateme is defined as absentation.[1] The story of "Caretaker" begins with the introduction of Chakotay, B'Elanna Torres, and Tuvok, who are Maquis rebels fighting an oppressive alien government and their own Federation's policies. Much like Native Americans, the Maquis are fighting for their homes because a distant government has made a treaty with the alien Cardassians. As they pilot their ship through an area of the galaxy known as "The Badlands" avoiding their Cardassian enemies, the characters mysteriously are brought by an unknown entity to a completely different side of the galaxy, the Delta Quadrant, some 70 years away from their homes. Eventually, Captain Kathryn Janeway of the *U.S.S. Voyager* will try to discover what happened to the Maquis and suffer the same fate in the Badlands. The rebellious nature of the Maquis crew could be considered a modern version of Propp's contention that often it is "the younger generation" which leaves at the start of the folktale narratives, for example to go visiting or gathering berries (26). The Maquis crew represents this "younger generation" who is rebellious against the system.

Propp discusses that the hero of the story often is provided some warning, either by parents or by the culture itself. By ignoring the interdiction, the villain of the narrative is allowed to take their first action against the heroes.2 Both Chakotay and then Captain Janeway are warned about the dangers of the Badlands. When Chakotay decides to utilize the Badlands to escape the Cardassians, Tuvok offers the interdiction, "Considering the circumstances, I question that proposal at this time." When Janeway tells Tom Paris of her intention to try and find the Maquis, Tom warns about the Badlands. "I wouldn't if I were you...I've never seen a Federation starship that can maneuver through the plasma storms." Both Chakotay and Janeway ignore the warning, one out of desperation (Chakotay), the other out of pride (Janeway tells Paris, "You've never seen *Voyager*."). The ignoring of the interdiction brings them into the region where there is a beam making it possible for the mysterious alien to move both the Maquis and Voyager crews 70,000 light years from the homes.

The villain of the episode is an alien entity the crews will eventually call "The Caretaker." Upon the crews going into the Badlands, the Caretaker scans their vessels, gathering information from the Maquis ship and *Voyager*'s database about humans and the Federation. Propp would call the Caretaker's scan his "reconnaissance" by which the villain learns information that encourages their malicious behavior (28). By learning about humanity, the Caretaker will be able to construct its illusions in the next scenes.3

As the *Voyager* characters scramble to repair the major damage their travel to the Delta Quadrant has caused their ship, the crew is mysteriously beamed to what appears to be a small town. There is a party going on, with dancing and singing. A banjo plays a happy tune. Confused, the crew tries to make sense of their situation. One of the townspeople is a beautiful woman who seduces Tom Paris. Another is a kindly, elderly woman who offers comfort and food to the crew. When his friend Harry Kim reminds Paris that the woman is probably an illusion, Paris responds "That is no reason to be rude." For Propp, the purpose of deception in Russian folktales is for the villain to be able to eventually take from the hero whatever they need, for example, a magic talisman or agent (28-29). In fact, one of his examples is of "a witch who pretends to be a "sweet old lady"" (29). Obviously, this episode of *Star Trek Voyager* utilizes this motif.4

Captain Janeway realizes that the Maquis have also been taken by the Caretaker when she and her crew discover the testing laboratory.

The Caretaker is conducting medical testing on the crews for a yet unknown purpose. Two characters, B'Elanna Torres and Harry Kim, are transported away from the Caretaker's array and sent to the planet Ocampa. While there, it is revealed they have tumors on their hands and faces as a result of the Caretaker's tests.5 They are told by the kindly Ocampan people who treat the Caretaker almost as a distant god figure that their disease is one for which they have no cure.

Propp charts 19 villainous acts of harm or injury that are usually expressed during this narrateme (31-34). For Propp, this is where the action and the conflict really begins, calling this narrateme "exceptionally important" to the narrative (31). Of the 19 villainous acts listed, the Caretaker engages most especially in expelling the fictional hero, casting a spell on someone (B'Elanna and Harry's disease could symbolically be seen as a spell, especially because the science of this is not fully explained), detaining the crews, and causing injury to the characters with his testing (31-34).

There is something wrong and the hero must help.6 As Propp described, this is the narrateme where the hero really starts to be the hero (36). During the next scenes of the episode, Janeway meets the Caretaker, who appears as a kindly elderly gentleman playing a banjo (symbolizing that he is the character in control, for he is "playing the music" or "composing" the events). The Caretaker has sent Harry and B'Elanna to Ocampa, and returned the Maquis and *Voyager* crews back to their ships. He is surprised they have returned to his home, which is called "the array."

He bemoans, "Oh, why have you come back? You don't have what I need." Janeway responds, "I don't know what you need, and frankly I don't care. I want our people back and I want us all to be sent home." The Caretaker's response shows he is dismissive of their misfortune that he has caused, "Oh, well, aren't you contentious for a minor bipedal species?" During their conversation and subsequent scenes, Janeway begins to learn about the reality of her situation.

The Caretaker and his symbolic wife are powerful aliens. They accidentally caused a terrible ecological disaster on the planet Ocampa which led to all its people having to move into caves to survive. He has been supplying the Ocampa with the power needed for their world, and trying to take care of them. It is, he reveals "a debt that can never be paid." Unfortunately, he is dying and trying to find a replacement who can be the next Caretaker. That is why he has brought the crews there, although they do not have what is required to be a Caretaker.

Janeway certainly expresses what Propp describes as the hero first showing their heroic qualities. Instead of getting angry, Janeway offers to help the Caretaker. She expresses the heroic quality of compassion for his situation, despite the harm he has inflicted on her crew and the Maquis. She appreciates his sense of responsibility, which is something that as Captain she shares with the Caretaker. The Caretaker refuses her help and Janeway teams with the Maquis Chakotay to retrieve their comrades and try to get home to the Federation.

Both Campbell and Propp recognize that there are often archetypal characters from myths whose purpose is to announce the journey to the hero. Campbell's name for these characters is "heralds" while Propp calls them "seekers" (36). *Star Trek Voyager* inverts this idea interestingly by having the villain character also be the herald or seeker. The Caretaker creates the situation that Janeway finds herself challenging, then announces to her the details of her journey. He is both villain and herald of the adventure for the fictitious heroes.

Janeway and Chakotay's respective crews begin their adventure. Propp discusses how during this initial phase of the journey, the hero is often presented with tests or challenges. The reason for this is to provide the "first function of the donor" or to introduce the character by which the hero will attain some advice or a talisman important to the journey (39). Simply, the hero must be kind to the frog because the frog actually has the magic that can save the day.7

Usually, the donor either creates challenges, or thresholds in Campbellian structural theory according to Henderson (30) or makes unusual requests of the hero to decide if the hero is worthy of help. It could be argued that this behavior by the donor characters are an inversion of the narrateme where the villain deceives the hero. Both the villain and the donor deceive, yet their purpose is different. One is to harm the hero, the other is to help. It is also important to note that heroes themselves deceive in mythology for noble purposes. During the episode, it is revealed that Tuvok is not actually a Maquis rebel. He is actually Janeway's close advisor and security chief sent on a mission to learn about the Maquis. Disguises and deceiving behaviors are common to hero, donor, mentors, and villains.

The donor character from "Caretaker" is Neelix, a scavenger who the crew meets on their way to the Ocampa planet. At first appearance, Neelix is gruff and aggressive. He threatens and challenges the Maquis and *Voyager* crews unless they leave his territory. Once he realizes they are indeed friendly, the real Neelix personality is revealed. Neelix is a kind, decent alien who is wise about the Delta Quadrant's resources and aliens. His own travels make him an excellent guide and he accepts the crew of *Voyager*'s promise of water and resources in exchange for his help navigating the region and for sharing his knowledge of the Ocampan people.

Propp defines magical agents as an animal, object, talisman, or ability which is bestowed on the hero by the donor character (43). The hero will utilize this magical agent to defeat the villain.8 Neelix provides an unusual magical agent to Captain Kathryn Janeway. Neelix leads the crews to meet the Kazon, a people temporarily living on the Ocampan planetary surface which he promises might help the heroes locate their comrades on the planet. However, this is a ruse (continuing the deceiving theme of the donor character). Neelix is actually bringing the Voyager crew there to make it appear that he has powerful friends. Neelix actually wishes to rescue his girlfriend, Kes, who is Ocampa, from the Kazon. Janeway must help rescue Kes in order for her and her crew to escape, yet they have now made an enemy of the Kazon.

While initially angry with Neelix, Janeway realizes that Kes possesses unique abilities and knowledge, and she is the science fiction equivalent of a magical agent. Kes is the only Ocampa who has ventured out from their home to the surface and she has the knowledge of how to get to the Ocampan community. It is also learned that Ocampa only live for nine years, aging very quickly. Various episodes of the show during the subsequent seasons, especially "The Gift" continue the idea that Kes is a magical agent. In "The Gift" her mental abilities are so great she able to help the crew move 10 years closer to home on their journey from the Delta Quadrant. Campbell teaches that the boons of mythology are often not tangible rewards or objects. ""What all the myths have to deal with is transformations of consciousness of one kind or another. You have been thinking one way, you now have to think another way"" (Henderson 44). The hero really earns enlightenment or family, not a Holy Grail or actual treasure. Propp agrees that the magical agent is not necessarily an object. It could be a belief or confidence. It could be a person with amazing abilities, and this is Kes, the Ocampa with mental abilities that helps save the crew.

Propp describes that the hero's boon or goal is "located in

"another" or "different" kingdom" (50). This is certainly the situation for the Maquis and *Voyager* crews as they must infiltrate the Ocampan city, which mimics the mythologically symbolic labyrinth in its maze design.9 It is here that Janeway and Chakotay are reunited with Harry Kim and B'Elanna Torres. Also relevant is the notion that Janeway and Chakotay, the two main heroes of the narrative, also gain knowledge as a boon during this sequence. For Janeway, it is knowledge that the Ocampa are a good people, which will help her to make an important decision at the narrative's resolution. She is also beginning to realize that she is going to need allies to survive during their journey home if the Caretaker does not send them back to the Federation with his array. Chakotay gains the awareness that the crew of the *Voyager* are honorable people when he is rescued by Tom Paris. These transformations of thought by Janeway and Chakotay allow the two crews to eventually act as a team for the journey home to the Federation.

As the crews escape the Ocampan community, there are two villains of concern.10 This is common to Russian fairytales. Propp discusses villains of the "first" and "second" variety (63). The Caretaker is the first villain, the Kazon the second. The Caretaker, who in a desperate attempt to provide for the Ocampa as much as possible before his demise, is sending waves of energy to the planet. The waves are creating tremors that challenge the crew. Janeway is intent on having the Caretaker send the crews home before he perishes. However, she must also face Jabin of the Kazon who does not want to permit Janeway access to the Caretaker or its array. The verbal combat between Janeway and Jabin is followed by a battle of their ships, the result of which allows Janeway to beam over to the array. As the Voyager and Maquis crews battle the Kazon, Janeway and Tuvok visit the Caretaker. Again, it is on the array that Janeway has a battle of wits with the Caretaker entity.

True to the motif of many *Star Trek* episodes, Janeway listens and begins to really appreciate that while his actions are not appropriate, the Caretaker is actually an entity of good conscience who is desperate to help the Ocampa before he perishes. During their talk, she is branded symbolically by a conversion of consciousness.11 She is converted to his cause of protecting the Ocampa. As with boons and magical agents, the branding of the hero need not be physical, although Propp's examples suggest as much. Janeway also teaches the Caretaker that his actions of

237

trying to find a replacement by bringing the crews to the Delta Quadrant were wrong, both because of the harm these actions caused, yet also because they were unnecessary, "Did you ever consider letting the Ocampa care for themselves? We are explorers, too. Most of the peoples we have encountered have overcome all kinds of adversity without the help of a Caretaker. It's the challenge to survive on their own that helps them to evolve."

When the Caretaker realizes his error, he is symbolically defeated. As Propp discusses, the defeat of the villain takes many forms, including something as innocuous as "he loses at cards" or "he is defeated in a contest" (53). The initial threat of the Caretaker is neutralized, and Janeway returns to the *Voyager*, her new home in the Delta Quadrant.

To define the *U.S.S. Voyager* as home is not actually a symbolic interpretation. In many episodes of the show, Janeway refers to the ship as a "home" most notably in "Year of Hell." Actress Kate Mulgrew describes Janeway's relationship with her ship. "I often talk to the ship. My deepest personal references are to the ship in the form of my captain's log. Although it will be filed and reported in the archives, it is essential to the ship itself. I do have a very visceral relationship with *Voyager*, no question about it" (Ruditis 61). For Janeway, the ship is her sacred place and her home.

Propp discusses various narratemes that represent the resolution of the narrative.12 Chakotay's smaller ship is no match for the Kazon, and while being pursued, he and his crew are rescued by the *Voyager*. With the Maquis crew now on her ship, Janeway talks with Jabin who presents himself as a "false hero" who is protecting the array. He is a false hero because his intentions are selfish and the array means the power to control the Ocampa people. However, Janeway's conversion of consciousness and her experiences with the Ocampa help her to be the true defender of the people. She vows to help the Ocampa by destroying the array. This is a very difficult task because it means stranding the Maquis and *Voyager* crews in the Delta Quadrant. Yet, she recognizes that if the crews use the array to get home to the Federation, it would allow the Kazon to control its power and the Ocampa.

As Janeway readies her ship to destroy the array, there is an interesting scene between the two Maquis B'Elanna Torres and Chakotay. It is an example of "the hero as unrecognized and hero as recognized" narrateme. When Janeway announces her intention to destroy the array, B'Elanna is furious.

> B'Elanna: What do you think you are doing? That array is the only way we have to get back home!
> Janeway: I am aware that everyone has family and loved ones back home that they want to get back to. So do I. But I'm not willing to trade the lives of the Ocampa for our convenience. We'll have to find another way home.
> B'Elanna: What other way home is there? (to Chakotay) Who is she to be making these decisions for all of us?
> Chakotay: She is the Captain.

This sequence is a good demonstration of the unrecognized-recognized motif of narrateme 23 and 27. Janeway must be recognized as the single authority figure for both crews, and Chakotay agrees that she is making the moral decision despite its negative effect on his crew.

The experiences of the hero usually lead to a transformation of identity according to Propp's narratemes.13 Because of Chakotay's conversion to Janeway's cause and his acquiescence of his authority as the Maquis leader is rewarded when he eventually earns back his commission as a Commander, he is Janeway's first officer and sheds his Maquis civilian clothes in favor of a Starfleet uniform.

The array is destroyed, and Jabin is defeated. He tells Janeway that she has made an enemy of the Kazon groups.14 Interestingly, Propp discusses that "Usually only the villain of the second move and the false hero are punished, while the first villain is punished only in those cases in which a battle or pursuit are absent from the story" (63). This is exactly what happens with the "Caretaker" episode. Jabin, the second villain, is punished by his being denied his prize, while the Caretaker is defined as a good entity who made bad decisions.

With the immediate dangers neutralized, the crews unite together in a symbolic marriage which is the thirty-first narrateme of Propp's theory.15 B'Elanna Torres will eventually be the Chief Engineer of the *Voyager*, and Chakotay as already mentioned will be First Officer to Janeway. As the episodes continue, there will be actual marriages, such as Tom Paris to B'Elanna Torres. Thus, the narrative is concluded.

Conclusion: The True Federation of Russian folktales and Star Trek

There is a real intellectual joy in being able to find commonality between Russian folktales and *Star Trek* despite the literal and figurative separation of space and time. Propp himself provides a reason why two dissimilar narratives could have structural sameness. "If we read through all of the functions, one after another, we observe that one function develops out of another with logical and artistic necessity" (64). Put simply, a yarn, properly told, has a logic to it that requires a certain sequential form, a kind of narrative syntax, be they about a Russian hero or a futuristic Captain, that transcends culture or history. And, of course, Russian folktales and *Star Trek* episodes are both good myths, good yarns, properly told.

Notes

1 "One of the members of a family absents himself from home" (Propp Narrateme #1)
2 "An interdiction is addressed to the hero" (Propp Narrateme #2)
   The interdiction is ignored (Propp Narrateme #3)
3 "The villain makes an attempt at reconnaissance" (Propp Narrateme #4)
   The villain gets his or her information (Propp Narrateme #5)
4 "The villain attempts to deceive" (Propp Narrateme #6)
   The hero is fooled by the deception (Propp Narrateme #7)
5 "The villain causes harm or injury" to the family of characters (Propp Narrateme #8)
6 "Misfortune or lack is made known" and the hero is summoned to action (Propp Narrateme #9)
   The hero agrees to or reacts to the summons (Propp Narrateme #10)
7 The hero begins their journey (Propp Narrateme #11)
   The hero is tested by the donor character (Propp Narrateme #12)
   The hero reacts to the donor character (Propp Narrateme #13)
8 "The hero acquires the use of a magical agent" (Propp Narrateme #14)
9 The hero is transferred to the object he or she has been seeking (Propp Narrateme #15)
10 The hero and the villain join in direct combat (Propp Narrateme #16)
11 "The hero is branded" (Propp Narrateme #17)
   "The villain is defeated" (Propp Narrateme #18)
   "The initial misfortune or lack is liquidated" (Propp Narrateme #19)
   "The hero returns" (Propp Narrateme #20)
12 "The hero is pursued" (Propp Narrateme #21)
   "Rescue of the hero from pursuit" (Propp Narrateme #22)
   "The hero, unrecognized, arrives home or in another country" (Propp Narrateme #23)
   "A false hero presents unfounded claims" (Propp Narrateme #24)
   "A difficult task is proposed to the hero" (Propp Narrateme #25)
   "The task is resolved" (Propp Narrateme #26)
   "The hero is recognized" (Propp Narrateme #27)
   "The false hero or villain is exposed" (Propp Narrateme #28)
13 "The hero is given a new appearance" (Propp Narrateme #29)
14 "The villain is punished" (Propp Narrateme #30)

15 The hero is married, the hero earns the throne (Propp Narrateme #31)

References

Campbell, Joseph. *The Hero With a Thousand Faces*. NJ: Princeton University Press, 1972.

"Caretaker." *Star Trek: Voyager*. Dir. Winrich Kolbe. Perf. Kate Mulgrew. 1995. DVD. Paramount Studios, 2004.

Doty, William G. *Mythography: The Study of Myths and Rituals*. Tuscaloosa, AL: The University of Alabama Press, 2000.

"The Gift." *Star Trek: Voyager*. Dir. Anson Williams. Perf. Kate Mulgrew. 1997. DVD. Paramount Studios, 2004.

Henderson, Mary. *Star Wars: The Magic of Myth*. NY: Spectra, 1997.

Leonard, Scott, and Michael McClure. *Myth and Knowing: An Introduction to World Mythology*. NY: McGraw Hill, 2004.

Memory Alpha. Web.

Pirkova-Jakobson, Svatava. "Introduction." *Morphology of the Folk Tale*. University of Texas Press, 1968.

The Power of Myth. Joseph Campbell and Bill Moyers. DVD. Mystic Fire Video, 2001.

"Prime Factors." *Star Trek Voyager*. Dir. Les Landau. Perf. Kate Mulgrew. 1995. DVD. Paramount Studios, 2004.

Propp, Vladimir. *Morphology of the Folk Tale*. University of Texas Press, 1968.

Ruditis, Paul. *Star Trek Voyager*. NY: Simon and Shuster, 2003.

Star Trek.com. Web.

"Year of Hell." *Star Trek: Voyager*. Dir. Alan Kroeker. Perf. Kate Mulgrew. 1997. DVD. Paramount Studios, 2004.

50 Years of *Trek* and the *Fascinating* Lessons We've Learned

Elizabeth A. Thomas

The Greeks had Aristotle and Plato. The Chinese had Confucius. Americans had *Star Trek*. It's been said that anything we might possibly face in our lives has already been experienced by the crew of the *U.S.S. Enterprise*. While this may sound simplistic, a deep review of the original series and the literature since reveals a wealth of logic and learning that exists amid the lore. The original *Star Trek* television series set clear examples for living a moral life. When we study the 50-year compilation of television, literature, film and fan culture, we learn that in each of *Star Trek*'s incarnations, each new episode, every novel, and every film contains a new or recurring life lesson we can appreciate.

Most fans know the basic lessons of *Star Trek* — non-interference is the prime directive, to boldly go where no one has gone before, Infinite Diversity in Infinite Combinations, the needs of the many outweigh the needs of the few (or the one). And upon deeper inspection, we have unlocked a vast universe of *Trek* teachings.

We begin with several lessons uncovered via Dave Marinaccio's 1995 publication, "All I Really Need to Know I Learned from Watching *Star Trek*."

Lesson 1: Everyone has their role to play – navigator, helmsman, science officer, engineer, doctor, communications specialist - leader. Hidden within the broader lesson is this directive: Do your own job and worry about your own duties. Everything will function much more smoothly if you do.

Lesson 2: Each person or species, no matter how alien, has the right to live their life as they wish (as long as they are not trying to take over the galaxy or eat you).

Lesson 3: Whatever you are doing, always answer a distress call. The most important time to help anyone is when they really need it.

Lesson 4: If you mess something up, you are responsible for fixing it. (For instance, if you go back in time and inadvertently cause the Nazis to win WWII, then you have to let Joan Collins walk in front of a car even though you're in love with her.)

Lesson 5: The more complex the mind, the greater the need for simplicity.

Lesson 6: If you can stay calm in a crisis then you've got a fighting chance.

Lesson 7: Never fear the unknown. Examine, study, understand and accept it.

Lesson 8: Close friends become family and family is the true center of the universe.

Lesson 9: End every chapter with a smile.

Lesson 10: And, finally, with time and patience, you can even learn something from the *Next Generation*.

From the writings of business consultant Jerry Smeding, we uncovered lessons taught specifically by each of the central characters on *TOS*. For instance, from Uhura we learned to keep all hailing frequencies open.

From **Pavel Chekov**, we learned that sometimes it's okay to be a little cocky, and it's always permissible to be proud of who you are and where you came from.

From **Sulu,** we learned to maintain a steady course and always keep our cool.

From **Scotty,** we learned to be dependable, to know our stuff and to love our jobs. Scotty also taught us that if a job is difficult, it's best to tell your boss that it's impossible---but do it anyway. Also, if you think a job is going to take 10 minutes, tell your boss it'll take an hour, then exceed all expectations.

From **Dr. Leonard McCoy**, we learned that is important to know our own limitations and always get to the point quickly. The doctor's most important lesson was to be honest; critique and praise our friends and coworkers even when we must tell then the hard truth.

From **Mr. Spock**, we learned that we must appreciate logic, but realize that life is not always logical. Don't let intellect get in the way of the ability to feel. Don't let intellect get in the way of spirituality.

From **James T. Kirk**, we learned that we must have confidence in ourselves. Trust our guts. Recognize opportunities and grab them. Kirk was committed to seeking out new life and new civilizations. He was always adventurous. He taught us to take a chance every now and then and never limit ourselves to the beaten path. Though Captain Kirk often found a way around a core lesson of the series, he did recognize that "non-interference is the prime directive." Finally, Kirk showed us the value of keeping our phasers set on stun. He demonstrated that we must always be prepared, expect the unexpected and not automatically shoot to kill.

Core Lessons We Learned Along the Way

* *Humans are highly illogical.*
* *Live long and prosper.*
* *Having a thing is not so pleasing as wanting it.*
* *Infinite Diversity in Infinite Combinations (IDIC).* This is the core of Vulcan philosophy. It's about tolerance and admiring and seeking alternative opinions - embracing the true beauty of diversity.
* *Tribbles hate Klingons* (and Klingons hate Tribbles). We can't get along with everyone. We don't have to get along with everyone. We weren't made to get along with everyone.
* *Don't put all your ranking officers in one shuttlecraft.* Don't put all your eggs in one basket (this is a core piece of common sense that many business owners today lack).
* *When your logic fails, trust a hunch.* In today's world, it's impossible to know everything. Every day brings new challenges and you won't always have a guide or decision rule to cover the situation, so learn to trust your gut.

From how to bandage a wounded silicon life form to how to make friends or navigate those pesky pubescent hormones, everything we need to know is in *Star Trek* somewhere. And if it comes cloaked in a cheesy costume, it's up to us to find the moral of the story.

Live Long and Prosper!

Make It So! Creating a Real-World Interstellar Civilization: The Future According to *Trek*

Kathleen D. Toerpe

Much of the discourse surrounding *Star Trek* through the last fifty years has centered on the possibilities and challenges of its physics, on duplicating its amazingly imaginative technologies, or on extracting its core ethical and philosophical tenets. We have made great strides in exploring the physics and the engineering, and—to a much lesser extent—the culture of the *USS Enterprise* and its crew, through individual episodes, series incarnations, novels, or original and reboot films. But real life is quickly catching up to Gene Roddenberry's science fiction world and initiatives through official agencies such as NASA (and its international counterparts), as well as through private organizations such as the British Interplanetary Society, 100 Year Starship, Tau Zero, Icarus Interstellar, and the Institute for Interstellar Studies, are today laying the foundations and creating the capabilities for real world interstellar travel as early as the next century. Roddenberry's vision is becoming realized and the world of *Star Trek* is quickly becoming our world, too. Are we ready?

For fifty years, *Star Trek* has compelled us to broaden our understanding of science fiction and to see in it a possible blueprint for creating our future. From the phones we carry in our hands, to the computer screens on our desktops, to the 3D printing that may someday replicate—or replace—the food that we eat, *Star Trek* has never been "just" a television show. Incarnated in multiple series, films, comic books, novellas, and mash-ups, Gene Roddenberry intended his vision of the future to offer social commentary on his own present-day 1960s. But something as compelling as humanity reimagined without prejudice and war, boldly exploring the galaxy, cannot belong to one scant decade alone. So, it is not surprising that fifty years after the charismatic, yet altogether fictional Captain James T. Kirk and crew first warped across the galaxy, twenty-first-century dreamers bent on truly exploring interstellar space hearken back to the now iconic *USS Enterprise* for inspiration and guidance.

No, we're not ready to build a starship yet, but we are engaged in laying the groundwork for the next generation—or two, or three—to physically engage a starship's thrusters and, in the words of the *Enterprise's* later captain, Jean-Luc Picard, to "Make it so!" Much of the media hype, not surprisingly, gravitates around creating faster-than-light (FTL) travel, a necessary prerequisite to leap frog the literally galactic and mind-boggling distances separating stars in the Milky Way. No FTL travel, no *Star Trek*, yet what the series can teach us extends far beyond astrophysics and technological innovations. If watched carefully, *Trek* also provides analogs in the *human dimension* of outer space, a field of increasing interest among sociologists, historians, psychologists, anthropologists, theologians, and others united under the umbrella of an emerging field called *astrosociology*.

On the face of it, *Star Trek* gives us an amazing range of analogous ideas to consider: embracing diversity amid close quarters and challenging situations; engaging and cooperating with other societies competing for resources; creating common goals that transcend boundaries of nation, language, or belief. Specifically, these are the type of questions that astrosociologists, social scientists, and humanists could ask about *Star Trek*:

* What can *Star Trek* teach us about how to create an interstellar civilization? What lessons should we follow? What pitfalls should we avoid?

* We know what life was like aboard the various incarnations of the *Enterprise*, but what could we know or infer about what life was like for those who remained on Earth? To what extent do we need to create that fictional Earth in the real world of today in anticipation of future exploration?

* How were the characters challenged and constrained by the politics and culture of their worlds? How can we use these fictional experiences as analogs for transcending similar limitations now in our own world?

* Many of the societies that the *Enterprise* encountered were tribal, agrarian, or pre-industrial—regressive in comparison to the technological advances of the Federation. Might real space explorers encounter similar societies, and how should they interact with them? Closer to home and our own time, how should Earth's most technologically advanced societies interact with developing nations?

* Do we need to institute a Prime Directive prohibiting human interference in extraterrestrial societies? If so, why haven't humans instituted a similar real-life directive for themselves here on Earth now?

* The humans of the 23rd century claim to have evolved beyond the prejudices of race, gender, and religion and, despite the Prime Directive, often encourage (even compel) extraterrestrial societies to do the same. Can we surmise how this "evolution towards tolerance" unfolded in their world, with an eye to creating it in our own?

* Intense curiosity about the universe abounds in the *Star Trek* canon. How has this curiosity been nurtured and sustained amid political and economic upheaval?

Of course, there are no real answers to any of these questions or to the hundreds more that could be posed. They are musings, nothing more. But by delving deeply into the backstory of *Star Trek*, we are confronting our own challenges that lay ahead of us. By understanding the fictional humans of the Federation and of the *Enterprise*, we gain an understanding of ourselves. By articulating the historic past of *Trek*-time, we are anticipating our own future. And our timeline—and that of *Star Trek*—will soon converge.

In *Trek* chronology, we are within shooting distance of that magical April 5, 2063 date in which the fictional Zefrem Cochrane and his *Phoenix* first achieved warp drive. In the *Trek* canon, of course, this was followed by the unanticipated and fantastical result of humanity's First Contact with an extraterrestrial civilization—the Vulcans, who detected the *Phoenix's* warp signature and initiated humans into the ranks of space-capable explorers. While it is still another eighty-eight years or so after that until Jonathan Archer's *Enterprise* leaves dry dock, we are now beginning to see the midpoint between real time and *Trek* time, with *Star Trek* celebrating its real-life 50th anniversary, while less than another fifty years remain to Cochrane's fictional mission. The chronologies are beginning to overlap and profound advances towards a *Trek*-like reality are being pursued.

There are many corporations, governments, and organizations, collaborating and competing in this era of real-life New Space exploration: Space X, Virgin Galactic, Bigelow Aerospace, XCOR, Orbital Sciences, Planetary Resources, Deep Space Industries, and Scaled Composites are some of the largest corporate players. Still fully in the game are also NASA, the European Space Agency, Japan's JAXA, Russia's Roscosmos, and the Chinese National Space Administration. Add to this mix educational, advocacy, research, or settlement organizations such as 100 Year Starship, SETI, the Tau Zero Foundation, The Planetary Society, The British Interplanetary Society, the Astrosociology Research Institute, Mars One, Icarus Interstellar, and the Institute for Interstellar Studies (to name only a few!) and space is getting very crowded before the first starship ever leaves dry dock! At the core of all these endeavors is the desire to create a space-faring civilization capable of the kind of human exploration envisioned by *Star Trek*—many vying to control space access and resources, realize faster-than-light propulsion, identify and locate both astrobiological as well as intelligent ET life, and create human missions and settlements on the moon, Mars, and even on exoplanets being identified by the thousands using data from NASA's Kepler mission. In each step of the process, real human lives will be affected on Earth and in space, and *Star Trek* just might offer us some lessons on how to do it well.

This big picture understanding of *Star Trek* engages participants by broadening our understanding of the science fiction phenomenon and considering its use as a possible blueprint for creating a future real world interstellar civilization. Confronting the challenges and possibilities of the human dimension of outer space exploration—and all that it implies for those of us who remain on Earth now and in our space-faring future—is no less audacious and no less laudatory than the achievement of warp speed, but like that holy grail of astrophysics, it, too, is necessary for us to "boldly go where no one has gone before."

Star Trek: Space and the Single Girl

Patricia Vettel-Becker

To dismiss the original *Star Trek* television series as sexist is commonplace, and looking back from the perspective of third-wave feminism it certainly is. However, I would like to suggest some alternative readings, hopefully providing insight into how the series may have resonated with female viewers at the time who were re-negotiating their own gender positions within a rapidly changing social and technological landscape.

Much has been made about Gene Roddenberry's liberal humanist vision, his belief that in the future humanity will have overcome the racial and ideological prejudices that characterized his present. However, his attempts to promote gender equality have not been widely celebrated, despite the fact that his first pilot for the series included a female first officer, his second pilot featured a professional woman as guest lead, and the series itself included at least one female bridge officer and numerous female guest stars playing roles from ambassadors, queens, and priestesses to scientists, engineers, and commanders. Instead, later detractors have focused on how the women regulars played secondary roles to the male leads; on how the women guest stars functioned primarily as sexual playthings for these same male leads, and on the fact that Starfleet women wore miniskirts.

After viewing the second pilot, NBC placed *Star Trek* on the fall 1966 schedule, with provision that the show be made more appealing. One decision was to change the women's uniforms from pants to the miniskirt, a design that at that time would have been seen as quite forward looking. In 1966 miniskirts were beginning to be adopted by women as a sign of their modernity and of their liberation from the domestic sphere. The exact origins of the miniskirt are disputed, but some have argued it originated within the context of American science fiction, with Helen Rose's clothing designs for the actress Anne Francis in the 1956 film *Forbidden Planet*. As Star Trek costume designer William Ware Theiss would later do, Rose placed her twenty-third-century character in a series of close-fitting dresses whose flared skirts ended just below the buttocks.

Another influence on Theiss's design for the female crew

members' uniforms may have been those of airline stewardesses, a contemporaneous example of single working women in space, or at least in the sky. In fact, it is possible that the highly publicized and admired position of stewardess may have inspired Roddenberry's entire conception of how a Starfleet woman should look and act, considering he had spent three years working as a pilot for Pan American. Deemed the most glamorous of all careers open to women in the 1950s and 60s, the role of stewardess was also among the most highly coveted. These careers lasted only a few years, however, because most airlines forced women to retire once they married or reached the age of thirty-two. This stipulation ensured the stability of the iconic symbol that the stewardess had become—the young, beautiful, world-traveling adventuress who would be romanced by the most desirable men in the world. Among the featured crew on the *U.S.S. Enterprise*, Janice Rand most closely fits the stewardess model. She was assigned to Captain Kirk as his personal yeoman, a junior officer performing chiefly clerical duties. Thus we see her in a service role, bringing him tapes to view, but also beverages to drink and food to eat. Also in keeping with the stewardess model was the prioritization of Rand's physical appearance. She was constructed as the ultra-feminine woman—pretty, pleasant, shapely and highly ornamented with make-up, nail polish, and elaborate hairstyles.

When *Star Trek* debuted in 1966, it offered the American viewing public a fantasy vision of female astronauts very different from the only one offered by reality—Soviet cosmonaut Valentina Tereshkova. In contrast, Starfleet women are the futuristic version of Helen Gurley Brown's "Single Girls." They do not cook, clean, raise offspring, or get married. They are professional women devoted to their careers who also delight in their femininity, the very model of single womanhood promoted by Brown in her best-selling books *Sex and the Single Girl* (1962) and *Sex and the Office* (1964). They are what Brown refers to as "female females," women who are glad they are women, not men, and who take pride in their appearance because they take pride in themselves. Nurse Chapel, Yeoman Rand and Lieutenant Uhura may have soothed cultural anxiety over the possibility of de-feminization by appearing and acting hyper-feminine, an overcompensation that may have been due as much to the fact that they had relinquished domesticity as that they had adopted scientific or technological career fields within an organizational structure patterned after the military.

That they could function within these roles while retaining physical markers of femininity may have suggested to American audiences at the time that gender equality will have been achieved by the twenty-third century. For many Americans, to empower women meant to empower women in their femininity, not to turn them into masculinized females, as it was believed the Soviet Union had done.

The most compelling model of the powerful but feminine woman to appear on *Star Trek* is the Romulan commander in "The Enterprise Incident." For women viewers in the 1960s, she would have functioned as a fantasy projection, a surrogate, a way for them to imagine themselves in such a position—commanding a starship and its crew while enjoying the pleasures of fashionable attire, comfortable furnishings, and sexual companionship on one's own terms. Whether they believed it inherent, an act to play, or a mixture of both, femininity was one tool sixties women had that men did not, and they did not want to lose it.

References
Patricia Vettel-Becker, "Space and the Single Girl: *Star Trek*, Aesthetics, and 1960s Femininity." *Frontiers: A Journal of Women Studies* 35:2 (2014): 143-178

My First Frontier – A Celebration of Fifty Years Of *Star Trek*

Karma Waltonen

I am in a sick bay, resting in an aqua chamber. As I am unable to use the holodeck, images are projected in front of me—keeping my mind off the healing.

In reality, I am in my stepfather's rarely used home office—there's a desk, a typewriter, some file cabinets. There's also a queen-sized waterbed—usually for guests.

It is the very early 1980s. I am around 7.

I am sick—sick enough to warrant being in a room with a television. When they weren't sure if I was ill, I was confined to my room—no TV. But this is one of the asthma times—I struggle to draw breath, counting the minutes until I can ease my lungs with another puff of the now-recalled Primatene mist emergency inhalers.

My stepfather is changing the channel for me—I'm too sick to get up, and this is before remotes. There aren't many choices—just three channels. He stops on a show—men in similar looking clothing—just different colors and an exotic locale.

"You should watch this."

"What is it?"

Star Trek.

He tells me it's famous. I don't yet hate him enough to just roll my eyes and reject his suggestions outright.

So I watch. I like it so much that we figure out from the paper *TV Guide* when the show will be on for the week I end up at home.

I find myself in the office in the back of the house frequently even when well, searching out the show.

I'm in love.

I am Spock, of course. I am a geek already—a misfit and a brain. I have hope that one day the only asset I can identify in myself—that brain—will be attractive to the right people. I assume I'll have to be older, when other people will need my brain and its superior homeworking abilities.

Years later, I am excited about *The Next Generation*. I am not jaded or angry that the Original will now be called the Original—it was always on repeat for me. Like *I Love Lucy* and *Bewitched*, it was never *mine*.

TNG was.

What did that younger me need that *Star Trek* gave?

I stayed a misfit and a brain. My asthma only got under control when I had access to insurance in my late twenties, so every fall and winter would see me in the back room for weeks at a time.

My mother and stepfather were volatile—drinking too much; fighting too much. I hid more and more in schoolwork. My natural teenage tendencies to pull away were exacerbated.

Star Trek is utopic, despite its imperfections—there's fighting and greed. There are unavoidable technical difficulties. There is a capricious god named Q, who had the benefit of seeming more approachable than the Southern Baptist god to whom I had been pledged—from whom I was fleeing.

Star Trek had a system in place: the Federation. I don't think I grasped, when I was younger, that the Federation was like a government agency—the military, the CDC, NASA combined. For me, it was our future—all of ours.

And it was glorious. The leaders were generally wise—and when they weren't, they could be relieved of command. Science and knowledge were embraced—the brainier the better. Class seemed to melt away—the uniform hid where you'd come from—resources on the ship were allocated equally. The replicator could provide you with food.

It could probably provide you with other essentials—a copy of *The Handmaid's Tale* when your stepfather wouldn't give you the money to buy it, leaving you to go up to the teacher during a break and explain. "Oh," she would whisper, "we set aside some books for kids like you."

And then there were the lessons. Having a Russian officer still mattered in reruns in the 80s. Having a black female officer still mattered in the deep south.

Saving the whales mattered.

Seeing what everyone could accomplish when poverty wasn't in their way mattered.

Seeing therapy as normal and necessary probably helped me reach out for it in graduate school.

But the moment I return to in memory the most was an episode in which Beverly Crusher fell in love with an alien, only to find out that the alien lived in host bodies. She found she could still love it when it jumped to another man. But she couldn't when it jumped to a woman.

I cried. Sobbed, really. And thought about—for the first time—how wrong it was to emphasize the type of body one loved.

It was a window into a world in which a woman might love someone in another woman's body—and how that was still love.

Human interaction—how we might work and play and love across our differences was much more interesting than the sliding doors and the hand-held communicators.

Today, I'm a teacher at UC Davis, where I teach writing, rhetoric, and critical thinking; as a non-tenure track faculty, I am part of the Academic Federation.

Jean-Luc Picard told me to "engage." And I did.

http://psychodrivein.com/first-frontier-celebration-fifty-years-star-trek/

Schedule for A Celebration of *Star Trek*

9:00–10:00

Idic: Philosophy and *Star Trek*
   Timothy Harvie, Matt Yockey, Nathanael Bassett, Jason Eberl,
   A. Bowdoin Van Riper, Scott Paeth
The Federation: Politics and *Star Trek*
   Patrick Smith, Michael MacLeod, Joy Ellison, George Gonzalez
Through the Wormhole: Reevaluating *DS9*
   Gordon Dymowski, Jennifer Cross, Matthew Peters, Sherry
   Ginn

10:15–11:15

**Academic Keynote: "'A dream that became a reality and spread
throughout the stars': History, Myth and American Culture in
Star Trek."**
   Dr. Lincoln Gergahty
History of the Klingon Empire, Part I
   Troy Pacelli
The Cultural Impact of Star Trek
   Elizabeth Thomas, Michi Trota, Caroline Siede, Kevin Yeargin,
   Andre Peltier
Trekkies, Trekkers, And Beyond: Fandom of *Star Trek*
   Ian Peters, Sarah Corse, Rick Worland, Jaime Hartless

11:30–12:30
Learn Klingon
   Jeremy Cowan
***Star Trek* and Gender**
   Patricia Vettel-Becker, Bruce Drushel, Kate Kulzick, Laura
Ammon
Llap: The Future According to *Star Trek*
   Allison Broesder, Shanna Gilkeson, Jody Lynn Nye, Kathleen
   Toerpe, Vivian Chin
Canon, Fanon, and In-Between: *Star Trek* Fan Works
   Jsa Lowe, Ian Peters, Cait Coker, Candace Benefiel
Generations of Trek: Film, TV, and the Evolution of *Star Trek*
   Michi Trota, Walter Podrazik, Jon Clarke, Danette Chavez

1:00–2:00
Producer Keynote
Brannon Braga

2:15-3:15
Writer Keynote
Lisa Klink
History of the Klingon Empire, Part II
Troy Pacelli
Debating The Future: Otherness and Privilege in *Star Trek*
Jennifer Cross, Kate Lansky, Keidra Chaney, Tanya Depass, Jonathon Lundy
Star Trek: Fan Phenomena
Bruce Drushel, Michael Boynton, Cait Coker, Elizabeth Thomas

3:30-4:30
Lecture: Leonard Nimoy Tribute
John Tenuto and Maria Jose Tenuto
Klingon: A Case Study af Conlangs in Mass Media
Jeremy Cowan
Beam Me Up: *Star Trek* Performance
Michael Boynton, Nick Wagner, Sean Kelly, Christopher Kidder-Mostrom
The Future Is Here: Science and Technology in *Star Trek*
Charles Adler, Nathanial Ramos, Liz Faber, Karma Waltonen

4:45-5:45
Klingon Christmas Carol
Christopher Kidder-Mostrom
Teaching Trek: Pedagogy and *Star Trek*
Carey Millsap-Spears, Robin Willey, Jim Mcintyre, Vickie Edwards, Melissa Csoke
Queer Identities in Cosplay And Fandom
Kimber Brightheart, Dommenique Dumptrux, Paige Elise, Ari Stanley, Leigh Hellman, Malice Aforethought.
Fantasy Draft Crew!
Kate Kulzick, Caroline Siede, Gordon Dymowski, Jon Clarke, Jody Lynn Nye, Nick Wagner

Screening Schedule

9:00–10:30 *Enterprise:* "In a Mirror Darkly, 1&2."
9:10–10:00 *Star Trek:* "Space Seed."
10:15–11:00 *The Next Generation:* "Relics."
10:30–11:15 *Deep Space 9:* "Far Beyond the Stars."
11:30–12:15 *Star Trek:* "Trouble with Tribbles."
1:00–1:45 *Deep Space 9:* "Soldiers of the Empire."
1:00–1:45 *Deep Space 9:* "In the Pale Moonlight."
1:00– 1:45 *Star Trek:* "Mirror, Mirror."
1:00– 1:30 *The Animated Series:* "More Tribbles, More Trouble."
1:30– 2:15 *The Next Generation:* "Cause and Effect."
1:45– 2:30 *Voyager:* "Timeless."
1:45– 2:15 *The Animated Series:* "Yesteryear."
2:30– 3:15 *The Next Generation:* "Darmok."
2:15– 3:00 *Deep Space 9:* "Trials & Tribble-ations."
3:00– 5:00 *Star Trek: First Contact*
3:30– 4:15 *"The Next Generation:* "The Inner Light."
4:15– 5:00 *Voyager:* "Year of Hell, I."
5:00– 5:45 *Voyager:* "Year of Hell, II."
5:00– 5:50 *Star Trek:* "City on the Edge of Forever."

HARRY
POTTER
and the Pop Culture Conference
DEPAUL UNIVERSITY

Introduction

Paul Booth

As I type this, we are still two months away from *Harry Potter and the Pop Culture Conference*, and so in some ways it seems a bit disingenuous for me to be discussing what hasn't happened yet (I wish I had a Time Turner, so I could attend the conference and then go back to now and actually write this!). At the same time, we seem to have so much already arranged for this event that I can't believe we have to wait a full **two months** before it happens; we've been living with this event for so long that I really can't believe it isn't here yet.

Probably the most notorious truth about this conference is that this little event got big—in a variety of ways. Not only do we have more people signed on to be on panels (at last count it was about 80), but we also have more people pre-registered to attend (right now we're sold out of free tickets, with an active waiting list, but we also are running out of tee shirt/donation tickets as well). Whether all these people end up attending is another thing (we often have more people register than attend) but it certainly has been an adventure with the tickets! This speaks to one of the truths of the Pop Culture Conference in general—as a self-described part fan convention and part academic conference, the Pop Culture Conference draws on two different worlds. Focusing this year on a children's book and film series has opened up a third category as well, the "fan event." From bookstore happenings to whole towns celebrating *Harry Potter*, the series has generated an enormous amount of activities for children—and while that's fantastic for the series and for those events, it's not something that the Pop Culture Conference ever tried to generated deliberately (in fact, given some of the content of the panels at this year's conference, some parents might not want their children to attend at all!).

Another consequence of "getting big" this year was the involvement of Warner Brothers during the planning of the event. Although the Pop Culture Conference has always skirted copyright issues (in fact, holding a scholarly conference about a pop culture text falls very squarely into the "fair use" clause of copyright), Warner Brothers did contact us quite early on in the planning with some requests, mainly about the promotion of the event. For instance, we had to change some of the images on the flyer and in the social media promotion because it conflicted with Warner Brothers. Astute attendees of multiple Pop Culture Conferences will notice that there are no screenings at this event—this is also at the request of Warner Brothers.

Not having screenings, however, also freed up the conference to feature some new and unique types of panels—it's great to be able to include "A Day at Hogwarts" classroom experience, and the Columbia College Renegades Quidditch club, to teach attendees how to play Quidditch. I'm also impressed by the sheer number of interesting panels topics we've been able to include this year, including:

* "The Religious Potter: Religion, Ethics, and Meaning in Harry Potter"
* "Discarding the Cloak of Invisibility: A Candid Look at the Whitewashing in the Potterverse"
* "The Harry Potter Alliance, Fan Activism, and Stories for Social Change"
* "Harry Potter and the Infinite Syllabus: How Harry Potter Has Shaped Education"
* "Are Metaphors Enough? Queer Readings of Harry Potter"
* "Expanding the Narrative: Spin-offs, Sequels, and the Harry Potter Canon"
* "The Occult Potter: Materiality and Wizardry in Harry Potter"
* "The Patronuses: Putting Harry Potter Activism into Practice"
* "The Historical Potter: Harry Potter, History, and Propaganda"
* "Inclusion and the Other in J.K. Rowling's Harry Potter"
* "Quidditch Through the Ages: Columbia College Quidditch Team"
* "The Banality of Evil: Collaborators and Appeasement in Harry Potter"
* "Fandom: Pilgrimages, Preferences, and Performances
* "The Political Potter: Harry Potter and the Political Situation"
* "From Representation to Resistance: Reimagining Harry Potter to Reflect Our Struggles"
* "The Importance of Memes in How We Understand the Harry Potter Franchise"
* "JK Who? Investigating Authorship in the Harry Potter Canon and Fandom"

It's also particularly gratifying to see so many students suggesting panels and topics—including undergraduate as well as graduate students in the roster.

Our Distinguished Keynote Speaker, Alanna Bennett, was such a treat to chat with before the event—I'm so pleased that we're able to bring in pop culture writers from a variety of outlets. Finding speakers specifically from *Harry Potter* proved to be difficult for this year's event, not just because there are fewer people involved in the process of writing a book than there are in a television show, but also because many of the people we contacted were not able to attend due to the mysteries and silences surrounding *The Cursed Child.* Many of the people involved with that stage show were sworn to secrecy and can't even talk about it over email! However, I'm really thoroughly pleased that Dr. Christopher Bell was also able to be our Academic Keynote for the event.

From Authorship to Quidditch, the *Harry Potter and the Pop Culture Conference* has been a joy to plan. Overall, I'm really so incredibly touched with how energized and excited people seem to be about the event this year—2017 is shaping up to be our biggest and best year yet! I hope you enjoy reading a selection of pieces from the event and hearing what some of the amazing speakers, scholars, and fans had to say about this popular book and film series. See you in 2018!

Keynote
Harry Potter and the Generational Aftertaste

Alanna Bennett

Think, right now, about the first time you picked up a *Harry Potter* book. Think about the first time you heard words from the series, whether you were reading it or being read to. Think about the first time—maybe a separate time, maybe not—when those words clicked together for you, in your head, and made a place for themselves. If you're reading this, chances are you have your own memories of these things. So many of us do. Because if there's one incontrovertible fact about *Harry Potter*, one that's been overstated to the point of exhaustion but still remains as true as the day someone first made the observation, it's that an entire generation has been shaped by the presence of the *Harry Potter* series. In fact, multiple have.

The entrance of *Harry Potter* into our world is practically a myth unto itself at this point: After a long road of rejection, depression, and financial catastrophe, Joanne "Jo" Rowling achieved her dream of being a published author, and *Harry Potter and the Philosopher's Stone* hit shelves in the summer of 1997. We were all, it seems fair to say, considerably younger then—if we'd even been born. And *Harry* was just getting started: That fated day in June snowballed into something far bigger than itself. That's a story most know pretty well, filled with record-breaking sales, movie deals, and such an intense force of fandom and phenomena that it was socially—and mentally—revolutionary.

When I first encountered *Harry Potter* I was seven, and I found the book sitting on the floor of my best friend's bathroom. When I first actually *read it*, I was ten, and the movies were about to be released. Flash forward to today, and I'm a woman in her mid-twenties whose entire career has been shaped by *Harry Potter*, as have several hopefully lifelong friendships. That's a momentous thing in itself: A thing has to be pretty powerful to shape careers and bring people together in a lasting and tangible way. And even though certain details of my story are rare, others are downright commonplace. Sit next to a stranger on a bus, and chances are they will have *something* to say about *Harry Potter*.

The evidence of this impact is tangible in several ways—in how conversations about the series have virtually never stopped, even once the books and movies (temporarily) ended, for sure—but in others it's a more tricky kind of subtle. Even in the pop cultural spheres not technically directly related to *Harry Potter*, the aftertaste the series left is palpable. Professionally and extracurricularly, I have spent much of my life in fandom spaces, and it's made one thing clear: As more and more conversations around what audiences demand from their media spread to the mainstream, it's clear those conversations stemmed in fandom. And it's clear that, at least in part, a lot of those conversations either stemmed from or were influenced by the way *Harry Potter*'s massive fandom grew up and evolved around the series. How it re-shaped it through fan works, and how it learned from that work to demand more from the creators who were actually getting paid to make media.

Harry Potter is, as a text, very interested in the challenging of authority figures and institutions. Is it any surprise, then, that the mass audience that formed around it are famous for taking inspiration from the series and spinning it out in all directions through fanfiction, cultural criticism, and other fan-created works? And that, by nature of this movement and its evolution, many of the fan communities involved took it upon themselves to challenge *Harry Potter* itself? One of the *Harry Potter* fandom's greatest triumphs has been in proving that the deep love fans hold for a series can co-exist with and *fuel* cultural criticism of the series itself. That's a credo fandom's run with (and then some)—and it's one that's spreading beyond the traditional fandom spaces like Tumblr, LiveJournal, and Archive Of Our Own. It's one that's rapidly spreading through the mainstream, and that's poised to define conversations around issues like representation and diversity, as people fight for a wider variety of voices, experiences, and identities to be present in the stories that they love.

Think, now, about your relationship to *Harry Potter* today, and how you've changed in the years since the series first marked you. Picture again that first image of yourself meeting Harry and his world, and Jo and her words—and place it side by side with your modern self. Maybe you picked up the series late, and it's not actually that wide a gap at all. Or maybe when you look back in time you see a child in a different world, and when you look at where you are now you see someone who's been through decades of experience, with all the daily drudgeries and time-consuming changes that entails. Picture what you wanted out of your stories when you first picked up the series. Picture what you want from them now.

I've reported before, in a piece for BuzzFeed called "The *Harry Potter* Fandom Is At A Crossroads," about the strange place in which the community around *Harry Potter* finds itself now. *Harry Potter* is continuing on in spin-off franchises, and it's unclear how long they'll last, how deeply they'll intersect with the original series, or if they will actually evolve with the world and include the wider variety of voices the fandom is demanding. We don't know where *Harry Potter* will be ten years from now. We don't know where *we'll* be. But what we can know, in the here and now, is this: In both the wistful and the more pragmatic ways, *Harry Potter* is all around us. There's a lot, still, for us to learn from it and the conversations around us. And there is absolutely no way to turn back the clock—the impact that it's made on the ways we see the world are here to stay, and the best thing we can do is look deeply at the ways it's changed us. It might just teach us how to build something that will continue to impact the generations that come after us.

Secret Languages and Sacred Tongues: A Rough History of an Idea and Its Influence

Nathanael Bassett

What is magic? In Harry Potter's world, wizards and other beings are able to channel forces beyond the natural. All beings are either imbued with this ability or not. A stark divide exists between the wizarding world and the "muggle" (mundane) world. Those fortunate enough to have these powers study and practice magic similar to a kind of scientific knowledge—Hogwarts and other institutions hold exams, award degrees and tutor in the proper use and knowledge of such skills. When magic is used, it comes from the will of the magician, typically uttered in special terms ("Alohomora," "Wingardium Leviosa" and so on). This use of a special language, a sort of pseudo-Latin, derives from the historical significance of sacred languages, but the concept is similar to a *forma locutionis*, or a perfect, formative language, where expression equaled form.

The term *forma locutionis* comes from Umberto Eco's "Search For The Perfect Language," which looks at Abulafia's and Dante's concept that all language is derivative of the means by which God spoke the world into being in Judeo-Christian mythology. The *forma locutionis* involves a direct correlation between modes of being (*modi esendi*) and modes of signifying (*modi significandi*). So the invocations of a secret language mean I do not just describe things, but I call them forth. In the very least I offer a perfect descriptor of a thing so that we can understand its true nature and important associations.

Gods of sky and air feature heavily into creation myths. Air is a classical Greek element and is closely related with spirit. In Biblical Greek this is *pneuma*, the wind and spirit God breathed into all living things. *Chokmáh*, or wisdom, is the *sephirot* on the Kabbalistic Tree of Life where intellect meets with creation. As Job. 28:12 notes, "Wisdom comes from nothingness." Likewise in the New Testament, John 3:8 reads, "the wind [*pneuma*] bloweth where it listeth, and thou hearest the sound thereof, but canst not tell whence it cometh, and whither it goeth: so is every one that is born of the Spirit [*pneuma*]." *Binah* (intelligence) and *Chokmáh* are the first children of *Kether* [crown], the highest emanation of the infinite divine.

After God breathed life into Adam, they spoke, and Adam was charged with naming all the animals. This is not just assigning arbitrary signifiers to what he perceives, but apprehending it, making it intelligible, bringing order to chaos. This fits with cosmological accounts where the creative power of a demiurge is passed down into creation. Creation myths typically are *ex nihilo*, *chaoskampfs*, or from *prima materia*. This is creation from nothing, creation from struggle with chaos, and creation from a first matter (the origins of the concept of a "Philosopher's stone").

Through these changes, some remnants of a divine essence remain, to be harnessed by others seeking to make changes in their own world. Prometheus steals the fire of Mount Olympus, so that humans might have a fraction of the power of the gods. Harnessing this power involves thaumaturgical or theurgical approach. This involves making direct changes in the world, or changes in oneself. Mystery religions, occult practices and various esoterica (not to mention institutional spirituality), are the study of these magicks, sometimes called the "Great Work" – questing for the "Holy Grail," climbing the Tree of Life, searching for the Philosopher's Stone. Complex frameworks are necessary to understand reality so that one can change it.

Some examples of this include the "Enochian" angelic language of John Dee, the *Ars Goetia*, the Kabbalistic study of the names of God, alchemy and sacred geometry. In less esoteric corners of thought, natural philosophy gave way to mechanical understandings of the world, and a heliocentric universe along with corpuscular philosophy lead to modern scientific rationalism and empiricism. But what is missing is still a clear understanding of our social and ecological relations. We seldom are fully aware of our *habitus*, the power dynamics of social relations in Bourdieu's terms. We are perplexed by *Dasein*, or Heidegger's thought on being-in-the-world and our conflicts with nature and *Das Men* (society). What we do have now is a rough map of the world through which we work our contemporary magics (technology) on society. But the dream of an Ademic language remains as a descriptive and prescriptive approach to understanding and affecting the world. It is the ultimate pipe dream for theorists.

Characters of fictional worlds sometimes have a level of self-awareness granted by their authors. In meta-fiction means, characters can take over the story and speak directly to the reader in a way conventional narrative doesn't allow. They sometimes struggle to change themselves or their world, with varying results. John Constantine of the *Hellblazer* comic series may be well aware he is written as a bastard, and that nothing can change that. Dream of the Endless, from Neil Gaiman's *Sandman* series, replaces his immutable existence in the death of a "point of view" about Dream. Other characters like Gaiman's Tim Hunter (very similar to Harry Potter), Alan Moore's Promethea, and Mike Carey's Tommy Taylor (also based on Harry Potter), struggle with varying levels of self-awareness and magical ability. Deadpool's absolute frustration with how Marvel Comics authors determine his existence is the subject of a short series where he murders all the other superheroes in his universe, before coming for the reader.

Perhaps the best example of this awareness of the creator's language is Vivec of "The Elder Scrolls: Morrowind" videogame. The player discovers a series of books in the game called *The 36 Lessons of Vivec*. A common theory among players is that these books and his dialogue indicate his awareness that he is an NPC, but that he could also access the command interface and change the game to his liking. Like Neo of *The Matrix*, he understands his reality and has the power to rewrite the source code, if he so chooses. But he's a character in a video game, so why bother?

The ultimate awareness these characters have is similar to the kind of knowledge we look for when we ask questions like "why am I here" and "what's the meaning of life?" This is often why people turn to magick and science, to explain and describe their world. Alchemy is often described as a sort of proto-chemistry, but Jung described it as an early form of psychoanalysis. The goal is not to turn lead to precious metals, but oneself into a better person. As the alchemist in Joderwosky's "The Holy Mountain" instructs, "You are excrement. You can make yourself into gold."

This is what we see in Harry Potter. The story begins with an orphan, who lives in a cupboard under the stairs in an abusive home. It ends with the same boy now grown, surrounded by friends and family. Although he spent a good deal of time studying magic, his actions and efforts to transform his reality came about through a deliberate force of will, something derived from J.K. Rowling's best wishes for him. Harry Potter's success as a magician doesn't come from a mastery of the arcane language used by wizards, but from the embrace of *habitus* and *daisen*. He has found his place in the world, and it is good.

Sharper Than a Serpent's Tongue: Parents and Children in the *Harry Potter* Series

Kate Behr

Love it or loathe it, *Harry Potter and the Cursed Child* is very much part of the Potter-verse, revisiting scenes from the past, questioning decisions made, and trying to reverse or restore past events. As readers and audience, we've been here before. Situated in but not of the Potter world, the play must draw on established characters, and with them come recognizable devices and established storylines. Familiar themes from the book series are reinforced, highlighting love, friendship, and family, as magic doesn't—can't—make everything right.

In revisiting familiar themes as they work themselves out in the next generation, the play shifts the focus—uncomfortably for some reviewers and fans—from mothers to fathers (Shepherd). In the book series, more attention was on the mothers who were almost invariably "good" and physically absent, while their mother love extended powerful but intangible protection. JK Rowling's 2011 interview makes this clear: from Lily Potter choosing to die in order to save her baby son to Narcissa Malfoy protecting Harry from Voldemort in order to protect her own son, mothers in the Potter series protect their children (Rowling). Motherlove gives them exceptional strength (Anelli Part One). Lily can die. Narcissa can defy Voldemort. Molly Weasley can epically defeat Bellatrix Lestrange in the last battle. All mothers in the book series are good mothers—except, perhaps, for Hagrid's giantess mother, whose neglect is, apparently, typical for giants, and Merope Gaunt, whose death doesn't protect her son but confirms his abandonment. Further, unlikeable characters can also be obsessive mothers: consider Petunia Dursley, an appalling mother-substitute for Harry (though she does grudgingly protect him), who passionately loves her piggish son. Protective motherlove is present, to death and through madness; Alice Longbottom's pathetic gifts of sweet-wrappers to her son demonstrate that love can survive torture (Anelli Part Three). Love is present but not always (like the sweet-wrappers, sweaters, or nagging Howlers) obviously potent.

Impotent families are necessary to the plot, which demands that children be outside the family protective circle so that action may happen. Mothers must be absent and fathers out of the picture. The boarding school genre effectively keeps the families at bay while allowing only tokens and remembrances signifying the life and love outside, within its walls. In this fictional world, responsible parenting means giving children agency—even allowing them to risk their lives (Winters). Here, *The Cursed Child* differs from the book series—fathers are seen actively and futilely working to impose their parental authority and "save" their children (Thorne 116).

In fact, as reviewers recognized, father/child relationships are the core of *The Cursed Child* (Kakutani, Memmott). Albus Severus Potter struggles with/against his father, Harry, and Scorpius Malfoy thinks he's a disappointment to his father, Draco (CC 141). Although there are father/daughter pairings as well, the plot diminishes them: one of the abortive trips into the past removes Rose Granger-Weasley completely, and we never see Delphi in any actual relationship with Voldemort. Instead all our attention is on the fathers and their sons, highlighting questions of identity, allegiance, and relationship already present in the book series that are given more force in the play as it's not Harry Potter who has to contend with the Harry Potter Legend, but the younger son who has unwillingly inherited it.

The parental paradigm in the book series was distant, but (at least initially) heroic and all-wise, a composite of dead James Potter, the Quidditch champion, and present father-substitute, headmaster Albus Dumbledore. This fits neatly into Jacques Lacan's idea of the symbolic father—largely absent, a paradigm of power, and the law-giver (67). This father is a social construct, what a father "ought to be" and rarely what an actual father is. The book series showed us how Harry struggled to reconcile the real James Potter (the reckless, occasional bully) with the heroic father he'd imagined.

How much harder, then, is it for Albus Severus Potter to establish his own identity when he's constantly overshadowed by the Harry Potter Legend and is even named after two dead father-substitutes? Especially as the legend doesn't match up to the awkward reality that Harry doesn't understand or communicate well with his son? The legend acts like a mirror, an external image of the body (remember Albus resembles Harry) wherein the child recognizes a part of himself that he doesn't equal, and so he measures himself against the "ideal," against the legend, and not against the real man.

Albus sees himself as an outsider, an unworthy child, and makes friends, almost in defiance of the legend, with a similarly struggling Scorpius Malfoy, who is ill-at-ease with his father, Draco, with his legacy as a Malfoy, and with the persistent rumor that he might be Voldemort's child (Thorne 17). It's the outsider quality, the flaws in the legend, that prompt Albus and Scorpius into trying to change the narrative. They want to heal a shattered father/son relationship by restoring Cedric Diggory to his grieving father, Amos, and "make one of his [Harry's] mistakes right" (Thorne 53).

In the end, the choices that Albus and Scorpius make bring their relationships with the fathers out of the imaginary stage. Instead of acting against authority figures, they work with their real parents in defeating Delphi and *not* using magic to change events as they witness the deaths in Godric's Hollow that ensured The-Boy-Who-Lived. In the book series, Lily chose to act and sacrifice herself to protect her baby; in the play, her son and grandson also make a heroic choice – not to act, to protect her choice and Voldemort's choice, which dooms him.

Early readers were disappointed by the script, many tweeting vehemently that the Harry Potter they *knew* from Rowling's books could never/would never have been a bad father (Shepherd). But what makes a father bad? Is it someone who fails to protect his son? Someone who fails to fight for him? Or is it someone who fails to live up to the "Name of the Father"? Someone who disappoints him? If the answer to those questions is yes, then Dumbledore, Sirius, and James Potter are all failures because Harry wants them to be better than they can be. The same is true in *The Cursed Child*. Harry Potter is not a bad father any more than he was an inadequate hero. The play confirms what the book series showed—even the best adults don't have all the answers and magic cannot fix anyone's mistakes.

References
Anelli, Melissa, and Emerson Spartz. "'The Leaky Cauldron and MuggleNet interview Joanne Kathleen Rowling: Part One." *The Leaky Cauldron*, 16 July 2005, www.accio-quote.org/articles/2005/0705-tlc_mugglenet-anelli-1.htm. Accessed 23 Feb. 2017.
"'The Leaky Cauldron and MuggleNet interview Joanne Kathleen Rowling: Part Three." *The Leaky Cauldron*, 16 July 2005, accio-quote.org/articles/2005/0705-tlc_mugglenet-anelli-3.htm. Accessed 23 Feb. 2017
Kakutani, Michiko. "Review:'Harry Potter and the Cursed Child' Explores the Power of Time." *New York Times*. 8-1-16. Nytimes.com/2016/08/02/books/harry-potter-and-the-cursed-child.htm. Accessed 3-8-2017.
Lacan, Jacques. *Ecrits: A Selection*. Translated by Alan Sheridan, 1977; repr. Routledge, 1989.

Memmott, Carol. "Review: 'Harry Potter and the Cursed Child." *Chicago Tribune.*
8-16-2016. Accessed 3-8-2017.

Rowling, JK. "The Women of Harry Potter." *Harry Potter and the Deathly Hallows: Part 2.* Warner Brothers, 2011. DVD.

Shepherd, Jack. "Harry Potter and the Cursed Child book: Why some fans really dislike JK Rowling's new script." independent.co.uk/arts-entertainment/books/news/harry-potter-and-the-cursed-child-book-why-some-fans-really-dislike-jk-rowlings-new-script-a7165991.html. Accessed 14 Mar. 2017.

Thorne, John, with John Tiffany and JK Rowling. *Harry Potter and the Cursed Child.* Arthur Levine Books, 2017.

Winters, Sarah Fiona. "Bubble-Wrapped Children and Safe Books for Boys: The Politics of Parenting in Harry Potter." *Children's Literature*, vol. 39, 2011, pp. 213–233.

Harry Potter and the Cursed Franchise

Gerry Canavan

In July 2016 the long-concluded Harry Potter franchise unexpectedly returned to life in a highly unusual form: as a stage play in London. Eventually released in screenplay format worldwide, *Harry Potter and the Cursed Child* revisits Harry's story nineteen years later, extending the narrative from a slightly revised version of the epilogue as his second son, Albus Potter, heads to Hogwarts for the first time. But Albus's story soon turns sour: he is sorted into Slytherin House, not Gryffindor or even Hufflepuff, a fact that ultimately leads to a break with his father and years of painful discord in their relationship. Nor is Hogwarts as safe as the "all was well" ending of Book Seven would suggest; even after Voldemort is defeated, his followers continue to linger and scheme, ultimately dragging the Potters into insidious time-travel machinations that threaten to retroactively undo their victory altogether.

As with other recent revivals of beloved franchises (most notably *Star Wars: The Force Awakens* from 2015, with which it shares a number of surprising structural parallels), the breakdown in traditional narrative structure caused by the profit-driven need to continually renew a commercial franchise inevitably produces a mood of misery and cosmic pessimism in texts like *The Cursed Child.* As narratives are forced to unnaturally stretch out, open-endedly, into forever, their heroes are no longer allowed to "win," or even earn a moment of rest. *The Cursed Child,* like *The Force Awakens,* thus turns what was once a fairytale ending into a sort of permanent nightmare for the characters, from which there is no hope or any possible escape. Our characters may *look* happy when the credits roll at the end of *Return of the Jedi* or *The Deathly Hallows,* but when we pick up the thread again we find them grown old and unhappy, their personal lives in tatters and their triumphs rendered partial, inadequate, or moot. In *The Cursed Child* the situation may be even worse than in *The Force Awakens,* as the revision to established canon regarding the previously ironclad limits on the use of Time Turners casts Harry's entire victory into permanent threat; at any moment some would-be follower of Voldemort could travel back in time and undo everything, just as Albus does.

The new political economy of the corporate franchise renders any sort of happy ending fragile at best; now no story truly "ends," but simply waits for the moment of its nostalgic revival ten or twenty years down the line. As the father of a five-year-old and a three-year-old I can't help but think of this in terms of my own parenting—of the way the well-intentioned desire to pass on the beloved artifacts of your youth and keep them relevant for your children has come to have the perverse effect of poisoning those happy memories. *Return of the Jedi* ended in smiles, a fireworks display, hugs, and a picnic—and, we have come to find out, the total failure of Luke's project to revive the Jedi Order, the corruption and collapse of the erstwhile New Republic, the return of the Empire, a bitter divorce, the loss of a child to the same addictive Dark Side that once destroyed his grandfather. Likewise, Harry, Hermione, and Ron may have defeated Voldemort, but the world they live in is still frighteningly corrupt, and essentially immune to any sort of lasting improvement or reform, while their psyches are battered by trauma and their personal lives frustrated and fractured— and through it all Voldemort's followers are still out there, lurking and unpunished, just waiting for another chance.

I think often of *The New Shadow,* the sequel to *The Lord of the Rings* Tolkien once briefly considered writing, which was to be set 100 to 150 years later during the reign of Aragorn's son Eldarion. *The New Shadow* reveals that the eucatastrophic ending of *The Return of the King* was extremely short-lived; with the Elves and the Wizards gone from Middle-earth, the Dwarves moving underground, and the Hobbits now isolated in what amounts to an enclave in the Shire, Men quickly fall back into their old bad habits. In fact by the time of *The New Shadow* the Men of Gondor already seem to have forgotten much of the details of the War of the Ring, even though it remains in living memory: they seem not to remember, or take seriously, the fact that they once strode with gods and angels in a war against pure evil, and were victorious. Instead, children play at being Orcs for fun; the death of Aragorn has been an occasion for political striving and reactionary plots; and something like a secret death cult of devil-worshipping rebels seems to be spreading through the elites of Gondor.

Tolkien wrote 13 pages. He later wrote:

I did begin a story placed about 100 years after the Downfall, but it proved both sinister and depressing. Since we are dealing with Men it is inevitable that we should be concerned with the most regrettable feature of their nature: their quick satiety with good. So that the people of Gondor in times of peace, justice and prosperity, would become discontented and restless — while the dynasts descended from Aragorn would become just kings and governors — like Denethor or worse. I found that even so early there was an outcrop of revolutionary plots, about a centre of secret Satanistic religion; while Gondorian boys were playing at being Orcs and going around doing damage. I could have written a 'thriller' about the plot and its discovery and overthrow — but it would have been just that. Not worth doing.

Franchise revivals like *The Cursed Child* and *The Force Awakens*—perhaps, already, the dominant narrative form of our cultural moment, at least in mainstream entertainment—necessarily have this same sinister, depressing character, almost by definition. They tell stories that don't end, that *can't* end, just like history doesn't ever end—which in a way can be thought of as a marker of their increased sophistication, but in another way can be seen as poisoning all their joy. That stories have happy endings, when history doesn't, is one of the nice things about stories—or it used to be. That's what Tolkien knew when he put *The New Shadow* away. *The scar had not pained Harry for nineteen years. All was well.* Well, not *really*, of course. *Once upon a time, they all lived happily ever after.* Sure, sure, until one day…

The Limits of Heroism: Reading *Harry P*
in Post-Truth America

Sarah K. Cantrell

For those of us whose racial, cis-het, or able-bodied privilege has been a shield against oppression, November 9, 2016 was a rude awakening. We now live in a country where freedom of the press, speech, assembly, religion, and other civil liberties are no longer assured. In the month following the presidential election, the Southern Poverty Law Center documented 1,094 hate crimes, 757 of which targeted immigrant, Black, Muslim, and LGBTQ + communities ("Hatewatch"). Yet as many of us searched for ways to protect our more vulnerable neighbors, patronuses from the *Harry Potter* books appeared on social media. Facebook users shared photographs of Rowling's pages, reminding us that we must also resist the "Dark Mark" of the current administration. In one example, a photo of the words "Dumbledore's Army" from *Order of the Phoenix* prompted viewers to defend the less privileged. Another post referenced Kingsley Shacklebolt's injunction that "[e]very human life ... is worth saving" (*Deathly* 440). As Hogwarts students conjure patronuses, their efforts model resistant, radical hope rather than violent revenge. Yet Rowling's text also problematically situates her protagonists as saviors of house-elves, Muggles, and less privileged "others." Such characters seem to function as magical "others" whose presence is merely a springboard for Harry and Hermione's own growth. Thus, Rowling's narrative raises the question: how might we advocate for endangered communities' needs without celebrating our own heroism?

The reappearance of his Dark Mark at the Quidditch World Cup in *Goblet of Fire* sanctions the re-emergence of hatred in the wizarding community. In such a climate, Draco Malfoy's early racism towards Hermione ("you filthy little Mudblood" [*Chamber* 112]) finds full-scale social and political support from Voldemort's followers. In *Deathly Hallows*, Bellatrix Lestrange tortures Hermione with the Cruciatus Curse just as the Carrows take delight in brutalizing resistant Hogwarts students (573). Neville Longbottom explains that Alecto Carrow's bigoted pedagogy is deliberately designed to dehumanize Muggles: "We've all got to listen to her explain how Muggles are like animals, pid and dirty…" (574). Rowling specifically incorporates racist characters like Draco, Bellatrix, and the Carrows to remind readers that bigotry is real. Alecto's ideology is also reminiscent of the current president's equations of Mexicans with criminals and rapists and Muslims with terrorists during his campaign. In this vein, Dumbledore's advice that Harry must "keep fighting, for only then could evil be kept at bay, though never completely eradicated" (*Half-Blood* 645) is instructive: we must acknowledge and combat racist intolerance.

In this climate of fear, Rowling's protagonists provide admirable examples of activism, laughter, and kindness. Their choices confirm scholar Jackie Horne's argument that Rowling's text models ways readers can "confront, eradicate, and ameliorate racism…" (76). For example, Hermione attempts to free Hogwarts' house-elves despite her peers' ostracism; she recognizes Dolores Umbridge as a threat to free inquiry, and she urges the formation of Dumbledore's Army to empower her peers. The Weasley twins turn Hogwarts into a swamp, provoking joyous chaos to thwart Umbridge's control. Such efforts inspire other students: Neville Longbottom creates the Room of Requirement in Harry's absence; Luna Lovegood leads her peers in producing patronuses that ward off Harry's despair; Colin Creevy chooses to die fighting rather than escape to safety. It is also worth noting that Luna, Colin, and Neville are outsiders whose mannerisms initially provoke their peers' irritation. As a result of their exclusion, they understand the dangers of hate in ways more privileged characters do not.

Yet even as Rowling's series calls for activist empathy, her text should also caution us against centering our own heroism. Like many white savior figures, Hermione assumes she knows best, and she attempts to liberate Hogwarts' house-elves without their involvement. As I note elsewhere, the series concludes with Harry hoping Kreacher will "bring him a sandwich" (*Deathly* 749), which maintains their master-servant relationship rather than abolishing it (61). Similarly, Kingsley celebrates "wizards and witches risking their own safety to protect Muggle friends and neighbors" (*Deathly* 440). This call to altruistic sacrifice is laudable and necessary. Yet Kingsley simultaneously characterizes Muggles as "ignorant of the source of their suffering" (440). His statement positions Muggles as helpless and denies their agency. Such wording also suggests an imperialist view whereby like house-elves, Muggles also require wizards to save them.

Moreover, the name "Muggle" evokes bumbling incompetency and an inability to engage in the divergent, creative thinking wizards like Dumbledore, Harry, and Hermione prize. As personified by the Dursleys, Muggles are childish blundering hysterics. Arthur Weasley's fascination with Muggle culture others them for laughs as he and Molly attempt to use electric plugs, telephones, and stamps. Nor does the text present any admirable, intelligent Muggles whose competency defies their magical limitations. Because readers identify with Rowling's heroes, such passages also endorse the view that readers know what vulnerable communities need, without ever having experienced marginalization themselves.

It is not my purpose to pillory Rowling's magnificent achievement. Such examples are not an argument against empathic engagement. Rather, they serve as a caution against the temptations of self-centered activism. We must stand with Persons of Color facing police brutality and deportation, with LGBTQ+ persons barred from jobs and restrooms, with Muslims banned from travel, with immigrants fleeing *our* country, with Jewish communities facing vandalism, and with the different-labled, especially when the president openly mocks them on live television. We must confront elected officials, barraging their offices with phone calls, letters, and emails. We must educate each other, rather than relying on communities experiencing discrimination to educate us. And we must do so without also erasing the voices of those whose safety we seek to secure. Such work is not convenient. It is not easy. Yet if Harry chooses to return to battle, to accept "pain and fear of more loss" (*Deathly* 722), so can we.

References

Cantrell, Sarah. "Harry Potter Goes to France: Exploring Erik L'Homme's *Le Livre des Étoiles (Book of the Stars)*." *The Lion and the Unicorn* 35 (2011): 47-66.

"Donald Trump Mocks CNN Reporter's Disability." *CNN Wire* 26 Nov. 2015, cnn.com 12 Mar. 2017.

"Hatewatch." *Southern Poverty Law Center*, 16 Dec. 2016, splccenter.org/hatewatch/2016/12/16 update-1094-bias-related-incidents-month-following-election 4 Mar. 2017.

Horne, Jackie C. "Harry Potter and the Other: Answering the Race Question in J.K. Rowling's Harry Potter." *The Lion and the Unicorn* 34.1 (2010): 76-104.

Johnson, Jenna. "Trump Calls for 'total and complete shutdown of Muslims entering the United States.'" *Washington Post* 7 Dec. 2015, washingtonpost.com 12 March 2017.

Trump, Donald. "Full Text: Donald Trump Announces A Presidential Bid." *Washington Post* 16 June 2015, washingtonpost.com 12 March 2017.

Harry Potter: A Saint for All of Us

Cynthia Cheshire

When the Harry Potter book series has been banned in schools, it's often been on religious grounds from conservative Christians taking issue with a positive portrayal of witchcraft. However, this ironically undermines one of the series' most striking elements: the portrayal of Harry Potter as a Christ figure himself. The *Harry Potter* series is the latest in a long and reputable line of allegorical fiction that pairs a secular vehicle with the messages of the Christian narrative—a synergistic relationship which benefits both secular and non-secular readers alike.

Giving an exhaustive account of the ways that the *Harry Potter* series and the Biblical narrative walk hand-in-hand is much like trying to compress *Hogwarts: A History* into these couple pages. For example: both Harry and Jesus of Nazareth are born into relative obscurity,[1] there are prophecies about both,[2] both endure an attempt on their lives within a couple years,[3] little is known about their early childhoods before they arrive on the public scene,[4] they both often act against the ruling powers of the day while fighting to protect the purity of the establishments they serve,[5] both gain a significant following but maintain only a few close friends, and both favor loyalty, compassion, and justice as chief virtues. The numbers seven and three factor largely in both bodies of literature. Friendship, sacrifice, and indeed, the combination of the two are consistent themes from *Sorcerer's Stone* on, as well as one of the hallmarks of Jesus' earthly ministry.[6] These are all notable, even quaint, points of similarity, but where the froth really hits the butterbeer is how both Harry and Jesus of Nazareth function in their respective narratives, and how death figures into the victories of both heroes.

The most striking element that qualifies Harry Potter as a literary Christ-figure is his death in the Forbidden Forest.[7] Rowling looks both back to the Biblical text and forward to the climax of her own series when, in chapter 16 of *Deathly Hallows*, Harry and Hermione read the inscriptions off of two gravestones in Godric's Hollow. The second belongs to Harry's parents:

Harry did not need to kneel or even approach very close to it to make out the words engraved upon it...*The last enemy that shall be destroyed is death.* Harry read the words slowly, as though he would have only one chance to take in their meaning, and he read the last of them aloud. '"The last enemy that shall be destroyed is death"...' A horrible thought came to him, and with it a kind of panic. 'Isn't that a Death Eater idea? Why is that there?'

'It doesn't mean defeating death in the way that Death Eaters mean it, Harry,' said Hermione, her voice gentle. 'It means...you know...living beyond death. Living after death.'8

The fact that the Bible is not attributed here is proof of how well the themes in this verse intertwine with the themes of the series; make no mistake, this is a direct quote.9 "The last enemy that shall be destroyed is death," found in 1 Corinthians, is the center of a long and heavy chapter on resurrection. In its original context, it references Christ of course; but on Lily and James Potter's gravestone, it references their son. Years later, Harry walks into that clearing prepared to die in order to bring the suffering—not just of the Wizarding world, but of the unknowing Muggle world as well—to an end, and *this* is the main function of a literary Christ-figure. Voldemort hits Harry with the Killing Curse, Harry enters another realm, and then returns to his earthly body. After his resurrection, Harry's sacrifice acts as a kind of shield for his people, and as a result, Voldemort's curses aren't as effective,10 even until his death a few pages later. It is a feat of modern storytelling, and it is also an allegory worthy of placement next to Lewis or Tolkien.

Why should Rowling use a resurrection narrative known to most of the Western world as the frame for her story? Because just as it is Harry's literary *function* that qualifies him as a Christ-figure, it is the *function of the allegory* to legitimize the series' ethical lessons. Whether we identify as Christian or not, the basic aspects of the Biblical resurrection narrative are ingrained into Western culture. Even the most devoted Atheist can recite its basic structure: there was a guy, he died, he didn't stay dead, the world changed afterward. Imagine a world in which Biblical narratives were unknown to our cultural consciousness. How would we read the final chapters of *Deathly Hallows*? With a grain of salt, I think. It would seem like a fantastic work of fiction, an ending fit for a fairytale but not real life, and everything that Harry stands for—bravery, sacrifice, loyalty, and especially hope—would have an accordingly distant application. But because Harry's victory is encompassed within a literary framework so central and familiar to the Western mind, we are instantly predisposed to accept not only the narrative, but also its ethics.

Indeed, its ethical element is part of why the *Harry Potter* series is so beloved. We learn from Neville that the weak become strong and from Draco that power and position do not guarantee love or integrity. From Ron we learn the power of loyalty, and Hermione the value of both knowledge and wisdom. Sirius Black teaches us to reconsider how we look at those the world has identified as criminals, and to reassess the institutions that label them as such. Professor Lupin, Dobby and Hagrid remind us that the outcasts still matter. Even Umbridge, Bellatrix, and Voldemort have their lessons to teach about evil, the corruption of power, and what can happen when "the other" automatically translates to "the enemy."

But these are Biblical values too. After 2,000 years of cultural distance and repetition—to say nothing of the damage inflicted by people who claimed to be followers of Christ while acting nothing like him—the truth of Jesus of Nazareth and the lessons he taught become faded to even Christian ears. By putting many of the same lessons—along with the Christ-figure narrative—in an engaging context, J.K. Rowling reinvigorates "the old, old story" for *all* readers, to take from it what they will.11

Notes

1 Although beloved and highly regarded by those who knew them, the Potters were not celebrities or wizarding royalty; Jesus gets made fun of for being raised in Nazareth in John 1:46

2 *Harry Potter and the Order of the Phoenix,* Chapter 37; Isaiah 7:14, 53:10-11; Micah 5:2

3 *Harry Potter and the Sorcerer's Stone,* p. 45; Matthew 2:16

4 "Nearly ten years had passed....The room held no sign at all that another boy lived in the house, too." *Harry Potter and the Sorcerer's Stone,* p. 14; Only two of the four canonical gospels recount Jesus' birth, while the other two pick up at his adulthood. No canonical source gives any information about Jesus between the ages of about 2 and 30.

5 Harry's consistent rule-breaking—especially being out of bed after hours to do things like, say, procure the Sorcerer's Stone—is a well established element of the series. Jesus' "Cleansing of the Temple" (John 2:13-25) and saving the woman caught

in adultery (John 8:2-11) were at the very least unappreciated by the Temple authorities of his time, and his public claims to be the Son of God ended up being part of the justification for his arrest and turnover to the Roman authorities.

6 "Greater love has no one than this, that one lay down his life for his friends" John 15:13, NASB

7 *Harry Potter and the Deathly Hallows*, pg. 691-704. For an excellent overview of the idea of literary Christ-figures, see: Downing, Christine. "Typology and the Literary Christ-Figure: A Critique." *Journal of the American Academy of Religion.* Vol 36, No. 1 (Mar., 1968), pp. 13-27.

8 *Harry Potter and the Deathly Hallows*, 328

9 Corinthians 15:22; The first gravestone was Ariana Dumbledore's (*Deathly Hallows*, 325) and contained a direct quote from Matthew 6:21 (c.f. Luke 12:34)

10 *Harry Potter and the Deathly Hallows*, "He was lifted into the air, and it took all his determination to remain limp, yet the pain he expected did not come." p.726; "'He beat you!' yelled Ron, and the charm broke, and the defenders of Hogwarts were shouting and screaming again until a second, more powerful bang extinguished their voices once more." p. 730; "In one swift, fluid motion, Neville broke free of the Body-Bind Curse upon him" p.733; "'Haven't you noticed how none of the spells you put on them are binding? You can't torture them. You can't touch them.'" p 738; 1 Corinthians 15:54-58; Romans 6:22-23

11 Rowling herself has acknowledged the Christian parallels in the series: "To me [the religious parallels have] always been obvious," [Rowling] said. "But I never wanted to talk too openly about it because I thought it might show people who just wanted the story where we were going." Source: http://www.mtv.com/news/1572107/harry-potter-author-jk-rowling-opens-up-about-books-christian-imagery/

Excerpt from Introduction to *Justitia Revelio!* Locating the Nexus of Harry Potter and a Lived Theology of Justice

Marissa P. Corliss

At the turn of the twenty-first century, there were few people in the Western world who had not heard of the boy wizard, Harry Potter.[1] "The boy who lived,"[2] along with his scar, his school, his spells, and his sidekicks, catapulted to the center of pop culture in the early 2000s, generating unprecedented success for author, J.K. Rowling, and changing the landscape of fantasy literature for children and adults alike. Within the imaginative layers of Rowling's magical coming-of-age tale exists an intricate moral ethos yielding ample fodder for reflection on the role of fantasy with regard to theology, justice, and the novel as inspiration for spiritual practice. Fantasy creates space for the in-breaking of hope within the everyday. This nexus of hope and imagination, situated within the world of *Harry Potter*, serves as a vista toward a lived theology of justice for readers who accompanied "the boy who lived" in his revolution for the deliverance of wizarding society. Just as the magical world exists subtly within our own, unnoticed by the untrained eye, so are notions of Catholic social teaching present within the novels, and revealed only to those plumbing the depths of Rowling's work for the sacred.

In the central arc of this seven book saga, the magical community rallies around and places their hope in protagonist Harry Potter, as he and his allies fight the resurgence of Lord Voldemort and his loyal "Death Eater" sympathizers. As this struggle develops over the course of Rowling's *Potter* books, themes, figures, and plot points offer entrees into a deeper understanding of a faith that does justice in light of the Christian tradition. This work will explore the ways in which the literary world of Harry Potter offers an entrée into a Christian understanding of a spirituality of justice modeled on Catholic social teaching through various elements of the series, and how this might be appropriated by Christian young adults within a contemporary context.

What does a Catholic social ethos of liberating justice look like? Where is there space in Christian spirituality for the fervent pursuit of righteousness? Drawing upon scripture, historical developments in Catholic thought, and contemporary themes at the intersection of liberation theology and a lived theology of justice, what it means to advance toward a horizon of a just society for Christians will be explored.

Now that the theological basis of a spirituality of justice has been set as a foundation, reference will be made to how this is illustrated in Rowling's *Potter* series, and the ministerial import of how fantasy literature, and *Potter*, in particular, can cultivate a deeper lived faith will be surveyed. While fantasy literature itself can serve as a spiritual resource, as our connections and communications with one another evolve with technological progress, so have the various ways in which fantasy literature can be shared, thus creating the opportunity for fresh pedagogical approaches. Concerning my pastoral project of a podcast that explores *Harry Potter* and a Christian spirituality of justice, I will explore the appropriation of literature, and Potter specifically, as a spiritual resource through emerging means.

Notes

1 Anatol, Giselle. *Reading Harry Potter: Critical Essays*. Westport, CT: Praeger, 2003. Ix. Print.
2 Rowling, J.K. *Harry Potter and the Sorcerer's Stone*. New York: Scholastic, 1997. 17. Print.

Teaching *Harry Potter*

Heather Easley

I'd had it on my mind to sneak *Harry Potter* onto a syllabus since I began teaching at DePaul six years ago. Viewing the series from a sociological standpoint was just so *easy*, but most of all, fun. You see, I'm one of "those" people. I can relate almost any scenario from real life to the magical world, because when I'm reading (and re-reading) the series, *I live there.* I brought the idea of creating a course that focused on Harry to my previous chair, Julie Artis, who said, "Great! I love it. But make it a focal point." She, along with Doug Long, director of DePaul's First Year Program, could not have given better advice. The experience of designing and teaching this course has been the most creative and rewarding job I've had here at DePaul.

Teaching using fiction is not a new idea for me. Some of the best courses that I remember from my own undergraduate experience (right here at DePaul) were courses that relied either solely or heavily on works of fiction to highlight societal, philosophical, political issues, and more. I endeavored to include fiction in nearly all of my courses, and, over time, students began to thank me for assigning reading that held such meaning for them. The *Harry Potter* course is the culmination of my love of fiction in and out of the classroom, and the students' reactions! Priceless. I've had the unique joy of teaching students who are almost entirely passionate about the series even before setting foot into the classroom. What I've most enjoyed, however, is when they tell me that their love of the series grew even beyond what they originally felt for these great novels. I had feared that dissecting the books to such a great degree might remove some of the magic of the reader's experience, but I am thrilled to find that the community we've created within the classroom, imbues the books with even more of what we love so much about this story: communities of friendship and family, the search for good, and faith in love.

Remembralls and Recognition: A Resistant Reading of Neville Longbottom as Disabled

Joy Ellison

When I met Neville Longbottom in the pages of J.K. Rowling's first *Harry Potter* book, I recognized him right away. Neville couldn't remember the password to Gryffindor tower or much of anything else. He tripped over his feet. His teachers yelled at him to try harder, but all his efforts seemed to be worthless. His gran wondered why he was not more like his parents. When Neville fell off his broom, I knew that I would have done the same if my childhood PE classes involved magic. I recognized his limited motor skills, tendency to reverse or confuse processes, and decreased short-term memory as like my own experiences of dyslexia. Neville is like me—a person with learning disabilities.

In this paper, I offer a "resistant reading" of Neville Longbottom in which I claim him as disabled. While I assert there is ample textual evidence to support my characterization of Neville as disabled, my decision to describe him as such also transforms the text. I do not argue that Rowling intended readers to understand Neville as disabled; if she did, then her description leaves much to be desired. By reading disability where none was intended, I am fashioning a representation of myself.

This approach to reading is not new. I draw on the work of underrepresented creators of Harry Potter fan fiction. These fan fiction writers have written stories that reimagined their favorite characters as representations of themselves: as queer, as trans, as people of color, as asexual, and as disabled. Pointing out that we have been left out of our favorite stories and creating representations of ourselves is a resistant act. In the case of Neville Longbottom, a beloved character who emerges as a freedom fighter, this resistant reading provides an opportunity to examine the meaning of resistance itself.

Reading Neville as Disabled

When Neville was a child, he showed few signs of magic. His family feared that he was a squib—a person born into a wizarding family but without magical abilities. Squibs, including the much-despised

285

Hogwarts caretaker Filch, experience oppression that mirrors ableism: they are objects of pity and second-class citizens denied the rights of able-minded witches and wizards. When Neville's magical abilities revealed themselves, he avoided becoming visible as disabled. Nonetheless, he was subjected to ableist attitudes. Professor Snape taunted him. Professor McGonagall urged him to try harder. They did not seek to understand how Neville's mind and body worked nor allow him access to adaptive tools and accommodations.

Neville's remembrall provides an important example of the specific ways ableism impacts people with learning disabilities. Remembralls glow red when the user has forgotten something. "The only problem is," said Neville, "I can't remember what I've forgotten." As a child, I received many remembralls: tools that were supposed to help me, but failed to address the specificities of my disability. I internalized messages that I was lazy, rather than disabled in a way that could not be "overcome" through hard work. Therefore, I did not realize that I could have looked for adaptive tools that suited me better. Like Neville, I wondered what was wrong with me.

Did finding a community of other people with disabilities help Neville to navigate his own? Perhaps Neville accepted the herbology book from Alastor Moody because Moody's physical disabilities stirred in him a feeling of kinship. Maybe Remus Lupin, whose werewolf status Rowling said is an analogy for chronic illness, advocated for Neville not out of kindness but from solidarity. I like to think so. Claiming my membership in disabled communities has allowed me to understand myself as like Neville—a part of a resistance movement.

Reading Neville's Resistance
In the fifth *Harry Potter* book, Dumbledore told Harry that the prophecy that made him the "chosen one" could have applied to Neville had Voldemort selected him instead. Curiously, in not choosing Neville, Voldemort provided Neville with what he needed to defeat him: the opportunity to mature in his own way and at his own pace. Neville becomes brave, determined, and willing to suffer for his beliefs. In his final year at Hogwarts, he leads an underground resistance movement against the Death Eaters that controlled the school. Of all the examples of resistance within *Harry Potter*, Neville's is the easiest to imagine applying to our own world. I like to imagine that Neville's experience of disability helped him develop the courage and compassion that

characterized his fight against Voldemort.

The scene in which Neville triumphs over Voldemort is uncannily familiar to me. When Neville steps forward to face the Death Eaters, he does so as a person who is finally valued by the people around him. As I have learned to navigate my own disability, I sometimes "pass" as able-minded and able-bodied. When I do, I find similar acceptance. Voldemort says to Neville, "You show spirit and bravery, and you come of noble stock. You will make a very valuable Death Eater. We need your kind, Neville Longbottom."

As a disabled person who can "succeed" in an ableist world, I am offered a similar bargain. Ableist ideologies and power structures now hail me as "valuable," and encourage me to separate myself from other disabled people. I could present myself as a symbol of inspiration, as someone whose hard work and determination have made me just like able-minded people. However, I know that is not true. I am still disabled, I always will be, and I am not afraid to be. I choose to claim a political community with other disabled people who face physical and structural violence because their lives are not considered valuable. Neville's story encourages me to remember my own and shout, "I'll join you when hell freezes over."

People with learning disabilities are rarely represented in popular culture. This is due in part to our ability to pass as non-disabled and the structural pressures we face to do so. By reading Neville Longbottom as disabled, we can fashion a representation of ourselves and claim our membership in a disabled resistance movement.

Resistance and Internalization: The Marginalization of House-Elves and Goblins in *Harry Potter*

Allie Fenson

Although the scene in the Great Hall at the end of J.K. Rowling's *Harry Potter* series seems to promise an inclusive future of unity for the magical community, some are still excluded from fully participating in that unity. Griphook makes clear to Harry and Hermione earlier in the *Deathly Hallows* that the fight for Muggle-borns does not promise equality for goblins, and the goblins are noticeably absent from the final battle. House-elves, on the other hand, are present in the final battle, but they remain slaves. Despite Harry's movement towards seeing house-elves as more autonomous, particularly in *Deathly Hallows,* he still wonders in the final line of the series "whether Kreacher might bring him a sandwich" (600), reinforcing the servitude of house-elves. Despite being rational beings capable of magic, which should make them equal to wizards, both goblins and house-elves are denied access from full participation in the magical community. They deal with this marginalization in radically different ways: goblins actively resist their oppression, while house-elves internalize theirs.

Goblins perhaps come the closest to equality with wizards of any other magical being. In Rowling's extracanonical *Fantastic Beasts and Where to Find Them*, goblins are always beings, never beasts. Here, we also learn of wizards' suspicion of goblins, who attempt to strengthen their voice through lesser creatures like trolls, teaching them basic sentences (xii). Recognizing their unequal treatment, goblins try everything to make their voice heard in the governance of the magical community. It is clear in this account that wizards are at the center of power in the magical community since they are the ones able to define who is included in the definition of "being." Rather than examining the historical marginalization and struggle of goblins, the account in *Fantastic Beasts*, framed as the work of wizard Newt Scamander, portrays their activist tactics as crafty and causing chaos. In *Deathly Hallows*, the unequal condition of goblins is made explicit. Once Gringotts is taken over, goblins like Griphook are forced to go on the run, since nothing is left under their control. When Harry talks to Griphook at the Shell Cottage, Griphook directly addresses issues of race and marginalization. He describes wizards as "wand-carriers" (394), and wands become a symbol of the magical and political power wizards withhold from them. Goblins, Griphook explains, have been denied wands and therefore the opportunity to enhance their power. The goblins' response to their marginalization follows what Jackie C. Horne describes as *radical/social justice antiracism*, which requires people "to examine the social, political, and economic structures in which they live. In particular, it draws upon the framework of oppression" (79). Griphook trusts Harry more than other wizards because he buries Dobby after digging the grave by hand, laying aside his wand, or the symbol of his superiority as a wizard, but this does not erase centuries of goblin mistreatment. For Griphook, Harry's individual treatment of him cannot overcome a lifetime of experience; Harry can never truly be an ally. Ron, as the representation of the dominant values of the wizarding world, continually expresses his distrust of Griphook, refusing to acknowledge that the struggle between wizards and goblins is an unequal one. The distrust goes both ways, but goblins are the ones confined to the margins of society.

Horne points out that hints of goblins' position in society have been threaded through the History of Magic lessons that Ron and Harry have been ignoring throughout the series. Mentions of goblin rebellions throughout the centuries are hidden in Professor Binns' lectures. Horne suggests the goblins' resistance "calls to mind actual historical and current-day political movements against racial and social class oppression in Great Britain—the Scottish insurgencies of the eighteenth century, the Chartist riots of the nineteenth, and the uprisings of the Irish in the twentieth" (90). The goblins do not merely accept their marginalized place in magical society, but actively fight against it. They are absent in the final battle which brings so many people and creatures together, indicating that the rift between wizards and goblins is still present and significant. Clearly, the wizards are the dominant group, although wizards and goblins work alongside each other in Gringotts. Goblins show themselves to be rational and possess magic, as wizards do. However, witches and wizards remain the centre of power in the magical community and withhold equal treatment from the goblins, viewing them instead with distrust and disdain.

House-elves, meanwhile, represent the most dangerous kind of oppression, where the oppressed have absorbed the ideology of the oppressor. Wizards and house-elves alike believe that all house-elves should be slaves and serve wizards, and they are defined by their subservience and devotion. It is not clear in the novels when the enslavement of house-elves began. Hermione notes that it "goes back centuries" (*Goblet of Fire* 198), suggesting that there was a time when house-elves were not enslaved and that devotion to wizards is not an innate, biological characteristic, but a learned, social one. Although Harry learns the importance of treating individual house-elves with respect and Dobby gains freedom from the Malfoys, the system remains ultimately unchanged. Dobby, although free, states that "he can obey anyone he likes" (*Half-Blood Prince* 394) and attaches his loyalty to Harry instead. Dobby makes decisions for himself only so far as he chooses who to serve.

Although respect for house-elves is advocated by the series, nothing directly challenges the problematic notion that the house-elves want to serve. Hermione's house-elf activism is framed as comic and idealistic, and, as Horne points out, "even Fred, George, and Hagrid all agree with Ron that the elves do not want to be freed" (87). While Hermione and Ron represent extremes of the discussion surrounding house-elves, Hermione attempting to trick them into freedom and Ron dismissing the issue entirely, Harry must negotiate between the two and lands on a perspective Horne describes as *multicultural anti-racism* which assumes "if we rid ourselves of prejudice (our own and others'), we will see how those of a different race are the same as we are, and will thus treat them fairly" (77), therefore emphasizing the fair treatment and not the liberation of house-elves. Dumbledore tells Harry that Kreacher's "existence has been as miserable as your friend Dobby's. He was forced to do Sirius's bidding because Sirius was the last of the family to which he was enslaved, but he felt no true loyalty to him" (*Order of the Phoenix* 733-34). In *Deathly Hallows*, Kreacher's attitude changes dramatically as soon as Harry treats him with kindness and respects his devotion to Regulus. However, Kreacher ultimately remains enslaved. Harry wonders after the Battle of Hogwarts "whether Kreacher might bring him a sandwich" (600). In the end, the dominant wizarding ideology that house-elves are meant to be slaves, perpetuated by not only wizards but by the house-elves themselves, wins out over Hermione's lonely voice of activism.

Both goblins and house-elves are rational and magical beings.

There is no apparent reason why they should be viewed as inferior to wizards and witches besides the social situation in which they find themselves. Goblins recognize their oppression and fight actively against it, alienating themselves from the rest of the magical community. Meanwhile, house-elves have internalized their oppression, and believe themselves that their duty is to serve wizards, making it impossible to escape their situation. Even when Dobby is supposedly free, he ends up serving Harry. The power of the wizarding community, symbolized in the wands that they withhold from goblins, prevents both goblins and house-elves from gaining full participation in the magical community.

References

Horne, Jackie C. "Harry and the Other: Answering the Race Question in J.K. Rowling's *Harry Potter.*" *The Lion and the Unicorn*, vol. 34, no. 1, 2010, pp. 76-104. *Project Muse*, doi:10.1353/uni.0.0488.

Rowling, J.K. *Fantastic Beasts and Where to Find Them*, Bloomsbury Publishing, 2001.

---. *Harry Potter and the Chamber of Secrets*, Raincoast Books, 1998.

---. *Harry Potter and the Deathly Hallows*, Raincoast Books, 2007.

---. *Harry Potter and the Goblet of Fire*, Raincoast Books, 2000.

---. *Harry Potter and the Half-Blood Prince*, Raincoast Books, 2005.

---. *Harry Potter and the Order of the Phoenix*, Raincoast Books, 2003.

---. *Harry Potter and the Philosopher's Stone*, Raincoast Books, 1997.

---. *Harry Potter and the Prisoner of Azkaban*, Raincoast Books, 1999.

The Problem of Werewolves: Remus Lupin and Ableism in J.K. Rowling's *Harry Potter*

Tea Gerbeza

The *Shorter Oxford English Dictionary* states that to be normal is to conform to and not deviate from a norm (Onions et al. 1413). Those that deviate from the norm are cast as abnormal. Socially constructed norms define disability, and because disabled bodies deviate from the norm, they are feared and marginalized. Tom Koch notes, "a social definition of disability [insists that] the importance of a physical difference lies solely in discriminatory social reaction to or ignorance of the effects of that difference" (370). Fiona Kumari Campbell argues that disability is "*always present…*in the ableist talk of normalcy, normalization, and humanness" ("Legislating," 109). Ableism is a network of beliefs and practices based on social norms that produce an ideal kind of self and body that is widely accepted as human. Disability, then, is viewed as a diminished state of being (Campbell, "Inciting Legal Fictions" 44). Ableism promotes the fear of the disabled body and suppresses any knowledge about it (Wendell, 43). In J.K. Rowling's Harry Potter series, Remus Lupin's status as a werewolf functions as a metaphor for disability.

Lupin's status as a werewolf deviates him from the norm, casting him as less than human. Roslyn Weaver argues that Rowling's metaphor is "an inherently flawed metaphor that cannot be sustained without serious objection, for the wolves in Rowling's world are not misunderstood people but are very real monsters who threaten the safety of humans. That is, there is some justification for fearing werewolves" (75). While it can be contested that Rowling's metaphor is flawed, she makes clear that it is not the condition that makes the witch or wizard afflicted inherently evil; rather, the evil comes from the person and their choices, as we see with Fenrir Greyback. Lupin's inability to control his transformations is the central reason for his marginalization, and this concept of control is "at the heart of oppression in disability in real life" (Weaver 73). Disabled people cannot help the way they are born or what happens when a chronic illness progresses and becomes disabling. Furthermore, werewolves are not given access to the services they need to function normally in society and are therefore excluded. The inclusion of werewolves depends on society's acceptance, and werewolves remain the other because the ableist attitudes toward werewolves are imbedded in every thought and decision.

The Wizarding society operates on a set of socially established norms, particularly the concept of control. Looking at both Nymphadora Tonks, a witch who is a Metamorphmagus,1 and Animagi, 2 the issue with Lupin appears to be what Weaver identifies as the choice and will (74) that comes with being a Metamorphmagus and an Animagi. Metamorphmagi and Animagi can control their ability to transform, whereas Lupin cannot. His inability to control his transformation induces fear because his condition represents the loss of choice and control. Lupin's inclusion into wizarding society depends on society providing him access to it. Accessibility creates the space for inclusiveness as it allows a disabled person to live normally and fruitfully in society without being othered by their condition. In Rowling's world, accessibility for Lupin is having access to the Wolfsbane potion. Taking the potion before the full moon allows Lupin to keep his rational mind when he transforms, and he curls up in his office, harmless (Rowling, *PoA* 258). Having easy access to the Potion would alleviate Lupin's guilt and shame of being a werewolf because he would be able to make his transformations safe for those around him, which would benefit the entire community as it eliminates the threat of death completely. However, it is easier for wizarding society to marginalize werewolves than it is to try to understand them and make the changes within itself to allow werewolves to live productively within the world.

The constant isolation from the outside world created the norm for Lupin, and taught him that he is a monster who should be locked away. As a student at Hogwarts, Lupin was terrified that the friends he made—James Potter, Sirius Black and Peter Pettigrew— would figure out what he was and desert him (*PoA* 259). However, when the three did figure out that Lupin was a werewolf, they "didn't desert [him] at all. Instead, they did something … that would make [his] transformations not only bearable, but the best times of [his] life. They became Animagi" (259). The transformation into Animagi points to another form of accessibility for Lupin, as these three friends figured out a way to make Lupin feel less like an outsider. Under their influence, Lupin confides that he became less dangerous; even though his body is still a wolf, his mind became less so while with them (260). The impact of this friendship illustrates the power of inclusiveness, as it shows the wizarding world that lycanthropy can be dealt with and managed in positive ways that allow werewolves to live harmoniously in society. However, this inclusiveness did not translate to the broader society, as in adulthood Lupin lived a "hand-to-mouth existence, taking jobs that were far below his level of ability" ("The Order" 2). He is forced to work at jobs below his skill level and leaves before anyone realizes his condition.

Once Lupin is back at Hogwarts to teach, his relationship with Harry differs from those with adults in society and is an integral relationship for Lupin. In fact, Harry's view of Lupin demonstrates the first step to eliminating ableism within the Wizarding community: he cares about Lupin's abilities as a wizard, not his condition. Harry is the example of how society should view and treat werewolves. He illustrates the ability to place individual intellect and talent above a person's difference, which can be used to guide the wizarding community to a better understanding of disability and make their world more accessible to werewolves. In *Prisoner of Azkaban*, the marginalization of werewolves is highlighted through different reactions to Lupin's status as a werewolf. For example, while at the Shrieking Shack, Hermione tells Harry and Ron that Lupin is a werewolf, to which Ron spits, *"get away from me, werewolf!"* (253). Ron's reaction to this information mirrors societal attitudes toward werewolves: fear and disgust. Harry, however, is not disturbed by this news; rather, his anger comes from Lupin's potential betrayal, as he is under the impression that Lupin has been helping Sirius, the accused betrayer of his parents. Harry's anger shows that he treats Lupin as a person, rather than a monster. After Lupin resigns from his teaching position, Harry exclaims, "You're the best Defence Against the Dark Arts teacher we've ever had! ... Don't go!" (309). The way that Harry values Lupin's talents as a teacher and wizard illustrates how access and inclusion into society would be to isolate Lupin only once a month when he transforms, rather than all the time.

Fenrir Greyback functions as a foil for Lupin, as he is the werewolf who is "ferocious and bloodthirsty and deliberately targets the weak and innocent" (Ward, "Cultural Contexts" 347), while Lupin is the opposite: a kind and talented man who is afflicted. This dichotomy suggests that Fenrir is a monster because he is a loyal supporter of Voldemort, and prides himself on his ability to be evil in service. Lupin describes this loyalty in *Half-Blood Prince* when he tells Harry that "Fenrir Greyback is...the most savage werewolf alive today. ... Voldemort has promised him prey in return for his services" (313-14). Fenrir's monstrosity does not come from being afflicted by lycanthropy; rather, the monstrosity is already fundamentally within him. Fenrir abuses the evil assets that come with his transformation, and remains evil when he is in human form. Dumbledore notices this evil when he says to Fenrir, "Am I to take it that you are attacking even without the full moon now? This is most unusual...you have developed a taste for human flesh that cannot be satisfied once a month?" (554). Dumbledore's speculation heightens the monstrosity of Fenrir; however, this fact illustrates that Rowling suggests that evil is not inherent in werewolves, as shown with Lupin, but that evil lies in the wizard. The problem of werewolves is not with the affliction itself; the problem is with the social norms and attitudes that surround it.

Notes

1. The ability to change her physical appearance at will (Rowling, *Order* 52).
2. The ability to change into an animal at will (Rowling, *Prisoner of Azkaban* 83-84).

References

Campbell, Fiona Kumari. "Legislating Disability: Negative Ontologies and the Government of Legal Identities" *Foucault and the Government of Disability.* Ed, Shelley Tremain. U of Michigan P, 2005.

---. "Inciting Legal Fictions: Disability's date with ontology and the ableist body of law." *Griffith Law Review*, vol. 10, 2001, pp. 42-62.

Koch, Tom. "Disability and Difference: Balancing Social and Physical Constructions." *Journal of Medical Ethics*, vol. 27, no. 6, 2001, pp. 370–376. *JSTOR*.

Onions, Charles Talbut., Jessie Coulson, Henry Watson. Fowler, G. W. S. Friedrichsen, and William Little. "Normal." *The Shorter Oxford English Dictionary: On Historical Principles.* 3rd ed. Vol. 2. Oxford: Clarendon, 1992.

Rowling, JK. *Harry Potter and the Deathly Hallows.* Raincoast Books, 2007.

---. *Harry Potter and the Half-Blood Prince.* Raincoast Books, 2005.

---. *Harry Potter and the Order of the Phoenix.* Raincoast Books, 2003.

---. *Harry Potter and the Prisoner of Azkaban.* Raincoast Books, 1999.

---. "The Order." *Short Stories from Hogwarts of Heroism, Hardship and Dangerous Hobbies.* Pottermore Limited, 2016.

Ward, Renee. "Cultural Contexts and Cultural Change: The Werewolf in Classical, Medieval, And Modern Texts." Ph.D Dissertation. University of Alberta, 2009.

Weaver, Roslyn. "Metaphors of Monstrosity: The Werewolf as Disability and Illness in Harry Potter and Jatta." *Papers: Explorations into Children's Literature*, vol. 20, no. 2, 2010, pp. 69-82.

Wendell, Susan. *The Rejected Body: Feminist Philosophical Reflections on Disability.* Routledge, 1996.

American Wizardry – Wands Not Included

C.J. Hawkins

When J.K. Rowling released her writings on 'Magic in North America,' the *Harry Potter* fandom rose from a dormant sleep, eager as always for any other scraps of information on the world that had given us so much. Though there were certainly those who devoured the new histories, instantly accepting them and meshing them with the canon we already knew, I felt cheated.

I felt like someone had taken the world I knew and loved, despite its flaws, and attempted to stretch it to fit their own ideas… but had botched it up. The writing felt lazy, forced, and so unlike the rich world-building I had come to expect. I grew up reading *Potter*, and as I aged, so did Harry. There are problems with the 'verse, as there are with any written work, and I came to terms with accepting them and still being able to love the series that brought me so much joy, and kept me going through my depression. But as much as I wanted to, I couldn't do that with the new pieces.

In the essays, Rowling describes Rappaport's Law, which made it illegal for wizards and Muggles to marry, befriend each other, or even speak to each other beyond what was absolutely necessary for daily interaction. This followed on magical legislation in the late nineteenth century stating, "every member of the magical community in America was required to carry a 'wand permit,' a measure that was intended to keep tabs on all magical activity and identify the perpetrators by their wands."

At this time in American history, we were led by Theodore Roosevelt, a president who put a huge premium on personal independence. Americans absolutely would not stand for such legislation. If American wizards are anything like real Americans, they would refuse to allow the government to decide whether they were using magic appropriately; there would be fights and protests. Rallies in the street. This is the group of people that were so adamant about not paying extra for tea that they wound up forming their own country. In the unlikely event it passed, I believe most American wizards would have simply decided to stop using wands. They would hone their innate skills without the aid of a stick to channel their powers. They would craft their own rules, blending into non-magical society and pretending to have been Muggles all along.

The Johnsons down the street never have any crabgrass, and the leaves on their maple tree always turn the best colors. Come to think of it, you've never actually seen them weeding or pruning, but their rhododendrons always look amazing. Magic in their family manifests as a "green thumb," and has been passed down from father to daughter as they kneel in the dirt together, fingers curling in the dirt, the magic sparking down their veins and back into the earth.

On hot and sticky South Carolina afternoons, everyone sits on the veranda in summer, sharing tidbits of news and town happenings, sipping on sweet tea. Eric sees Aunt Peggy down the street, shooting Aunt Jane next to you a dirty look for winning 'Best Jam' at the county fair. He presses his hand to his chest, drawling out, "bless her *heart*," before taking another long sip of tea. Suddenly, the suffocating press of heat and humidity vanishes. MeeMaw's sweet tea has that effect on the weather. It's a recipe that's been handed down for generations, and has a place of pride in the family potion—er, recipe—book.

Florida is a haven for vacationing purebloods. American pureblood families have worked out how to blend in, but that doesn't mean they always feel like putting in the effort. Thankfully, the Muggles have written off the particular brand of strange that comes from the Sunshine State a long time ago.

Every kid knows that you jinx someone if you both say the same thing, and payment must be made to remove it. When little Jimmy tells a lie, he knows that crossing his fingers will protect him from retribution. Rebecca knows that her grandfather's soup will always make her colds go away, and Tanesha runs inside to show her mother her skinned knee. One kiss, and it won't hurt anymore. It'll be like it never happened, and it will be all better. Peter is alone in his kitchen and makes himself a peanut butter and banana sandwich. He cuts off the crusts, just like his father used to, and then cuts the sandwich into triangles. As he bites into it, he can hear his father's voice, and he knows that his father would be proud of him, and for a minute, it doesn't feel like his whole world has been turned upside down.

Just because the bulk of American magic is performed without wands doesn't mean it's all performed without *schools*. Having a single school for Great Britain is workable; the country isn't that big. But a single school for all of the United States (to say nothing of Mexico, Canada, and the entirely of Latin America) just isn't feasible.

Up in New York, Sleepy Hollow High School is loud and proud, the Horseman himself as their mascot, and every day they laugh because MACUSA hasn't worked out that it's not a joke. Hiding in plain sight has always been their strategy, and they've embraced the weird. So has Portland, and it's worked pretty well for them as a wizarding mecca. There are three schools there. The magical population far outnumbers the Muggles, but honestly, even if they have worked it out, the ones who live there seem to embrace it.

Ranger Ranch is only a few miles outside of Austin, but Texan wizarding families decided a long while ago that it was better than sending the kids off to some hoity-toity school up in Massachusetts. Wizards in Big Sky country learn from the giants. It's called Big for a reason. Paul Bunyan may be tough headmaster, but he's fair.

There are a few excellent institutions scattered over the South with afterschool groups. Common workshops include disguising snark for civility, and how to get the perfect mix of tang and tart in Carolina Style barbeque sauce.

We could have had a brand new take on wizarding education, and an integration of magic with the cultural melting pot of America. But instead of a celebration of the vibrancy and diversity of American culture, and an opportunity to take a hard look at the parts of our history often swept under the rug, we were given a homogenization of North American magic, and a Hogwarts knockoff. We deserved better.

When Do Harry Potter Metaphors in Public Argumentation Become Polarizing?

Ashley Hinck

In many ways, activism and politics are central to the Harry Potter fandom. Andrew Slack built the Harry Potter Alliance (HPA) into a powerful network of activist fans, reaching audiences across the world. Leaders in the fan community like wizard wrockers Paul DeGeorge and Matt Maggiacomo have lent their support to the HPA, helping build it from the ground up and serving as board members and staff. Fans have also long used Harry Potter as a frame for campaign communication, including "Republicans for Voldemort" and "Voldemort 2012" bumper stickers and "Wizards for Obama" t-shirts. Between the relatively liberal themes in the Harry Potter story, the central role the HPA plays, and JK Rowling's own political activism on Twitter, it's no wonder that scholars have found social scientific evidence demonstrating that the Harry Potter books have influenced fans' political beliefs.1

As someone who studies fan activism and fan-based citizenship like the HPA's, I often get asked about the ways in which *Harry Potter* metaphors deployed in politics may function to polarize citizens or minimize moral complexity and ambiguities (for example, see Cassie Brummit's comment here: http://mediacommons.futureofthebook.org/imr/2016/11/14/trump-voldemort-metaphors-2016-us-presidential-election). Here, I want to argue that division, simplification, and polarization are possible when Harry Potter metaphors are invoked, but don't always occur. Rather it depends on a number of factors, including the metaphors constructed and the possibilities inherent in the source text.

The case of Japan and China's 2014 editorials provide an example of Harry Potter metaphors that may simplify complex moral issues, gloss over ambiguities and ultimately further divide two opposing camps. In a 2014 *Telegraph* op-ed, Liu Xiaoming, Chinese ambassador to the UK, criticized Japanese Prime Minister Shinzo Abe's December 26, 2013, visit to the Yasukuni Shrine and argued that such visits were problematic.2 Liu said, "In the Harry Potter story, the dark wizard Voldemort dies hard because the seven Horcruxes, which contain parts of his soul, have been destroyed. If militarism is like the haunting Voldemort of Japan, the Yasukuni Shrine in Tokyo is a kind of Horcrux, representing the darkest parts of that nation's soul."3 By calling Japan Voldemort in its official diplomatic discourse, China locks itself into the role of enemy with Japan. Indeed, Liu encourages the audience to view his diplomatic discourse through such extremes. He says, "At stake is the credit of that country's [Japan's] leaders in observing the purposes and principles of the UN Charter and upholding peace. It is a choice between aggression and non-aggression, between good and evil and between light and dark."4 As Robert L. Ivie notes, images of the other side as "savage" slip easily into justifications for war.5 A discourse reduced to questions of villains and evil deeds leaves little room for regional talks, international summits, or compromise. Indeed, Voldemort is a character who never redeemed himself—Harry gave Voldemort the opportunity to show remorse and Voldemort rejected it each time.6 The only way to defeat Voldemort and his Horcruxes was to destroy Voldemort himself. By calling Japan Voldemort, China is already inviting us to imagine Japan as unremorseful and to imagine a future in which it is nearly impossible for Japan to change its course. Voldemort was only defeated when Harry took violent action. China asks us to envision a similar future for Japan. In the end, the way in which China and Japan constructed their Harry Potter metaphors encourage division and a simplification of moral complexity.

Yet, China and Japan might have constructed their metaphors differently—in ways that could have still drawn on Harry Potter while maintaining moral complexity. For example, rather than calling Japan Voldemort, China might have chosen to call Japan Regulus Black. Regulus at first rushed to support Voldemort, but shortly after, began to question Voldemort's unethical methods.7 As a result, Regulus worked to destroy the locket Voldemort used as a Horcrux, and eventually gave his life doing so. By drawing a comparison with a character who struggled internally to determine whether he supported Voldemort or not, China could have called Japan to make a similar change. While the metaphor of Regulus Black may be more ethical, it may also be less effective. Regulus as a character is less visible and memorable than Voldemort, and a metaphor that relies on Regulus might find a smaller audience than a metaphor that relies on Voldemort.

The *Harry Potter* story includes many characters and story arcs that embrace moral ambiguity and complexity. While Voldemort is, in the end, ultimately evil, and must be destroyed, his followers and the heroes contain moral gray areas. While Voldemort may appear black and white, the rest of the *Harry Potter* story is gray. Thus, *Harry Potter* is a source text well-suited to metaphors that embrace complexity and avoid polarization or unnecessary simplification. Of course, not all stories may be so rich. Metaphors that invoke fan-objects may be constrained by the possibilities of their source text. Thus, Japan and China's *Harry Potter* metaphors demonstrate the complexity inherent in *Harry Potter* metaphors used in civic discourse. Whether they drive citizens farther apart or show us the moral complexity of the opposing side may depend on how the metaphor is constructed and the possibilities inherent in the source text. Ultimately, *Harry Potter* metaphors hold great power in civic discourse. Hopefully, we can use them wisely.

Notes

Anthony Gierzynski, *Harry Potter and the Millennials: Research Methods and the Politics of the Muggle Generation* (Baltimore: The Johns Hopkins University Press, 2013); Diana C. Mutz, "Harry Potter and the Deathly Donald," *PS: Political Science and Politics* 49, no. 4 (2016): 722–29.

2 "China and Britain Won the War Together," *The Telegraph*, January 1, 2014, sec. Op-Ed, http://www.telegraph.co.uk/comment/10546442/Liu-Xiaoming-China-and-Britain-won-the-war-together.html.

3 Ibid.

4 Ibid.

5 Robert Ivie, "Images of Savagery in American Justifications for War," *Communication Monographs* 47 (1980): 279–91.

6 J.K. Rowling, *Harry Potter and the Deathly Hallows* (New York NY: Arthur A. Levine Books, 2007), 741.

7 Ibid., 176–200.

"I 'ave big bones!": Gender Performance and the Treatment of Half-Humans in J.K. Rowling's Wizarding World

Katherine Hughes

Giants and Veela are unique in the wizarding world: they are the only magical, humanoid beings that are able to have children with humans. The perception of these beings within the wizarding community is greatly divided between these two beings, with Veela perceived positively and Giants are cast negatively. This carries over to the way their children are treated, especially in relation to the gender roles they perform. Giants are portrayed in masculine, monstrous terms, while Veela only exist in a feminine form, using their beauty to entice and entrance men. When characters perform their roles to the satisfaction of the dominant wizarding society, they can pass for that dominant group. Kimberlyn Leary theorizes that passing "occurs in the context of a relationship: it requires... a subject who does not tell and... an audience who fails to ask. Passing occurs when there is a perceived danger in disclosure ("Passing, Posing, and 'Keeping it Real'" 85). Fleur and Maxime are unsuccessful in their passing attempt because their performances as fully human are questioned and speculated upon. It is only through performing their feminine societal roles that they are accepted in the wizarding society. By comparing the attitudes toward the half-human children of Veela and those of Giants, the adherence to social standards of gender performance is the defining factor in their inclusion or exclusion in the dominant wizarding society. In essence, if the half- or quarter-human is able to perform the accepted gendered role for the dominant group, it is much easier for the children to integrate into the dominant society. Because Fleur is better able to conform to the gender roles of the dominant society, she is more readily accepted, while Maxime must work harder to be viewed as the powerful woman she is.

The case of Madame Maxime highlights the issue of gender performance: she is the headmistress of a prestigious wizarding school in France, yet she denies her Giant heritage in order to further her career because Giants are stigmatised as exceptionally volatile (a traditionally masculine quality). Hagrid tries to make a build a relationship with her, confiding in her his relationship with his parents and Giant mother in particular, but Maxime denies having any Giant blood, instead saying that she simply has "big bones" (*GoF* 373). Despite Maxime's initial insistence to the contrary, Rowling uses other characters to out Maxime as a half-Giant, stating that "Harry had only ever seen one person as large as this woman in his life, and that was Hagrid… Yet somehow…. this woman… seemed even more unnaturally large" (214). Harry's descriptions of Maxime as being "unnatural," "large," sporting a "beaky nose" (214), as well as his comparison of her self-proclaimed big bones to that of a dinosaur (374), all work to dehumanize as well as defeminize her. She is described in these inhuman, exaggerated, masculine terms, weakening her attempts to pass for the dominant society, and drawing her identity into question. Bethany Barratt notes in *The Politics of Harry Potter* that by not coming out and saying she is half-Giant, she may be preserving her reputation, but she is ultimately hurting her fellow half-Giants by "refusing to do the one thing she could that would further opportunities for her kind in the future" (80). While there is some merit to this argument, further interactions in later novels disprove Barrett's point. In *Order of the Phoenix*, Maxime partners with Hagrid to talk to the remaining Giants in the mountains, and their relationship becomes extremely supportive. Hagrid tells the Harry, Ron, and Hermione, "An' I'll tell ya this, she's not afraid of roughin' it, Olympe. Yeh know, she's a fine, well-dressed woman, an' knowin' where we was goin' I wondered 'ow she'd feel abou' clamberin' over boulders an' sleepin' in caves an' that,' but she never complained once" (*OotP* 376). Maxime performs the gender role of well-dressed, refined woman when the occasion calls for it, but she can also fall into more typically masculine roles when she is required to. Because she is half-Giant and half-human, she is able to perform one side of her being or the other, depending on the situation; her role as headmistress requires more refined mannerisms while hiking through mountains to meet with Giants requires the more masculine elements of her being to come through. By existing in both spheres at the same time, Maxime is a liminal character, promoting the visibility of half-Giants because of her inability to pass for one group or the other.

On the feminine end of the spectrum, Veela are able to pass for women because of the conventional beauty they possess. Even when the bloodline has been diluted once or twice, the mesmerizing effect Veela-human children have is just as strong. When Fleur is announced as the Triwizard champion for Beauxbaton, she is described as possessing graceful and sweeping movements (*GoF* 237), as well as having "large, deep blue eyes, and very white, even teeth" (222). During her wedding to Bill Weasley, her beauty is said to enhance the beauty of other women in her presence, differing from its typical overshadowing effects on others (*DH* 121). While she is not "passing" as purely human per say, she is able to fit in with the dominant wizarding society because she performs, or exceeds, the beauty standards, raising her social standing among particularly the male characters who fawn over her and her cousins.

When comparing the ways in which Madame Maxime and Fleur are described and the responses to their presence, especially the responses made by male characters, it is easy to assume that the Veela have an advantage because they are considered to be traditionally beautiful and seductive, but Maxime is the headmistress at a wizarding school, a very prestigious position that requires an immense amount of talent and political clout. Given the disparaging remarks made by Ron, it seems unlikely that another half-Giant would be able to hold such a position especially considering the social context provided in the British school. This is due in part to the fact that the reader is only provided with the context of Hogwarts, while both Fleur and Maxime are from France. The differing attitudes to half-humans may be due to the different social contexts of the schools, and is certainly the case when we look to *Fantastic Beasts and Where to Find Them: The Original Screenplay* with its suited Giant in a bar in Harlem (192). Whether this was a joke Rowling wanted to make about New York Giants or it was to show the backwards attitudes British wizards hold towards Giants, especially when compared to the inclusion of other humanoid beings in France, further publications may clarify. For now, readers will have to be content knowing that the inclusion of such beings varies from country to country, and there is a place for everyone be included no matter their heritage. Maxime may not be successfully passing as a full-human, but her prominent position in the text highlights her ability to perform her role as a powerful woman to the satisfaction of the dominant wizarding society, despite the masculine lens through which other characters see her, while Fleur's role has been prescribed to her based on her beauty, and her performance as female is better received.

References

Barratt, Bethany. *The Politics of Harry Potter*. New York: Palgrave Macmillan, 2012. Print.

Leary, Kimberlyn. "Passing, Posing, and "Keeping It Real."" *Constellations* 6.1 (1999): 85-96. Web. 15 Mar. 2017.

Rowling, J.K. *Harry Potter and the Deathly Hallows*. Vancouver: Raincoast, 2007. Print.

Rowling, J.K. *Harry Potter and the Goblet of Fire*. Vancouver: Raincoast, 2000. Print.

Centaurs and Merfolk United: Gender Performativity and Othering in the *Harry Potter* Series

Kaleigh Johnson

Greek sociologist Yiannis Gabriel says that "Othering is the process of casting a group, an individual or an object into the role of the 'other' and establishing one's own identity through opposition to and, frequently, vilification of this Other." That is, the role of the Other helps to dictate what the "norm" society is; there cannot be the cultural norm without those that fall outside of it. As such, we will look at two humanoid races in the Harry Potter series that fall within this category of the Other—merfolk, and centaurs—and how they both accept this Othering, or try to mimic the normative group.

There is a clear connection between both the merfolk and the human wizards and witches. Most interesting is how they are described by Harry himself in *Goblet of Fire*, as he interacts with the merfolk of the Black Lake during the second trial. In his description, issues of gender arise, in particular those concerned with gender performativity— a term coined by Judith Butler coined in her text *Gender Trouble: Feminism and the Subversion of Identity*. Gender performativity is the idea that gender is culturally constructed and based on performative acts, and that the culture dictates what is "masculine" and what is "feminine" (7). Typically, legends of merfolk focus on the feminine form—the mermaids, that is. Even in the Prefects' bathroom as he puzzles out the golden egg, Harry notices the portrait of the blond mermaid dozing on a rock (399). The only merfolk in the Black Lake are identified as men, and it is worthwhile to observe just what they are noted as doing: "He swam swiftly towards a seven-foot-tall merman with a long green beard and a choker of shark fangs, and tried to mime a request to borrow the spear. The merman laughed and shook his head. 'We do not help,' he said in a harsh, croaky voice [...] and [Harry] tried to pull the spear away from the merman, but the merman yanked it back, still shaking his head and laughing'" (433). Later, when Harry attempts to save Hermione, there is the comment that "several pairs of strong grey hands seized him. A half-a-dozen mermen [...]" (433). Both of these instances where Harry observes that the merfolk are male are masculine actions—holding a spear and showing strength by taking it back, and physically restraining Harry. Not once is there mention of a mermaid in this scene, and this might be due to the mere fact that Harry finds the merpeople of the Black Lake so hideous (he does, after all, think that they are nothing like the portrait in the Prefects' bathroom). Butler's theory of gender performativity is shown through Harry's projecting of his known culture, in this case, human culture, and the gender binary of male and female present there, complete with what he feels is "masculine" and what he feels is "feminine."

Merfolk are not the only race that are Othered in the series; centaurs are as well, but in a much different way. While some might not think to link centaurs and merfolk together, Rowling would argue otherwise. Like merfolk, centaurs are seen as the Others in the wizarding world. In *Fantastic Beasts and Where to Find Them*, there is mention of the connection between centaurs and merfolk in the section entitled "What is a Beast": "The centaurs, who under Muldoon had been classified as 'beasts' and were now under Madame Clagg defined as 'beings,' refused to attend the Council in protest at the exclusion of the merfolk, who were unable to converse in anything except Mermish while above water" (xxi-xxii). Also, later, there is mention of their similarities in a footnote: "The centaurs [...] declared that they would manage their own affairs separately from wizards. A year later the merfolk made the same request" (xxiii). The centaurs themselves are Othered by the wizarding community, but they are proud of such. In *Order of the Phoenix*, one centaur says: "'We are a race apart and proud to be so,'" followed quickly by another saying, "'We are an ancient people [...] We do not acknowledge your superiority'" (667). Centaurs strongly oppose any wizarding influence on their culture, which is understandable, when their lands are being diminished by the Ministry of Magic.

Othering is important in the wizarding world because it shows the different cultures and gendered representations, and that there are a multitude of them—as opposed to a single, solitary culture and community. Centaurs and their pride in the Othering the wizarding community has taken to regarding them, as well as gender performativity and how Harry puts his viewing lens as a human on the merfolk, both show there are differences between both the centaurs and the merfolk in comparison to the wizards, despite their humanoid appearance and some of their cultural practices. At the same time, while separated from each other, the wizarding world shows us that there is the possibility for different cultures to coexist, even if it means leaving one another alone and to their own lifestyles.

References
Butler, Judith P. *Gender trouble: Feminism and the Subversion of Identity.* New York: Routledge, 1990. Print.
Gabriel, Yiannis. "The Other and Othering - A Short Introduction." *Yiannis Gabriel.* Blogger, 9 Sept. 2012. Web. 1 Mar. 2017. <http://www.yiannisgabriel.com/2012/09/the-other-and-othering-short.html>.
Rowling, J. K. *Fantastic Beasts and Where to Find Them.* New York: Bloomsbury, 2009. Print.
---. *Harry Potter and the Goblet of Fire.* Vancouver: Raincoast Books, 2000. Print.
---. *Harry Potter and the Order of the Phoenix.* Vancouver: Raincoast Books, 2003. Print.

The Hogwarts Generation

Alena Karkanias

"We are people of this generation, bred in at least modest comfort, housed now in universities, looking uncomfortably to the world we inherit."

This is how, in June of 1962, the Students for a Democratic Society began their Port Huron statement expressing their frustration and anxieties at the contemporary state of affairs in America's political, social, and cultural climate. The sentiment resonates profoundly with me now, as I feel a shared sense of urgency and responsibility with my peers to assess how our culture has dealt with engaging, working through, and addressing a number of cultural anxieties. The SDS wrote their statement in response to their fears about many serious issues that continue to endanger life today. Key among those for me is the fear of the development and power of totalitarian states and fascist movements, which once again threaten the modern world.

As we know from Newcomb and Hirsch, media provides a "cultural forum" through which a society can raise questions about, talk through, and come to conclusions about pressing anxieties (47). History and popular media thus have a dialectical relationship, as those who create media construct it, to paraphrase Newcomb and Hirsch, in response to contemporary events, shifting attitudes and values, and challenges to social structure (47), and thus contribute significantly to the ways in which cultural memories of historical events form, and societies process profound moments of their past.

Fascism has never been absent long (arguably, ever) from screens or public conversation since its initial rise before the first world war, and thus has an outstanding place within the cultural forum. However, I have noticed a warping of the cultural forum's traditional use with regards to fascism: rather than its prominence being evidence of deep cultural engagement with the subject, the particular ways in which fascism is present speak instead to society's inability to process the movement, its historical and cultural legacy, and its implications about human nature, leaving media instead to continually raise its specter without ever putting it to rest or preparing for its true resurrection.

I contend that while early historical, humorous, and

metaphorical portrayals of fascism may have helped audiences recognize it and, particularly, learn to fight it with demonstrations of resistance, as time went on these modes of representation may have contributed to the fictionalization of fascism that makes it hard for people to reconcile it with and recognize it in real-life events. This is an obviously timely issue, as the American public is beginning to question the idea that fascism is only a thing that exists *elsewhere* – in other countries, in the past, and in fictional worlds – and therefore, crucially, confront the reality that it has the potential to develop in every human and every society. Despite these grim realities, it gives me hope to see critical thinking and productive action coming from young people, often deeply informed by their engagement in their media such as *Harry Potter*, as it speaks to a rehabilitation of media as a cultural forum, and to the promise of the people of this generation.

In another work, I go in depth on the ways in which different engagements with fascism eventually resulted in its devaluation as a legitimate threat. In summary — portrayals of historical fascism are commendable for not allowing it to disappear from cultural memory, but have also framed fascism as something of the past for audiences to come to terms with but not consider with relevance to the future, while humorous portrayals are significant for revealing powerful, terrifying forces like fascism as weak or foolish, thereby undermining them as the inevitable victor in a conflict, but over time these humorous depictions shifted from a specific power play into something of farce, making the very notion of real fascist movements laughable and not worth taking seriously as a continually relevant threat. Countless other works also use the trappings of fascist rhetoric and aesthetics to characterize their villains, reducing these antagonists to "a few easily identifiable and immutable traits" (Hake 39-40). While this allows filmmakers to thus make their positions explicitly clear in opposition to fascism through their protagonists' victories, it also devalued fascism as a legitimate threat by making it and its followers simply the blatantly "deviant, deficient, and dangerous" (40). Thus, audiences were able to view fascism as something located only in obvious 'outliers' of their communities, in everyone from isolated and demonstrably abnormal humans to literal aliens, and simplistically easy to defeat in a single blow, rather than accepting that it could develop in the common-place ideas and conversations at large happening between average citizens in average communities and was thus just as complicated to control and conquer.

Franchises such as *Star Wars*, *Captain America*, and *Harry Potter*, in which fictional groups operate within the media's closed universe in heightened parallels to the ways in which Nazis and other fascist movements operated historically, belong to this class of film. However, particular choices in characters and narratives in these works, especially *Harry Potter*, allow audiences to engage more complexly with fascist threats by making them continually relevant rather than only relegated to the past.

Harry Potter's protagonists, like those in the other listed franchises, actively fight against named groups who champion and advertise their allegiance to specific ideologies, rhetorics, and agendas that align with and echo specific and general themes and movements of fascism. Further, all three of these sagas also positioned fascist movements as things that had been previously defeated, but were now returning, or more accurately had never truly gone away but just been willfully ignored. Further significantly, all of these films focus explicitly on the protagonists' development of specific counter ideologies and tactics with which to fight the threat's rise and influence. Over the seven books and films, and especially in the last four (five), the *Harry Potter* series deals intently with issues of authority, power, responsibility, and resistance, exploring in multiple dimensions the ways they are exemplified and abused individually, in interpersonal relationships, and in the society as a whole. We see these issues reflected in SPEW, the DA, in Umbridge and resistance to her, and in so many other themes and concepts explored in the books, including young people being ignored by those older and/or in power, government irresponsibility, the relationship between media, politics, and journalism, underground communication channels, education rights, purity movements, casual bigotry, blind loyalty, fear tactics, and many more. In many such ways, these media works like *Harry Potter* thus demonstrate a much more complex engagement with the complexities and nuances of fascism than more traditional depictions.

Newcomb and Hirsch's model of media analysis sees popular media as central to the creation of "public thought" as a process of social construction and negotiation of reality (47). Media opens up the possibility for new discussions by "commenting on ideological problems" and bringing audience's attention to these issues to an "intense and obvious level" (49). As a society, we ought to be able to use this quality of media to discuss fascism, but instead, we see it used to put fascism out of sight and mind, as it is relegated to the past and to fictional landscapes, and its legitimate threat of continued real existence is thus made absurd.

Douglas Kellner notes that media is crucial for forming one's identity, saying it "provides the materials out of which we forge our very identities [by] providing the symbols, myths, and resources through which we constitute a common culture" (7). While he was speaking specifically to the ways in which media operates for the individual, it is applicable as well to looking at the way that cultural identity forms for a society as a whole, which is reflected in the ways that media has engaged with and thus shaped our cultural memory of, relationship with, and ownership of fascism. Many historical films, while striving to preserve the reality of fascism's existence, go too far and cement it in the past, while other films make light of its overbearing power in an effort to undermine its control, but consequently delegitimize it as a serious threat, and others still demonstrate a recognition of its power as a force of destructive change, but locate it such a way that detaches it from its very human roots. In sum, instead of media being a way for us to come to terms with a problem, it has become a way for us to push it away. It allows us to say that Hitler was a fictional villain, that the holocaust was a closed historical event, that fascists are aliens—in other words, things that exist only elsewhere and in others—and not something that's potential lives inherently in every human, in every culture, and that could easily happen again. It is a way for us to get away from the guilt that owning the past gives us but it also makes us irresponsible with regards to the future.

In their reflection on the state of the world, the SDS noted that "we might deliberately ignore, or avoid, or fail to feel all other human problems," but that some are "too immediate and crushing in their impact, too challenging in the demand that we as individuals take the responsibility for encounter and resolution" to continue to ignore. Decades later, I feel a similar call to action to begin a conversation about the ways in which, while media has been complicit in this process of creating a cultural identity that does not take fascism seriously as a threat to modern life, works like *Harry Potter* demonstrate the crucial role media can play in helping individuals recognize and engage with the complexities of fascism, speaking to the need for us as scholar, as fans, and as people of this generation to move away from the pattern of complacency we have developed and harness media in the hopes of doing some good in the world.

References

Students for a Democratic Society (U.S.). The Port Huron Statement (1962). Chicago, Ill.: C.H. Kerr, 1990. Print.

Hake, Sabine. *Screen Nazis: Cinema, History, and Democracy*. Madison: University of Wisconsin Press, 2012.

Kellner, Douglas. "Cultural Studies, Multiculturalism, and Media Culture." *Gender, Race, and Class in Media: A Critical Reader*. Ed. Gail Dines and Jean M. Humez. Los Angeles: Sage, 2015. 7 – 19.

Newcomb, Horace M. and Paul M. Hirsch. "Television as a Cultural Forum: Implications for Research." *Quarterly Review of Film Studies*, 1983, p. 45 – 55.

Ministry of Misinformation: *Harry Potter* and Propaganda

Christine Klingbiel

"The Prophet? You deserve to be lied to if you're still reading that Muck, Dirk. You want the facts, try the *Quibbler*" says Ted Tonks in J. K. Rowling's *Harry Potter and the Deathly Hallows* (299). In the *Harry Potter* series, there are many things that are not what they seem; even when the facts are uncovered people choose to believe something else. Sometimes the reader is misled as well, as in the case of Sirius Black in *Harry Potter and the Prisoner of Azkaban*. Other times, the reader knows the truth along with the protagonist. Harry is not Slytherin's heir, Voldemort has returned, Dumbledore has not lost his mind. And that is when readers feel most frustrated with the citizens of the wizarding world. Why are they so blind, dumb, gullible, and willing to be misled? J.K. Rowling, in her Harry Potter books, offers up a few explanations as well as numerous examples of how rhetoric works. As a rhetorician, a writing instructor, and an average citizen who has to negotiate a world filled with people, political parties and corporations trying to get me to behave in a certain way (buy X, vote for Y, do Z) I am interested in how language works to influence my thinking. I am interested in the everyday propaganda, the obvious and subtle ways we are influenced. In today's world, where journalism is rapidly changing, consumerism is the air we breathe, and PR firms make millions, we need to be aware of how we are being manipulated for the good or bad. As Wendell Potter put it in his insightful book *Deadly Spin: An Insurance Company Insider Speaks out on How Corporate PR is Killing Healthcare and Deceiving Americans*, you need "to understand why you believe some of the things you believe and do some of the things you do." (45). As the Harry Potter books teach us, words have power. But it's not just the magic words. It's the everyday words whether they are coming from Rita Skeeter, that master spin doctor, or Harry himself, "the way an object is described and the manner in which a course of action is presented direct our thoughts and channel our cognitive responses concerning the communication" say Anthony Pratkanis and Elliot Aronson in their book, *Age of Propaganda: The Everyday Use and Abuse of Persuasion* (44). Propaganda will not disappear. If anything it is more prodigious in the media-saturated modern world. The wizarding world can help us spot it, thereby helping us choose consciously if we want to be persuaded or not. As Mad-eye Moody says, "constant vigilance!"

Psychologists Anthony Pratkanis and Elliot Aronson regard propaganda as the *abuse* (not just use) of language, the abuse of persuasion as the title of their book suggests. Jawett and O'Donnell, as they define propaganda mention it uses "strategies of questionable ethics" (4). This suggests there is a right way and a wrong way of using persuasion. It would be impossible to cover every propaganda technique in this essay and some of them may fall into a few different categories, but here are a few examples:

The Propagandist's Spellbook

How do propagandists fool us? Like with a spell, they choose the right words or conjure up convincing images.

1. **Labels**. Just by the words you use, you can influence how people view something. People often make decisions based on a name or the adjectives that surround the name. Pratkanis and Aronson say, "Through the labels we use to describe an object or event, we can define it in such a way that the recipient of our message accepts our definition of the situation and is thus pre-persuaded even before we seriously begin to argue" (44). Companies carefully consider their names and the names given to the products they sell. This is what marketing companies call branding. Tom Riddle did his own kind of branding when he changed his "foul, common muggle" name to Lord Voldemort, as he says, "a name I knew wizards everywhere would one day fear to speak" (*CoS* 314). A lord is definitely not a common person and "Voldemort" contains the word "morte" French for death. It did indeed become a name wizards and witches feared. Just saying the name brings out an emotional response (pathos) in listeners. Throughout the series, wizards and witches are so afraid they flinch, jump, yelp, fall and drop things when the name is spoken. Harry is also given the labels: "The Boy Who Lived" and later on "The Chosen One" marking him out as special. The Ministry calls him "Undesirable Number One" in *DH* when they want to turn public opinion against him. This label marks him as the enemy, while "The Chosen One" makes him the people's savior.

2. **Glittering generalities** are "attractive sounding but vague terms" (Jackson and Jamieson, 39). Sometimes these are also called "purr

315

words" (Pratkanis and Aronson, 45). These words work because they sound good and they are so vague they can mean anything; that leaves it up to the listener to apply their own meaning. Politicians often say: "Stand up for America!" Many companies make products or sell services "for a brighter future." In *OotP*, Dolores Umbridge, Senior Undersecretary to the Minister, comes to Hogwarts and gives a speech that includes: "Let us move forward, then, into a new era of openness, effectiveness, and accountability, intent on preserving what ought to be preserved, perfecting what needs to be perfected, and pruning wherever we find practices that ought to be prohibited" (213-214). Harry finds her speech loaded with "waffle." And most of the other students' eyes glaze over and they cannot follow what she says. It is only Hermione who is able to sift through the generalities to see that the Ministry intends to interfere in the school.

3. **Weasel Words** "suck the meaning out of a phrase or sentence, the way that weasels supposedly suck the contents out of an egg, leaving only a hollow shell" (Jackson and Jamieson, 49). Stores do this all the time. There is an advertised sale "up to 50% off." That's half off, most people think. The weasel words here are "up to." There could be one item for 50% off, the rest could be 10% and the store would technically be telling the truth (Jackson and Jamieson, 49). Orange juice "made with real orange flavor" doesn't have to contain a single orange, the weasel word being "flavor." When Rita Skeeter writes her article entitled, "Harry Potter 'Disturbed and Dangerous,'" she gets others to do some weaseling for her. She writes, "It is possible, say top experts at St. Mungo's Hospital for Magical Maladies and Injuries, that Potter's brain was affected by the attack...he might even be pretending...this could be a plea for attention" (*GoF*, 612). While these "top experts" sound like credible sources, none have examined Harry, and they use words like "it is possible," "might" and "could" to not make any claim at all, yet it still sounds like they are. Also, just who are these experts? What are they experts in? For all we know, they could work in the hospital cafeteria and make a mean treacle tart.

4. **FUD Factor.** FUD, according to Jackson and Jamieson, stands for "fear, uncertainty, and doubt" (26). Playing upon an audience's fear is also a technique advertisers do all the time. You might lose friends or people will not want to be around you if you do not use our brand of deodorant or breath mints! Is your family safe from germs? Buy our anti-bacterial wipes and be sure! "If it's scary, be wary," Jackson and

Jamieson say (26). In The *Harry Potter* series, Voldemort epitomizes the FUD factor technique. He instills fear to get what he wants. Sirius says, "In the old days he had huge numbers at his command; witches and wizards he'd bullied or bewitched into following him" (*OotP*, 5). When Harry asks why everyone was afraid of the dark mark that was sent into the sky at the Quidditch World Cup, Mr. Weasley answers, "You-Know-Who and his followers sent the Dark Mark into the air whenever they killed...the terror it inspired ... you have no idea, you're too young. Just picture coming home and finding the Dark Mark hovering over your house, and knowing what you're about to find inside...everyone's worst fear ... the very worst." (*GoF*, 9). And when Voldemort finally does take over the Ministry, Lupin says he "is playing a very clever game. Declaring himself might have provoked open rebellion: Remaining masked has created confusion, uncertainty, and fear" *(DH,* 208). Wendell Potter, in his book *Deadly Spin* states, "Organizations with the most to lose are most likely to resort to fear mongering. Their information may mention the loss of jobs, a threat to public health, or a general decline in social values, standard of living, or individual rights. It may also vilify a specific cause or even a specific person in order to create the desired point of view (52). Voldemort and other Pure-blood families vilify muggles and muggle-born wizards and witches and say they are responsible for a decline in standards in the wizarding world. Jackson and Jamieson also call this propaganda technique, "the blame game," pointing a finger at an unpopular group and hoping to divert attention from the weakness of his own evidence" (37). Sirius says about his family: "they thought Voldemort had the right idea, they were all for the purification of the Wizarding race, getting rid of Muggle-borns and having purebloods in charge" (*OotP,* 112).

5. **Images.** We are not just persuaded with words but images also shape how we think. Lockhart knew a winning smile would get him what he wanted. A lot goes into the marketing of a product. Not only what the product looks like, but the images associated with it. That is why beer commercials have sexy models or depict a fun party atmosphere or why trucks in commercials are covered in mud or drive through the rugged countryside. They say a picture is worth a thousand words and they are an effective way of implying something without saying it. Politicians often use pictures. He or she might be seen visiting a local factory with his or her jacket off and shirt sleeves rolled up, implying they are ready

to work hard for their constituents. Symbols are used in their photographs and ads; the American flag is often in the background. The Ministry of Magic uses symbolic images to shape what people think. Rowling draws our attention to the fountain at Ministry headquarters a couple times. First, in the *OotP*, the statues in the fountain are described as "…a noble-looking wizard with his wand pointing straight up in the air. Grouped around him were a beautiful witch, a centaur, a goblin, and a house-elf. The last three were all looking adoringly up at the witch and wizard" (127). Dumbledore recognizes it as propaganda when he says, "The fountain we destroyed tonight told a lie. We wizards have mistreated and abused our fellows for too long…" (834). The statues were destroyed when Dumbledore dueled with Voldemort in *OotP*, and what replaces it—a giant statue of black stone labeled "Magic is Might"—later in *DH* is even more slanted propaganda. To Harry, "what he had thought were decoratively carved thrones were actually mounds of carved humans: hundreds and hundreds of naked bodies, men, women, and children, all with rather stupid, ugly faces, twisted and pressed together to support the weight of the handsomely robed wizards" (242). This is symbolic of wizards ruling over muggles. Why wizards are right to rule over muggles ties back to the FUD factor. It is rumored that they are stealing magic from wizards. Or as Voldemort suggests, they will somehow taint Pure-Bloods. (Notice also how "Pure-blood" and "Mudblood" are propaganda labels.) The pamphlet that Harry sees workers at the Ministry putting together is entitled, "MUDBLOODS and the Dangers They Pose to a Peaceful Pure-Blood Society;" it has "a picture of a red rose with a simpering face in the middle of its petals, being strangled by a green weed with fangs and a scowl" (*DH*, 249). As with most images crafted for propaganda purposes, the message is pretty obvious.

Constant Vigilance!

Do we have more propaganda today or just more mediums to deliver (and receive) it? James Combs and Dan Nimmo in *The New Propaganda: The Dictatorship of Palaver in Contemporary Politics* say, "Propaganda today is complete. It surrounds us like the air we breathe. Propaganda is everywhere, is all pervasive and all penetrating. To live in contemporary times is to be showered with the seeds of suasive ideas, seeds encountered by chance, seeds planted in us, seeds scattered over us" (15). The very reason why we need to be aware of it is also the reason it is so hard to distinguish. Fiction has long allowed us to examine our reality. It is easier to see the propaganda when it is not aimed at us. The *Harry Potter* series can show us how language and images can manipulate us especially when there is an organizing, intentionally deceitful effort behind it. Be aware of language. Ask yourself, why was it said that way and would it make a difference if it was said another way? Know yourself; how your background shapes your thoughts and what biases you have, as we all have biases. Harry didn't just learn magic at Hogwarts, he learned more about himself. He was able to defeat Voldemort (a master at manipulation) not by having greater magical skills but by knowing more. During their final duel in *DH*, Harry says, "I know things you don't know, Tom Riddle. I know lots of important things that you don't" (738).

Fiction also allows us to see multiple perspectives. In the series, there are two views on death, Voldemort's and Dumbledore's. Voldemort declares in OotP, "There is nothing worse than death" (814). Voldemort fears death so much that he willing tore apart his soul to never die. Dumbledore, on the other hand, says, "to a well-organized mind, death is just the next great adventure" (*SS*, 297). Viewing things from multiple perspectives can help us avoid confirmation bias. That does not mean we will agree with every point of view, but knowing there are other views will help us see the spin. As Jackson and Jamison say, "look for general agreement among experts" which means more than one source is necessary (159). A little bit of research goes a long way, so does a healthy dose of skepticism. Hermione is a great example of this. While I absolutely love Luna Lovegood as a character, Hermione proves to be right more often. Hermione weighs the facts. She asks the right questions, even when others don't like it, as was the case with Lavendar Brown's rabbit. While most of the students take it as a sign of Trelawney's prognostication powers, Hermione says, "Well, look at it logically...Binky didn't even die today...and she can't have been dreading it, because it's come as a real shock" (*PoA*, 149). Hermione tries to caution Harry from believing Creature and running into a trap at the Ministry in *OotP*, and she slows them down enough so that Harry thinks twice about going after the Hallows in *DH*. So be skeptical, but not cynical. A cynic just gives up. "They're all crooks. They're all the same. I don't know who to believe," say a cynic. That just plays into the propagandist's hands. Negative campaigning, for instance, is often meant to keep people from voting at all. Or, if you give up on finding the facts, you are more likely to settle for confirmation bias. So as Mad-Eye Moody said in *GoF*, "you need to be prepared. You need to be alert and watchful" (212). And remember that Mad-Eye Moody was an imposter, a death eater in disguise.

References

Aufderheide, P. (2007). *Documentary Film: A very short introduction*. Oxford, England: Oxford University Press.

Birk, N. P., & Birk, G. B. (1977). "Selection, slanting, and charged language." In G. Goshgarian (Ed.), *Exploring language* (13th ed., pp. 4-11). Boston, MA: Little, Brown.

Combs, J. E., & Nimmo, D. (1993). *The new propaganda: The dictatorship of palaver in contemporary politics*. New York, NY: Longman Publishing Group.

Enos, R. L. (1993). *Greek rhetoric before Aristotle*. Prospect Heights, IL: Waveland Press, Inc.

Heil, E. (2012, March 12). Rick Santorum spokeswoman's Dutch treat. *The Washington Post*. Retrieved January 31, 2015.

Jackson, B., & Hall Jamieson, K. (2007). *Unspun: Finding facts in a world of disinformation*. New York, NY: Random House.

Jowett, G. S., & O'Donnell, V. (1992). *Propaganda and persuasion* (2ndnd ed.). Newbury Park, CA: Sage Publications.

Kennedy, G. A. (1991). *Aristotle on rhetoric: A theory of civil discourse*. New York, NY: Oxford University Press.

Potter, W. (2010). *Deadly Spin: An insurance company insider speaks out on how corporate PR is killing health care and deceiving Americans*. New York, NY: Bloomsbury Press.

Pratkanis, A. R., & Aronson, E. (1991). *Age of Propaganda: The everyday use and abuse of persuasion*. New York: W.H. Freeman and Company.

Rowling, J.K. (1997). *Harry Potter and the sorcerer's stone*. New York: Scholastic.

Rowling, J.K. (1998). *Harry Potter and the chamber of secrets*. New York: Scholastic.

Rowling, J. K. (1999). *Harry Potter and the prisoner of Azkaban*. New York: Scholastic.

Rowling, J. K. (2000). *Harry Potter and the goblet of fire*. New York: Scholastic.

Rowling, J.K. (2003). *Harry Potter and the order of the phoenix*. New York: Scholastic.

Rowling, J. K. (2005). *Harry Potter and the half-blood prince*. New York: Scholastic.

Rowling, J.K. (2007). *Harry Potter and the deathly hallows*. New York: Scholastic.

Shermer, M. (1997). *Why people believe weird things: Pseudoscience, superstition, and other confusions of our time*. New York, NY: W.H. Freeman and Company.

Walshe, S., & Friedman, E. (2012, July 26). "Romney in London for Olympics: Candidate angers Brits." In *ABC News*.

Harry Potter and the Control of the Creator of the Canon

Stacey M. Lantagne

The saga of *Harry Potter* begins on a night a decade before the events of the rest of the book, although, by the end of the saga, it's clear it really began many, many decades before that, as the ample use of Pensieve flashbacks helpfully fills in for the reader. Much like Harry Potter, contemporary debates over copyright authorship and who gets to control a piece of creativity have much earlier roots, with the age of Internet fandom presenting just the latest challenge to how we think about legal authorship versus creative ownership.

The story begins, frankly, with the printing press, but to jump forward a century or two, it's important to think about photographs. In the nineteenth century, photography was a new technology that was challenging the way courts thought about creativity. Were photographs something that could be copyrighted? And, if they could, who owned the copyright? Unlike, for instance, a book, a photograph was a piece of creativity that seemed to involve multiple people in its creation, including, at a minimum, the photographer and the subject (it was before the age of the ubiquitous selfie, in which the two merge together).

Courts decided that photographs were copyrightable creations, and courts chose to give the ownership of the copyright to the photographer. However, this in itself led to complications. The owner of a copyright is generally, unless an exception applies, also the "author" of the copyrighted work at issue, which also, generally speaking, means the photographer is also the "creator" of the work. But what about if the photographer just set up the photo but didn't actually push the button? In the late nineteenth century, when photographs were carefully staged instead of snapped quickly out a car window for posting on Snapchat, it wasn't unheard of for the "photographer" to arrange the subject but leave the operation of the complicated camera equipment to assistants.

An 1884 Supreme Court case called Burrow-Giles Lithographic Co. v. Sarony decided that photographs could be protected by copyright, and also introduced to U.S. copyright law a concept that would develop into what is known as the "mastermind" theory. In the case, the "photographer" didn't press the button but did pose the subject, choose the subject's costume and surrounding props, and adjust the lighting of the photograph. Basically, the Court seemed to conclude and other courts have subsequently agreed, the "photographer" was the "mastermind" and thus the creator, author, and owner...and thus the person who could control what happened to the creative work.

The "mastermind" theory of copyright has been challenged through the years. The effect of the theory places copyright control in the hands of only a few people, and arguably has devalued the contributions of the people who don't often achieve supervisory "mastermind" positions, such as people of color or gender minorities. And perhaps no one has more energetically challenged the idea that every creative work has a single "mastermind" who gets to control it than Internet fandoms.

Most *Harry Potter* fans, if asked, would acknowledge that J.K. Rowling is the legal owner of *Harry Potter*. Indeed, many works of *Harry Potter* fanfiction contain disclaimers to that effect. Many fans might even grant her the position of *original* mastermind. However, fans are reluctant to grant that mastermind determination too much power. Rowling might own *Harry Potter*, but the fans consider themselves to be entitled to decide if she's doing him justice or not, reserving the right to re-write the story to what they want and to ignore her directives. One characterized fans as having "earned [the] privilege" of being able to write their own endings for the characters. It is as if Rowling masterminded the creation of the characters, but, by consuming them, the readers gained their own creative power over the versions of the characters that exist in their heads. The readers became their own masterminds of a plethora of alternative universes in which to plop Rowling's original characters, and, indeed, sometimes resented when Rowling would return to try to exert some power and influence.

The fans shipped different characters than Rowling's "canon" books, and unapologetically continued to do so even after the books had reached a conclusion. In fact, many fans pushed the books farther into the future to undo the broad strokes Rowling had painted in the epilogue, or ignored the epilogue altogether in such large numbers that it became its own fic subgenre: "Epilogue? What Epilogue?" Fan reaction to *Harry Potter and the Cursed Child*, the first major "new canon" in years, crystallized how much fans considered *Harry Potter* to have left Rowling's control and entered theirs. One fan wrote, "I worked hard to ignore every announcement and tidbit JKR & Co released about the characters and the world. . . . I could spend the rest of my life deep in *Harry Potter* land without hearing another word from its author." Once *Cursed Child* was released as "canon," many fans responded with attitudes similar to "lol it's not actually." Many were explicit: "I refuse to accept anything [about] the [C]ursed [C]hild as canon." Indeed, *Business Insider* helpfully rounded up many of the "not-canon" pronouncements in an article headlined "Some *Harry Potter* fans are so disappointed with the new story that they're refusing to call it canon."

These fans are, in their way, challenging the "mastermind" theory of copyright. While ownership may still reside with Rowling, she is not considered the final word on what happens to her creation. Indeed, one could argue she's no longer even seen as *the* "mastermind," instead of just one of the voices speaking on *Harry Potter*. She might speak more authoritatively than most, but fans still choose to accept or reject her statements.

The word "canon" entered fandom circles as a reference to Biblical scripture, as if the word from the original creator was the word of God. However, the reaction of *Harry Potter* fans reflects a growing atheism: Canon is no longer what the Creator God tells us it is, but what the fans decide, upon individual consideration, to accept. It's interesting to consider how this has resulted in a splintering of the legal perception of the creator and the cultural perception: Rowling may have the copyright registrations, but it isn't necessarily because fans consider her the ultimate "mastermind." She may be the original author, but her authority over *Harry Potter* extends only so far. The fandom's skepticism toward Rowling's "mastermind" status is a skepticism toward the scale and scope of Rowling's rights as the copyright owner. It's the fandom who ultimately controls who *Harry Potter* is to them, and the fandom who pushes at the bounds of Rowling's copyright protections with every re-imagining they place on the Internet.

Finding Harry: What Are Fans Looking for on *Harry Potter* Fan Pilgrimages?

Katherine Larsen

The concept of pilgrimage is most often associated with religious rituals—going to Mecca or Canterbury, or walking the Camino de Santiago. It's associated with paying respect at sacred places, venerating relics, communing with one's god. It is also, of late, increasingly associated with fandom. We go to Elvis' birthplace and Penny Lane, we seek the reality behind the fantasy by visiting filming locations in Vancouver and London. We seek the fantasy behind reality by journeying to Hobbiton in New Zealand or Tatooine in Tunisia.

While I have of late been considering (and then reconsidering) the connections between religion and fandom, I'm not intending to go down that particular rabbit hole here. That said, there are undeniable connections between religiously motivated pilgrimages and those undertaken in connection with a fanned object, and there are similar questions to ask about what we are seeking, and what impediments might lay in the way of our finding those things.

Fan pilgrimage, as we understand it today, is certainly not a new phenomenon. The spotlight shone on Shakespeare and his works by the 18thC actor David Garrick initiated a steady stream of visitors to Stratford-upon-Avon. More recently the graves of James Dean and Jim Morrison, the tree in Barnes where Marc Bolan's car crashed, and Amy Winehouse's home in Camden have all drawn the faithful. Not all pilgrimages are to mourn, however, and what I'd like to consider here is the experience of fans who want to immerse themselves in the fictional/mythic world they love.

For some, this process of immersion is easy. If you are a *Sherlock* fan, a casual stroll through London will bring you through Trafalgar Square, Chinatown, Baker Street, St.Barts Hospital, the Tate Modern and the South Bank, all easily recognizable sites from the series and easy to locate on one's own. For fans of *Supernatural, Smallville, The X-Files* or any other of the many series filmed in Vancouver the search is somewhat more difficult since the fan is seeking the real places that have been used as stand-ins for their fictional counterparts. Places "in" Missouri, Kansas, Ohio, Virginia, etc are more difficult to find in the

Vancouver landscape but not impossible and diligent pilgrims will be rewarded with the opportunity to immerse themselves in the series they love. In fact, they might feel more authentically "in" Lawrence, Kansas for instance while in Vancouver than they would if they were in Kansas itself since the real place will not correspond to the fictional representation.

But what of the *Harry Potter* fan who goes looking for places that do not, cannot, exist in our Muggle world? Where do they go and how do they access the Wizarding World? In some cases, we are provided points of intersection between the real and the fantasy world, mostly around London. A *Harry Potter* walking tour will take you to the Millenium Bridge, Piccadilly Circus, the entrance to Diagon Alley, the outside of the Ministry of Magic, and of course, Kings Cross Station. The problem with such a tour though is that we are always on the wrong side of the looking glass—perennially Muggles trying to peer through the veil. How do we get to Hogwarts?

Once solution might be to leave London for the Warner Bros Studio tour in Levensden or go even farther afield to Universal Studios in Orlando. (I'll leave aside the cognitive dissonance of trying to experience wintery Scottish landscapes in the middle of hot and humid Florida.) Here we can climb aboard the Hogwarts Express, stroll through Hogsmeade, walk down Diagon Alley. But of course, the closer we get to the "real" experience the farther we get from an *authentic* experience. We are wandering through sets, simulacra of the "real" places we are looking for, and the corporate presence providing that experience is never far from view. The magic behind both the Wizarding World and the movie world is revealed to us, special effects are explained, we are simultaneously transported and dislocated.

One exception to the dynamic was Platform 9 ¾ in Kings Cross Station. Despite the fact that for exterior shots it was replaced by the nearby and more photogenic St Pancreas station in the films, fans made their way Kings Cross in order to find the portal to Hogwarts for themselves. Once the first film was released a large plaque was installed on the floor of the area between platforms 9 and 10 (even though the filming site was several platforms over between tracks 4 and 5). When more and more fans started turning up and interfering with the operation of the station they were redirected to a nearby wall onto which a half a luggage trolly had been affixed with a Platform 9 3/4 sign above it. Due to massive refurbishment of Kings Cross, this makeshift pilgrimage site was moved several times over the years but what always remained was the ability of fans to relate to the space on their own terms. It was theirs to find, theirs to imaginatively interact with in much the same way that those visitors to Vancouver could be "in" Lawrence, Kansas. Many YouTube videos attest to the playful interactions of people reenacting the process of passing through the wall to the magical platform beyond.

However, when Kings Cross reopened in 2012, fans in search of Platform 9 ¾ were directed to a site far removed from the actual platforms. No longer a makeshift half trolly provided by the station management, the space had become a corporatized photo-op run by Warner Brothers. In exchange for the intimacy of experience which I'd argue is one of the most important aspects of the pilgrimage experience, the fans got realistic props (Harry's trunk and Hedwig's cage now grace the half trolly embedded in the wall), costumes (fans are given their choice of which house scarf they want to have their pictures taken with), a "flipper" (a WB employee who will flip your scarf at the moment your picture is snapped to make it look like you are running toward the wall), and of course the opportunity to buy that photo around the corner at the newly opened Harry Potter gift shop.

The comments on Trip Advisor testify to the mixed reactions fans had to the co-opting of what had once been "their" space. Some loved it and welcomed the "realistic" props and help from the staff to get just the right picture. More resented a variety of aspects including the long lines, the cost of the photograph (though to be fair no one is required to buy the photo from the WB and people are free to take their own as well), the distance of this iteration of Platform 9 ¾ from the actual platforms, and the overall intrusion of the WB in general.

So, the questions I've been grappling with and which I hope to discuss further here: What matters most to fan pilgrims? What constitutes an "authentic" experience? To what extent does the corporatization of fandom enhance or interfere with a fan's experience?

Further Reading

Aden, Roger C. *Popular Stories and Promised Lands: Fan Cultures and Symbolic Pilgrimages*. Univ. of Alabama Press, 1999.

Brooker, Will. "Everywhere and Nowhere Vancouver, Fan Pilgrimage and the Urban Imaginary." *International Journal of Cultural Studies* 10, no. 4 (December 1, 2007): 423–444.

Couldry, Nick. *Media Consumption and Public Engagement: Beyond the Presumption of Attention.* Consumption and Public Life. Basingstoke, Hampshire; New York: Palgrave Macmillan, 2007.

Kruse, II. "The Beatles as Place Makers: Narrated Landscapes in Liverpool, England." *Journal of Cultural Geography* 22, no. 2 (Spring 2005): 87–188.

Larsen, Katherine. "(Re)Claiming *Harry Potter* Fan Pilgrimage Sites." In *Playing Harry Potter: Essays and Interviews on Fandom and Performance,* ed. Lisa Brenner. Jefferson, NC: MacFarland, 2015.

Leaver, David, and Ruth A. Schmidt. "Before They Were Famous: Music-based Tourism and a Musician's Hometown Roots." *Journal of Place Management and Development* 2, no. 3 (September 10, 2009): 220–229.

McElroy, Ruth. "'Putting the Landmark Back into Television': Producing Place and Cultural Value in Cardiff." *Place Branding and Public Diplomacy* 7, no. 3 (August 1, 2011): 175–184.

Norman, Alex. "Celebrity Push, Celebrity Pull: Understanding the Role of the Notable Person in Pilgrimage." *Australian Religious Studies Review* 24, no 3 (December 2011): 317-341.

Reijnders, Stijn. "Stalking the Count: Dracula, Fandom and Tourism." *Annals of Tourism Research* 38, no. 1 (January 2011): 231–248.

Harry Potter and the Historical Anachronisms

Walter Metz

One of the most startling things about J.K. Rowling's world of wizards and witches is the importance placed on material objects, both by the author and her characters. When the basilisk is terrorizing the school after being released from the Chamber of Secrets, Colin Creevey survives only because he is looking at the serpent indirectly through a camera. In the film, while investigating the object, Dumbledore opens the case and the film explodes once exposed to light. If the books and films are set in the contemporary moment, which they seem to be (Hermione's muggle parents are dentists, and live in a nicely furnished flat in a suburban neighborhood; Mr. Dursley manufactures drills), why would Colin not have an iPhone like every other privileged kid in Western civilization? The film in the camera is an historical anachronism, and this slippage in history strikes me as one of the most interesting things about the world of Harry Potter.

In *Harry Potter and the Goblet of Fire*, Professor McGonnagall is teaching the children how to dance in preparation for the Yule Ball, a Christmas celebration. The scene in the film is introduced via a close-up on a gigantic phonograph, as out of proportion with the humans as the beloved Hagrid, a half-giant who befriends Harry. McGonnagall's nineteenth-century machine, which mechanically reproduces sound from wax embedded on a piece of plastic, is one of the series' most fascinating material objects. Surely she could magically summon up music for the children to dance to. And yet, instead, she stages an emotional drama in the center of which is the record player, a hearth to this seemingly insignificant yet in the end completely crucial filmic experience. Throughout *Harry Potter and the Goblet of Fire*, Harry, Ron, and Hermione squabble like the fourteen-year-olds they are. They discover love, and jealousy, and indifference, just like the rest of us. The phonograph serves as the material linkage that grounds the Imaginary drama back in the world of the Real. The adult wizards engage in the same pettiness that will set the world on fire, and our beloved teens are in training to wield power in this world come the ascension of the next generation.

For this reason, it strikes me that the most significant anachronistic object in all of Harry Potter's world is the radio in *Harry Potter and the Deathly Hallows*, a device Ron uses to try to learn of the fate of his parents while Voldemort's minions wreak havoc across Britain. So clearly evocative of the function of the radio in World War II Britain as the nation endured the German bombing night after night, the sequences remind us of Rowling's absolute hatred of our adult world, a world that produces willful pain and suffering.

A story that lurks in the background of the seven Harry Potter novels and films, Albus Dumbledore's greatest moment, his defeat of the dark wizard, Gellert Grindlewald, comes to the fore in the newest Rowling film, *Fantastic Beasts and Where to Find Them*. Here, we see the rise of Grindlewald in the United States, and assume that the sequels will lead us to the 1945 battle in which Dumbledore finally brings the evil reign of Grindlewald to an end. The 1945 date, of course, links Grindlewald allegorically to Adolf Hitler; the 1920s American setting of *Fantastic Beasts* links the British boarding school fantasy of the Harry Potter works to the necessary Anglo-American pact that allowed Nazism to be defeated in the 1940s.

Like its predecessors, *Fantastic Beasts* is obsessed with the materiality of the wizarding world. In this paper, I will study the significance of the film's material objects as they develop a new understanding of Rowling's world in the context of the 1920s United States. I will focus on three objects: the ocean liner on which Newt Scamander (Eddie Redmayne) arrives at Ellis Island; what I read as an electric chair, used to torture ex-auror Tina Goldstein (Katherine Waterston) for helping Newt; and an under-construction skyscraper, whose I-beams the aurors must reconstruct, but not finish the construction of the building, at the end of the film.

These objects' function in *Fantastic Beasts* results in an engagement with modernity different from the Harry Potter world's bucolic vision of the British countryside. The film traces the shift from the British boarding school of the nineteenth century to the United States' rise to global superpower in the twentieth century. Unlike the British wizards' replication of the role of Prime Minister, the Americans have a purportedly more democratic Congress of magical folk. In Rowling's most canny anachronistic move, the President of the American wizards, Seraphina Picquery is played by Carmen Ejogo, heretofore most famous for playing Coretta Scott King in *Selma* (Ava

DuVernay, 2014). Half Nigerian and half Scottish, Ejogo is the film's most radical representation of Rowling's commitment to diversity. In the midst of Jim Crow in the non-magical United States, the wizards' president is a black woman.

Indeed, the Grindlewald action plot pales in comparison to the film's subtle engagements with identity politics. Despite the American wizards' seeming forward thinking approach to racial difference, Newt calls attention early in the film to our backwardness when it comes to wizard/human interaction. In a subplot, non-magical Jacob Kowalski (Dan Fogler) develops a relationship with Queenie (Alison Sudol), Tina's sister of the auror befriended by Newt, serves as Rowling's plea for tolerance. Forty years before the Supreme Court decision, *Loving v. Virginia* (1967) would relegate anti-miscegenation laws to the dustbin of history, Kowalski and Queenie fall in love. As in the Harry Potter novels, this is Rowling's greatest gift to us as an artist. Whatever our failings, wizards and human beings alike have the capacity to love, if we can only overcome our bestial instincts, those exploited by the Voldemorts, and Grindlewalds, and Trumps of our base material world.

Opening Minds Young and Old to Complexity: The Gift of *Harry Potter*

Christina Hoover Moorehead

"We've all got both light and dark inside us. What matters is the part we choose to act on. That's who we really are."
- J.K. Rowling, Sirius Black, *Harry Potter and the Order of the Phoenix.*

Fairy tales.
Fables.
Cartoons
Pop culture film and comic book characters.

It's an endless list of fuel that cultures around the world feed children. And tucked within these entertaining permutations of storytelling are lessons.

Some lessons are overt, spelled out in no uncertain terms, and at times summarized at the end of the tale, as in "Aesop's Fables."

Other lessons? Not so obvious.

But the thread connecting all our stories is this:

Everything is either good OR evil.
Light OR dark.

We wrap our children in a mental diet of simplistic opposites, only to try to undo the damage as they get older.

I would argue that the damage goes far deeper than we can ever imagine.

And herein lies the gift that J.K. Rowling gave the world when she looked up from her life's worry, and sadness and began writing *Harry Potter and the Sorcerer's Stone.*

For *Harry Potter* in its entirety is not just a tale of fantasy, although it certainly is that.

Harry Potter is an undoing of the simplicity of seeing the world as always a struggle between pure good and pure bad. It does not matter much to me whether or not J.K. Rowling consciously or unconsciously embedded in each subsequent *Harry Potter* book increasingly complex lessons. What matters to me is that she did.

Think about it.

In the first book, *Harry Potter and the Sorcerer's Stone (Philosopher's Stone),* she lures the young 9 or 10-year-old reader (and to be honest, readers of any age who remember being 9 or 10) into a world of recognizable fairy tale and fantasy extremes. Good versus evil. Dumbledore and the Weasley family against the Dursleys, Voldemort and Professor Snape. Along the way, we meet characters recognizably good and recognizably evil, as seen through Harry's eyes.

But then *Harry Potter and the Chamber of Secrets* emerges, the readers slightly older, the story itself slightly more complex and the story starting to make us question the ideas of good and evil. Acromantulas are bad...right? Popular, shiny, handsome professors such as Gilderoy Lockhart are good...right?

Suddenly we aren't so sure.

And here is J.K. Rowling's brilliant gift throughout the series.

She gives us complexity.
She forces us to question our preconceived notions of good and evil.

She helps us to untie our stubborn life-long clutch on seeing the world through binary lenses and encourages us to see the shadows, the hues, the dark and the light, the good and the bad.

When we plant the seeds in our young people for understanding our world as always and only a fight between two extremes, I believe all of us unwittingly also are planting the seeds for our adult prejudices.

Mine versus yours.
Black versus white.
My people versus your people.
My sexual orientation versus your sexual orientation.

I could fill pages with examples of our simplistic assumptions.

It is no mistake that *Harry Potter* fans of all ages have been found to be more open-minded, more accepting of differences, more globally aware. For in embracing *Harry Potter*, in allowing his world to share space in our imaginations with our own frequently confusing and painful reality, we are opening ourselves up to seeing the world not as a constant battle between extremes, but as something more nuanced.

I just turned 50 years old this year. When the first *Harry Potter* book came out I was already 31 years old with a four month old son.
And yet, I bought that first book.
And I read it.
I read it again.
And again.
And I did the same thing with each book that came out, eagerly anticipating each new book, obsessively reading and re-reading it, absorbing the textures and complexities and relationships, savoring how each book grew with the reader.

I appreciated beyond belief being able to watch my own children grow and began reading these books for themselves…watching them absorb, as I absorbed, how the world of *Harry Potter* offered no easy answers.

Just like our real world offers no easy answers.

Our world is complex and challenging and demands us to constantly question our assumptions and actions.

In reading *Harry* Potter we are led to the realization that none of us is all good or all evil. Nothing about our existence is as simple as that.

Sirius was right. He was so, so right —
"We've all got both light and dark inside us."

Riddikulus!

Andrea Morales

Power, throughout the *Harry Potter* series comes from unexpected sources. The most unexpected and inexhaustible source of power is humor, which can either bring laughter or pain. Characters use humor as a weapon for evil and as a weapon to fight evil.

One of the most prominent philosophical theories of humor is Thomas Hobbes's superiority theory. Hobbes's theory asserts that humor is a tool employed in times of others' suffering in order to feel superior: "that the passion of laughter is nothing else but sudden glory arising from some sudden conception of some eminency in ourselves, by comparison with the infirmity of others, or with our own formerly" (Smutes). J.K. Rowling illustrates this theory by demonstrating how humor can belittle for evil purposes, but also demonstrates how the opposite can be achieved. Rowling reveals that humor can bring about goodness through the belittlement of evil actions and people.

The Riddikulus charm deploys humor to conquer boggarts, shape shifters that prey on a person's deepest fear to paralyze them. Riddikulus, which resembles the word *ridiculous*, conquers fear by labeling the feared object as extremely silly and unreasonable. The charm is not the only tool it takes to conquer a boggart, however: "the thing that really finishes a boggart is laughter..." (*Prisoner*, 88; ch. 7). For example, Neville's boggart resembles Snape because Snape constantly tortures and demeans him. When the boggart transforms into the terrifying professor with greasy hair, jet-black cloak, a crooked nose, and a hatred that burns in his eyes, Neville faces his fear and removes its power through the Riddikulus charm and humor: "Snape stumbled; he was wearing a long, lace-trimmed dress and towering hat topped with a moth-eaten vulture, and he was swinging a huge crimson handbag" (*Prisoner*, 90; ch. 7). Belittling Professor Snape in this ridiculous way makes him less frightening. As the class sees the humorous version of Snape, "There was a roar of laughter..." (*Prisoner*, 90; ch. 7), and the boggart is truly defeated. Laughter, like fear, is a powerful psychological process. But while fear causes a surge in cortisol — the stress hormone in the brain, humor causes a surge in dopamine — the "feel good" hormone of the brain. Laughter decreases the stress that comes during a fear-provoking situation, and this allows a person to face and conquer their fears. Making fears appear ridiculous and humorous strips the boggart of its power, revealing the power of humor.

Fred and George's ability to belittle fear further expands Hobbes's theory. Fear is a palpable emotion in the Weasley's home after George returns from the Battle of the Seven Potters with only one ear. Mrs. Weasley is terrified for her son's health, Ginny fears for her brother, Harry blames himself, but Fred is the most terrified as he sees his twin lying in front of him. Despite his injury, George immediately cracks a joke that lightens the mood:

> "'How do you feel, Georgie?' whispered Mrs. Weasley. George's fingers groped for the side of his head….'Saintlike,' repeated George, opening his eyes and looking up at his brother. 'You see . . . I'm holy. Holey, Fred, geddit?'" (*Deathly*, 74-75)

Through a single joke, the atmosphere in the room shifts from terror to relief: "Mrs. Weasley sobbed harder than ever. **Color flooded Fred's pale face**" (*Deathly*, 74-75). George's joke further demonstrates the power of humor against evil by transforming an act meant for evil to something good.

The greatest example of the twins' ability to use humor to fight evil is Potterwatch. Harry, Ron, and Hermione have been camping for months and are losing hope in their mission. When things seem darkest, they hear Fred's familiar voice over the radio:

> "'*Rodent*'?' said yet another familiar voice, and Harry, Ron, and Hermione cried out together:
> "Fred!"…"I'm not being 'Rodent,' no way, I told you I wanted to be 'Rapier'!" (*Deathly*, 443)

Fred's joke about his desired code-name is not unexpected, but this particular joke has unforeseen power. 'Rodent' connotes traitor, weak, and dirty, while 'Rapier,' in contrast, is a sword that is sharp, light, and thin. The name fits Fred, whose weapon is his humor: often light, but simultaneously sharp enough to pierce and diffuse tense situations. Fred's more powerful joke, however, is his scorn of Lord Voldemort himself:

> "'So, people, let's try and calm down a bit. Things are bad enough without inventing stuff as well. For instance, this new idea that You-Know-Who can kill with a single glance from his eyes. That's a basilisk, listeners. One simple test: Check whether

the thing that's glaring at you has got legs. If it has, it's safe to look into its eyes, although if it really is You-Know-Who, that's still likely to be the last thing you ever do'

For the first time in weeks and weeks, Harry was laughing: He could feel the weight of tension leaving him" (*Deathly*, 443)

By belittling Voldemort, Fred diminishes the fear gripping the wizarding community. Fred's joke diminishes not only Harry's fear, but fear of Lord Voldemort himself.

In the *Chamber of Secrets*, after Harry is accused of being the heir of Slytherin, Fred and George:

"found all this very funny. They...shout[ed], 'Make way for the Heir of Slytherin, seriously evil wizard coming through...'

'Harry's in a hurry.'

'Yeah, he's off to the Chamber of Secrets for a cup of tea with his fanged servant,' said George, chortling" (*Chamber*, 137; ch.12)

Labeling Harry the heir of Slytherin belittles Harry's humanity. In contrast, the twins' humor reinforces Harry's humanity by diminishing the rumor to an absurd statement. Further, by calling the monster in the chamber Harry's "fanged servant" (*Chamber*, 137; ch. 12), the twins undermine Voldemort's power to instill fear by diminishing the monster to something silly. Though simple and ordinary the joke reveals humor's fascinating power to fight evil. Fred and George's joke undermines Voldemort's power while also reassuring Harry's identity and humanity.

Rowling juxtaposes humor for good by showing how Bellatrix Lestrange corrupts humor into an evil weapon. Bellatrix corrupts the power of riddikulus when she mocks Harry's deepest fear of losing those he loves, "'come out, little Harry!' she called in her mock baby voice" (*Order*, 607; ch. 36). Her inhumanity and incapacity to feel love is revealed as she preys on Harry's capacity to do just that, "'Aaaaaah... did you love him, little baby Potter'" (*Order*, 607; ch. 36). Bellatrix further mocks the idea of love as a ludicrous, childish weakness and this brings Harry to a dangerous line: "Hatred rose in Harry as he had never known before... [he] bellowed 'Crucio!'" (*Order*, 607; ch. 36). Harry, who hates the inhumanity of Voldemort, suddenly finds himself driven to that inhumanity through Bellatrix's evil humor.

Bellatrix and *riddikulus* both deploy humor to demean fear. The two use completely opposite capacities of humor to do so, however. Bellatrix uses humor to belittle fear in an effort to bring about evil. As she derides Harry's fear and grief, she generates evil within Harry. *Riddikulus*, in contrast, belittles fear in an effort to empower a person. *Riddikulus* derides fear to reveal that the wizard carries the strength to conquer their deepest fears. Through these two capacities of humor, Rowling draws a distinct line as to when humor is used for good and when it is not.

Moreover, Harry grows up in a family who use humor to diminish Harry to less than human. Dudley's complaint of Harry accompanying them to the zoo demeans Harry to nothing more than a nuisance: "'…He always sp- spoils everything!' He shot Harry a nasty grin through the gap in his mother's arms" (*Sorcerer*, 17). Dudley also uses humor to prey on one of Harry's worst memories: "Dudley gave a harsh bark of laughter then adopted a high-pitched, whimpering voice. "'Don't kill Cedric! Don't kill Cedric! Who's Cedric — your boyfriend?'" (*Order*, 15). Dudley mocks the greatest loss of Harry's life---the loss of his parents: "'Dad! Help me, Dad! He's going to kill me, Dad! Boo-hoo!'" (*Order*, 15). While Dudley has never experienced loss or pain Harry, he continues to mock Harry's misfortunes. As a result of growing up amidst the Dursley's evil humor, Harry faces an adolescence filled with confusion, timidity, and uncertainty.

In contrast to the distinct line as to when humor is used for good and when it is not, Rowling also reveals that a translucent line exists line as to when humor is good and when it is evil when it is belittling others. James, Sirius, and Dudley clearly demonstrate that humor used to demean others is evil. However, when Fred and George belittle Dudley the question arises if humor is being used for good or for evil. The argument can be made that Fred and George are belittling Dudley in order to avenge Harry. However, their humor still brings about a victim: Dudley. Is Fred and George's use of humor justified? This translucent line raises important questions as to the nature of humor.

While Dudley uses his humor to belittle Harry to less than human, Fred and George use their humor to build Harry up by belittling Dudley and his humor. When the twins come to take Harry from the Dursley's in the Goblet of Fire, and one of their ton--tongue toffees "accidentally" slips out of Fred's pocket Dudley, of course, eats one of the candies: "[Dudley] was gagging and sputtering on a foot-long, purple, slimy thing that was protruding from his mouth. One bewildered second later, Harry realized [it] was Dudley's tongue" (*Goblet*, 29-30; ch. 4). The tongue is Dudley's weapon since it is what creates the words that belittle Harry. Fred and George belittle Dudley through their humorous invention by taking away Dudley's weapon, and simultaneously build up Harry. Nevertheless, the twins demean a human being through their humor. Throughout the first six novels, Dudley fails present himself in a positive light; instead, he constantly tortures Harry and mocks his tragedies. In the *Deathly Hallows,* however, Dudley redeems himself as he acknowledges Harry's humanity. The twins are demeaning a character capable of redemption. Fred and George victimize Dudley in the same manner he victimizes Harry. To readers', their actions are justified because of the way Dudley treats Harry; however, the twins' actions victimize Dudley. Hagrid also belittled Dudley when he gave him a pig's tail. Again, to readers' this action seemed justified; this action, however, may have been what fueled Dudley's fear of wizards, which fueled Dudley's torture of Harry. People often deride others in fear, and the twins' actions may have further fueled Dudley's fear of wizards. This increasing simply fueled the vicious cycle that is hatred. The twins' joke avenges Harry's torture at the hands of the Dursleys undermining its power by reassuring Harry that he does have a family who cares for him.

James Potter and Sirius Black are two characters that demonstrate that, while humor can be used for good, it can also be used for evil. As Harry experiences Snape's childhood memory in the pensieve, he discovers the cruel nickname James and Sirius used to degrade Snape: "'*Snivellus*'..." (*Order,* 645) which deprecates Snape's manhood by associating Snape with something considered "womanly" or childish—sniveling. Although not seen as humorous by readers, James and Sirius believe their nickname is humorous because it allows them—like Hobbes's theory suggests—to feel superior at the expense of another person. James and Sirius's taunts continue as people begin to watch:

> "Snape lay panting on the ground. James and Sirius advanced on him, wands up, James glancing over his shoulder at the girls at the water's edge as he went...
> 'How'd the exam go, Snively?' said James
> 'I was watching him, his nose was touching the parchment,' said Sirius viciously. 'There'll be great grease marks all over it, they won't be able to read a word.'
> Several people watching laughed" (*Order,* 645)

James and Sirius tease Snape about his looks in front of a large group of students. James and Sirius's humor derives its power from belittling Snape into an undesirable friend: "Snape was clearly unpopular" (*Order,* 645). When Snape attempts to defend himself, James and Sirius's torture continues:

"'You — wait,' [Snape] panted, staring up at James with an expression of purest loathing. 'You — wait. . . .'

'Wait for what?' said Sirius coolly. 'What're you going to do, Snivelly, wipe your nose on us?'

Snape let out a stream of mixed swearwords and hexes, but his wand being ten feet away nothing happened.

'Wash out your mouth,' said James coldly. 'Scourgify!'

Pink soap bubbles streamed from Snape's mouth at once; the froth was covering his lips, making him gag, choking him" (*Order,* 645-646)

Again, James and Sirius use cruel humor to belittle Snape by insinuating that Snape enacting revenge on them is ridiculous and that he is a weak man who few desire as a friend. From petty nicknames to jinxes meant to harm, James and Sirius reveal that humor can be used for evil.

It would be inaccurate to say that James and Sirius's evil humor was the sole cause of Snape's venture into the dark arts; it does appear, however, to be a contributing factor. Snape loses the friendship of Lily Evans—the only friend he had—because of James and Sirius's taunts.

"'LEAVE HIM ALONE!'" Lily shouted...

'you're lucky Evans was here, Snivellus —' [James said]

'I don't need help from filthy little Mudbloods like her!' [Snape shouted]

Lily blinked. 'Fine,' she said coolly. 'I won't bother in future.

And I'd wash your pants if I were you, Snivellus'" (*Order,* 648)

After he loses Lily's friendship, and with no one else to turn to, Snape turns to the Dark Arts for comfort. James and Sirius's evil humor apparently pushes Snape over the edge.

Another way James and Sirius's humor has unforeseen, evil consequences, is the way it destroys Harry and his sense of self. Harry grows to develop a sense-of-self that is directly tied with his father and, when Harry sees Snape's memory his sense-of-self is broken:

"What was making Harry feel so **horrified and unhappy**...it was that he knew how it felt to be humiliated in the middle of a circle of onlookers, knew exactly how Snape had felt as his father had taunted him, and that judging from what he had just seen, his father had been every bit as arrogant as Snape had always told him" (*Order,* 650). When James and Sirius use humor for evil they fail to understand the depth or breadth of the consequences of their actions.

The dichotomy Rowling presents through her novels reveals humor's power. Humor can both bring-about and combat evil. As the Dursleys, Bellatrix, James, and Sirius reveal, humor can cause destructive evil. James and Sirius further reveal that humor can bring evil to more than just the humor's intended target. Simultaneously, however, Fred and George and the spell *Riddikulus* reveal the immense power of humor for good. Humor is a double-edged sword. The *Harry Potter* series raises this important question about the nature of humor while also revealing that humor has the capacity to be used both as a weapon for evil and a weapon to fight evil. By having humor be a double-edged weapon, Rowling reveals that within all of us lies the capacity for both good and evil. A person's choice is ultimately what determines which capacity humor embodies.

Magical Memory: The Creation of Collective Memory Through *Harry Potter* Tourist Attractions

Ryan Rigda and Victoria Stiegel

For fans of *Harry Potter*, trips to the Wizarding World in Universal Studios Orlando or to the Warner Bros. Studio Tour in London are ways to relive the magic of J.K. Rowling. When the final installment of the *Harry Potter* series was published, the story of *Harry Potter* became a piece of history. When fans visit places like these, they facilitate the public memory of the *Harry Potter* series. Walking past the Hogwarts Express, for example, brings up memories of Harry meeting Ron and Hermione for the first time, chocolate frogs jumping out windows, and a spell to turn a rat yellow. Despite the story of *Harry Potter* being a work of fiction, the creation of theme parks and studio tours treats the story as if the events that happened in it were real. Much like other museums and monuments around the world, *Harry Potter* tourist attractions help to facilitate the public memory of the life of *Harry Potter*. For scholars of *Harry Potter*, this allows for a critical moment to understand the ways in which fans' experiences with and their memories of a text can create mediated collective memory.

The concept of collective memory refers to "recollections that are instantiated beyond the individual by and for the collective" (Zelizer, 214). Rather than being determined by individuals alone, these recollections are instead created through group interaction. Drawing from the work of Alison Landsberg, Blair, Dickinson, and Ott explain "prosthetic memories" to be a product of the historically- and culturally-specific nature of memory as situated in modern society with its mass media technologies. They are named "prosthetic" memories because they are not gained via lived experience but instead "are derived from engagement with a mediated representation" – for example, by watching a film or television series (as cited in Blair et al., 11-12). We argue that fan communities develop shared prosthetic memories while engaging with a text (in this case, the *Harry Potter* novels and films) and with each other in fan communities. The prosthetic memory is not the memory of doing the reading or watching the film. Instead, *Harry*

Potter fans develop prosthetic memories of attending Hogwarts, shopping in Honeydukes, or having a pint in the Leaky Cauldron. Attractions such as the Wizarding World of Harry Potter or the Warner Bros. Studio Tour reinforce these collective prosthetic memories by allowing fans to actually experience them.

The Wizarding World of Harry Potter opened as part of Universal Studios Orlando in June 2010. Originally, the park included the Hogwarts castle and selected shops from Hogsmeade Village. Today, the park has expanded to include a working Hogwarts Express and a replica of Diagon Alley. Each attraction is modeled after a specific place in the books, allowing fans to relive the memory of *Harry Potter*. When visitors enter the Hogsmeade Village in Islands of Adventure, for example, they are instantly transported into the wizarding world. Guests are greeted by a large scarlet steam engine, which is unmistakably the Hogwarts Express. In the distance, the Hogwarts castle looms over the village, drawing visitors to it. They way in which fans interact with each individual piece of the park rely on specific cultural and prosthetic memory. In this way, visitors become *part of* the memory. Despite the story of *Harry Potter* being fiction, fans dress in robes, carry their wands, and participate in the creation of prosthetic memory.

The Warner Bros. Studio Tour in London provides a different way for fans to recreate their *Harry Potter* prosthetic memories. The Studio Tour is located in two purpose-built soundstages in what is currently known as Warner Bros. Studios, Leavesden, a fully-operational film studio purchased formally by Warner Bros in 2010. Unlike the Wizarding World, which is completely focused on providing an immersive experience, the Studio Tour by its very nature consistently reminds the visitor that they are visiting an exhibit about a film series. Visitors are let into the exhibit in metered groups, though after a short movie about the making of the films and a brief spiel from a docent in the Great Hall, you are permitted to wander at your own pace through the rest of the tour. Though some portions are more immersive in the story—such as the Great Hall, interior sets of Number Four Privet Drive, and being able to interact with the imposing "Magic is Might" sculpture from the Ministry of Magic (see Image 2)—for the most part, visitors are always aware they are visiting an exhibit about the making of a film. Whereas the Wizarding World of Harry Potter immerses visitors in physical manifestations of the prosthetic memories developed while reading or watching the series, the Studio Tour reminds visitors of the way they obtained those memories. Simultaneously, it gives visitors the opportunity to take photos on the Knight Bus, walk through Diagon Alley (though you cannot enter the shops), and drink butterbeer. Therefore, Studio Tour visitors are encouraged to both relive and separate themselves from their prosthetic memories, thus memorializing both the memories and the process by which they are created.

Both the Wizarding World of Harry Potter and the Warner Bros. Studio Tour allow fans of *Harry Potter* to relive their experiences with the text. Through their interaction with each exhibit and attraction, fans reinforce the prosthetic memory of the wizarding world, despite the fact that these events are works of fiction. However, it is the relationship between the fictional nature of *Harry Potter* and the physical representation of the text that allow for the blending of memory studies and fandom studies. We consider this project a call for further study of this intersection.

References

Blair, C., Dickinson, G., & Ott, B. (2010). Introduction: Rhetoric/memory/place. In G. Dickinson, C. Blair, & B. Ott (Eds.), *Places of public memory: The rhetoric of museums and memorials* (pp. 1-54). Tuscaloosa, AL: University of Alabama Press.

Landsberg, A. (2004). *Prosthetic memory: The transformation of American remembrance in the age of mass culture*. New York, NY: Columbia University Press.

How The Harry Potter Alliance Turned Me Into a Fan Activist

Anny Rusk

When Donald Trump won the election, half of us were devastated. I was in that half.

I took a day to mourn, and then realized that Hillary's loss contained a silver lining. Those of us like me, who did some good, but were complacent in other areas, would be galvanized to do more, a lot more!

Shortly after that epiphany, I found a group that a kidlit writer from CA, Erin Dionne, had started on Facebook called the Order of the 1460. (There are 1460 days in a four-year presidential term.) The mission is to "combat hatred, misogyny, fear, racism, anti-Semitism, anti-immigrant, anti-Muslim, homophobic rhetoric. Every day for the 1460 days of Trump's presidency. Peacefully. Thoughtfully. Responsibly."

Perfect, I thought. I'd quickly passed through the stages of grief and wanted to find an outlet that allowed me to use "The Donald" as a force for positive change.

A couple of weeks after I'd joined the group, someone posted, asking whether any of us had heard of the Harry Potter Alliance. No one had, which shocked me since we are kidlit writers, after all.

I googled HPA, and to my delight, found a group devoted to using fantasy to change reality—something I'd been doing my whole life. I'd always believed that the arts had a responsibility beyond just entertaining us. That they needed to enlighten and educate us too, but without being preachy, which is a hard line to walk as a creator!

PA took my idea one step further by turning fans into activists. "The Harry Potter Alliance turns fans into heroes. We're changing the world by making activism accessible through the power of story. Since 2005, we've engaged millions of fans through our work for equality, human rights, and literacy. Our vision: A creative and collaborative culture that solves the world's problems."

I'd found my realm; my activist tribe....I couldn't wait to get started.

I searched Chicago for the HPA chapter nearest me and there

wasn't one. The closest group was the Flourish and Blotts chapter in Beverly, which was at least an hour south of me without traffic.

I was hesitant to start a Chicago group because though I'd been an active volunteer, I hadn't been an active leader for a while. But when I read about some of the amazing things HPA had already done, like send 5 cargo planes full of life-saving supplies to Haiti, or disseminate 250,000 books to underserved areas like villages in Ghana (One village has a chapter called the Chocolate Frogs). I was hooked! I had to start one, but I couldn't do it alone.

Reading HPA's values helped me pinpoint the type of folks I needed to recruit:

* We believe in magic.
* We believe that unironic enthusiasm is a renewable resource.
* We know fantasy is not only an escape from our world, but an invitation to go deeper into it.
* We celebrate the power of community—both online and off.
* We believe that the weapon we have is love.

Basically, I needed folks who'd remained tethered to the child inside of them. Who were willing to jump into flights of fancy be it a game of Quidditch, or walk through a wardrobe into a land called Narnia. Who believed in the power of story and were willing to wield that power to help others. I needed other kidlit writers!

On December 10, 2016, a group of us sat down and christened The Patronuses. The next step was to figure out what HPA meant by 'fan activism.' Before we got a chance to make use of HPA's vast resources on how to turn fans into heroes, a campaign came to me. Comics Education Outreach, a group whose mission is to make comics and graphic novels a part of mainstream curriculums across the U.S., decided to create a lending library.

The CEO Lending Library is a program designed to put comics/ graphic novels into the hands of students in need. CEO Classroom Kits comprised of classroom sets of certain graphic novels and/or comics along with instructional materials needed to teach the unit. The school keeps the kit for a month, and then returns it back to CEO so that it can be sent out to the next school. In addition, individual books may be sent along as well to allow teachers to set up a literary reading circle along a similar topic/theme as the kit. The Library will focus on books/comics that teach/model social change/justice.

#TheLendAHandLikeKamalaKhan book drive campaign was born.

We chose Kamala Khan, who is the newest Ms. Marvel, because she fights for social change, in part by being a positive role model for millions of girls who'd never had a superhero who looked like and acted like them, but mainly because she blasted Muslim stereotypes. She struggles with basic teenage issues of identity, how to fit in when you're different, should you even try to fit in, and most importantly to me, she shows readers that not all Muslims going to strap a bomb to their chests and blow up New Jersey, or wherever. (She lives in Jersey.) In fact, she shows us another side of Islam; they can choose to be heroes, too.

To learn more about the history behind Kamala Khan's creation, check out this Tedx talk by her co-creator Sana Amanat. https://youtu.be/o9lev9739zQ

Through our campaign, we learned that 'fan activism' in its simplest form meant doing in the real world what an admired fictional character was doing in their universe. We are turning their fantasy into our positive reality.

For more info on how to fan the flames of fan activism, go to HPA and check out their fandom forward toolkits. http://www.thehpalliance.org/fandomforward

And if you're curious, our book drive is off to a good start, but it's far from over. To learn more about the books CEO needs and how you can help go to: www.popcultureclassroom.org/ceo

"Help us win the hard way -- the right way -- not with hate, not with retribution, but with wisdom and hope. Help us become champions."
                                    - Kamala Khan

Welcome to Hogwarts: Entering the Story through Wizard Rock

Anne Collins Smith

According to Peter Lamarque and Stein Haugom Olsen in *Truth, Fiction, and Literature*, readers take an active role in the practice of fiction. "An integral part of responding to fiction involves a reader's imaginative supplementation of the explicit content of the fictive utterances.... Much of the pleasure of reading fiction derives from the imaginative 'filling in' of character and incident" (Lamarque & Olsen, 90). As part of the practice of reading fiction, readers may adopt what Lamarque and Olsen call an "internal perspective," which means that "readers project themselves into imaginary 'worlds' and observe them, as it were, subjectively from the point of view of an observer or participant" (Lamarque & Olsen, 153). As such, readers become "travellers in worlds of the imagination" (Lamarque & Olsen, 153).

Some fictional worlds are easier to enter than others. Jonathan Lewis observes that "children's classics often offer readers the possibility that if they get caught in the right wind or walk into the proper mirror, wardrobe, or the right train platform, they will somehow cross both the fictive barrier and the thresholds into these magical worlds" (Lewis, 44-45). The *Harry Potter* series is especially conducive to this kind of imaginative entrance. After all, any one of us who grew up in a Muggle household might suddenly discover, like Harry or Hermione, that we have hitherto unsuspected magical powers. We can hope that any trip to the mailbox will reveal a yellowish parchment envelope addressed in emerald-green ink, with the Hogwarts seal on the back.

This open invitation to enter the story finds a warm response in one of the subgenres within the multifaceted world of Wizard Rock, pop music written, performed, and enjoyed by Harry Potter fans. The idea of music based on fantasy and science fiction universes is not a new one; for decades, fans (including myself) have enjoyed "filk" music ranging from original science fiction in musical form to commentaries and extrapolations based on their favorite books or shows. Despite the obvious similarities, Wizard Rock evolved separately from filk and displays some intriguing differences.

Many Wizard Rock performers take on the role of canonical characters and sing from their point of view; popular examples include Harry and the Potters, Draco and the Malfoys, and the Moaning Myrtles. However, some groups take on their own new identities as non-canonical characters who participate in the story.

The Parselmouths, for example, write and perform as a couple of delightfully bratty Slytherin girls who recount their own adventures at Hogwarts. In "Who Are These Boyz?" we get to follow them on a predictably disastrous double date with Crabbe and Goyle, which they agree to in the mistaken belief that it's the only way to stop these annoying boys from repeatedly asking them out. A year later, in "Freaking Ask Me to the Yule Ball," they demonstrate increased confidence and maturity by deciding not to worry about being invited to the Yule Ball, proclaiming, "I don't need no stinking date to dominate this ball!" Listeners can share their adventures—and their confidence.

The Gryffindor Common Room Rejects strike an especially sympathetic chord with listeners who are still in school in their bouncy piece, "Before OWLs," in which the narrators fret about upcoming exams and how hard the courses at Hogwarts are for students who are not especially brainy. "Professors just don't understand, I'm not Ravenclaw for a reason!" In a more serious piece, "The Wisdom of Luna," the narrators describe their initial dismissal of Luna Lovegood as someone not worth taking seriously, and their gradual realization of the value of Luna's alternate perspective. Listeners can all put themselves in the place of these unnamed characters, finding cause to commiserate and rejoice.

The Basilisk in your Pasta also take on the personas and describe the adventures of non-canonical characters. In their song "Muggletown," students who were born and bred in the Wizarding World sneak out of Hogwarts after curfew to sample the forbidden delights of a Muggle pub. Those of us listening can enjoy a whole new perspective on our own world as an exotic locale filled with curiosities, and chuckle as the witches are baffled by cell phones, whiskey, and televised Quaffle-less sports.

Clearly, the Wizard Rockers themselves adopt Lamarque and Olsen's "internal perspective" and project themselves into the wizarding world. Moreover, in doing so, they create works into which their own readers—or in this case, listeners—can enter. When we enjoy these songs, we are invited to enter the Wizarding World through secret tunnels not marked on the original Marauders' Map. What's more, we enter them in a special way, not merely by reading/listening, with all the responsibilities that activity entails, but also by singing along. We may sing along at the top of our lungs at a live Wizard Rock concert; we may sing in a normal register to the Wizard Rock coming from our car stereo, or we may sing along silently inside our heads to the Wizard Rock playing on our office computer. However we sing along, we sing ourselves into the story.

References

Gryffindor Common Room Rejects. "Before O.W.L.S." and "The Wisdom of Luna." *Still Recruiting*. Wizard Parselmouths. "Who Are These Boyz?" *Illegal love potion*. Wizard Rock EP of the Month Club, 2007.

Lamarque, Peter, and Stein Haugom Olsen. *Truth, fiction, and literature*. Oxford: Clarendon Press, 2002.

Lewis, Jonathan. "If Yeh Know Where To Go: Vision and Mapping in the Wizarding World" in *Scholarly Studies in Harry Potter: Applying Academic Methods to a Popular Text*. Ed. Cynthia Whitney Hallett. Lewiston, NY: Edwin Mellen Press, 2005.

Parselmouths. "Freaking Ask Me to the Yule Ball." *Pretty in Pink (and Green)*. Cheap Rent, 2008.

Parselmouths. "Who Are These Boyz?" *Illegal love potion*. Wizard Rock EP of the Month Club, 2007.

The Basilisk in Your Pasta. "Muggletown." *I Ate My Frog (Again)*. Wizard Rock EP of the Month Club, 2008.

Harry Potter and the Great Canon Debate

Laura Springman

In 2001 *Harry Potter and the Philosopher's Stone* was released in theaters and unintentionally sparked a debate within fandom that still exists to this day. When watching the film, many fans noticed that it differed in significant ways from the books, failing to show specific scenes and ignoring certain characters altogether. This raised a very important question for fans, did the books or the movies reflect the true canon in *Harry Potter*? This fandom, in particular, has a very hard time figuring out what is canon, as it is comprised of 7 books, 8 films, a play, a new movie series, supporting books, an interactive website and more. With all these sources to draw from fans often argue over what is the true canon, book versus movie, original books versus the play, or a hybrid of all or some. With the advent of social media, these lines have blurred further, offering a platform for creators to share new facts that were never in the original media. With so many varying forms of information to draw from, the process of uncovering what counts as canon is up to each individual fan to decide. The debate goes further, raising questions about what level of authority fans have in making decisions about canon. Although they are not the original content creator, fans have just as much right to decide canon as a creator, and *Harry Potter,* because of its vastness, is the perfect environment for fans to do so.

Defined on Fanlore.org as "a source or sources considered authoritative by the fannish community... canon is what fans agree 'actually' happened."1 Canon is rarely straightforward and often leads to intense arguments. It is difficult to agree on what happened in *Harry Potter* when there are so many different versions of the events. Was Draco and Harry's meeting the one in the books at Madame Malkin's, or on the stairs of Hogwarts like in the films? Does Peeves exist? The list goes on and on. On a *Harry Potter* sub-Reddit a user asked "do you consider the movies canon?" to which most fans replied with passionate "no's."2 One fan said "I only consider canon something penned directly from JK Rowling" which in turn would mean that *Fantastic Beasts* is *Harry Potter* canon but *Harry Potter and the Prizoner of Azkaban* (2004) is not.3 Another post brought up the idea that because the films are adaptations of the books, "they are two different canonities."4 Even though JK Rowling oversaw the creation of the films, to fans, because she did not directly pen the screenplays, they are not canon. The *Harry Potter* Lexicon has put the movies after tertiary canon, putting them in the same category as fanfiction.5 Deciding what counts is up to each fan, and one sees this practice often in fanfic, where authors will combine aspects of the films and the movies into a new hodgepodge of canon.

In addition to asking what forms of media count as canon, one must also ask who gets to decide the specifics of canon? Is it up to the original author, the fans, or both? JK Rowling's writings have not ceased with the end of the seventh book. She has continued to discuss the world and characters she created in talks, tweets, and the website Pottermore. From huge announcements, like the information that Dumbledore was gay, to mundane tidbits of information like how students pay for tuition at Hogwarts, JK Rowling has continued to exert her authority over *Harry Potter.*6 This has further blurred the lines of canon and has bothered many fans. A new question is raised with her continued discussion; does it count as canon because JK Rowling said it but didn't write it in the books? Most fans seem to feel that interviews or tweets are just miscellaneous information and Pottermore is below the books in the hierarchy of canon.7 But by continuing to pen new information extending the canon of *Harry Potter*, JK Rowling has, perhaps inadvertently, curbed fan authority. As one fan wrote, "When JK Rowling posts a tweet with new HP information, I feel like it's taking away my agency as a reader to interpret the text."8 While it's enjoyable for fans to learn more about the depth of the world JK Rowling created, it also works to undermine fanon and fan interpretation by removing grey area from the works.

Every fan interprets *Harry Potter* differently and through this they create their own unique blend of canon. To some fans grey spaces, or areas JK Rowling didn't mention explicitly, are the perfect space to create their own facts.9 For example, one popular manifestation of this practice is racebending, or drawing and headcanoning characters as non-white. JK Rowling never said Harry Potter was white, and in many ways, the comments about his mother's eyes would make more sense if he was non-white. So, fans have taken to reimagining him as Black or Indian, creating their own canon that is not necessarily diametrically opposed to JK Rowling's. Other fans, instead of looking at grey area, outright remove sections of the books or movies because they don't like it. Epilogue What Epilogue or Not Epilogue Compliant are common tags in the *Harry Potter* section of Archive of Our Own, totaling at least 5,000 different fics.10 Many fans were unhappy with the ending of the books and as such have rewritten it to create their own canon. Another focus of canon deviation for fans is in the practice of shipping, some will acknowledge canon ships as past relationships that then become new non-canon ships, while others will completely ignore the couples depicted in the books or movies. Most notably in the practice of shipping queer relationships, as there are none explicitly shown in the books or films.11 Fans have taken on a new form of authority, deciding for themselves what counts as canon and reworking or rewriting canon that they do not enjoy. Fans are challenging the hierarchy of content creation by taking the beloved characters into their own hands.

Although fans are united through their love of *Harry Potter,* each fan has experienced the books and films differently, and as such have different views of canon. My Harry, Ron, and Hermione are vastly different from that of my sister's, even though we read the books together, often on the same couch. My mom thinks the movies count as canon while my sister and I scoff at the idea, arguing staunchly as seven book purists. However, while we may differ in our consumption of the media and our views of canon, we each have just as much authority to hold these views as any other fan. Or JK Rowling herself. While her consistent practice of expanding canon through the sharing of new facts on social media illustrates a creator's need to exert authority over their content, canon is not a one-way street. It is a cooperative process between creator and fans, and hopefully will continue to be this way. There should not be a supreme control over content, canon becomes vastly more rich and interesting when others apply their unique points of view. Half my love for *Harry Potter* is rooted in the fanfiction and fanart created by fellow fans, and my view of the world is forever colored by my experience with fanon.

Notes

1 "Canon," Fanlore, accessed March 2, 2017, https://fanlore.org/wiki/Canon.

2 "Do You Consider the Movies Canon?," Reddit, accessed March 2, 2017, https://www.reddit.com/r/harrypotter/comments/1qdr9a/do_you_consider_the_movies_canon/

3 IMalwaysJK, "Do You Consider the Movies Canon?," accessed March 2, 2017, https://www.reddit.com/r/harrypotter/comments/1qdr9a/

do_you_consider_the_movies_canon/

4 TVjoker, "Do You Consider the Movies Canon?," accessed March 2, 2017, https://www.reddit.com/r/harrypotter/comments/1qdr9a/do_you_consider_the_movies_canon/

5 "Sources Used by the Lexicon," Harry Potter Lexicon, accessed March 2, 2017, https://www.hp-lexicon.org/sources-used-by-the-lexicon/

6 "JK Rowling outs Dumbledore as Gay," BBC, October 20, 2007, accessed March 7, 2017, http://news.bbc.co.uk/2/hi/7053982.stm and Charlotte Alter, "JK Rowling Says Hogwarts is Free," July 17, 2015, accessed March 7, 2017, time.com/3963231/j-k-rowling-hogwarts-harry-potter/

7 "Which Harry Potter works are Considered Canon?," Science Fiction & Fantasy Stack Exchange, December 29, 2016, accessed March 10, 2017, http://scifi.stackexchange.com/questions/117948/which-harry-potter-works-are-considered-canon

8 Emily, "The Canon Debate: In Which I Change Sides," August 11, 2016, accessed March 10, 2017, http://www.mugglenet.com/2016/08/canon-debate-change-sides/

9 Melusina, "More Than You Ever Wanted to Know About Canon and Fanon," accessed March 8, 2017, http://www.culturalinfidelities.com/Meta/more-than-you-ever-wanted-to-know.htm

10 http://archiveofourown.org/tags/HP:%20EWE/works and http://archiveofourown.org/tags/Harry%20Potter%20-%20J*d*%20K*d*%20Rowling/works

11 The most popular ship for the Harry Potter fandom on Archive of Our Own is Harry/Draco with over 22,500 fanfictions, https://archiveofourown.org/tags/Draco%20Malfoy*s*Harry%20Potter/works.

"Accio, Author!": Dispersal and Convergence of Authorships in the *Harry Potter* Franchise

Lesley Stevenson

The name "Harry Potter" instantly conjures up an exact, shared mental picture of the same actors in the same black robes in the same castle with the same noseless villain. The image seems to come from one place alone (the "queen of our lives," J.K. Rowling), yet the *Potter* fandom is seeing ever more frequently a *dispersal* of origins and authors.1 Rowling maintains—and her collaborators often give her— total ownership of the metatextual universe, regardless of the extent of her involvement in individual parts. This is the tension at the heart of Rowling's Wizarding World—or at least how it lives in the public consciousness. In 2014, Warner Bros. established a team to oversee the brand across existing and emerging platforms2—and there are many.3 Taking stock of all these influencers forces an elastic notion of authorship that underscores the significance of author forms and functions, a complex best seen in the *active, visual representations* of the wizarding world—in other words, how it looks and sounds. The unprecedented convergence of authorship theories ultimately upends the notion that any one entity could claim sole authorship of the wizarding world. From there, we can assess who, alongside or in place of Rowling, actually deserves credit for bringing Harry to life.

Consider three authorship theories: the auteur, the death of the author, and the author-function. An auteur's works capture his/her personal vision, rooted in Romantic-era theories of a solitary genius controlling every aspect of the work.4 Roland Barthes interrogated that perspective through "the death of the author," shifting agency to the reader, whose experiences and preferences endow texts with personal meaning.5 In Michel Foucalut's "author-function," entities beyond the writer can occupy the liminal space between reading and interpreting the text.6 For example, Tony Bennett suggests the character of Bond serves more of an authorial role than Ian Fleming himself because it unites and defines all elements of the transmediated franchise.7 Few people would say Sam Mendes' recent films directly result from Fleming's original vision—but we take this for granted about *Potter*.

Rowling's unprecedented cultural and critical success cemented er as a singular genius to whom even huge directors, producers, and studios defer.8 One film critic remarked that *Sorcerer's Stone* treated "J.K. Rowling's debut novel with a reverence that wasn't even accorded to the Bible."9 Incidentally, her complete map of the Hogwarts grounds —a spontaneous sketch during her first meeting with production designer Stuart Craig—became known as his team's bible, guiding construction for the entire series.10 She approved every official prop, food, beverage, and piece of merchandise. She also indicated the Sorcerer's Stone looks like "an uncut ruby" and, when asked by executive producer David Heyman about the Black family, "faxed him a complete family tree for the house of Black, with over seventy-five names going back over five generations, all with births and deaths, marriage details, and even the family crest and motto."11 These exchanges confirm Rowling as Author, the ultimate source of knowledge—but simultaneously they reveal the importance of individual craftspeople.

Digging deeper, we can see the relative impact of Rowling to the films' designers. Heyman, the producer who first discovered Rowling's then-unpublished *Philosopher's Stone*, personally selected each director *and* represented Rowling's voice as well. Like a TV showrunner or an heir, he was entrusted with safeguarding Rowling's vision.12 But instead of hiring any ol' director and having Harry, like James Bond, be the focal point of all transmediated content,13 Heyman chose each for very specific reasons when the series reached very specific points—in effect encouraging each director to articulate his own personal vision alongside Rowlings's.14 Christopher Columbus, seasoned children's director, privileged textual fidelity in the first two films.15 One critic called them historical reenactments; many said he captured them too literally, instead of translating the essence of Rowling's words to the screen.16 *Azkaban* director Alfonso Cuarón developed an emotional landscape absent in the first two films, and *Goblet*'s Mike Newell fleshed out the artifacts of the wizarding world. Finally, David Yates, known for political dramas, underscored the sociopolitical conflict in the last four films through literal darkness and escalating references to fascism. Heyman, as "guiding hand," championed his directors' freedom of interpretation.17

But they weren't alone. Stuart Craig, production designer for all eight films and the *Fantastic Beasts* series, deserves almost as much if not equal credit as Rowling for building the world of *Harry Potter* as we see it. Selecting sets, props, costumes, and locations, Craig had primary influence over the realized look and feel of the series.18 Yes, he received input from Rowling and others, but in terms of initial designs and finished products, he stands alone as the central player in the envisioning process. When we think of *Harry Potter*, we think of the visual landscape that he developed. The theme parks further support this fact. A Universal Creative executive told me:

> In every iteration we've done of the Wizarding World, the books are always given first priority in design. More specific than that, we only use the U.K. Bloomsbury editions of the books when we look for descriptions, terminology, spelling, and grammar. For the buildings themselves, [team members] relocated to London for nearly nine months to work with Stuart's team at Leavesden Studios to hand-draft hundreds of sheets detailing all of the Hogsmeade shops. Since Stuart had already established himself as the man J.K. Rowling trusted to develop her world, his direction was typically the only word we would seek when it came to the overall look.

This executive gives Craig almost complete credit for the park's design while simultaneously claiming that the books (and of course, the more authentic British books) served as the ultimate source material. His remarks illustrate the confluence of book versus movie, wherein J.K. as Author provided compulsory framework, but Craig's author-function drove the actual construction. When I asked the same executive whether he himself felt any artistic ownership (read: authorship) over the series, he tellingly replied:

> I don't really consider much of what was done to be my own in any way. … I'd be wary of anyone claiming to be responsible for it as their own creation—aside from Stuart. As 'Universal Parks and Resorts,' we effectively paid for and built a real-world version of Stuart's designs as opposed to creating anything ourselves.19

So, in talking about *visual authorship*, that is, how the metaverse actually looks, Craig played a far more hands-on role than anyone else, even Rowling herself, across the entire franchise.

One vital group of authors remains: the fans.20 Videos, performances, and events in the "fanon" constantly reference the books, the movies, and each other, remixing Rowling's works and challenging her exclusivity as Author.21 Simultaneously, consumption of the

Wizarding World effectively leads fans, without knowing it, to picture *Craig's* world, not just Rowling's, when they visualize the series. Fans want to experience *Potter* on their own terms, but few realize how much of that experience they owe to Craig.

J.K. Rowling as Author is certainly not dead. But she does not deserve sole recognition for the way the world sees Harry. David Heyman and the directors guided a series that stayed thematically true to the books *and* respected each director's artistic style. Almost magically, Stuart Craig built a visually cohesive world and carried that vision beyond the movies. Although Rowling first conceptualized *Potter* herself, an elastic notion of authorship reveals the envisioning process to be highly collaborative—even if she doesn't see it that way.

Notes

1 Ellie Bate, "J.K. Rowling Has Released New Backstory On The Potter Family Along With The Redesigned Pottermore" *BuzzFeed*. BuzzFeed, Inc., 22 Sept. 21 Apr. 2016.

2 Georg Szalai, "Warner Bros. Unveils 'Harry Potter' Global Franchise Development Team." *The Hollywood Reporter*. The Hollywood Reporter, 30 Jan. 2014. Web. 12 Nov. 2015.

3 The multi-franchise Wizarding World now includes a new film series, *Fantastic Beasts and Where to Find Them*; the Warner Bros. Studio Tour; three Wizarding World theme parks; Pottermore; a two-part play; the scripts, published as "the eighth story in the Harry Potter canon;" the globe-traveling Exhibition; and illustrated editions books—and these are only the official texts and products, not fan-created material.

4 Andrew Sarris, "Notes on the Auteur Theory in 1962." *Film Theory and Criticism: Introductory Readings*. Ed. Leo Braudy and Marshall Cohen. London: Oxford University Press, 1974, 563; Andrew Sarris, "The Auteur Theory Revisited." *Critical Visions in Film Theory: Classic and Contemporary Readings*. Ed. Timothy Corrigan, Patricia White, and Meta Mazaj. Boston: Bedford/St. Martin's, 2011, 361; Timothy Corrigan, "The Commerce of Auteurism." *Critical Visions in Film Theory: Classic and Contemporary Readings*. Ed. Timothy Corrigan, Patricia White, and Meta Mazaj. Boston: Bedford/St. Martin's, 2011, 418; Jim Collins, *Bring on the Books for Everybody: How Literary Culture Became Popular Culture*. Duke University Press, 2010, 13.

5 Roland Barthes, "The Death of the Author." *UbuWeb Papers*. UbuWeb. Web. 6 Nov. 2016, 2-6

6 Michel Foucault, "What Is an Author?" *Bulletin De La Société Française De Philosophie* 64.3 (1969): 73-104. Rpt. in *Screen*. By Donald F. Bouchard. 1st ed. Vol. 20. N.p.: n.p., 1979, 19.

7 Tony Bennett, "'The Bond Phenomenon." *Southern Review* 16.2 (1983): 211.

8 Gary Wiener, "J.K. Rowling: A Biography." *Readings on J.K. Rowling*. Ed. Gary

Wiener. San Diego: Greenhaven Press, 2003, 20-21.

9 Adrian Hennigan, "Harry Potter and the Philosopher's Stone." *BBC*. 6 Nov. 2001. Web. 12 Mar. 2016.

10 Bob McCabe, *Harry Potter: Page to Screen, The Complete Filmmaking Journey*. New York: Harper Design, 2011, 28.

11 Stephenie McMillan, Interview. WB Studio Tour London. Leavesden, U.K. Audiovisual tour; qtd. in McCabe 99.

12 Nick Curtis, "Pulling Power: Meet David Heyman, the Super-Producer behind Gravity." *London Evening Standard*. N.p., n.d. Web. 29 Apr. 2014; Sean Smith, "Harry's' Guiding Hand." *Newsweek*: 18 June 2007: 16. *Expanded Academic ASAP*. Web. 30 Apr. 2014.

13 MP Allen, and A Lincoln, "Critical Discourse and the Cultural Consecration of American Films." *Social ForcesL* 82, no. 3 (2004): 877-878.

14 Amy Anderson, "Movie Magic: From Struggling Producer to Keeper of the Harry Potter Film Franchise, David Heyman's Business has Taken Flight." *Success*: 66. 4 July 2011. Web. 30 Apr. 2014.

15 Harry Haun, "Sophomore Sorcery: Chris Columbus Sets Sail again for Hogwarts." *Film Journal International* 105.11 (2002): 8+. *Expanded Academic ASAP*. Web. 31 Mar. 2014.

16 Philip Nel, "Bewitched, Bothered, and Bored: Harry Potter, the Movie." *Journal of Adolescent & Adult Literacy* 46.2 (2002): 172; Jeff Jensen, and John Young, "There Will be ' Half- Blood'." *Entertainment Weekly*. 22 Aug. 2008: 36-41. Web. 1 May 2014.

17 Smith.

18 McCabe 28-29, 97-98.

19 Personal interview.

20 Actors, as well—but it is simply too difficult to determine (at least in this space) to what extent individual performers shaped their characters. Plus, they didn't cast themselves; Heyman did. They didn't clothe themselves; Craig did.

21 Mark JP Wolf, *Building Imaginary Worlds: The Theory and History of Subcreation*. New York: Routledge, 2012, 279.

The Magic of Re-Reading (in) the *Harry Potter* Books

Virginia Zimmerman

On the twentieth anniversary of the publication of *Harry Potter and the Philosopher's Stone*, as many of us look back on our first meeting with the boy wizard, it seems appropriate to consider the topic of re-reading. Some will take this anniversary as an occasion to re-read, perhaps experiencing as an adult a book first experienced as a child. Many have already re-read that first book and all the others more times than they can count.

For some of us, re-reading the *Harry Potter* books has become a part of life like visiting family at Thanksgiving or going to church. Thanks to e-readers, many of us carry all seven books around at all times and relish the chance to delve into favorite passages while waiting for the bus or the dentist. Many of us know exactly where our hard copies of the books wait for us, at the ready on the shelf, and I suspect most of us can name without hesitation the chapters we turn to when we need strength or comfort or a reminder of who we are. Those of us who identify as readers likely also identify as re-readers. We learned in childhood the joy of returning to a much-loved book. Along with *Harry Potter*, other books and series have grown soft and ragged as we have read them until they literally fell to pieces.

Re-reading is an important kind of reading that doesn't get a lot of attention. When we return to a book, we appreciate not just the story but how the story is told. A famous example from *Harry Potter* is J.K. Rowling's strategic placement of the vanishing cabinet in *Chamber of Secrets* when she didn't really need it until *Half-Blood Prince*, four books and seven years later. When they re-read the earlier book, fans appreciate the author's deft management of detail, but they also learn something about how stories work. Most writers know the mantra, "the end must be in the beginning." When thoughtful readers return to a book, they, too, know the end in the beginning, and they watch the author maneuver people and plots toward that end. Think how often in the very first book of the series Harry hears how he has his mother's eyes.

Re-reading also offers an opportunity for self-reflection as people measure their own growth against books when they return to them. For example, between the first and fifth times through the series, a reader may become a parent and therefore understand Harry's mother differently, or Ron's. A reader may suffer unrequited love or struggle with a cruel administrator, both experiences that will alter relationships to characters and plots. And an older reader may discover that her values, her notions of friendship or of bravery, even her sense of self are rooted in the *Harry Potter* books.

As if Rowling anticipated how these books would be re-read, she artfully makes careful scrutiny of certain textbooks central to the plot. Re-reading is essential in the sixth book in which a battered potions text bears evidence of much careful reading in the copious annotations inscribed by the Half-Blood Prince; enchanted with this textual artifact, a palimpsest of sorts, Harry reads and re-reads those notes, modeling the behavior of Rowling's readers who pore over the unauthorized annotations on myriad fan sites and the authorized ones from canonical sources, such as Pottermore. Hermione is the character most frequently depicted reading, and she returns often to certain texts, such as Bathilda Bagshot's *History of Magic*. This book appears for the first time in *Philosopher's Stone* and resurfaces throughout the series, moving out of the margins in *Deathly Hallows*. In this final book, Hermione keeps *History of Magic* in her magical handbag where it is always available for reference.

Deathly Hallows features several significant acts of re-reading, such as Harry's many returns to Elphias Doge's "Albus Dumbledore Remembered" and Rita Skeeter's "Dumbledore—The Truth at Last?" The last book in the series also introduces the *Tales of Beedle the Bard*, a collection of stories that Harry and Hermione encounter for the first time and that Ron has already read many times, having grown up in a wizarding household. Interestingly, Ron's experience of re-discovering these stories parallels that of real-world readers who find the Harry Potter books contain much more than they'd realized when they were younger. Throughout *Deathly Hallows*, all three characters re-read "The Tale of the Three Brothers," and their analysis guides them as they weigh the search for horcurxes against the search for hallows. The tale also guides Harry, Ron, and Hermione as they assess the value of the three hallows. And astute readers will notice that re-reading the tale offers insight into the themes of the series.

The 2008 publication of the *Tales of Beedle the Bard* enables fans to emulate the characters as they read and re-read the tales. What's more, there is a wickedly clever temporal dimension to this text-within-the-text: just as Rowling plants the vanishing cabinet long before Draco Malfoy needs it, she plants *Tales of Beedle the Bard* for readers to discover long before Dumbledore bequeaths the book to Hermione. When *Deathly Hallows* was published in 2007, no real person had ever read *Tales of Beedle the Bard*, but readers who come to that last book in the series now, may do so having already read the interpolated tales. For these readers, the first encounter with the tale in the final book of the series may already be an act of re-reading. Just as the third brother in "The Tale of the Three Brothers" greets Death as an old friend, readers great the tale as an old friend, as we do each book of the series.

Harry Potter and the Philosopher's Stone is our oldest friend, one we've known for twenty years and by different names. It is a time-turner that carries us back to our younger selves, a pensieve that holds cherished memories, and a portkey that transports us to a magical home. It may not be for sale at Flourish and Blotts, but it is a magical book all the same, one that charms and transfigures us with each re-reading.

Schedule for *Harry Potter and the Pop Culture Conference*
9:15–10:15
Expanding the Narrative: Spin-offs, Sequels, and the *Harry Potter* Canon

Kate Behr, Gerry Canavan, Lynnette Porter, Jen Wojton, Virginia Zimmerman

The Banality of Evil: Collaborators and Appeasement in *Harry Potter*

Jen Cross, Kate Lansky, Matthew Peters, Michi Trota

The Harry Potter Alliance, Fan Activism, and Stories for Social Change

Eti Berland, Ashley Hinck, Anny Rusk, Annie Sugar

The Occult Potter: Materiality and Wizardry in *Harry Potter*

Nathaneal Bassett, Jason Winslade, Megan Zimmerman

10:30–11:30
K Who? Investigating Authorship in the *Harry Potter* Canon and Fandom

Lauren Camacci, Stacey Lantagne, Andrea Morales, Laura Springman, Jose Soto, Lesley Stevenson

Discarding the Cloak of Invisibility: A Candid Look at the Whitewashing in the Potterverse

Kenzie Allen, Sushella Bhat, Jen Cross, Matthew Peters, Michi Trota, Suzanne Walker

The Patronuses: Putting *Harry Potter* Activism into Practice

Eti Berland, Leanne Statland Ellis, Christina Hoover Moorehead, Ilana Ostrar, Anny Rusk

Quidditch Through the Ages: Columbia College Chicago Renegades Quidditch

Matt Coyle, Ben Dib, Sareh Ma'ani, Karen Ortega, and Ben Peachey

11:45–12:45
Academic Keynote

Dr. Christopher Bell

1:00–2:00
Beyond the 7 Potters

Megan Ammer, Monica Chapman, Tabitha Rees, Katie Utke

Are Metaphors Enough? Queer Readings of Harry Potter
    Tanya DePass, Kate Lansky, C.J. Hawkins, Suzanne Walker
The Political Potter: *Harry Potter* and the Political Situation
    Sarah Cantrall, Amanda Dougherty and Tiffany Ford, Alena
    Karkanias, Kate Kulzick
The Portraits are Moving: Students Examine Art and *Harry Potter*
    Ryan Cantrell, Jamie Grimston, Andrew Thompson, Mariam
    Mackar, Melanie Wong; Instructor: Heather Easley, Beth
    Sutton-Ramspeck

2:15–3:15
Critical Keynote
    Alanna Bennett

3:30–4:30
The Importance of Memes in How We Understand the *Harry Potter*
Franchise
    Kirsten Dillender, Erica Salmonson, Kelly Schloss
Harry Potter and the Infinite Syllabus: How Harry Potter Has
Shaped Education
    Eti Berland, Heather Easley, Leanne Statland Ellis, Rebecca
    Johns-Trissler, Jessica Kander, Christine Reyna
From Representation to Resistance: Reimagining Harry Potter to
Reflect Our Struggles
    Joy Ellison, Kennedy Healy, Cynthia Medrano,
Fandom: Pilgrimages, Preferences, and Performances
    Michael Boynton, Katherine Larsen, Michelle Maloney-
    Mangold, Ryan Rigda, Anne Collins Smith, Victoria Stiegel

4:45-5:45
The Religious Potter: Religion, Ethics, and Meaning in *Harry Potter*
    Larissa Carneiro, Cynthia Cheshire, Marissa Corliss, Joel
    Garver, Scott Paeth
Studying *Harry Potter* in the United Kingdom
    Rebekah Buchanan, Kirsten Dillender, Haley Helgesen, Ashley
    Hill, Max Keil, Maric McLean, Klaira Strickland, Maggie Wallace
Inclusion and the Other in J.K. Rowling's *Harry Potter*
    Allie Fenson, Tea Gerbeza, Kate Hughes, Kaleigh Johnson

The Historical Potter: *Harry Potter*, **History, and Propaganda**
Christine Klingbiel, Barbara Kulesza-Gulczyńska, Walter Metz,
Amanda Dougherty and Tiffany Ford

Event Schedule
A Day at Hogwarts
Jennifer Jones (Conference long Harry Potter classroom
experience)
Reading Rowling (Conference long fan-reading of the HP series)

Screening Schedule
2:15–3:45 "Wizard People, Dear Reader."

CPSIA information can be obtained
at www.ICGtesting.com
Printed in the USA
LVOW12s2228080517

533793LV00003B/212/P